LABOR
IN AMERICA
Fifth Edition

Arthur S. Link
GENERAL EDITOR FOR HISTORY

LABOR
IN AMERICA
A History, Fifth Edition

FOSTER RHEA DULLES
MELVYN DUBOFSKY
State University of New York at Binghamton

HARLAN DAVIDSON, INC.
Arlington Heights, Illinois 60004

Library of Congress Cataloging-in-Publication Data

Dulles, Foster Rhea, 1900–1970.
    Labor in America: a history / Foster Rhea Dulles, Melvyn Dubofsky.—5th ed.
        p.   cm.
    Includes bibliographical references (p. 407) and index.
    ISBN 0-88295-900-X (paper).
        1. Labor—United States—History.   2. Working Class—United States—History.
3. Trade-unions—United States—History.
I. Dubofsky, Melvyn, 1934—   II. Title.
HD8066.D8 1993
331.88'0973—dc20
                                                                                    92-16104
                                                                                    CIP

Cover photo: Striking meatpackers jeer at replacement workers, Hormel strike, 1986. Courtesy
UPI/Bettmann Newsphotos, #UPI86134074.

Cover design: DePinto Graphic Design

Manufactured in the United States of America
97 96 95 94 93 1 2 3 4 5 EB

CONTENTS

	Preface	*vii*
I.	COLONIAL AMERICA	1
II.	THE FIRST UNIONS	21
III.	THE WORKINGMEN'S PARTIES	35
IV.	LABOR STRENGTH IN THE 1830s	51
V.	THE IMPACT OF INDUSTRIALISM	70
VI.	TOWARD NATIONAL ORGANIZATION	90
VII.	AN ERA OF UPHEAVAL	108
VIII.	THE RISE AND DECLINE OF THE KNIGHTS OF LABOR	120
IX.	THE AMERICAN FEDERATION OF LABOR	142
X.	HOMESTEAD AND PULLMAN	157
XI.	THE PROGRESSIVE ERA	175
XII.	THUNDER ON THE LEFT	200
XIII.	THE FIRST WORLD WAR—AND AFTER	215
XIV.	LABOR IN RETREAT	233

XV.	THE NEW DEAL	255
XVI.	THE RISE OF THE CONGRESS OF	
	INDUSTRIAL ORGANIZATIONS	278
XVII.	LABOR AND POLITICS	301
XVIII.	THE SECOND WORLD WAR	319
XIX.	FROM TAFT-HARTLEY TO THE MERGER OF	
	THE AFL AND THE CIO	343
XX.	DISAPPOINTED HOPES	363
XXI.	AN UNCERTAIN FUTURE: LABOR SINCE	
	THE 1970s	385
	Further Reading	*407*
	Index	*423*
	Photographic Essay *following page*	*214*

PREFACE

In the decade that has passed since I initially revised Foster Rhea Dulles's history of American labor, the world has been turned upside down. Not only did the Soviet Union loosen its grip on Eastern Europe and tolerate the reunification of Germany under Western hegemony; not only did the former Soviet Union under the leadership of Mikhail Gorbachev first renunciate Stalinism and the centrality of class struggle, and subsequently eliminate the Communist Party as the source of all power and itself as a national entity to be replaced by a new and freer association of autonomous republics; not only had the United States waged three "small" overseas wars, in Grenada in 1983, Panama in 1989, and Iraq in 1991; but some savants have even proclaimed "the end of history," or in the title of an essay by the Anglo-Polish philosopher Leszek Kolakowski, "The Demise of Historical Man."

Yet the purpose of this revision remains true to the goal of the first edition which appeared in 1949, for history to be "the stuff of which this book is made." When Dulles first conceived the project and through its first three editions down to 1966, that history, in Dulles's words, sought "to give a comprehensive and general account of the rise of American labor since colonial days." By the time I started preparing a revised fourth edition in 1980, teleological histories narrating the rise of labor had become passé, and one could even conceive of the history of labor in the United States as a process of decline and fall. In fact, at the end of the 1980s, David Montgomery, one of the nation's leading scholars of labor, titled his history of American workers from 1865 to 1925, *The Fall of the House of Labor.*

To be sure, organized labor, which is what Montgomery meant by the phrase "the house of labor," has fallen as often as it has risen. When I completed my revision, which appeared in print in 1984, labor seemed poised, once again, on the brink of decline. Since then, the contemporary house of labor has experienced a series of crises and traumatic blows to its self-esteem and influence in society. Just as the universe of the Cold War, which dominated global affairs from 1945 to 1985, has come tumbling down, the world of American labor has been turned upside down since the mid-1970s. The post–World War II accord between capital and labor, which produced a generation of sustained economic growth, rising standards of living, and national affluence, gave way to new forms of antagonism between management and labor, economic stagnation, and declining real standards of living for many working people. Through it all, the face of labor itself changed, as more women worked outside the home, new immigrants entered the job market in numbers not seen since the era, 1881–1921, nonwhites became the fastest growing sector of the labor force, and the definition of work itself altered with fewer employees producing goods and more providing services and knowledge.

Basically what I have tried to do in this fifth edition is to offer readers a fuller description of the changes which have transformed work, workers, and unions since the 1970s and to set those changes in the perspective of history. Thus I have completely rewritten the final chapter (XXI) but made no substantive changes elsewhere in the text except to update one anachronistic footnote concerning the Teamsters' Union. To be sure, this means that some of the language in the text as written originally by Dulles in the 1940s sounds anachronistic to contemporary ears. This is especially the case with terms that refer to gender, an issue to which Dulles appeared oblivious. Such terms are treated with more sensitivity in the new chapter. I also had to revise the suggestions for "Further Reading." The blossoming of labor history to which I referred in the preface to the fourth edition has continued apace. The number of books, articles, and essays published on the subject since 1980 has been astounding, and the redefinition of the subject matter to encompass gender, race, culture, and language has been more remarkable still. Therefore, I have added what I consider the best of the new literature to the bibliographical essay. Otherwise the book remains true to the purpose Dulles conceived in his first edition of 1949 and to which I rededicated the fourth edition of 1984. *Labor in America* intends today, as in the past, to enlighten another generation of college students about the history of work, workers, and worker movements in the United States, to help those students learn for themselves the story of those who built the United States and who will rebuild it in the future.

Melvyn Dubofsky

Binghamton, New York

I

Colonial America

In the first two and a half centuries of colonization, the area of the New World now known as the eastern United States was an overwhelmingly rural society. Especially during the colonial period (1619–1776), and for some time afterward, upwards of 90 per cent of the people lived in the countryside. Not only did the mass of the people dwell in rural areas; the vast majority of free people were also self-employed, either as independent farmers, artisans, or in a host of urban retail trades and professions.

But from their beginnings, the American colonies included a number of bustling seaport cities, from Boston in the North to Charlestown in the South. In the cities a real need existed for both casual day laborers and hired craftsmen who were paid wages. Moreover, as the southern colonies shifted their agricultural base from the production of food crops for local consumption to cash crops (first tobacco and rice, and then cotton) for sale in the world market, the need for laborers mounted as well.

To satisfy the rising demand for labor in a new land, potential employers turned mostly to indentured servants and African slaves. Free workers included carpenters and masons; shipwrights and sailmakers; tanners, weavers, shoemakers, tailors, smiths, coopers (barrel makers), glaziers (glass makers), and printers.

The skilled craftsmen among these workers at first plied their trades independently, but as the centers of population grew, master workmen set up small retail shops and employed journeymen and apprentices who worked for wages. By the close of the eighteenth century, these journeymen were beginning to form local trade societies—the genesis of the first unions and of what was to become, in time, the organized labor movement.

The simple economic pattern of those distant days provides no real basis for comparisons with the complex industrial scene of the twentieth century. The status of a small handful of independent artisans and mechanics does not have any valid relation to that of the huge mass of industrial workers in our modern society. The occasional and sporadic instances of labor protests in the colonial period could hardly be further removed from the nationwide strikes which in recent years have halted production in the coal mining, steel fabrication, and automobile manufacture on which our closely knit economy is so wholly dependent. Nevertheless, certain underlying conditions were operative in colonial days that would strongly influence the whole course of American labor.

From the first, the history of labor in America was affected by the availability of virgin land. As long as land was abundant, which was the case in the seventeenth century, and the first half of the eighteenth, and from the end of the American Revolution to the close of the nineteenth century, life for the majority tended to be salutary. Regardless of class, most New World residents enjoyed more material comforts, better health, and greater life expectancies than their Old World counterparts. The abundance of land also made it more difficult for the colonial upper class to transport English feudal patterns, which required common people to defer to their social betters, to the new environment. This reality encouraged plain farmers and common artisans to assert their own independence and equality and to become active participants in a vigorous movement for broader democracy. No matter how much America changed in the course of the nineteenth and twentieth centuries, workers retained their belief that they should be free and equal citizens in a democratic republic. Such beliefs endowed American workers and their institutions with a distinctive character.

The early settlers had no more than landed in Virginia and Massachusetts than they realized the imperative need for workers in the forest wilderness that was America. In the first voyage to

Jamestown and three succeeding expeditions, the Virginia Company had sent over to the New World a motley band of adventurers, soldiers, and gentlemen. In growing despair of establishing a stable colony out of such unsatisfactory material, Captain John Smith finally entered a violent protest. "When you send again," he wrote home emphatically, "I entreat you rather send but thirty carpenters, husbandmen, gardeners, fishermen, masons, and diggers of trees' roots, well provided, than a thousand such as we have."

Plymouth fared better. Artisans, craftsmen, and other laborers largely made up the little band of Pilgrims, and the Bishop of London rudely characterized even their leaders as "guides fit for them, cobblers, tailors, feltmakers, and such-like trash." The Puritan settlers of Massachusetts Bay in 1630 also had a majority of artisans and tillers of the soil. In spite of this advantage, the founders of New England soon felt, as had those of Virginia, the scarcity of persons content with performing the humble tasks of society. Governor Winthrop of Massachusetts wrote despairingly in 1640 of the difficulty of keeping wage earners on the job. They were constantly moving on to frontier communities where pay was higher, or else were taking up land to become independent farmers. Cotton Mather made it "an Article of special Supplication before the Lord, that he would send a good servant."

While tillers of the soil and "diggers of trees' roots" were a primary consideration in these early days of settlement, the demand for skilled workers rapidly mounted. The colonists were compelled to become carpenters and masons, weavers and shoemakers, whatever their background, but both on southern plantations and in New England towns, trained artisans and mechanics were always needed.

The ways in which the labor problem was met varied greatly in different parts of America. The circumstances of early settlement and natural environment led New England to rely largely on free workers. The South was ultimately to depend almost wholly on slaves from Africa. In the majority of colonies during the seventeenth century, and continuing on through the eighteenth in the middle colonies, the bulk of the labor force was recruited from indentured servants. It has been estimated, indeed, that at least half, and probably more, of all the colonists who came to the New World arrived under some form of indenture and took their place as wholly free citizens only after working out their terms of contract.

There were three sources for such bound labor: men, women, and children whose articles of indenture were signed before leaving the Old World; the redemptioners, or so-called free-willers, who agreed to reimburse their passage money by selling their labor after landing in the colonies; and convicts sentenced to transportation to America. Once in the colonies, these various groups coalesced into the general class of bound servants, working without wages and wholly under their masters' control for a set term of years.

So great was the demand for labor that a brisk trade developed in recruiting workers. Agents of the colonial planters and of British merchants scoured the countryside and towns of England, and somewhat later made their way to the continent, especially the war-devastated areas of the Rhineland, to cry abroad the advantages of emigrating to America. At country fairs they distributed handbills extravagantly describing the wonders of this new land, where food was said to drop into the mouths of the fortunate inhabitants and every man had the opportunity to own land. The promises held forth were often so glowing and enthusiastic that the poor and aspiring gladly signed articles of indenture with little realization of the possible hardships of the life upon which they were entering. The "crimps" who worked the English countryside, and so-called "newlanders" operating on the continent, did not hesitate at fraud and chicanery.

Thousands of persons were "spirited" out of England under these circumstances, and far from trying to prevent such practices, the local authorities often encouraged them. The common belief that England was overpopulated led them to approve heartily of the overseas transportation of paupers and vagabonds, the generally shiftless who might otherwise become a burden upon the community. Indeed, magistrates sometimes had such persons rounded up and given the choice between emigration and imprisonment. It was also found to be an easy way to take care of orphans and other minors who had no means of support; the term "kidnaping" had its origin in this harsh mode of peopling the colonies.

In 1619 the Common Council of London "appointed one hundred Children out of the swarms that swarme in the place, to be sent to Virginia to be bound as apprentices for certain yeares." The Privy Council inquired into this matter, and, after commending the authorities "for redeeminge so many poore Soules from misery and ruyne," authorized the Virginia Company to "imprison, punish and dispose of any of those children upon any disorder by them committed, as cause shall require; and so to Shipp them out for Virginia, with as much expedition as may stand for convenience."

Some forty years later, the Privy Council appears to have become aroused over the abuse of this practice by the Virginia Company. Two ships lying off Gravesend were discovered to have aboard both children and other servants "deceived and inticed away Cryinge and Mourning for Redemption from their Slavery." It was ordered that all those detained against their will—"a thinge so barbarous and inhumane, that Nature itself much more Christians cannot but abhor it"—should be released at once.

In these circumstances, the line between voluntary and involuntary transportation—especially when it involved young children and the poor—was very hard to draw. There were undoubtedly many bound servants in the colonies who might have echoed the pathetic lament of the young girl described in the "Sot-Weed Factor, or, a Voyage to Maryland," a tract published in London in 1708:

> In better Times e'er to this Land
> I was unhappily Trapann'd;
> Perchance as well I did appear,
> As any Lord or Lady here,
> Not then a slave for twice two Year
> My clothes were fashionably new,
> Nor were my Shifts of Linnen Blue;
> But things are changed, now at the Hoe
> I daily work, and Barefoot go,
> In weeding Corn or feeding Swine,
> I spend my melancholy Time.
> Kidnap'd and Fool'd, I thither fled,
> To shun a hated Nuptial Bed,
> And to my cost already find
> Worse plagues than those I left behind.

As time went on, prison contributed an increasing number of emigrants who crossed the Atlantic as "His Majesty's Seven-Year Passengers." They were at first largely made up of "rogues, vagabonds and sturdy beggars" who had proved "incorrigible." However, during the eighteenth century more serious offenses were added to the list for which transportation overseas was meted out. The prerevolutionary roster of such immigrants in one Maryland county, adding up to 655 persons and including 111 women, embraced a wide range of crimes—murder, rape, highway robbery, horse-stealing, and grand larceny. Among the women, there were many whom contemporary accounts succinctly described as "lewd."

The colonies came to resent bitterly this influx of the refuse from English prisons—"abundance of them do great Mischiefs...and spoil servants, that were before very good"—and they found it increasingly difficult to control them. But in spite of their protests, the practice was continued, and in all some fifty thousand convicts are believed to have been transported, largely to the middle colonies. In Maryland, which seems to have been a favored dumping ground, they made up the bulk of indentured servants throughout the eighteenth century.

"Our Mother knows what is best for us," a contributor to the *Pennsylvania Gazette* ironically observed in 1751. "What is a little Housebreaking, Shoplifting, or Highway-robbing; what is a son now and then corrupted and hanged, a Daughter debauched, or Pox'd, a wife stabbed, a Husband's throat cut, or a child's brains beat out with an Axe, compared with this 'Improvement and Well peopling of the Colonies?'" Benjamin Franklin bitterly declared that the policy of "emptying their jails into our settlements is an insult and contempt the cruellest, that ever one people offered another." Its consequences were reflected, from quite a different point of view, in Dr. Samuel Johnson's famous remark on Americans: "Sir, they are a race of convicts, and ought to be content with anything we allow them short of hanging."

Although contemporaries and subsequent scholars emphasized the involuntary aspects of colonial immigration and the role played in the migration stream by paupers and criminals, the most recent research discloses a different reality. First, in the New World, indentured servitude largely replicated English patterns of rural employment with variations to adapt it to colonial conditions. Second, the immigration of indentured servants proved a rational response to the realities of seventeenth and eighteenth century markets for skilled and unskilled labor; it effectively redistributed labor from a sated English market to a hungry colonial one. Third, the indentured servants were a cross-section of the English laboring classes. As the economist David Galenson observes in his 1981 book, *White Servitude in Colonial America,* "the indentured servants probably came in significant numbers from all levels of the broad segment of English society bounded at one end by the gentry, and at the other by the paupers" (p. 78).

Whatever their Old World circumstances, the emigrants to the New World experienced great discomfort and suffering on their voyage across the Atlantic. They were indiscriminately herded aboard the "white guineamen," often as many as three hundred passengers on little vessels of not more than two hundred tons burden—overcrowded, insanitary, and with insufficient provisions. Typhus and other diseases invariably took a terrible toll of lives. The mortality rate was sometimes as high as 50 per cent, and young children seldom survived the horrors of a voyage which lasted anywhere from seven to twelve weeks.

"During the voyage," reads one account of the experiences of redemptioners recruited from the German Palatinate, "there is on board these ships terrible misery, stench, fumes, horror, vomiting, many kinds of seasickness, fever, dysentery, headache, heat, constipation, boils, scurvy, cancer, mouth rot, and the like, all of which come from old and sharply-salted food and meat, also from the very bad and foul water, so that many die miserable.... Add to this want of provisions, hunger, thirst, frost, heat, dampness, anxiety, want, afflictions, and lamentations, together with other trouble, as *e.g.*, the lice abound so frightfully, especially on sick people, that they can be scraped off the body. The misery reaches a climax when a gale rages for two or three nights so that everyone believes that the ship will go to the bottom with all human beings on board. In such a visitation the people cry and pray most piteously."

Nor did the hardships of the immigrants necessarily end when port was finally reached. Those for whom contracts had already been arranged were handed over to their unknown masters. If the redemptioners did not immediately find employment themselves, they were put up for sale by the ship captains or merchants to whom they owed their passage money. Families were often separated when spouses and offspring were auctioned off to the highest bidder. The terms of servitude varied with age and might run from one to seven years. More generally, those over twenty without specific articles of indenture were bound out for four years "according to the custom of the country."

The colonial newspapers often carried notices of prospective sales.

On March 28, 1771, the following announcement appeared in the *Virginia Gazette:*

> Just arrived at Leedstown, the Ship Justitia,
>   with about one Hundred Healthy Servants.
>
> Men, Women and Boys, among which are many
> Tradespeople—viz. Blacksmiths, Shoemakers,
> Tailors, House Carpenters and Joiners, a
> Cooper, several Silversmiths, Weavers,
> A Jeweler, and many others. The Sale will
> commence on Tuesday, the 2nd. of April, at
> Leeds Town on Rappahannock River. A
> reasonable Credit will be allowed, giving
> Bond with Approved Security to
>   Thomas Hodge

If the sales were not concluded at the port of entry, groups of the redemptioners were taken to the backcountry by "soul drivers," who herded them along the way "like cattle to a Smithfield market" and then put them up for auction at public fairs.

The importation of servants was highly profitable. A fifty-acre headright was granted the planter in some of the colonies for each immigrant, and there was always the sale of the indenture. In the case of sturdy farm hands and particularly skilled artisans, prices might run high. William Byrd reported to his agent in Rotterdam, in 1739, that he was in a good position to handle heavy shipments. "I know not how long the Palatines are sold for who do not pay passage to Philadelphia," he wrote, "but here they are sold for Four years and fetch from 6 to 9 pounds and perhaps good Tradesmen may go for Ten. If these prices would answer, I am pretty Confident I could Dispose of two Shiploads every year."

The treatment accorded bound servants varied a great deal. In John Hammond's seventeenth-century account, in "Leah and Rachel, or, the Two Fruitful Sisters Virginia and Mary-land," their labor was said to be "not so hard nor of such continuance as Husbandmen, nor Handecraftmen are kept at in England." The hours of work were reported as those between the rising and setting sun, but with five hours off in the heat of the day during the summer, Saturday half holidays and "the Sabbath spent in good exercises." George Alsop, himself an indentured servant, wrote home in 1659 almost glowing accounts of life in Maryland. "The servants of this province, which are stigmatiz'd for Slaves by the clappermouth jaws of the vulgar in England," he declared, "live more like Freemen than the most Mechanical Apprentices in London, wanting for nothing that is convenient and necessary."

Other accounts, however, give a harsher picture of general conditions. While colonial laws called upon masters to provide their servants with adequate food, lodging, and clothing, there were many instances where the diet was as meager as the labor was exhausting. Moreover, the servants were rigidly confined to the immediate vicinity of the place where they were employed, tavern keepers were not allowed to entertain them or sell them liquor, their terms of service might be extended for a long list of minor offenses, and they were subject to whippings and other corporal punishment by their masters for disobedience or laziness. Servant girls could be held in longer bondage because of bastardy, and their masters were sometimes not above conspiring to this end. "Late experiments shew," read one report, "that some dissolute masters have gotten their maides with child, and yet claim the benefit of their services."

The indentured servants were recognized as fellow Christians and were entitled to their day in court—in these respects, at least, their status was quite different from that of African slaves. But their masters' quasi-proprietary rights naturally made it extremely difficult for indentured servants to secure redress for any injuries or indignities. While humane masters undoubtedly treated their servants well, it is not difficult to believe the report that they were often subjected to "as hard and servile labor as the basest Fellow that was brought out of Newgate."

Court records concerned with instances of willful ill-treatment are revealing if not typical. A certain Mistress Ward whipped her maidservant on the back so severely, with the added pleasantry of putting salt in the wounds, that the girl shortly died. On the finding of a jury that such action was "unreasonable and unchristianlike," Mistress Ward was fined 300 pounds of tobacco. In another case, Mistress Mourning Bray defiantly told the court that in no circumstances would she allow her servants to "go to play or be Idle," and the unlucky complainant was stripped and given thirty lashes. A third trial resulted more favorably for another maidservant. She was discharged from the further employ of a master who had climaxed frequent beatings by hitting her over the head with a three-legged stool when he found her reading a book on Sunday morning. "Youe disembling Jade," the court records report him as having shouted, "what doe youe doe with a booke in your hand?"

One sorely beset servant took his own revenge. According to his story, he had "an ill-tongued Mistriss; who would not only rail, swear and curse at me within doors, whenever I came into the house casting on me continually biting Taunts and bitter Flouts, but like a live Ghost would impertinently haunt me, when I was quiet in the Ground at work." Driven to distraction, he one day seized an axe and murdered not only his ill-tongued mistress but also his master and a maidservant.

Advertisements often appeared in the colonial newspapers for runaway servants. One such notice referred to an English servant-man who had "a pretty long visage of a lightish complexion, and thin-flaxen hair; his eye tooth sticks out over his lower teeth in a remarkable manner," and another to a shoemaker and fiddler who "loves to be at frolics and taverns and is apt to get in liquor and when so is subject to fits." Other advertisements offered special rewards for runaway bricklayers, tailors, carpenters, and even schoolmasters. Occasional descriptions of their clothes give a vivid glimpse of multicolored vests and blue, green, and yellow coats. One runaway was said to have been wearing "a double-breasted cape coat, with white metal buttons, and an old jacket of bluish color, good shoes, and large white buckles, and no stockings except he stole them."

A more cheerful notice appeared in the *Maryland Gazette* on September 6, 1745. John Powell was able to report that the man who had previously been advertised as a runaway had been found to have "only gone into the country a cyder-drinking." Since he had returned to his master, the notice continued, all gentlemen and others with watches or clocks needing repair could now have them done "in the best manner, and at reasonable rates."

For the servant who faithfully served out the term of his indenture, there were substantial rewards. Grants of land were the exception rather than the rule, but in some cases, at least, the industrious were given "a competent estate," and there was universal provision for some form of "freedom's dues." In Massachusetts, for example, the law specifically stated that all servants who had served diligently and faithfully for seven years should not be sent away empty-handed. What this meant varied, of course, not only from colony to colony but in terms of individual articles of indenture. The freedom's dues generally included at least clothing, tools of some sort, and perhaps such livestock as would enable the servant to start farming on his own account. Typical indentures called for "a pigg to be pay'd at every years end" and "double apparell at the end of the term."

Those indentured servants who survived the rigors of the ocean crossing, the seasoning period in a new environment, and the experiences of enforced servitude in relatively good health could then seek to make a free life of their own. Once they had established their freedom, Hugh Jones wrote in 1724, they might "work Day-Labour, or else rent a small Plantation for a trifle almost; or turn overseers, if they are expert, industrious and careful, or follow their trade...especially Smiths, Carpenters, Taylors, Sawyers, Coopers, Bricklayers, etc."

Some of the indentured servants succeeded as independent farmers or artisans, their once unfree status long forgotten. Others were less successful. They drifted off to the rough frontier where they seldom achieved landowning status. Instead, they formed what rapidly became a large, discontented rural class of poor whites. Still others became the casual day laborers needed in seaport cities. Whatever their ultimate destinies, the indentured servants were vital to the economic development of colonial America.

Free labor in the colonies was made up of immigrant artisans and mechanics who had been able to pay their own passage money and of recruits from the ranks of bound servants who had served out their terms of indenture. The available supply of such labor at first failed to satisfy the demand for it, which is why all the colonies sought and used both indentured servants and bound slaves. Not till the mid-eighteenth century, when the supply of available land diminished, especially in the New England and middle colonies, did labor scarcity somewhat abate. In the quarter century before the Revolution, the number of urban poor grew apace, and the gap between rich and poor widened in the seaport cities.

"The genius of the People in a Country where every one can have Land to work upon," a colonial official reported to the Board of Trade in 1767, "leads them so naturally into Agriculture, that it prevails over every other occupation. There can be no stronger instance of this, than in the servants imported from Europe of different trades; as soon as the Time stipulated in their Indentures is expired, they immediately quit their Masters, and get a small tract of land, in settling which for the first three or four years they lead miserable lives, and in the most abject Poverty; but all this is patiently borne and submitted to with the greatest cheerfulness, the Satisfaction of being Land holders smooths over every difficulty, and makes them prefer this manner of living to that comfortable subsistence which they could procure for themselves and their families by working at the Trades in which they were brought up."

In New England, where relatively few indentured servants were available, this situation led to such high wage rates and such an independent attitude on the part of both skilled and unskilled workers that the colonial authorities felt compelled to act. It must be remembered that at this time all the colonies were but fragments of England, and that colonial rulers looked to the Old World for the proper patterns of social organization. Those who ruled seventeenth-century England believed that a society prospered insofar as its laborers received only a *minimum* subsistence income. Only dire necessity compelled common people to toil hard, and high wages would cause indolence. Colonists carried such beliefs across the ocean. The result was the first labor legislation in America affecting free workers. Maximum wages were established by law, changes in occupation prohibited, and various class distinctions in dress and deportment prescribed to keep the lower classes in a subordinate role.

As early as 1630, the General Court in Massachusetts undertook to enforce a wage ceiling of two shillings a day for carpenters, joiners, bricklayers, sawyers, thatchers, and other artisans, and of eighteen pence for all day laborers, with the further provision that "all workmen shall worke the whole day, alloweing convenient tyme for food and rest." To combat what appears to have been a prevailing practice of supplementing such wages with allowances for liquor ("without which it is found, by too sad experience, many refuse to worke"), the Court further decreed that anyone who gave wine or strong liquors to any workmen, except in cases of necessity, would be fined twenty shillings for each offense.

Forty years later, another law reaffirmed these general wage rates, stating more specifically that the working day should be "10 houres in the daye besides repast," and extended its provisions to additional artisans. Carpenters, masons, stonelayers, coopers, and tailors were to be paid two shillings a day, special piece rates were established for shoemakers, coopers, and smiths, and, finally, the new statute declared "that whereas it appears that Glovers, Sadlers, Hatters, and Several other artifficers doe at present greatly exceed the rules of equitie in their prizes, they are all required to moderate the same according to the rules prescribed to others."

These maximum wages were in part compensated by the regulation of the prices of certain basic commodities to hold down the cost of living, but the clear intent of the General Court was both to help employers and to keep the workers in their place on grounds of public policy. "The excessive deerenes of labour by artifficers, Labourers, and Servants" was felt to have highly unfortunate consequences in the puritanic eyes of the New England fathers. "The produce thereof," they sternly declared, "is by many Spent to mayntayne such bravery in Apparell which is altogether unbecomeing their place and ranck, and in Idleness of life, and a great part spent viciously in Tavernes and alehouses and other Sinful practices much to the dishonor of God, Scandall of Religion, and great offence and griefe to Sober and Godly people amongst us."

The idea that low wages and long hours were conducive to the workers' well-being flowed directly from the reality of work in preindustrial times. Both in the city and the country, workers set their rhythms by nature, not the machine. Custom, not the clock, determined the pace of work and its daily length. Bouts of intense toil alternated with long periods of idleness. It was not uncommon for toilers to break their workday for a period of hard drinking or heavy eating or to observe "St. Monday," a day off after a long weekend of drinking or feasting. Such customs and work habits were obstacles for those who planned to use the labor of others to enrich themselves. Hence long hours and low wages were necessary to reduce idleness and protect workers from the temptations of tavern, cockpit, and playing field.

An even more direct restriction on what might be called conspicuous consumption by the workers was laid down in another law regulating just what they should wear. "We declare our utter detestation and dislike," this edict read, "that men and women of mean condition should take upon themselves the garb of gentlemen." The ban included "wearing gold or silver lace or buttons, or points at their knees, or to walk in boots, or women of the same rank to wear silk or tiffany scarfs, which though allowable to persons of greater estates, or more liberal education, yet we cannot but judge it intolerable in persons in such like conditions."

These laws could not be enforced. Although the authorities continued to link the demand for higher wages with intemperance,

Sabbath-breaking, gaming, and mixed dancing as among "the Mischievous Evils the Nature of Man is prone unto," they could not control the situation. The General Court ultimately relegated the task to the local town governments, but even then material realities proved to be a more decisive factor than arbitrary legislation in determining wage rates and social customs.

Although the bulk of settlers tilled their own land and provided through home manufactures most of their immediate needs, craftsmen and artisans played an increasingly important economic role as the eighteenth century advanced. Many of them were itinerant workers, going from town to town to work at whatever job was offered or making on order anything which the farm families might need. One man sometimes plied several trades. A blacksmith would be also a toolmaker, a tanner a shoemaker, or a soap boiler a tallow chandler (candle maker). How far a craftsman might be prepared to extend his services is suggested by an advertisement in the *New York Gazette* in June 1775. John Julius Sorge announced that he could make artificial fruit; do japan work; manufacture cleaning fluid, toilet water, soap, candles, insecticides, and wine; and remove hair from ladies' foreheads and arms.

With the further growth of colonial towns, the demand for artisans increased. There were more and more of the small retail shops in which a master workman employed a number of journeymen workers; that is, artisans or mechanics who worked for wages, and also trained boys as apprentices to whatever trade was being practiced. Printing shops, tailoring and shoemaking shops, hat shops, cabinet-making shops, and bakeries were among such establishments. The work was generally done on order—so-called "bespoke work"—and the shop might often be the master's home where the journeymen and apprentices could board as well as work. At the same time, the expansion of the building trades led master carpenters and master masons to employ journeymen and train apprentices.

In both New England and the middle colonies, there were also all manner of little mills needing both skilled and unskilled wage earners, and shipyards, ropewalks (rope factories), distilleries, breweries, and paper and gunpowder factories. On the large plantations of the South, home manufactures created a need for skilled labor. Robert Carter had a smithy, a fulling mill, a grain mill, salt works, and both spinning and weaving establishments on his plantation, where he employed free white workers as well as African slaves.

There was at least a beginning of manufacture on a larger scale. By the middle of the eighteenth century, ironworks had been established in Pennsylvania, Maryland, and New Jersey which employed a considerable number of men. One set up by Peter Hasenclever, the best known colonial ironmaster, included six blast furnaces, seven forges, and a stamping mill, and he is said to have brought five hundred workers over from Germany for their operation. The glass works of Henry Steigel, at Mannheim, Pennsylvania, must have had a considerable labor force, since they included a plant so large "that a coach and four could turn around within the brick dome of its melting house." Linen factories with as many as fourteen looms foreshadowed mounting employment in textile mills. In 1769, a "manufacturing house" in Boston had four hundred spinning wheels, and six years later the United Company of Philadelphia for Promoting American Manufacture employed four hundred women in the production of cotton goods. Some of these latter enterprises provided work for the indigent and for orphans—without wages—as a service to the community.

Besides those in manufacturing establishments, other groups of wage earners were of growing importance. The most numerous were sailors and fishermen, and every town also had its quota of day laborers. Household servants were never available in sufficient numbers to meet the needs of the more wealthy members of the community. "Help is scarce and hard to gett, difficult to please, uncertaine," remained a familiar complaint in colonial society. This is why in all the colonies, including Puritan New England, the urban upper class turned to African slaves for domestic help.

With the approach of the Revolution, the increasing opportunities for wage earners and a diminishing labor supply as men were drafted for military service drove up wages. The earlier attempts to fix maximum rates and control prices were consequently renewed. The Articles of Association adopted by the Continental Congress stressed the importance of such regulations, and several of the new state governments undertook to enforce them. At a convention held in Providence in 1776, attended by delegates from Massachusetts, New Hampshire, Rhode Island, and Connecticut, agreement was reached on a general program of price and wage control. Farm labor was not to be paid more than three shillings and four pence a day (almost three times the rate of a century earlier), and the wages of artisans and mechanics were to be so fixed as to maintain their normal relationship to farm wages at this new rate. The states concerned acted promptly on this resolution—an early example of an interstate compact—and, when the matter was brought before the Continental Congress, it referred to the remaining states "the propriety of adopting similar Measures."

Other conventions, however, were not as successful as the one held at Providence in reaching mutual agreement upon prices and wage scales. The South was already showing its reluctance to fall in line with standards set in the northern states, and the experience of different sections was confused and conflicting. While further action was taken locally in some instances, the Continental Congress finally decided that the whole program was not only impractical "but likewise productive of very evil Consequences to the great Detriment of the public Service and grievous Oppression of Individuals." It advised the states to repeal existing laws, and this first attempt at a controlled economy made no further headway.

Although the material conditions of colonial life made for greater comfort and health for common people than prevailed generally in the Old World, workers still lacked basic political rights. The right to vote was restricted to property owners, and skilled artisans and mechanics were as helpless in asserting their rights as day laborers. By the 1780s, however, there was a growing demand for broader privileges on the part of workers in seaboard towns. In supporting the movement which led to American independence, these workers were protesting not only against oppression by a distant England, but also against the controls exercised by the ruling class at home.

The role of small tradesmen, artisans, and mechanics in promoting the revolutionary cause was particularly important in Massachusetts. Again and again, when the ardor of merchants and farmers appeared to be subsiding, the "rage of patriotism" was stimulated by the zeal of those whom the Tories derisively called the "Mobility" or the "Rabble." The popular party in Boston, so astutely led by Sam Adams, was in large part made up of wharfingers (wharf operators), shipwrights, bricklayers, weavers, and tanners who were equally opposed to rule by British officials or colonial aristocrats. The Sons of Liberty, and later the local Committees of Correspondence, were generally recruited from workers from the docks, shipyards, and ropewalks. The famous "Loyall Nine," which was to instigate the mob action which led to the Boston Massacre and the Boston Tea Party, included two distillers,

In spite of the high promise of the Declaration of Independence, the political status of the wage-earning class in American society had thus not materially improved. Its standard of living remained high in comparison with Europe, but with advancing prices in the post-revolutionary period, workers in the little towns strung along the Atlantic seaboard seldom had very much of a margin over extreme poverty. While John Jay complained bitterly in 1784 of "the wages of mechanics and labourers, which are very extravagant," the pay for unskilled workers hardly ever exceeded fifteen shillings a week—barely subsistence level.

"On such a pittance," John Bach McMaster has written, "it was only by the strictest economy that a mechanic kept his children from starvation and himself from jail. In the low and dingy rooms which he called his home were wanting many articles of adornment and of use now to be found in the dwellings of the poorest of his class. Sand sprinkled on the floor did duty as a carpet. There was no glass on his table, there was no china in his cupboard, there were no prints on his walls. What a stove was he did not know, coal he had never seen, matches he had never heard of. Over a fire of fragments of boxes and barrels, which he lit with the sparks struck from a flint, or with live coals brought from a neighbor's hearth, his wife cooked up a rude meal and served it in pewter dishes. He rarely tasted fresh meat as often as once in a week, and paid for it a much higher price than his posterity.... If the food of an artisan would now be thought coarse, his clothes would be thought abominable. A pair of yellow or buckskin or leather breeches, a checked shirt, a red flannel jacket, a rusty hat cocked up at the corners, shoes of neat's-skin set off with huge buckles of brass, and a leather apron comprised his scanty wardrobe."

For all the hardships which such a way of life implied, America remained a land of opportunity for many persons. Artisans and mechanics were citizens in a "people's" republic and could use their citizenship to advance their material interests and to seek to build a society of free and equal, independent, self-employed craftsmen. The ideals of that greatest of American revolutionary pamphleteers, Tom Paine, resonated among urban artisans. In a society still based upon agriculture and handicraft industries, moreover, the craftsman had a recognized and respected status. His way of life may have been simple, but it also seemed to the artisan to be customary, sensible, and satisfying.

Over the horizon were far-reaching changes which would vitally affect both the society in which workers lived and their own status. In the name of progress, these changes would open up the possibilities of a far higher standard of living than wage earners had ever before enjoyed in this or any other country. But these changes also demanded adjustments which were to prove highly difficult, and nineteenth-century labor often felt itself cut off from the benefits that industrial progress appeared to promise. In the face of new barriers to the realization of their hopes and aspirations, the nations's workers were to find that only through organization could they secure the rights and privileges to which they believed they were entitled.

II

The First Unions

The real beginnings of labor organization awaited the transformation in economic society brought about early in the nineteenth century by the rise of merchant capitalists who established business on a wholesale basis. The master workmen in the colonial period, who brought together journeymen and apprentices for work on common projects or joint enterprises, and paid them wages, had not created an employer-employee relationship in any modern sense. There was no real differentiation between the interests of the journeymen and those of the masters who labored side by side with them. The price lists set up for "bespoke work" determined wages, and, to a very considerable extent, the functions of merchant, master, and journeyman were united in the same person.

In such circumstances, masters and journeymen acted together to maintain the standards of their craft, uphold price lists, and generally protect themselves from unfair competition. There were occasions when journeymen protested against the controls exercised by masters in their capacity as employers. In occupations which did not bring them together in close and natural association, disputes sometimes arose that led to sporadic strikes and incipient labor revolt. But, generally speaking, the extremely simple economic organization of the seventeenth and eighteenth centuries precluded any significant concerted action on the part of workers.

The earliest record of what might be considered a labor disturbance goes back to 1636. A group of fishermen employed by one Robert Trelawney at Richmond Island, off the coast of Maine, were reported to have fallen "into a mutany" when their wages were withheld. Some forty years later the licensed cartmen of New York, ordered to remove the dirt from the streets for threepence a load, not only protested such a low rate of pay but "combined to refuse full compliance." Other comparable incidents occasionally were noted in the colonial press during the eighteenth century, and in 1768 a "turn-out" of journeymen tailors in New York—perhaps the first really authentic strike against employers—has an almost modern ring. Some twenty workers struck because of a reduction in their wages and publicly advertised that, in defiance of their masters, they would take private work. They would be on call at the Sign of the Fox and Hound, their notice in the papers read, at the rate of three shillings and six pence per day, with diet.

That masters themselves sometimes joined forces to protect their interests is revealed in a somewhat earlier account of trouble among Boston barbers which appeared in the *New England Courant*. Thirty-two master barbers "assembled at the Golden Ball, with a Trumpeter attending them," and jointly agreed to raise their rates for shaving from 8s. to 10s. per quarter, and "to advance 5s. on the Price of making common Wiggs and 10s. on their Tye ones." It was also proposed that "no one of their Faculty should shave or dress Wiggs on Sunday morning," a resolution which led the *Courant* to observe censoriously that "it may be concluded, that in times past such a Practice had been too common among them."

The Revolutionary period, with its wartime inflation, stimulated further protests on the part of workers who found living costs rising much faster than wages. The New York printers were a case in point. In November 1778, the journeymen demanded—and received—an increase in pay under circumstances which have a very modern flavor except for the courtesy with which the printers voiced their demands.

"As the necessaries of life are raised to such an enormous price," read the journeymen's protest as it appeared in the *Royal Gazette*, "it cannot be expected that we should continue to work at the wages now given; and therefore request an addition of Three Dollars per week to our present small pittance; it may be objected that this requisition is founded upon the result of a combination to distress the Master Printers at this time, on account of the scarcity of hands; but this is far from being the case; it really being the high price of every article of life, added to the approaching dreary season. There is not one among us, we trust, that would take an ungenerous advantage of the times—we only wish barely to exist, which it is impossible to do with our present stipend."

To this letter James Rivington, the well known Tory printer and publisher of the *Gazette*, briefly replied: "I do consent to the above requisition."

There were other concerted protests or strikes in these and the immediately following years—on the part of seamen in Philadelphia in 1779, New York shoemakers in 1785, and journeymen printers in Philadelphia in 1786. "We will support such of our brethren," these printers declared, "as shall be thrown out of employment on account of their refusing to work for less than $6 per week." The employers at first refused to meet their demands, but the turn-out was ultimately successful.

The members of the building trades were also restive, and a long smoldering conflict broke out in 1791 between journeymen and master carpenters in Philadelphia. The former declared that their employers were trying to reduce wages "to a still lower ebb, by every means within the power of avarice to invent." They specifically demanded a shorter working day and additional pay for overtime. They bitterly complained that they had heretofore "been obliged to toil through the whole course of the longest summer's days, and that too, *in many instances*, without even the consolation of having our labour sweetened by the reviving hope of an immediate reward."

What settlement may have been reached in this dispute is not known. The masters blamed the conditions of trade for the low wages and declared that they "had in no instance, discovered a disposition to oppress or tyrannize."

These strikes and turn-outs did not in any case involve an organization which could be termed a labor union. The workers merely joined on a temporary basis to press their demands or to take joint action to protect their interests. Such trade societies as did exist, and there were a number of them in the latter part of the eighteenth century, had been formed, not to promote economic aims, but for philanthropic purposes. They were mutual-aid societies, often including both journeymen and masters, which provided various sickness and death benefits for their members. Almost every important trade in such cities as New York, Philadelphia, and Boston had such a society by the 1790s, and in some instances there were organizations of broader scope—the General Society of Mechanics and Tradesmen in New York, the Association of Mechanics of the Commonwealth of Massachusetts, and the Albany Mechanics' Society.

In supporting such members as might by accident or sickness be in need of assistance and aiding the widows and orphans of those who died in indigent circumstances, these societies sought to free both masters and journeymen from "the degrading reflection arising from the circumstances of being relieved. . . by private or public charity." The workers were self-respecting and proud. Thus early in American history they were prepared, as the charter of one society stated, "to demand relief. . . as a *right.*"

Many mutual-aid societies also had social features and provided meeting rooms and recreation. The house rules of the Friendly Society of Tradesmen House Carpenters, organized in Philadelphia in 1767, reveals both the scope of such activities and also the strict regulations governing the deportment of members. A fine of sixpence had to be paid into the common stock of the society by any member who presumed "to curse or swear, or cometh disguised in Liquor and breeds Disturbance. . . or promoteth Gaming at Club Hours."

Although economic activity fell generally outside the scope of the New York Society of Journeymen Shipwrights (its charter stipulated automatic dissolution if the organization made any attempt to fix wages), it was inevitable that these societies should in time become concerned about problems of employment. The line between mutual-aid societies and bona fide trade associations thus becomes almost impossible to distinguish. The Federal Society of Journeyment Cordwainers (shoemakers), established in Philadelphia in 1794, has, however, been called the first "continuous organization" of wage earners in the United States and is perhaps entitled to be considered the original trade union. Its membership was solely made up of journeymen shoemakers, it conducted a strike and picketed the masters' shops in 1799, and it remained in existence for twelve years.

A few months after the Philadelphia cordwainers organized, the journeymen printers in New York formed what was to be the first of a long line of unions in that trade, and two years later there was also established in New York a relatively long-lived society of Journeymen Cabinet Makers. The latter organization published in the papers a complete price list—which in effect meant wage scales—with the further provision that the journeymen chairmakers would "work ten hours per day; employers to find candles."

These tentative beginnings of organization pointed the way toward the more general growth of trade societies—as the first unions were long called—that followed upon the rise of the merchant capitalists. It was not until the retail shop and custom-order work gave way to wholesale business, and the old easy relationship between master and journeyman was broken down, that the workers really felt compelled to combine against their employers. But with the beginning of the nineteenth century, the skilled artisans and mechanics in trade after trade followed the earlier examples of printers and shoemakers in forming societies whose avowed purpose was to guard their interests against "the artifices or intrigues" of employers and to secure adequate reward for their labor. These societies remained united by mutual-aid benefits, but now they added specifically economic goals to their more customary fraternal obligations.

As capitalism developed apace in the early nineteenth century, the gap between employers and workers widened. Merchants who sought direct control over the supply of goods which they marketed, and ambitious artisans who used the labor of others to enrich themselves, combined to enlarge the scale of production. Responding to the opportunities of widening domestic markets, these early entrepreneurs struggled to reorganize traditional methods of artisan manufacture, to lower the costs of production, and to discipline the actual producers. To the extent that they succeeded, the aspiring capitalists put the higher-cost, limited-market, custom-craft shops out of business. Capitalists, who employed labor to manufacture goods for the market, steadily displaced petty commodity producers, who produced for customers only on special order.

The development of improved means of transportation—canals, turnpikes, and steamboats—widened the market further and expanded business opportunities. The "transportation revolution" opened the growing American interior to the products manufactured on the eastern seaboard. A national market was in the making which would overshadow the old local markets dependent upon retail trade and "bespoke work," and it set the pace for economic progress. The eclipse of the master artisan's custom shop by the capitalist's hired hands foreshadowed the local manufacturing plant and the industrial combinations and mergers of the 1880s and 1890s.

Under constant pressure to reduce costs in meeting the highly competitive conditions of this new world of business, employers sought to hold down wages, lengthen the working day of their employees, and tap new sources of cheap labor. They tried to break down the restrictions of the traditional apprenticeship system; they began to employ both women and children wherever possible; they introduced the sweatshop and the practice of letting out contracts to prison labor. For skilled craftsmen, whatever their trades, such moves were a threat not only of lower standards of living, but also of loss of status. They were at once aroused to combat such developments and realized that only through concerted action could they hope to protect their rights.

For a time the artisans and mechanics mounted an effective resistance to the "new capitalism." The rapid growth of the nation between 1800 and 1819 and again from 1824 to 1837 kept labor relatively scarce. As Alexander Hamilton noted in his famous *Report on Manufactures:* "The objections to the pursuit of manufactures in the United States represent an impracticality of success arising from three causes: scarcity of hands, dearness of labor, want of capital." And as population moved west, the new towns of the interior offered higher wages and prices to attract resources and labor.

Newspapers of the period afford constant evidence of this demand for workers. There were frequent advertisements of jobs: "Wanted, two or three journeymen coopersmiths; liberal wages will be paid," "Wanted, six or eight carpenters; will be allowed the use of tools," and "Wanted, four or five journeymen bricklayers." The contractors building the City Hall in New York in 1803 were forced to advertise for stonecutters in the papers of Philadelphia, Baltimore, and Charleston, and to promise high wages, repair of all tools, and to assure that, although there was yellow fever in other parts of the city, the workingmen need have no fear of it.

Nevertheless, the skilled workers soon found themselves fighting a defensive war against the mounting resources of the employers. Although data on real wage rates and standards of living for the early nineteenth century are far from complete and much in dispute, it seems clear that for most workers wages barely kept pace with prices. The general average about 1818 was probably not more than $1.25 a day, except in a few special trades such as that of ship carpenters. New York typesetters, for example, were earning $8 a week and journeymen tailors in Baltimore $9. In comparison, the great demand for laborers on canals and turnpikes and, in the construction of buildings and on other comparable projects, had driven up the wages of day laborers from about $4 a week at the close of the Revolution to $7 a week and sometimes more. When they were fed and lodged, their actual pay might amount to more than artisans and mechanics could command. An advertisement for men to work on the road being built from the Genesee River to Buffalo promised $12 a month, with food, lodging, and whiskey every day.

Although the skilled craftsmen maintained a wage advantage over other workers, they realized that conditions were changing to their disadvantage and that it was going to grow harder rather than easier for them to maintain old standards. The organizations that sought, under these circumstances, to safeguard the status of the skilled workers were most general among printers, cordwainers, tailors, carpenters, cabinetmakers, shipwrights, coopers, and weavers. Especially important were the journeymen printers and cordwainers. It has already been noted that they were union pioneers and suc- ceeded in maintaining active societies throughout the first twenty years of the nineteenth century, not only in New York and Philadelphia, but also in Boston, Baltimore, Albany, Washington, Pittsburgh, and New Orleans. The members of the building trades were also organized in almost every city, and among other societies were those of millwrights, stone-cutters, handloom weavers, and hat- ters. Prior to 1820, there were no organizations among factory opera- tives—although some 100,000 persons were employed in cotton mills by that year—and there is no evidence of women taking part in the burgeoning labor movement.

These early trade societies were in effect closely restricted craft unions, wholly local in character and necessarily small in membership. The workers who belonged to them were bound to conform to strict rules and regulations, to keep union proceedings secret, agree under oath to abide by established wage scales, and always to assist fellow members to get employment in preference to any other workers. Ini- tiation fees were about fifty cents, with monthly dues amounting to six to ten cents. Attendance at regular meetings was required, with fines for unjustified absence. Moreover, rigid discipline was enforced and union members could be expelled for such lapses as frequent intoxication, gross immorality, or "giving a brother member any abusive language in the society-room during the hours of meeting." The societies were deeply concerned with maintaining the standards of the crafts which they represented and thereby providing assurance that their membership included all the best workmen in the community.

The early local unions already sought, among their other objectives, those most commonly associated ever since with movements of organized workers—higher wages, shorter hours, and improved working conditions. The attempts on the part of employers to lower standards by hiring untrained workers—foreigners and boys, eventually women—also led to vigorous efforts to enforce what today would be called a closed shop. The New York Typographical Society complained bitterly that the superabundance of learners, run-away apprentices, and halfway journeymen undermined the wage rates of "full-fledged workers." In common with many other societies —probably with most of them—it maintained a strict rule that none of its members should work in any shop which employed workers who did not belong to the organization. There were many turn-outs in this and later periods against employers who tried to take on artisans or mechanics who were not union members in good standing, and the society regulations were rigidly upheld. The pressure being exerted against the craftsmen appears, in fact, to have led to a more concentrated effort to establish the principle of the closed shop than in any later period. The Journeymen Cordwainers of New York not only had a specific provision in its constitution against working in any non-union establishment, but was also prepared to impose fines upon any journeyman who came to the city and did not join the society within a month.

In their dealings with employers, the societies introduced the principles of collective bargaining. In the case of the Philadelphia shoemakers, a deputation had "waited upon the employers with an offer of compromise" as early as 1799, and many instances might be cited of journeymen submitting a price list and coming to terms after protracted negotiations. When agreements had been reached between a society and the employers, a member of the former was often designated "to walk around" from shop to shop to see that it was being kept. In other instances, "tramping committees" were set up to supervise enforcement of the contract.

The strikes, or turn-outs, as they were more frequently called—whereby the workers sought to uphold their interests when wage negotiations failed, employers refused to abide by the terms of an agreement, or nonmembers of the society were employed—were generally peaceful during this period. The employees simply quit their jobs and stayed at home until some sort of settlement could be reached. The struggle appears often to have been fought out in the newspapers rather than in violent action. Workers and employers would put their respective cases before the public through notices in the press.

There were, however, occasions when strikers took more forceful measures. Six journeymen stayed on the job during a turn-out of Philadelphia shoemakers and were kept hidden in their employer's garret. The strikers kept up a sharp eye for them and, when they briefly emerged one Sunday night to visit a nearby tavern, beat them up severely. On another occasion, when a shop was boycotted because of refusal to accept the prescribed wage scales and the employer advertised for fifty new journeymen, the strikers established what was in effect a picket line and forcefully maintained it. There was deep resentment against nonunion workers who would take the place of strikers, and attacks were not unusual upon persons already being called "scabs."

Noisy demonstrations and sometimes violence marked the rather frequent turn-outs of sailors. During one strike in New York, in which the seamen demanded an increase in wages from $10 to $14 a week, so much disturbance was created that a parade of strikers finally had to be broken up by the constables. Another time, the sailors tried to board and rifle a vessel whose owner had especially aroused their ire. Learning of the planned assault, a group of citizens took over the defense of the vessel and, when the strikers moved in behind a drum and fife corps with colors flying, "they were three times repulsed, with broken and bloody noses."

The growth of journeymen societies and their militant activity were matters of mounting concern to employers. They in turn soon began to cooperate to block demands for higher wages and to combat the closed shop. While the journeymen had organized in self-defense as changing economic conditions undermined their former independent status, the masters also found themselves hard pressed to maintain their position in an increasingly competitive capitalist society. When they were unable to meet the challenge of organized employees on their own ground, they sought protection through the courts and attacked the journeymen societies as combinations or conspiracies in restraint of trade.

The first of such actions was the prosecution, in 1806, of the Journeymen Cordwainers of Philadelphia. The case grew out of one of the recurrent strikes for higher wages on the part of these aggressive shoemakers, and the trial judge proved to be a sympathetic supporter of the employers. In his charge to the jury, he characterized the strike as "pregnant with public mischief and private injury" and left the twelve good men and true little choice as to the verdict which he expected them to bring in.

"A combination of workmen to raise their wages," the judge declared, "may be considered in a two-fold point of view; one is to benefit themselves...the other is to injure those who do not join their society. The rule of law condemns both." The grounds for such a decision were found in the old common-law principle that, wherever two or more persons conspired to do something jointly, even though they were individually entitled to take such action, the public interest was endangered. While its application to labor organizations which sought no more than an increase in wages would appear to have raised some doubts even in the judge's own mind, he quickly brushed them aside. "If the rule be clear we are bound to conform to it," he stated, "even though we do not comprehend the principle upon which it is founded. We are not here to reject it because we do not see the reason for it."

Four years later, the Journeymen Cordwainers of New York, and then in 1815 another organization of Pittsburgh shoemakers, were indicted on similar charges of criminal conspiracy. On both occasions the court again found for the employers. The emphasis, however, had somewhat shifted from outright condemnation of any combination to raise wages. The New York judge did not wholly deny the right of workingmen to organize for such a purpose, but he declared that the means which they were employing "were of a nature too arbitrary and coercive, and went to deprive their fellow citizens of rights as precious as any they contended for." In the Pittsburgh case a further point was stressed. A combination of workingmen attempting to enforce their demands by concerted action against an employer was said to be an illegal conspiracy, not only because of its injurious effect upon the employer, but also because it was prejudicial to the interests of the community. The judge in this instance dismissed the question of whether the journeymen or the masters were the oppressors as irrelevant and condemned the former's society because it tended "to create a monopoly or restrain the entire freedom of trade."

These conspiracy cases aroused widespread resentment among the workingmen. Were all other combinations, among merchants, politicians, sportsmen, "ladies and gentlemen for balls, parties, and banquets" to be permitted, they asked, and only the poor laborers combining against starvation to be indicted?

"The name of freedom is but a shadow," read one appeal to the public, "if, for doing, what the laws of the country authorize, we are to have taskmasters to measure out our pittance of subsistence—if we are to be torn from our firesides for endeavouring to obtain a fair and just support for our families, and if we are to be treated as felons and murderers only for asserting our right to take or refuse what we deem an adequate reward for our labor."

The issue was injected into local politics. Federalists and Jeffersonian Republicans were at the time engaged in a bitter controversy over the general use of English common law in the United States, and the latter considered the application of what they termed its undemocratic principles to labor unions a challenge to the whole cause of liberty. The right of association could not be divorced from other fundamental rights, the Republicans declared, and they zealously took up the workingmen's cause.

"Would it be believed," an editorial in the *Philadelphia Aurora*, the leading Jeffersonian paper, stated in 1806, "at the very time when the state of the negro was about to be improved attempts were being made to reduce the whites to slavery? Was there anything in the Constitution of the United States or in the Constitution of Pennsylvania which gave one man a right to say to another what should be the price of labor? There was not. It was by the English common law that such things became possible."

The controversy was to continue for many years to come, but the decisions against the workingmen stood. They did not stop the further organization of labor societies nor wholly prevent the use of strikes and boycotts. When employers resorted to the courts, however, workingmen were hard pressed to defend themselves against charges of conspiracy.

If these cases were a first blow at the early movement for labor organization, the new unions were soon confronted by a much more serious threat to their existence. In 1819, the country suffered a severe depression. As business activity was curtailed and the demand for labor automatically declined, even skilled workers found it increasingly difficult to get jobs. They could no longer afford to hold out for higher wages or seek to enforce a closed shop. They were driven to accept whatever jobs were offered, regardless of wages or working conditions. In such circumstances, the young labor unions could not maintain their membership and rapidly broke up. While some of them managed to survive, the great majority fell by the wayside as economic distress spread throughout the country.

This was to be a recurrent phenomenon during the nineteenth century. Labor unions thrived in periods of prosperity when the rising demand for workers gave their members effective bargaining power. They dwindled away whenever depression and the scarcity of jobs forced every man to look out for his own interests, no matter how it might affect those of workers generally. The first time that labor succeeded even partially in maintaining union strength during hard times was in the 1890s.

This was far in the future, however. The newly organized unions of the opening years of the century were so local in scope and so weak that they had no chance whatsoever of holding the line when employers aggressively took advantage of every opportunity to break down wage scales and undermine the closed shop. But in what was to become a familiar pattern, returning prosperity after 1822 led to a reemergence of unionism. The few societies of artisans and mechanics which had somehow managed to survive the depression took a new lease on life as the bargaining position of their members was strengthened, and new organizations sprang up to replace the ones which had succumbed.

Not only were the societies of journeymen printers and cordwainers, tailors and carpenters, and other skilled workers revived, but for the first time there was a tentative beginning of organization among factory workers in the textile mills of New England. Moreover, these new unions were especially active and did not hesitate to resort to strikes and boycotts to enforce their demands. Successful turn-outs for both higher wages and shorter working hours were reported in contemporary newspapers on the part of tailors in Buffalo, ship carpenters in Philadelphia, cabinet makers in Baltimore and journeymen painters, tailors, stonecutters, and even common laborers in New York. The organization of mill hands also led to a first strike on the part of female workers when the weavers at Pawtucket, Rhode Island, turned out in 1824. The meeting at which the women agreed on this action was reported in the *National Gazette*:

"It was conducted, however strange it may appear, without noise, or scarcely a single speech."

Even more significant than the revival and militancy of these local labor societies was a further step in the organization of labor which went beyond limited craft lines. In 1827 a Mechanics' Union of Trade Associations was established in Philadelphia. In the terminology of today, this meant, rather, an association of unions, or a city central. It was the first labor organization in the country which brought together the workers of more than a single craft, and it was to make possible concerted action by workers in Philadelphia on a citywide basis.

This new association grew out of a strike of carpenters who were demanding a ten-hour day and had obtained the support of such other members of the building trades as the bricklayers, painters, and glaziers. The strike failed, but the experience in working together led to a call for more permanent organization. All existing labor societies were asked to join the association, and those trades which had no unions were requested to organize at once and send delegates.

The Mechanics' Union was not primarily concerned with such limited goals as higher wages and shorter hours, even though it had grown out of a strike for the ten-hour day. A new note was introduced into the activity of labor societies when the broad issue of equality for producers in general was raised. The changes effected by the new economic order had aroused among the workers increasing concern over their social as well as economic status. The Philadelphia labor leaders sought some means to maintain the position of workers in the face of what appeared to be newly developing class lines. They thought of themselves as the real producers, in contrast to the emerging parasitic capitalists who neither toiled nor benefited society. In fact, they believed that labor produced all value and that labor was both prior to and superior to capital. Committed to an embryonic labor theory of value, these Philadelphia workers argued that the labor movement promoted the prosperity and welfare of the entire community.

"If the mass of people were enabled by their labour to procure for themselves and families a full and abundant supply of the comforts and conveniences of life," the preamble of the new organizations' constitution stated, "the consumption of articles, particularly of dwellings, furniture and clothing, would amount to at least twice the quantity it does at present, and of course the demand, by which employers are enabled either to subsist or accumulate, would likewise be increased in an equal proportion. . . . The real object, therefore, of this association, is to avert, if possible, the desolating evils which must inevitably arise from a depreciation of the intrinsic value of human labour. . . and to assist, in conjunction with such other institutions of this nature as shall hereafter be formed throughout the union, in establishing a just balance of power, both mental, moral, political and scientific, between all the various classes and individuals which constitute society at large.''

Such aims had definite political implications. The Mechanics' Union of Trade Association of Philadelphia, indeed, never engaged in direct trade-union activity but turned at once to politics. It appealed to the artisans and mechanics of Philadelphia to "throw off the trammels of party spirit, and unite under the banner of equal rights." It also called for the nomination of candidates for local office who would represent the interests of the working classes.

III

The Workingmen's Parties

In urging its members to nominate candidates for public office, the Mechanics' Union of Trade Associations in Philadelphia broke fresh ground for labor and inaugurated what was to become a widespread political movement of workingmen's parties. It soon spread to other towns in Pennsylvania; to New York, where wide popular support developed, not only for local parties in New York City itself, but also in many upstate localities; and into Massachusetts and other parts of New England. Ultimately, workingmen's parties were established in at least a dozen states. As far west as Ohio, as well as along the Atlantic seaboard, local groups of farmers, artisans, and mechanics named their own political candidates and in some instances elected them. For a brief time they were highly important because they sometimes held an actual balance of power between the major parties in local elections.

An equally widespread growth of labor newspapers took place in the early 1830s, with no less than sixty-eight such journals upholding the workingmen's cause and agitating for labor reforms. Their enthusiasm and assurance knew no bounds. "From Maine to Georgia, within a few months past," commented the *Newark Village Chronicle* in May 1830, "we discern symptoms of a revolution, which will be second to none save that of '76." "Throughout the vast republic," the *Albany Working Men's Advocate* stated shortly afterwards, "the farmers, mechanics and workingmen are assembling...to impart to its laws and administration those principles of liberty and equality unfolded in the Declaration of Independence."

These developments were early expressions of both the producer ethic enunciated by the Philadelphia labor leaders and the swelling popular democratic movement, which would be partly absorbed by Jacksonian Democracy. The country was rapidly expanding in these years. The opening up of new western territory, the building of turn-pikes and canals, the steady growth of manufactures, and rise of cities everywhere created a spirit of buoyant confidence. What the workers of the country basically sought was that the capitalist class would not monopolize for itself the boundless opportunities. They had newly obtained political power through the removal of property qualifi-cations for voting, and were ready to use their votes to insure that producers received a proper share of the wealth which they created.

There was little question that the general status of labor was con-tinuing to deteriorate as a result of the changes wrought in the American economy by the rise of merchant capitalism. The ordinary divisions within society were deepening. Contemporary critics saw, on the one hand, the producing masses, made up of the laboring poor, and, on the other, a wealthy nonproductive aristocracy bulwarked by special privilege. Banking and other monopolies accentuated this cleavage, and the great majority of the country's workers saw little im-provement in the conditions under which they labored, even though trade and commerce expanded and the nation as a whole grew more prosperous.

Wages rose but not in proportion to the rise in the cost of living. Twelve to fifteen hours remained the usual day's work. During the summer, artisans and mechanics were on the job as early as four in the morning, took an hour off for lunch at ten and another for dinner at three, and then quit work only with sunset. They were often paid in depreciated currency whose value was constantly fluctuating. Should their employer fail and be unable to pay them, they had no redress. Yet when they could not meet their own obligations, they were liable to imprisonment for debt.

Moreover, the workingmen felt that government was wholly on the side of the aristocracy and that its policies were helping to perpetuate the conditions which were depressing the position of all labor. They had no faith in either major party, whatever its professions of goodwill, because the men chosen for public office were invariably representatives of the class that they had come to believe was oppressing them. Heretofore they had been politically helpless to do anything about redressing a balance of power which they saw swinging steadily against them. Armed with the vote, they declared themselves unwilling any longer to accept passively policies which in government, finance, or business sought to reserve special privilege for the favored few at the expense of the great majority.

In forming their own parties, the workers tried to secure participation in government by members of their own class—the producers—and they were convinced that, in doing so, they were serving the best interests of the people as a whole. Their party platforms vigorously attacked every instance of special privilege, particularly banking monopoly. Indicative of their general objective of equal citizenship, their foremost demand was invariably for free public education. Seeking to secure representation for "the plain people" in every governmental process, they recognized that education for the masses was a first step toward an effective democracy. On more specific grounds, the workingmen also demanded abolition of imprisonment for debt and mechanics' lien laws; the revision of a militia system which bore heavily upon the poor; the direct election of all public officials; greater equality in taxation; and the complete separation of church and state.

The political agitation of the workers and the formation of their local parties occurred simultaneously with the emergence and rise of Jacksonian Democracy. Although Jacksonian Democracy arose largely in response to agrarian interests, including the large slaveholders, it contained a core of antimonopolism and producer ideology which appealed to some urban workers. Arising independently of Jacksonianism, the local labor parties did occasionally march behind Jackson's banners, especially when the General and his supporters lauded "the humble members of society" and attacked capitalistic parasites.

The local parties formed by the workers were to become inextricably involved in the complex and shifting political patterns of the 1830s. Whatever their ultimate fate, however, their influence in quickening the demand for reform and promoting progressive principles was important. Commenting on the course of one workingmen's party in Massachusetts, a Whig newspaper sourly charged that there was no distinction between "Working-Menism and

Jacksonism." If this was not necessarily true, it did reveal the link between the more radical antientrepreneurial side of Jacksonian Democracy and the influence of working-class politics.

The significance of the growing political power of the workingmen was demonstrated in other ways. In opposition to Jackson's espousal of the cause of the common man, the newly organized Whigs for a time sought to uphold Federalist traditions which favored government by the rich and the well-born. Whigs especially attacked the proposition of "throwing open the polls to every man that walks." But when they found themselves unable to stem the growing political power of small farmers and urban workers, they began to shift their ground. Attacking Jackson for emphasizing class distinctions, they maintained that there was no warrant for setting off aristocracy and democracy as opposing forces in American national life. "These phrases, *higher and lower orders,*" one Whig editor declared, "are of European origin and have no place in our Yankee dialect." However conservative their ideas might still be, it was no longer politically feasible for them to uphold aristocratic principles, and they were compelled to recognize the right of all classes in society to share in government.

By the end of the Jacksonian period, the original workingmen's parties had long since fallen by the wayside, but the producing masses of the nation had won the political recognition that had been their first objective. Both major parties were continually angling for labor support. When, in 1836, the editor of the *Ohio People's Press,* to cite a single example, shifted his political allegiance from Jackson to William Henry Harrison, he called for support of the latter on exactly the same grounds on which he had originally backed the former. The program advocated by Harrison, he maintained, would "restore to the farmer, the mechanic and the working-man their proper station and influence in the Republic." The extension of the franchise and the growing political awareness among workers caused the major political parties to appeal, as never before, directly for labor's vote.

Among the various local workingmen's parties, the experience of the one organized in New York is at once most revealing of the influence which they were temporarily able to exert and of the complicated factors that brought about their collapse. This party grew out of a meeting of "mechanics and others" that had been summoned on April 23, 1829, to protest against any lengthening in the prevailing ten-hour day already won in that city by the early trade unions.

Deciding to broaden the scope of their activity, the delegates sent out a call for a larger meeting. It was attended by some 6,000 persons, and a set of resolutions was adopted dealing with the broad principles of workingmen's rights. Consideration of ways and means for implementing this program was then delegated to a Committee of Fifty, and, on October 19, it brought in a report, (of which 20,000 copies were subsequently circulated) which vigorously attacked the existing social order and called for a convention to nominate for the New York assembly political candidates from among those "who live by their own labour *And None Other.*" Four days later, this convention was held. After all nonworkers, "such as bankers, brokers, rich men etc.," had been expressly warned to leave the hall, the workingmen agreed upon an assembly slate which included a printer, two machinists, two carpenters, a painter, and a grocer.

From the very first, however, rivalry and intrigue over the leadership of the new workingmen's party threatened to split its ranks. It was to be dominated by several highly individualistic reformers whose philosophy and ideas caused heated controversy. Four such persons stand out especially for their influence on the labor party in New York and on the course of workingmen's political activity in general.

In its earliest stages, the party was largely influenced by Thomas Skidmore, a machinist by trade, who had been instrumental in persuading the workers to broaden their program as a means of "coercing their aristocratic oppressors" into maintaining the ten-hour day. Wholly self-educated, he was totally committed to the workers' cause and had developed a radical philosophy that questioned the entire basis for existing property rights. He believed that, in giving up his original and natural right to land to become a smith, a weaver, a builder, or other laborer, every man was entitled to a guarantee from society "that reasonable toil shall enable him to live as comfortably as others." Any system which failed to provide such social security was inherently wrong in his opinion, and he hoped to lead a workingmen's revolt in favor of basic political reforms.

Skidmore's views were shortly to be set forth in a formidable treatise which he comprehensively entitled *The Rights of Man to Property; Being a Proposition to Make it Equal among the Adults of the Present Generation; and to Provide for its Equal Transmission to Every Individual of Each Succeeding Generation, on Arriving at the Age of Maturity.* Skidmore specifically proposed that all debts and property claims should be at once canceled, and that the assets of society as a

whole be sold at public auction, with every citizen having equal purchasing power. After such a communistic division of property, the
maintenance of equality would be assured by doing away with all
inheritance.

Not perhaps understanding all the implications of this radical program, the members of the New York Workingmen's party allowed
Skidmore to draw up their original platform. It was based upon the
forthright premise that "all human society, our own included as well
as every other, is constructed radically wrong," and it condemned
both the private ownership of land and the inheritance of wealth. Its
more specific provisions, however, set forth the objectives which were
fundamental to the workingmen's movement everywhere: communal
education, abolition of imprisonment for debt, mechanics' lien laws,
and the elimination of licensed monopolies.

A second leader, who accepted at least in part Skidmore's program
but was to be far more influential in the workingmen's movement in
these and later years, was George Henry Evans. A printer by trade, he
founded the *Working Man's Advocate,* perhaps the most important
labor journal of these years, as the organ for the New York party, and
he turned out a continuous stream of articles and editorials. Reflecting the influence of Skidmore, his paper first carried the slogan: "All
children are entitled to equal education; all adults to equal property;
and all mankind, to equal privileges." But his views were to be later
modified, although he remained throughout his life a strong advocate
of basic property reforms.

As if such leadership were not enough to condemn the Workingmen's party in the eyes of all conservatives, it was further damned
by the participation in its activities of another brace of radical
reformers: Robert Dale Owen and Frances Wright. Having but
recently moved to New York from the cooperative community at New
Harmony, Indiana, where the former's father, the English reformer,
Robert Owen, had attempted to put into practice his socialistic program for replacing the factory system, these two naturally seized upon
the workingmen's movement as a medium for promoting their own
particular brand of reform. They had founded a paper, the *Free Enquirer,* to publicize their ideas, and it was soon campaigning vigorously in support of the new party.

Robert Dale Owen was twenty-eight at this time—a short, blue-
eyed, sandy-haired young man whose idealism and earnest sincerity
gave him a very real influence. In spite of a rasping voice and clumsy

gestures, he was a forceful speaker at workingmen's meetings, and he was also a prolific and able writer. He believed strongly in a more equitable distribution of wealth, was opposed to organized religion, and advocated more liberal divorce laws, but his primary interest was in free, public education. He single-mindedly believed that it was the only effective means to regenerate society, and he had developed an elaborate educational program which called for a system of "state guardianship."

All children, whether of the rich or of the poor, according to this scheme, were to be removed from their homes and placed in national schools where they would receive the same food, be dressed in the same simple clothing, and taught the same subjects in order to promote the general cause of democracy. "Thus may luxury, may pride, may ignorance be banished from among us," read one report on state guardianship; "and we may become what fellow citizens ought to be, a nation of brothers." While the workers did not wholly approve this particular program, Owen contributed a great deal to their educational ideas.

Frances Wright was at once the most zealous, the most colorful and, in the eyes of contemporaries, the most dangerous of the reformers associated with the Workingmen's party. Although a free thinker and so outspoken an advocate of women's rights and easier divorce that she was generally accused of advocating free love, she did not look the part of a radical agitator. Tall, slender, with wavy chestnut hair, she completely dazzled the workingmen's audiences she constantly addressed. Conservatives were as much shocked by the daring effrontery of a female in appearing on the lecture platform as by her unorthodox views, but few of those who actually heard her speak were wholly immune to her charms. "She has always been to me one of the sweetest of sweet memories," Walt Whitman, taken to one of her meetings by his carpenter father, was to write in later years. "We all loved her; fell down before her: her very appearance seemed to enthrall us...graceful, deerlike.... She was beautiful in bodily shape and gifts of soul."

Fanny Wright was born in Scotland and, falling early under the influence of the English reformer, Jeremy Bentham, became even as a young woman the militant champion of reform that she was to remain throughout her life. On first coming to the United States, she had taken up the cause of enslaved blacks and established at Nashoba, Tennessee, a colony where she tried to prepare groups of slaves, purchased at her own expense, for freedom and eventual colonization outside of the United States. When this project failed, she joined the community at New Harmony and then accompanied Robert Dale Owen to New York to cooperate with him in editing the *Free Enquirer*.

Undaunted by her disappointments at Nashoba and New Harmony and with her zeal for reform in no way abated, Wright enthusiastically adopted the workingmen's movement. She saw in it not only a protest against social inequality but also a basic revolt on the part of the oppressed for which history offered no parallel. "What distinguishes the present from every other struggle in which the human race has been engaged," she wrote in the *Free Enquirer*, "is, that the present is, evidently, openly and acknowledgedly, a war of class. . . . It is the ridden people of the earth who are struggling to throw from their backs the 'booted and spurred' riders whose legitimate title to starve as well as work them to death will no longer pass current; it is labour rising up against idleness, industry against money; justice against law and against privilege."

The newspapers railed against Fanny Wright. They attempted to dismiss her as "an exotic of some notoriety"; they called her "the great Red Harlot of Infidelity." But no matter what abuse they flung at her, she boldly continued to express her "alarming principles" on public platforms and in the press.

When the Workingmen's party took the field under such sponsorship in the New York elections of 1829, with its slate of tradesmen and artisans, the conservatives were nonplussed. They at first attempted to dismiss any possible threat to their own interests, but, as the vote of the laboring classes appeared to be swinging heavily behind the new party, they became thoroughly aroused. "We understand with astonishment and alarm," the *Courier and Enquirer* protested, "that the 'Infidel Ticket,' miscalled the 'Workingmen's Ticket,' is far ahead of every other Assembly ticket in the city. What a state of things we have reached! A ticket got up openly and avowedly in opposition to social order, in opposition to the rights of property, running ahead of every other!" Even more shrill were the outcries of the *New York Commercial Advertiser:* "Lost to society, to earth and heaven, godless and hopeless, clothed and fed by stealing and blasphemy . . . such are the apostles who are trying to induce a number of able-bodied men in this city to follow in their course."

In the result, such fears proved to be exaggerated. The Workingmen's party did not sweep the city. Nevertheless, it polled some 6,000 votes, out of a total of 21,000 cast in the election, and sent one of its candidates—a carpenter—to the assembly. "The sun of liberty has not pursued his steady and unchanging course for half a century in vain," George Henry Evans began a rhapsodic editorial in the *Working Man's Advocate*, and then abruptly dropping his metaphor, observed more moderately that the result has proved "beyond our most sanguine expectations, favorable to our cause—the cause of the people."

Nevertheless, a growing divergence in the views of the party's self-constituted leaders, and a revolt on the part of the rank-and-file membership against Thomas Skidmore, soon led to internal dissension and factional fights. At a meeting in December 1829, a resolution was adopted in which the workingmen explicitly stated that they had "no desire or intention of disturbing the right of property in individuals, or the public." As Robert Dale Owen then moved in to try to take over Skidmore's repudiated leadership, opposition also arose to his program of state guardianship. The workingmen were ready to make education their foremost party plank, but they would not support "any attempt to palm upon any man, or set of men, the peculiar doctrines of infidelity, agrarianism, or sectarian principles." They declared that the school system should be based "upon a plan that shall leave to the father and the affectionate mother the enjoyment of the society of their offspring."

The consequences of these inner conflicts, in part promoted by politicians who sought workingmen's support for their own purposes, was a three-way split in the original organization. Skidmore and the few followers he could hold in line established a straight-out Agrarian Workingmen's party. Another faction, whose interests were promoted by George Henry Evans in the *Working Man's Advocate* and which was still supported by the Owenites and Wright, struggled to maintain the original party. A third group broke away under new leadership, with the support of the *Evening Journal*, another labor news sheet, and became known as the North American party, after the name of the hotel where its meetings were held.

Between the last two groups especially there was embittered and continuing strife. They were soon endorsing rival politicians, putting rival tickets in the field, flinging verbal brickbats at each other through the pages of their respective organs, and breaking up each other's meetings. The original Workingmen's party, finding itself under attack because of the radical views of Owen and Wright, frantically denied the implications of these charges. "The cries of Infidelity and Agrarianism are mere political scarecrows," it asserted, "such as were formerly set up to terrify the democrats of 1801." The North American party was accused of selling out to local politicians, and workingmen were called upon to avoid "the political trimmer, the pettifogger, the office hunter." Unity was essential if they were to make their influence felt—"Yoke not, therefore, the noble war horse with the ignoble ass."

While the intraparty contest raged in New York, local parties sprang up in such cities as Albany, Troy, Schenectady, Rochester, Syracuse and Auburn. Plans were made to hold a state convention of workingmen and to nominate candidates for governor and lieutenant governor. It was finally summoned, with seventy-eight delegates from thirteen counties, but the split in New York City proved disastrous when rival delegations attended the convention. The professional politicians took over and succeeded in winning the workingmen's vote in support of a Democratic office-seeker. "The Working Men Betrayed," shrieked the *Advocate*, and declared that its adherents would nominate their own slate.

In the resulting confusion, the election of 1830 found three factions of workingmen each putting forward its own nominees in the city elections and endorsing rival candidates for the governorship. Without cohesion or unity, the Workingmen's part as originally constituted was an easy prey to professional political influences and the blandishments of Tammany Hall, and it broke up. The Democrats won both the state and local elections, and there was an end to any further effective organization among the forces of labor in New York. *The Working Man's Advocate* insisted that nothing could so effectually prevent the final accomplishment of labor's objectives as a coalition with any other party for the temporary purpose of electing particular men. The workers' votes, however, had already swung over to Tammany.

If the experience of the New York artisans and mechanics in trying to set up an independent political organization was short-lived, very much the same story might be told of the activities of other workingmen's parties. In many instances, particularly in Pennsylvania and Massachusetts, they succeeded for a time in aligning the labor vote behind their own candidates and exercising an important and occasionally decisive influence in local politics. But just as in New York, internal friction and external pressures led to factionalism and gradual disintegration. Self-constituted leaders sought to promote their own individual panaceas of reform, which, as in the case of the programs promoted by Skidmore, Evans, Owen, and Wright, sometimes conflicted with the vital interests of the workers. And when reformers were ousted, politicians were quick to move in to take over control and try to swing the workingmen's votes for one or another of the major parties.

In Massachusetts, an attempt to bring about a broader political organization of workers came in 1832 with the formation of the New England Association of Farmers, Mechanics, and Workingmen. The successes won by this group in local elections inspired the nomination of a governor, but the association was soon deeply involved in the larger political struggles of the day with its own gubernatorial candidate urging the working class to rally in support of the Democrats.

In spite of the failure of the workingmen's parties themselves, they did cause both Whigs and Democrats to appeal for the labor vote by adopting several of the workers' specific demands. Generally, Democrats proved more adept than Whigs in attracting worker support. When Jackson vigorously indicted monopoly and special privilege in his war against the Second Bank of the United States, many workers cheered him on. More working-class voters than not probably supported Jackson in the election of 1832 as the foe of monopoly and the friend of producers.

The conservatives gave warning in terms that were to be repeated often in the future. "Elect Jackson," one factory owner told his employees, "and the grass will grow in your streets, owls will build nests in the mills, and foxes burrow in the highways." But many workers turned out nevertheless to help return Jackson to office. In New York they marched to the polls singing:

> Mechanics, cartmen, laborers,
>   Must form a close connection,
> And show the rich aristocrats,
>   Their powers at this election...

Yankee Doodle, smoke 'em out
The proud, the banking faction
None but such as Hartford Feds
Oppose the poor and Jackson.

The twists and turns of politics in the 1830s were one thing. However, another was the steady growth of progressive principles and the practical achievement of the reforms which workers sought. As the popular support for the original aims of the workingmen's parties gathered increasing force, the major parties responded. Steady progress was made in meeting the demands that first flared forth in the labor press.

A first case in point was educational reform. At the head of the editorial column in almost every workingmen's newspaper was the demand which figured so prominently in the campaign of the New York party—Equal Universal Education. At this time, only the vaguest consideration was being given to the needs of children whose parents were unable to afford private institutions. New England was ahead of the rest of the country in having tax-supported schools, but even in such populous and wealthy states as New York, New Jersey, Pennsylvania, and Delaware (to say nothing of the new states in the West or the states of the South), the only provision for the children of workingmen and other poor families was the charity school—inadequate, inefficient, and socially degrading. The Public School Society of New York reported in 1829 that there were over 24,000 children between the ages of five and fifteen in that city who had no schooling whatsoever, or almost the same number as that enrolled in all charity and private schools. Some years later, a more extensive report in Pennsylvania declared that 250,000 out of the 400,000 children in that state did not attend school. For the country as a whole, overall estimates placed the total at over a million, with a corresponding measure of complete illiteracy.

The workingmen resented equally the lack of opportunity for an education as reflected in these figures, and the odium attached to such public schools as there were because they were charitable institutions. Without going so far as to accept all the doctrines of Robert Dale Owen and Frances Wright, they universally agreed with them in insisting upon the importance of free, republican education which would be available on terms of complete equality for the children of both the rich and the poor. The workingmen based their position on the philosophy of equal rights inherent in the Declaration of Independence and bulwarked it with the unassailable argument that, as future citizens, it was imperative that all children have the education which would enable them to vote intelligently. Never have a people had greater faith in education—"the greatest blessing bestowed upon mankind"—than this generation of Americans. The workers could not have been more determined in demanding it for their children as a right to which they were morally entitled.

"It appears, therefore to the committees," read a typical report of a workingmen's group in Philadelphia, "that there can be no liberty without a wide diffusion of real intelligence; that the members of a republic should all be alike instructed in the nature and character of their equal rights and duties, as human beings, and as citizens." This report also argued that only an effective system of public schools could prevent children from being exposed too early to the pernicious influences of society and thereby "yield an abundant harvest for magdalens and penitentiaries" or fall victim to intemperance—"that assassinator of private peace and public virtue." The major emphasis was invariably placed, however, on the importance of education as the very foundation of the democratic forms of government which America exemplified. "A system that shall unite under the same roof the children of the poor man and the rich, the widow's charge and the orphan," was the demand put forward by the reorganized Workingmen's Party of New York in 1829, "where the road to distinction shall be superior industry, virtue and acquirement, without reference to descent."

Opinions differed as to the type of education which should be provided, but stress was in most instances laid upon the importance of practical training as well as the liberal arts. Public institutions, it was urged in another report of the Philadelphia workingmen, should be "so located as to command health, exercise at the various mechanic arts, or argiculture, at the same time [that] a knowledge of the natural sciences, and other useful literature is taught."

Of course, the educational campaign also had support outside the working class. It was taken up by many reformers and attracted increasingly wider attention. Even conservatives began to speak out in favor of public education. If common people were to vote—as they did—then they had to be taught in public schools to respect social distinctions and property rights, asserted Daniel Webster, the

Massachusetts Whig. In other words, public education could accomplish conservative as well as liberal ends.

Soon, this campaign waged so vigorously for Equal Republican, Scientific, Practical Education began to bear fruit. State legislatures took the issue under more serious consideration than they ever had before and new laws were gradually adopted, first authorizing and then requiring local communities to levy taxes for public education. The turn perhaps came when Pennsylvania, where the workingmen had been so active, finally adopted a free, tax-supported system in 1834. The bill embodying this program narrowly missed defeat. In response to a protesting petition with 32,000 signatures, the Senate tried to substitute a provision "for the education of the poor gratis." But the principle of a public school system free to all on terms of equality triumphed. Other states fell into line, and the victory for which the workingmen had so long contested was ultimately won.

Another issue for which labor battled hard and successfully during this period was abolition of imprisonment for debt. The antiquated practice of throwing a man into jail when he could not meet his financial obligations was still in almost universal effect in the 1820s. The Boston Prison Discipline Society estimated, at the close of the decade, that some 75,000 persons were being imprisoned annually for debts and that, in at least half of the cases, the sums involved were less than $25. In one instance, a woman was taken from her home and the care of her two children for a debt of $3.60; in another, a man was thrown into jail for a $5 debt owed his grocer, even though it had been contracted while the debtor was ill. Thirty-two persons were found in one prison for debts which in every case were less than $1.

Obviously this system bore most heavily on the poor, and its injustice rankled deeply. "A law that makes poverty a crime," one workingman political candidate declared, "and a poor man a felon, after these very laws have made poverty inevitable, is not only cruel and oppressive, but absurd and revolting." Adding to the miseries of the situation, the debtors' jails were shockingly overcrowded and insanitary, and there was often no provision for feeding the prisoners, who remained wholly dependent upon private charity. In New Jersey, according to one report, there were "food, bedding and fuel" for criminals, but for the debtors only "walls, bars and bolts."

The workingman's drive first led to the passage of laws whereby the poor debtor could win release by taking a bankruptcy oath, and then to limitations upon the amounts for which he could be imprisoned. But soon the states were one by one forced to accept the inescapable logic of abolishing the system altogether. Ohio took this step in 1828, and the next decade saw its example followed by New York, New Jersey, Connecticut, Virginia, and other states. The practice still lingered on in some parts of the country, but its complete disappearance was clearly foreshadowed by the end of the 1830s.

The attack upon the militia system, largely promoted by the workingmen's parties, was also successful. In most states, attendance at annual drills and parades, generally lasting three days, was compulsory for every citizen. The militiamen had to pay all their own expenses and provide their own equipment, while failure to attend was punished by fines or imprisonment. For the workingmen, such regulations meant not only a loss in wages while attending the drill, but also what were for them heavy expenses. The rich, on the other hand, could easily afford to escape their obligations by paying the fines without difficulty. After 1830, compulsory service was either modified or completely abolished. President Jackson called attention to the issue in his Annual Message in 1832, urging that wherever the old system still prevailed—as in New York—its inequalities should be carefully examined.

Other instances of economic or social advance owed much to the workers. Their demand for mechanics' lien laws[1], at once taken up by Tammany Hall in New York, led to widespread adoption of such legislation. Their opposition to the existing auction system, to general incorporation laws, to the issuance by local banks of small currency notes, and to other economic abuses was an important factor in the passage of remedial laws.

The rise of the workingmen's parties did not represent a class movement in the Marxist, or socialist, sense. But it did signify a realization by many workers that capitalism bore down on them unfairly, and it did place in question society's dominant property relations. It added to the political agenda many demands associated with the labor theory of value.

As internal dissension and the manipulations of major party politicos disrupted the labor parties, the workers' movement began to focus on winning improved material conditions. The rapid economic growth of the years 1829–1836 increased the demand for labor and suggested to workers that trade-union economic action offered far

---

[1]Laws which protected the wages of workers in the event of employer's bankruptcy.

greater possibilities for success than politics. It even led the *National Laborer* of Philadelphia to assert prematurely, "The Trades' Unions never will be political because its members have learned from experience that the introduction of Politics into their Societies has thwarted every effort to ameliorate their Conditions."

Yet political action had produced several substantial gains for workers. Memories of such success would in the future lead to further instances of labor political action. But the history of labor parties in the Jacksonian era also carried less positive lessons. It showed how internal divisions among working-class leaders sowed dissension among the rank and file, and how the major parties could preempt labor's demands. Politics, moreover, revealed a split personality among many workers. On the one hand, many wanted to reform or abolish capitalism as it then existed. On the other hand, an equal and perhaps larger number merely wanted to share in the benefits of an emerging capitalism.

Unlike their contemporaries in Europe, American workers did not have to unite behind radical or socialist leadership to obtain the vote. It was already theirs to use when worker movements began to emerge on a broader scale. The continued buoyant growth of the economy, the spreading of population across the continent, and persistent infusions of new immigrants from abroad combined to keep American workers and the movements which they built internally divided.

If for a time the workingmen's parties of the 1830s seemed to foreshadow the possible creation of a labor party, their decline disclosed the limits of independent working-class political action.

IV

Labor Strength in the 1830s

The original workingmen's parties rose and fell within a very brief span of time. Whatever may be claimed for their political influence, their existence as distinctive political organizations was too ephemeral to figure prominently in the history of the labor movement. The return of the trade societies to economic action was in many ways a far more significant development. During these years, in which marked progress was being made in social reform in the country as a whole, and particularly during Jackson's second administration from 1833 to 1837, union activity was more widespread and more militant than it would be again for several decades.

The workingmen continued to experience, as their excursion into politics had already demonstrated, a degradation of their changing social position. The revived trade unions were to be concerned primarily with wages and hours, but they also reflected the desire of their members to regain status in the community. The old society which they had known appeared to be dissolving, with formerly independent craftsmen sinking to the level of wage earners, and artisans and mechanics more than ever hoped through union membership to reaffirm the dignity of labor and to win greater public recognition of its social as well as economic values.

"As the line of distinction between employer and employed *wid-ened*," wrote one labor leader in 1834, "the condition of the latter inevitably verges toward a state of vassalage...hostile to the best interests of the community, as well as the spirit and genius of our government." The trade societies sought to combat this trend by creating a solidarity among the workers which would safeguard them from complete and helpless subordination to the employing class.

Conditions in the early 1830s encouraged the growth of unions. On the one hand, mounting prosperity strengthened the bargaining power of the workers; on the other, determined efforts on the part of employers to hold down wages in the face of rising prices forced them to organize in self-defense. Not only did trade societies among almost all classes of workers multiply rapidly, but further attempts were made to link these local unions in citywide federations to promote labor unity. Still broader organization began which foreshadowed the establishment of a truly national labor movement. Moreover, the aggressive attitude of the members of these unions led to a wave of strikes which provided a dramatic chapter in the long struggle of the workers to establish their rights.

So general did this activity become that no trade appeared to be immune to its contagious militancy. "The barbers have struck," the *New York Times* exclaimed in April 1836, "and now all that remains for Editors is to strike, too."

Never before in time of peace had there been such a rapid increase in the cost of living as resulted from the wildcat boom of the early 1830s, with all its speculation and extravagant inflation. The easing of bank credit and the profligate issue of paper money, which were the immediate consequences of Jackson's successful attack upon the Second Bank of the United States, forced prices up all along the line. In New York, flour went from $5 a barrel in 1834 to $8 in April 1835, and then to $12 a year later. Other foodstuffs followed the same upward spiral, clothing and household goods rose phenomenally, and the advance in rents was from 25 to 40 per cent. It was generally estimated that the cost of living increased some 66 per cent between 1834 and 1836.

Wages invariably lagged behind in this upward march, and the further measures taken by employers to hold down their own costs constituted an even greater threat to the workers' living standards. With the virtual collapse of the apprenticeship system in many trades, young half-trained boys were taken on at lower wages than the prevailing rate for journeymen.

Also, women were joining the paid labor force in increasing numbers. Employed most commonly as tailoresses, seamstresses, and shoe binders, they now began to find work as printers, cigar makers, and in other trades. Because employers paid women less than men for comparable labor, a committee of the Philadelphia general trades assembly declared in 1836 that "of fifty-eight societies, twenty-four are seriously affected by female labour, to the impoverishment of whole families, and the benefit of none but the employers." Finally, the use of convict labor was becoming widespread. Mechanics and artisans complained bitterly that, through this developing practice of letting out contracts to prisons, whatever the benefits for the convicts themselves, articles were manufactured at prices "from 40 to 60 per cent below what the honest mechanic, who supports himself and family, can afford."

In such circumstances, there was hardly an urban community in which the workingmen were not driven to act together in mutual defense of their interests. In Philadelphia, the cordwainers reorganized, the handloom weavers formed a new society, and bricklayers, plumbers, blacksmiths, cigar makers, comb makers, and saddlers, among other tradesmen, were unionized. The older societies in New York were revived, with the printers, cordwainers, and tailors once again in the lead, and with cabinet makers, hat finishers, basket makers, locksmiths, piano makers, and silk hatters joining the union ranks. The organizations in Baltimore included bootmakers, stonecutters, coopers, carpet weavers, and coach makers. The same story could be told of every other city on the Atlantic seaboard, and also of upstate New York, Washington, Pittsburgh, Louisville, and other manufacturing centers in the West.

The further organization among workers other than the traditional mechanics and artisans was making at least some headway. By this time, there was a rapidly developing textile industry in Massachusetts and Rhode Island, factories in Connecticut were turning out clocks and watches, and iron foundries in Pennsylvania presaged the further growth of large-scale industry. In addition to the employees in such establishments, other new groups of wage earners included machinists and engineers, freight handlers, firemen on steamboats, stage drivers, and gatekeepers on turnpikes and canal bridges. While these workers still remained largely unorganized, pioneering unions among the cotton factory operatives, tinplate and sheet iron workers, and many other groups won increasing support.

Women also eagerly founded their own trade societies. Baltimore had a United Seamstresses Society; New York its Ladies' Shoebinders and Female Bookbinders, as well as a female Union Association; and Philadelphia a Female Improvement Society. In the cotton textile industry, the first large-scale type of machine factory, young single women, especially in Massachusetts, dominated the labor force. They, too, organized themselves, forming in 1833 the Female Society of Lynn and Vicinity for the Protection and Promotion of Female Industry, and a year later, the Factory Girls' Association.

A picturesque view of the trade societies as they existed in New York about this time is found in the description of a spectacular demonstration in that city celebrating the triumph of the French Revolution of 1830. Although Tammany Hall took over control of the affair, the unions dominated it. Their delegations were the most prominent feature in a parade whose line of march was some three miles long and which was watched by crowds estimated at thirty thousand persons.

The elaborate floats, as described in the *Working Man's Advocate*, were the sensation of the day. The printers had two elegant presses ("tastefully gilded and ornamented") which they had borrowed from the manufactories of Messrs. Rust and Hoe and set up on two separate cars drawn by four horses. The butchers, in dress described as characteristic of their profession and mounted on prancing white horses, were also on hand. On one of their floats the skin of an ox had been so stuffed as to take on a life-like appearance and had been gaily decorated with ribbons and cockades. On another, a butcher's stall had been erected where "sausages were manufactured to the great amusement of the people."

The cordwainers had made extensive and elegant preparations for the demonstration, and two young ladies were busily engaged in binding shoes on one of their floats. The manufacturers of steam engines exhibited a perfect steam engine ("the smoke from the pipes ascended, the water wheels revolved"), and the cabinet makers had such splendid specimens of furniture that the *Advocate's* reporter found himself unable to describe them. The carvers and gilders were in the line with portraits of Jefferson and Lafayette in superb gilt frames; the tobacconists won the applause of the admiring crowd by distributing small plugs of tobacco; the saddlers and harness makers had mounts furnished with the most shining examples of their ware; the bookbinders boasted a float in the form of a mammoth book hauled by four sturdy horses; and the chair makers graciously built on route a "Grecian Post Maple Chair."

The shouts and huzzas, the waving pennants, tricolored cockades and "star spangled banners" made for a great occasion. Only a small part of the throng could be accommodated about the reviewing stand where the venerable ex-President James Monroe had the place of honor until the "chilly state of the atmosphere" compelled him to leave. There were fervid speeches, and an ode, written by Samuel Woodworth, printer, was sung to the tune of the *Marseillaise* with the accompaniment of the orchestra from the Park Theatre:

> Then swell the choral strain,
> To Hail the blest decree.
> Rejoice, rejoice, the Press shall reign
> And all the world be Free.

That night the various societies held commemorative banquets (a dinner was sent in to the inmates of the debtor's prison by the sympathetic delegates of the ninth ward), and a large group of workingmen assembled at the Masonic Hall. After a sumptuous entertainment had served as prelude "for the enjoyment of the mental repast," a glowing address was delivered on the success of the French revolutionary movement and the part played in it by workingmen.

"Move on then, mechanics and working men," the speaker of the evening declared in his eloquent conclusion, "in your glorious career of mental independence, with republican education for your polar star, union and firmness your sheet anchor, and the day is not distant which shall crown your noble effort with victory, and your country shall stand redeemed from the poison of fashion and the canker worm of party—and in their place shall spring up the tree of pure republicanism, yielding the choice fruits of real equality of rights; then man shall be judged by his actions and not by his professions; by his usefulness to society as an industrious citizen and not by the texture of the garb which covers him."

The address was followed by toasts—fourteen formal toasts and thirty-one volunteer toasts—happily "interspersed with appropriate songs, odes and recitations." The enthusiastic diners toasted the workingmen of Paris and of New York; they drank to the memory of

Jefferson and Lafayette, to true democrats, universal education, free
enquiry; they toasted "the Original Working Men—May they not
oblique to the right or the left," and the "Simon Pures—May they not
be frightened by the cries of Fanny Wrightism, Agrarianism or any
other *ism*, but stick to true republicanism."

There were forty-five toasts, as the bottles circulated and the workingmen cheered. "The greatest hilarity and unanimity," concludes
the account of the *Working Man's Advocate* "characterized the proceedings of the evening, and the company separated at an early hour,
much gratified with the manner in which they had been entertained."

The rapid growth and development of the trade societies led
naturally to the movement for closer association to promote common
aims. A precedent for such cooperation had been established by the
Mechanics' Union of Trade Associations in Philadelphia, but, as we
have seen, this group had almost immediately become absorbed in
politics. What the workingmen now sought in forming "trades'
unions"—that is, unions of local trade societies which represented in
modern terminology central trades councils—was a basis for joint
economic activity.[1] The trades' union, in the words of the constitution of one of these new organizations, was a "compact, formed of
Societies and Associations of Mechanics and Working Men, which,
having discovered that they were unable to combat the numerous
powers arrayed against them, united together for mutual protection."

The General Trades' Union of New York was the most important
of these new central trades councils, but there were comparable
organizations in Philadelphia, Boston, Baltimore, Washington, Cincinnati, Pittsburgh, Louisville, and other manufacturing cities. Their
number had grown to thirteen by 1836, with fifty-two associated
societies in New York, fifty-three in Philadelphia, twenty-three in
Baltimore, and sixteen in Boston.

----

[1]The terminology of labor organization in this period is confusing. The "trade
societies," as suggested in the text, were the equivalent of modern "trade unions," and
the new "trades' unions" corresponded more nearly to today's "central trades
councils" established in the cities by the AFL and the CIO. At this very time, however,
the "trade societies" were beginning to be called "trade unions," although "trades'
unions" were the association of the local societies.

One of the earliest examples of the use of "union" in the modern sense of the term,
in a pamphlet, *Dialogue Between Strike and Steady* (1836), had this interesting comment: "My objection to your Union is, that you wish to use the very compulsion, you
will not yourselves endure."

The final coordinating step in this activity came in 1834, when the summons went out to establish a national organization embracing all trades. Representatives of local societies in New York, Brooklyn, Boston, Philadelphia, Poughkeepsie, and Newark met in New York and formed the National Trades' Union. Its purposes were to advance the welfare of the laboring classes, promote the establishment of trades' unions in every part of the country, and publish such information as would be useful to mechanics and workingmen. In the light of the failure of the workingmen's parties, its leaders were determined that the new organization should not be drawn off into political activities. The workingmen "belonged to no party," one Massachusetts labor leader declared; "they were neither disciples of Jacksonism nor Clayism, Van Burenism nor Websterism, not any other ism but workeyism."

National organization of the workers was not to be really effective at this time. It was to wait upon the nationalizing of business in the years following the Civil War. But the attempt to form such a federation attests the strength and vitality of the labor movement of the 1830s. As the result of the zeal of local societies, city trades councils, and the National Trades' Union, there were in the country as a whole an estimated 44,000 to 131,000 unionized workers in the mid-1830s, the lower estimate being the more likely number.[2] On a relative basis, so large a number of wage earners would not again be enrolled in union ranks for half a century. In New York, some two thirds of all the city's workers were said to be members of one or another of its fifty-odd labor unions.

In increasingly active defense of their rights, trade union members did not hesitate either to threaten or actually go out on strike when their employers refused to meet what they felt were their legitimate demands. When employers tried to hold down wages or bring in untrained workers at lower pay, there were turn-outs in almost every trade and in every city. Printers and weavers, tailors and coachmakers, masons and bookbinders walked out. Carpenters in New York earning $1.50 a day struck for $1.75 and, having won it, promptly struck again for $2.

---

[2]Maurice Neufeld, "The Size of the Jacksonian Labor Movement: A Cautionary Account," *Labor History*, XXIII (Fall, 1982), 599–607.

The girls working in New England cotton mills again went on strike. "One of the leaders mounted a pump," the *Boston Transcript* reported, "and made a flaming. . .speech on the rights of women and the iniquities of 'monied aristocracy' which produced a powerful effect upon her auditors, and they determined to have their own way, if they died for it." As in the first waves of strikes instigated by the original trade societies, such turn-outs were almost always peaceful, but they became so general that the business community became increasingly alarmed. Between 1833 and 1837, no less than 168 strikes were recorded in contemporary newspapers.

As in later periods, the employers sought to attribute these disturbances, not to labor's legitimate grievances, but to the activity of radical and subversive agitators, generally supposed to be foreigners. "I fear the elements of disorder are at work," a conservative New Yorker, Philip Hone, former mayor, noted in his diary; "the bands of Irish and other foreigners instigated by the mischievous councils of the trades union and other combinations of discontented men, are acquiring strength and importance which will ere long be difficult to quell." Whatever the workers' complaints (and Hone noted himself the tremendous increase in the cost of living), he felt that any strike, however orderly, was an "unlawful proceeding."

The demand of workers throughout the East for a ten-hour day came to a head during this period in a concerted outbreak of strikes. There had been earlier agitation for such a reduction in the hours of work. It had been the background for the formation of the Mechanics' Union of Trade Associations in Philadelphia in 1827, and of the Workingmen's Party in New York two years later. But the workers were now ready to use their strongest weapon as a means to coerce employers to grant their demands.

"All men have a just right, derived from their creator," stated a resolution of the journeymen carpenters in Philadelphia, "to have sufficient time each day for the cultivation of their mind and for self-improvement; Therefore, resolved, that we think ten hours industriously imployed are sufficient for a day's labor."

On this same note, New England workingmen also demanded a shorter day and, surprisingly, found support from such a conservative paper as the *Boston Transcript*. "Let the mechanic's labor be over," it urged, "when he has wrought ten or twelve hours in the long days of summer, and he will be able to return to his family in season, and with sufficient vigour, to pass some hours in the instruction of his children, or in the improvement of his own mind."

In other periods of labor's long struggle for shorter hours, stress would be laid upon the ill effects of prolonged, exacting toil on the workers' health and wellbeing, or upon the importance of spreading work to combat the danger of unemployment. In the 1830s, however, the emphasis upon time for self-education, which was considered essential to enable the newly enfranchised laboring classes to fulfill their obligations as citizens, was a great deal more than merely a facile argument. There is compelling evidence that the workers were deeply interested in education for themselves as well as for their children. The crowded workingmen audiences at the popular lyceum lectures of these years, the growing vogue for circulating libraries, and the insistent demand for free, public schools all attest to a deep concern born of the idealistic belief that education alone could provide the basis for a successful democracy.

"We have been too long subjected," a circular of striking workingmen in Boston in 1835 stated, "to the odious, cruel, unjust and tyrannical system which compels the operative Mechanic to exhaust his physical and mental powers.... We have rights, and we have duties to perform as American citizens and members of society, which forbid us to dispose of more than Ten Hours for a day's work."

Such arguments did not, however, carry much weight with employers. The proposal for a ten-hour day, one newspaper declared, "strikes the very nerve of industry and good morals by dictating the hours of labour.... To be idle several of the most useful hours of the morning and evening will surely lead to intemperance and ruin." A statement published in the *Boston Courier* by a group of merchants and shipowners further emphasized the serious loss to the community in any reduction of the working day and deplored the "habits likely to be generated by the indulgence of idleness." However deeply grounded was the real objection to shorter hours because of its effect upon business profits, it was, indeed, this professed fear that leisure would undermine the workers' morals and foster intemperance that became the chief stock in trade of the conservative opposition to any change in the traditional sun-up-to-sunset system.

The organized workingmen in city after city refused, however, to be persuaded by such arguments and stood their ground. Their universal demand was for a working day from six in the morning until six in the evening, with an hour off for breakfast and another for dinner. In Baltimore, the members of seventeen trades joined forces in a strike for this reform in 1833. Two years later, the carpenters of Boston, with the support of masons, stonecutters, and other workers in the building trades, walked out with similar demands. Both of these movements failed. In Philadelphia, on the other hand, an even more widely organized and popularly supported strike won a resounding victory in 1835 and had wide repercussions.

This strike was initiated by coal heavers and other common laborers, but they were soon joined by cordwainers, handloom weavers, cigar makers, saddlers, printers, and members of the building trades. A circular relating the experiences of the Boston workers had an electric effect in unifying those of Philadelphia and strengthened their determination not to give in. Workers of all trades paraded through the streets, with fife and drum and banners emblazoned "from 6 to 6."

"We marched to the public works," wrote their leader, John Ferral, a handloom weaver and fiery labor agitator, "and the workmen joined in with us. . . . Employment ceased, business was at a standstill, shirt sleeves were rolled up, aprons on, working tools in hand were the order of the day. Had the cannon of an invading enemy belched forth its challenge on our soil, the freemen of Philadelphia could not have shown a greater ardor for the contest; the blood-sucking aristocracy, they alone stood aghast; terror stricken, they thought the day of retribution was come, but no vengeance was sought or inflicted by the people for the wrongs they had suffered from their enemies."

The common council of the city was the first to give in and established a ten-hour day for all public servants. The master carpenters and master cordwainers followed, and other employers then quickly fell in line until the ten-hour day prevailed throughout the city. "The mechanics of Philadelphia stood firm and true," Ferral wrote; "they conquered, because they were united and resolute in their actions. The presses which could not retard the progress of public opinion, nor divert it from its just objects, viz. the adoption of the ten-hour system. . . now proclaim the triumph of our bloodless revolution."

The movement spread to other parts of the country and in many instances won a corresponding success. Soon the ten-hour day had widely replaced, for artisans and mechanics, the former sun-up to sunset. In the factories that were being established for the New England textile industry, and in many other manufacturing industries, the work day was long to remain twelve hours and more. In some trades, the gains of the 1830s were to be lost. But a very real victory had been won for the workers by their concerted stand in the strikes of Philadelphia and other cities. Moreover, the federal government was soon to be induced to establish a ten-hour day for all public works. Congress had refused to take any notice on the frequent memorials addressed to it on the subject, but when striking shipwrights appealed directly to Jackson in 1836, the system was installed at the Philadelphia navy yard. Four years later, President Martin Van Buren even more directly admitted his debt to the workingmen for their political support by an Executive Order which established ten hours as the work day on all governmental projects.

The employers held out as long as they could in combating the workers' demands for both higher wages and a shorter working day. They continued whenever possible to undermine their employees' bargaining power by drawing upon cheaper sources of labor. But where skilled artisans and mechanics were concerned, employers found it increasingly difficult to maintain their position. The craft unions succeeded in enforcing a closed shop which tied the employers' hands. Through public cards listing as "unfair" any journeyman who did not join a union and designating as "foul" any establishment where an "unfair man" was given work, they largely controlled the labor market. Of course, this was not always true, but the records of the time reveal an unexpected power on the part of the organized workers in the skilled trades.

In these circumstances, employers turned more and more to mutual protective associations which were prepared to act together in opposing "every injurious combination" of the workingmen. In New York, a group of employers, curriers, and leather dealers took up arms against the General Trades' Union and mutually agreed that they would not employ "any man who is known to be a member of that or any other society which has for its object the direction of terms or prices for which workmen shall engage themselves." In Philadelphia, the master carpenters took the lead and called for the formation of an Anti-Trades' Union Association. A set of resolutions was adopted which delcared the trades' union to be arbitrary, unjust, mischievous, and a powerful engine of the leveling system that would reduce masters to the status of journeymen. Employers had every right, it was maintained, to make whatever contracts with their employees they chose—without the interference of any workingmen's society.

When the employer associations were again unable to hold out against the labor societies, court action was once more in order. The drive to break up unions as conspiracies in restraint of trade was vigorously renewed, and, as in the opening years of the century, the employers found willing allies among conservative members of the bench.

The case of *People* v. *Fisher,* decided in New York Supreme Court in 1835, was an important demonstration in this period that the opposition of the courts to labor unions had not changed. A society of journeymen cordwainers in Geneva, New York, was prosecuted for conspiring to raise wages and thereby, as claimed by the plaintiffs, committing an act injurious to trade and commerce and a misdemeanor under existing laws. The presiding judge ruled in the employers' favor. On the theory that the interests of society were best served when the price of labor was left to regulate itself, he declared that, in combining to raise wages, the cordwainers were working a public injury because "a conspiracy for such an object is against the spirit of the common law."

"Competition is the life of trade," the decision concluded. "If the defendants cannot make coarse boots for less than one dollar per pair, let them refuse to do so; but let them not directly or indirectly undertake to say that others shall not do the work for a less price.... The interference of the defendants was unlawful; its tendency is not only to individual oppression, but to public inconvenience and embarrassment."

The effect of this decision was to encourage other employers to seek to suppress the trade societies even though they did not engage in strikes, and, when the courts continued to follow a flagrantly antilabor policy, a storm of protest arose among workingmen and their sympathizers. It came to a head in New York after a further case in 1836 where the presiding judge strongly charged the jury to find a society of journeymen tailors guilty of conspiracy in restraint of trade.

"They were condemned," William Cullen Bryant wrote in vehement defense of the tailors in the New York *Evening Post,* "because they had determined not to work for the wages offered them! Can any thing be imagined more abhorrent.... If this is not Slavery, we have forgotten its definition. Strike the right of associating for the sale of labor from the privileges of a freeman, and you may as well at once bind him to a master or ascribe him to the soil."

The outraged labor leaders of New York distributed throughout the city circulars, inscribed with a coffin, which called upon all workingmen to attend court on the day set for sentencing the convicted tailors.

"On Monday, June 6, 1836," the circulars read, "these Freemen are to receive their sentence, to gratify the hellish appetites of the Aristocracy. On Monday, the Liberty of the Workingmen will be interred! Judge Edwards is to chant the requiem! Go! Go! every Freeman, every Workingman, and hear the melancholy sound of the earth on the Coffin of Equality! Let the court-room, the City Hall—yea, the whole Park, be filled with Mourners!" The crowd which actually turned out does not appear to have reached the hoped-for proportions, and it was entirely peaceful. A week later, however, after the tailors had been duly sentenced, another mass meeting was held which drew some 27,000 persons. The offending judge was burned in effigy.

The reaction against these trials was in fact so strong that juries could not fail to be influenced by it, and in two other conspiracy cases during the same summer verdicts of not guilty were returned. Finally, in 1842, Chief Justice Lemuel Shaw of the Massachusetts Supreme Court rendered an important decision in *Commonwealth* v. *Hunt* which appeared to provide a firm basis for the legality of unions.

The case was that of the Journeymen Bootmakers' Society of Boston, whose members had agreed not to work for any person who employed a journeyman who did not belong to their organization. Shaw stated that the manifest purpose of the society was to induce all those engaged in the same occupation to become members, and that this could not be considered unlawful. Nor could he see that, in attempting to accomplish it by refusing to work for any employer who engaged a journeyman not a member, the bootmakers were employing criminal means. He cited as a possible parallel a society whose members might undertake to promote the highly laudable cause of temperance by agreeing not to work for anyone who employed a user of strong spirits. In other words, agreement for common action to achieve a lawful object was not necessarily a criminal conspiracy. "The legality of such an association," the decision concluded, "will . . . depend upon the means to be used for its accomplishment."

Since the labor societies might still have to prove that the means which they adopted to attain their ends were in every case lawful, this decision was not a complete victory for labor. It had, indeed, turned upon certain technicalities in the indictment. But both union

organization and even the principle of the closed shop had nevertheless received substantial support. It would not be until a much
later period that labor again found itself on the legal defensive,
fighting renewed conspiracy charges under the antitrust laws and the
arbitrary use of injunctions against strikes and boycotts.

In the ten-hour movement, the revolt against the conspiracy laws,
and in their strikes, the workingmen of the 1830s had the full and active backing of their general trades' unions. These organizations were
ready to render whatever assistance they could, both in supporting the
local societies in their demands and in extending financial assistance
when workers went out on strike. In New York, Philadelphia,
Boston—wherever general trades' unions had been formed—there
was close cooperation among the workers as a result of this leadership. Monthly dues were paid to the central organization, making
possible the creation of a strike fund, and in many instances additional union appropriations aided the members of other societies out
on strike. Occasionally such aid was extended from one city to
another. When a delegation of Philadelphia bookbinders appealed to
New York's General Trades' Union for aid in February 1836, a resolution favoring such action was at once adopted. It called upon all
members to support "their fellow mechanics who are at this incle-
ment season driven to a stand for their rights against aristocratical
tyranny." Varying sums of money were sent to the bookbinders not
only by unions in New York but also by those of Washington,
Baltimore, Albany and Newark.

The National Trades' Union, which had met first in 1834 and held
conventions in the two succeeding years, did not have the close
organization of the general trades' unions. It remained little more
than an annual conference which debated labor issues and occasionally addressed memorials to Congress—on the ten-hour day, prison
labor, or public lands. It also went on record, although it refused to
enter upon direct political action, in support of many of the reforms
being promoted by the Jacksonian Democrats. It attacked "this
American banking system, this rag-money system, this system of
legalized monopolies which makes the rich richer and the poor
poorer." It was in no sense a class-conscious movement, however.
"Our object in the formation of the Trades' Union," declared its
organ, the *Union*, on April 21, 1836, ". . . was not to create a feeling of
enmity against the non-producers; . . . [but] to raise in the estimation

of themselves and others, those who are the producers of the
necessaries and luxuries of life."

Perhaps the greatest contribution of the National Trades' Union to
the cause of labor was to bring together the workingmen's leaders
from various parts of the country. It gave them a sense of common
purpose and of support for their activities which encouraged them, as
in the case of the ten-hour movement, to keep up their local struggles
for labor's rights.

John Ferral, the aggressive handloom weaver who led the successful
ten-hour strike in Philadelphia, was a prominent figure at union conventions. No one more strongly urged direct economic action by labor
societies or warned more often of the danger of their being diverted
from their main purposes by political blandishments. "The office
holders and office seekers of all parties have tried to lure us into the
meshes of their nets," he wrote, "but experience came to our aid, and,
coy as the young deer, we shied off from their advances; we felt
grateful for their proffered aid, but told them 'we knew our own
rights, and knowing dared maintain them.'" His initiative and energy
were perhaps the most important factors in the organization of the
Philadelphia General Trades' Union. He served as chairman of one of
its original organizing committees, was constantly involved in its
activities, and references to his "spirited addresses" run through all
the proceedings of the union.

Another Philadelphia delegate was William English, for a time
secretary of the General Trades' Union. He was a journeyman
shoemaker and a radical, highly erratic champion of the workers'
cause. His critics declared that he did not have an idea which he had
not borrowed or stolen from someone else, but his impassioned
addresses always held popular attention.

The principal representative of the New England workingmen was
Charles Douglas, one of the founders of the New England Association of Farmers, Mechanics, and Other Workingmen, and editor of
the *New England Artisan*. His opposition to political activity was no
less pronounced than that of John Ferral. Douglas' special interest
was the status of factory operatives in the textile mills, and he was one
of the first spokesmen for this class of workers.

Attending at least one National Trades' Union meetings was his
coworker in this cause, Seth Luther, the so-called "Traveling Agent"
of the *Artisan* and a prototype of many later labor agitators. He was
one of the most picturesque leaders of this period, a tall lanky,

tobacco-chewing Yankee, in a bright green jacket, who toured through the factory towns calling upon workers to defend their rights. "You cannot raise one part of the community above another unless you stand on the bodies of the poor," he repeatedly declared, and, in support of this thesis, he issued a stream of pamphlets which depicted the harsh life of the women and children who worked in the cotton mills under the lash of factory managers. His style was grim, sardonic, and highly colored. "While music floats from quivering strings through the perfumed and adorned apartments...of the rich," Luther wrote, "the nerves of the poor woman and child, in the cotton mills, are quivering with almost *dying agony*, from *excessive labor* to support this splendor."

The first president of the National Trades' Union was Ely Moore. Originally a student of medicine, he had abandoned that profession to become a journeyman printer and then entered actively into the labor movement. He suffered from ill health, which was eventually to force his retirement from the political scene, but not before he had proved himself both an able organizer and effective administrator in union activities. Tall, handsome, with curly black hair brushed back over a broad forehead, invariably well dressed and habitually carrying an ivory-headed cane, he possessed, according to contemporaries, a thrilling power of eloquence. He headed the General Trades' Union in New York before taking over his post in the National Trades' Union, and in the former capacity had sounded the keynote of the developing labor movement in addressing the workingmen as Pioneers in the Great Cause.

"To you, then, gentlemen, as the *actual* representatives of the Mechanic interests throughout the country," Moore declared, "the eyes of thousands and thousands are turned; for should the experiment succeed here, and the expectations of the friends of the 'Union' be realized, other Unions of a kindred character will be formed, in every section." But should they fail, he then went on to warn his audience, "the haughty aristocrats of the land will hail the event with exulting hearts and hellish satisfaction."

Moore soon made his position in labor circles a springboard for entry into active politics, and, with the support of the unions and Tammany Hall, he was sent to Congress the same year that saw him chosen head of the National Trades' Union. There he won national prominence as a spokesman for the interests of labor and played a notable part in introducing the various memorials addressed to Congress by the union. Whenever he spoke, he seems to have commanded rapt attention for his pleas in behalf of workingmen's rights and his vehement attacks upon "the heartless cupidity of the privileged few."

During the aftermath of the popular excitement aroused in New York by the conspiracy trial of the journeymen tailors, Moore rose on one occasion in April 1836 to defend labor under unusually dramatic circumstances. A representative from South Carolina had warned of a possible workingmen's insurrection. Although he was so ill that he had to steady himself by leaning on his cane, Moore addressed his audience in a ringing voice that reached to every corner of the House. How could the interests and safety of the state be plotted against, he asked peremptorily, by a group composing three fourths of the state? "Sir," he declared, glaring at the Speaker as his audience listened intently and one southern congressman was heard to murmur that the high priest of revolution was singing his swan song, "there is much greater danger that capital will unjustly appropriate to itself the avails of labor, than that labor will unlawfully seize upon capital."

"My eye was fixed upon him," wrote a reporter who described the scene for the *Democratic Review*; "I saw him grow paler than ever; till a deadly hue swept over his face; his hands were arrested in the air—he grasped at emptiness—a corpse seemed to stand with outstretched hands before the agitated crowd—his eyes were closed—he tottered, and amid the rush and exclamations of the whole house, fell back insensible into the arms of one of his friends."

Moore recovered from this attack of illness but he would not again address the House. His friends felt that he was in too poor health to undergo the strain which public speaking imposed upon a person of his excitable, nervous temperament. But his oration went rapidly through four editions and played its part in arresting the drive to outlaw unions by court action. Public opinion was more and more swinging to their support. "What but a general revolt of all the laboring classes is to be gained," William Cullen Bryant asked in the New York *Evening Post*, "by these wanton and unprovoked attacks upon their rights?"

The labor movement of the 1830s, to be sure, differed substantially from the one which emerged a century later. It originated in a society in which the great mass of workers were either skilled artisans and their apprentices in small-scale shops, or unskilled fetchers and haulers. Hence the founders of most early trade societies, or unions, thought of themselves as respectable, independent mechanics, men who preferred to obtain a just price for their product rather than a fair wage for their labor.

The lines which the artisans drew in American society were between rich and poor, parasites and producers, aristocracy and democracy, as well as between employers and employees. They were greatly aroused, as was stated in an address of the New England Association, by "the low estimation in which useful labor is held by many whose station in society enable them to give the tone to public opinion." They resented the trend whereby all those who could, sought to find some means of living without hard work and condemned the more useful and industrious portion of the community to a life of constant toil—"stripped of the better share of their earnings, holding a subordinate, if not degraded situation in society, and frequently despised by the very men, and women and children who live at ease upon the fruits of their labour." The dignity of labor, and the respect due to workingmen, were as much the concern of the labor unions of the 1830s as improvement in actual working conditions.

Whatever may be said of the high purpose of the labor unions of the 1830s, and whatever progress they made in achieving both their broader and more immediate aims, their days were numbered. In 1837, the prosperity which had provided the background for their growth and accomplishments came to a sudden end. The bubble of speculation was rudely punctured. As prices plunged precipitately downward, hard times again swept over the entire nation. Trade and commerce dried up, manufacturing sharply declined, and business stagnated in the formerly prosperous towns and cities of both the Atlantic seaboard and the West.

The workingmen again faced what depression has always meant for them—declining wages and unemployment. When the alternative to work was starvation for themselves and their families, they deserted the unions as they had in 1819 for fear of employer retaliation, and they did not dare to strike to protect the gains they had won when things were going well. With few exceptions, the journeymen societies which had seemed so powerful completely folded. They were crushed by economic circumstances, and in their collapse their newspapers and their federations also disappeared almost overnight. The depression of 1837 brought the emerging labor movement to a halt, as the Panic of 1819 eighteen years before had broken up the original trade societies.

Had organized labor survived this financial and economic panic, its subsequent history might have followed a quite different course. Strong unions would perhaps have been able to cope with the new needs and new problems which confronted labor when the full impact of the industrial revolution made itself felt in American society. Its long shadow was falling over the land in the 1830s and the new class of factory operatives was constantly growing. The skilled workers, already organized, were prepared to cooperate with these weaker wage earners, and they could have helped to promote at this early stage of industrialization the establishment of effective unions among the unskilled. But this was not to be. As the steady expansion of manufactures tended to depress the wage-earning class, labor failed to develop for the workers as a whole any program which could successfully defend their interests.

V

The Impact of
Industrialism

In the course of his American tour in 1842, the English novelist, Charles Dickens, visited Lowell, Massachusetts, where the new textile manufacturers of New England had established one of the country's first factory towns. The young women and girls who made up most of the working force appeared to him paragons of virtue—happy, contented, and exemplary in their conduct. With their neat and serviceable bonnets, warm cloaks and shawls, "they were all well dressed, but not to my thinking above their station. . . . From all the crowd I saw in the different factories that day, I cannot recall or separate one face that give me a painful impression."

The English traveler also admired the well-ordered rooms in the factories, some of which had plants growing in the windows, and the fresh air, cleanliness, and comfort; he was impressed with the boarding houses where the young women lived under careful chaperonage; and he was particularly struck with what he reported as three startling facts: there were pianos in many of the houses, nearly all of the young ladies subscribed to circulating libraries, and a magazine was published—the *Lowell Offering*—that was entirely made up of stories and articles by the factory operatives. Gazing happily upon this industrial paradise, Dickens compared it with the manufacturing centers of England and earnestly begged his countrymen "to pause and reflect upon the difference between this town and those great haunts of misery."

Although it could also have been pointed out, even in 1842, that the factory girls worked incredibly long hours, were badly overcrowded in their boarding houses, and found their lives wholly ordered and controlled by the paternalistic factory owners, the picture that the enthusiastic Dickens drew of Lowell was not wholly out of keeping with the facts. Other visitors confirmed his general impressions. They, too, wrote of the pleasant atmosphere, of the cultural opportunities of circulating libraries and lecture rooms, and of the gay appearance of the young ladies with neat bonnets over their carefully curled ringlets and wearing silk stockings and carrying parasols. Lowell may not have been amusing, as the French traveler, Michael Chevalier, wrote, but it was "clean, decent, peaceful, and sober."

Because of the relative scarcity of labor in New England, the textile mills of Massachusetts at first avoided the most unwholesome aspects of the early stages of the industrial revolution as it had developed in Europe. The Massachusetts capitalists who established the first textile mills had to attract their labor force from the New England countryside. In order to recruit young rural women of strict Protestant background, the mill owners created a clean, controlled environment.

The mill girls had to live in the boarding houses, where they were under strict supervision and the doors were closed at 10 p.m. They were expected to attend church. Not only was discharge an immediate consequence of immodesty, profanity, or dancing—to say nothing of more serious lapses from morality—but, concerning male workers, the Lowell Manufacturing Company stated that it would not "continue to employ any person who shall be wanting in proper respect to the females employed by the company, or who shall smoke within the company's premises, or be guilty of inebriety."

Although the long hours of tending looms in the mills could be oppressive to them, the mill girls also found new opportunities. In Lowell and similar towns, they met hundreds of young girls just like themselves, fresh from the farms of Vermont and New Hampshire. They talked to each other, socialized, and built bonds of sisterhood. For the first time, many experienced liberation from the bondage of repressive patriarchical families. Indeed, the wages they earned, small as they may have been, offered them a measure of economic independence. Their savings could be used for frivolous purchases as well as to support their rural families or amass a dowry.

Equally important, the mill girls of the 1820s and 1830s did not form a permanent factory proletariat. Few entered the mills with the intention of remaining. Some hoped to save enough money for their marriage dowry, others to obtain enough cash to finance a move west, and still others the funds to preserve the family farm. Moreover, throughout the period, in slack times and boom times, the girls moved constantly back and forth between farm and factory. They were neither firmly attached to the mills nor wholly dependent on them.

Such an exceptional work situation was of short duration. Far-reaching changes were already well under way at the time of Dickens's visit to Lowell. As competition increased in the textile industry, the original concern of the mill owners for their employees gave way to stricter controls which had nothing to do with the well-being of the workers. Employers reduced wages, lengthened hours, and inten-sified work. For a work day from 11½ to 13 hours, making up an average week of 75 hours, the women operatives were generally earn-ing less than $1.50 a week (exclusive of board) by the late 1840s, and they were being compelled to tend four looms whereas in the 1830s they had only taken care of two. When the manager of one mill at Holyoke, Massachusetts, found his hands "languorous" because they had breakfasted, he ordered them to come before breakfast. "I regard my work-people," an agent at another factory said, "just as I regard my machinery. So long as they can do my work for what I choose to pay them, I keep them, getting out of them all I can."

Embittered complaints began to take the place of earlier satisfac-tion as these conditions grew steadily worse. "These ladies have been imposed upon egregiously by the aristocratic and offensive em-ployers, assuming to be their lords and masters," wrote the *Lynn Record*. Orestes Brownson, radical friend of labor, declared that "the great mass wear out their health, spirits and morals without becoming one whit better off." In the *Voice of Industry*, a new labor newspaper devoted to the cause of mill workers, there were frequent attacks upon the policies which the employers were following.

"Your factory system is worse by far than that of Europe," stated an open letter in this journal addressed to the mill owner, Abbott Lawrence. "You furnish your operatives with no more healthy sleeping-apartments than the cellars and garrets of the English poor. . . . The keepers are compelled to allow . . . but one room for six persons and generally crowd twelve and sometimes sixteen females into the same hot, ill-ventilated attic. . . . You shut up the operatives two or three hours longer a day in your factory prisons than is done in Europe. . . You allow them but half an hour to eat their meals. . . .You compel them to stand so long at the machinery. . .that varicose veins, dropsical swelling of the feet and limbs, and prolapsus uter, diseases that end only with life, are not rare but common occurrences."

The factory girls themselves resented more and more "the yoke which has been prepared for us" and tried to combat the reductions in wages and increase in work. Even in the 1830s, as we have seen, they had experimented with strikes, and now, a decade later, they pledged themselves not to accept additional looms without wage increases and called for shorter working hours. But they made little headway. A number of former farm girls remained in the mills permanently, but the number of new recruits from the countryside fell precipitately. The promise of easy work and high wages no longer lured masses of farm girls.

Yet the mill owners were not left without an abundant labor force. Hard times in Europe and the potato famine of the 1840s drove millions of Irish and German immigrants to the United States. In New England especially, immigrant Irish families, and particularly their women, supplied the textile mills with a needy labor force. Since they lived on the edge of starvation, the immigrant Irish took whatever wages or hours the mill owners offered. The infusion of cheap immigrant labor, as a committee of the Massachusetts legislature noted in 1850, was causing "an entire modification and depression of the state of society in and about manufacturing places."

While the textile trade provides a striking example of what happened to working conditions with increasing industrialization, the same thing was taking place in other trades. The Lynn shoemakers had enjoyed a high degree of independence in the 1830s with their own workshops and the opportunity to fall back on farming or fishing should trade fall off. "When the spring opened," read one perhaps too idyllic account of a worker's life, "the horizon of his hopes expanded. Less clothing and fuel were needed. The clam banks discounted more readily; haddock could be got at Swampscott so cheap that the price wasn't worth quoting. The boys could dig dandelions. . . . Then if the poor man had his little 'spring pig' that he had kept through the winter, 'pork and dandelions' were no small item in the bill of fare while 'greens' lasted." But the masters steadily tightened their control over manufacturing, and wages were reduced and paid in store orders rather than cash. The shoemakers gradually found themselves forced from their own workshops, from their fishing and farming in off hours, into the new factories with whose machine processes they could no longer compete.

The *Awl*, a journeymen shoemakers' paper, repeatedly expressed resentment against manufacturers who pretended to pay the workers a living wage but "did by other means reduce them to degradation and the loss of that self-respect which had made the mechanics and laborers the pride of the world." The protesting shoemakers of Lynn called upon their fellow artisans in the larger cities to take concerted action to demonstrate "that we are not menials or the humble subjects of a foreign despot, but free, American citizens." Nothing came of this agitation. A way of life was inevitably passing, and the shoemakers as well as the textile workers were inextricably caught in the toils of the factory system.

The printers' trade was also being revolutionized by the invention of new presses and the use of steam power. These developments not only tended to throw men out of work and to depress wages, but also encouraged the transfer of control over their trade from the printers themselves to outside management. A highly independent profession was transformed through the widened gulf between employer and employee. Their long record of organization helped the printers, and they were to continue to enforce union rules governing apprentices and working conditions with considerable success, but they were facing new forces which made it increasingly difficult to maintain either their wages or their general status.

Among other trades, the introduction of power looms worsened conditions for the hand-loom weavers whose weekly wages, never very high, were virtually halved by the mid-forties; the relatively well-paid journeymen hatters suffered a decline in their pay, between 1835 and 1845, from about $12 to $8 a week, and the cabinetmakers found themselves compelled to work longer and longer hours to earn as much as $5 a week in the face of competition from the wholesale production of German immigrants who were said to "work rapidly, badly and for almost nothing."

The greater supply of cheap labor, indeed, was as important as the introduction of machinery in cutting wages, not only in the New England cotton mills, but throughout industry. In the first half century of American national history, approximately one million immigrants entered the country, but in the single decade from 1846 to 1855, the total was almost three million. Famine in Ireland and suppression of the revolutionary uprisings on the continent accounted for a swelling stream of workers crossing the Atlantic. They tended to settle in the East, drawn to the rapidly growing cities and manufacturing centers, where the demand for labor was greatest and both the skilled and the unskilled might find employment. Immigration was for the first time, but not the last, providing American employers with an abundant supply of labor, which acted to depress wage rates. This process was to repeat itself on an even more massive scale between 1881 and 1914.

The general conditions among workers in the seaboard cities graphically revealed the effect of such immigration. Two separate estimates of a workingman's family budget in the early 1850s, the one in the *New York Times* and the other in the *New York Tribune,* gave a minimum for essential expenditures, for rent, food, fuel and clothing, which amounted to approximately $11 a week. "Have I made the workingman's comforts too high?" asked Horace Greeley in commenting on this budget. "Where is the money to pay for amusements, for ice-creams, his puddings, his trips on Sunday up or down the river in order to get some fresh air?" But except for persons in the building trades, whose relatively high wages just about met this budget, there were few urban workers who even approached it—not the factory operatives, not the workers, men and women, employed in the clothing trades, and most assuredly not the common laborers. Shortly before publishing his budget, Greeley had actually estimated that "the average earnings of those who lived by simple labor in our city—embracing at least two thirds of our population—scarcely, it at all, exceed one dollar per week for each person subsisting thereon."

Contemporary descriptions afford ample evidence of the part that inadequate wages played in creating the slum areas of such cities as New York, Philadelphia, and Boston. Overcrowding, lack of sanitary conveniences, dirt, filth, and disease already stood in stark and glaring contrast to the comfortable, spacious, well-furnished homes of the wealthy. There was in New York a cellar population, estimated to total over 18,000, crowded into damp, unlighted, ill-ventilated dens with anywhere from six to twenty persons—men, women and children—living in a single room. In the notorious Five Points, hundreds of families were squeezed into ramshackle buildings, their only sanitary conveniences outside privies. Boston had equally depressing and unhealthful slums. "This whole district," a Committee on Internal Health reported in 1849, "is a perfect hive of human beings without comforts and mostly without common necessaries: in many cases huddled together like brutes without regard to sex, age or a sense of decency, grown men and women sleeping together in the same apartment, and sometimes wife, husband, brothers and sisters in the same bed."

The situation which Thomas Jefferson had foreseen when he spoke of the mobs of great cities adding just as much to pure government "as sores do to the strength of the human body," appeared to have materialized. The workers themselves began to protest against immigration as creating "a numerous poor and dependent population." The abject condition they had known in their own countries, the *Voice of Industry* declared, made such immigrants all the more helpless victims of exploitation in the United States, satisfied to work "fourteen and sixteen hours per day for what capital sees fit to give them."

The harsh effect of industrialism and the mounting tide of immigration served in large measure to prevent any reconsolidation of the ranks of labor. The workingmen did not resume on a comparable scale either the political or trade-union activity which had had such dynamic drive before the Panic of 1837. Workers split themselves along ethno-religious lines. American-born Protestant workers participated in broad evangelical reform movements or more nativistic groups, while immigrant Roman Catholic workers withdrew into insular ethnic communities. In the absence of general trade unions, which linked workers across the boundaries of nationality and religion, workers also fractured politically. Many American-born Protestants supported nativistic Whigs or a straight-out Native American (Know-Nothing) party. Immigrant Catholics increasingly swung to the Democratic party. Protestant workers participated actively in a myriad of general reform activities (many led by middle-class evangelicals), from temperance to dress reform to general social purity. On such social issues as drink, religion in the public schools, Sabbath observance, and many others, American-born and immigrant workers went their separate ways.

The decade of the 1840s was preeminently one of perfectionist moral reform and romantic utopianism. The perfectionist reformers and utopians repeatedly sought support from working people. They descended in droves upon every meeting or convention that might be summoned to consider labor issues, and sometimes they succeeded in wholly dominating it. The first formal meeting of the New England Workingmen's Association in 1844, called to inaugurate a revived ten-hour movement, had only a scattering of delegates from labor societies in comparison with the brilliant array of reformers. George Ripley, of Brook Farm; Horace Greeley and Albert Brisbane; Wendell Phillips and William Lloyd Garrison; Charles A. Dana, William H. Channing, and Robert Owen were all on hand, eagerly seeking to win new disciples. The meeting was thrown open with sweeping enthusiasm "to all those interested in the elevation of the producing classes and Industrial Reform and the extinction of slavery and servitude in all their forms." However generous the impulses behind such activity, they could not have been more vague and diffusive.

The imagination of some of the workers during this period was caught by the glowing promises of the "Associationists." Through the formation of independent, socialistic communities—all of whose members would work toward a common end—the Associationists promised an escape from the consequences of the industrial revolution and actually hoped to recreate the simpler society of an earlier day. This idea was primarily derived from the utopian socialism of the French reformer, Charles Fourier, with its elaborate system of phalanxes, designed both to dignify labor and increase production. Fourierism had been introduced to the United States by Albert Brisbane. In 1840 Brisbane published *The Social Destiny of Man*, a detailed exposition of Fourier's program, but far more important in spreading the gospel of Association were his writings in the column which Horace Greeley placed at his disposal in the *New York Tribune*.

Greeley was, indeed, to do everything possible to promote this tempered form of socialism as one phase of his general support for the interests of workingmen. An idealistic Yankee, who had come to New York as a farm boy to enter the printing trade, Greeley was a familiar figure at labor gatherings, and his round moon face, with its fringe of whiskers, was known to thousands of workers. "Why should those by whose toil ALL commodities and luxuries are produced or made available," he asked, "enjoy so scanty a share of them?" He realized, perhaps more than any of his contemporaries among public men, the effects of the exploitation of the workingmen which resulted from the industrial revolution, and he felt that any lasting betterment for society depended upon their organization. He not only opened the columns of the *Tribune* to Albert Brisbane but also ran a weekly letter dealing with socialism for a European correspondent—Karl Marx.

Fourierism, in any event, won many converts through the *Tribune*. Even before Brisbane laid out his own plan for a North American phalanx, a group of workingmen launched the Sylvania phalanx in western Pennsylvania. Other communities quickly followed on the heels of this experiment, and even the idealistic founders of Brook Farm, whose colony represented an intellectual revolt against the spirit of the times, were persuaded to adopt the form and organization of a Fourierite community. In all, some forty phalanxes, with perhaps 8,000 members, were established during the 1840s.

They were not a success. One by one they fell by the wayside, the North American plalanx itself ceasing operation in 1854. Community living and community production did not prove practical. Nor did they in any way meet the needs of labor. In spite of the enthusiastic propaganda, the answer to industrialization did not lie in an attempt to escape from it. The hopeful dreams of the Associationists foundered on the rock of economic and social forces which could not be so easily withstood or diverted.

As the phalanxes collapsed, some attempt was made to provide a partial substitute in the interests of the workingmen by establishing both consumers' and producers' cooperatives. "The direction and profits of industry," the proponents of cooperation declared, "must be kept in the hands of the producers." In Massachusetts, New York, and other parts of the country, protective unions were organized which undertook to set up self-employing workshops whose products were to be sold at wholesale prices for the benefit of the union's members. There were other instances of cooperatives, such as the Journeymen Molders' Union Foundry, which established a plant near Cincinnati, the Boston Tailors' Associative Union, and a Shirt Sewers' Cooperative Union Depot in New York. But whether consumers' or producers' cooperatives, these early ventures were no more successful than the phalanxes. Various factors accounted for their failure, but basically the conditions of American life, perhaps the American temperament, did not provide a fertile soil for the growth of cooperation. They lent themselves, rather, to competition and individualistic striving to make the most of the opportunities of a young and growing country. Cooperation was to be revived again and again in the future and to have some limited success, but neither in the 1840s nor later could it provide any real solution to the problems which confronted the laboring classes.

Another and more significant reform which won widespread labor support was a new agrarianism. The original workingmen's parties had been in part wrecked by the internal friction and external attacks resulting from their flirtation with the radical agrarian ideas of Thomas Skidmore, but the new revelation did not involve the assault upon all property which Skidmore had launched so vigorously in *The Rights of Man to Property*. The agrarianism of the 1840s and 1850s was far more moderate. Its thesis was that the people as a whole had a natural right to the existing public lands, and that they should be equally distributed in farm lots of 160 acres which would be both inalienable and exempt from seizure for debt. Through such a program, it was maintained, the workingmen would be assured of his just share in the national wealth and be freed from his complete dependence on the masters of capital.

The high priest of this reform was George Henry Evans. After the dissolution of the Working Men's party in New York, he had retired in 1836 because of ill health to a farm in New Jersey, and only emerged with his new message in 1844. Reestablishing the *Workingman's Advocate*, his old paper, he dedicated himself to agrarianism and in season and out demanded action by Congress to promote his program. "This is the first measure to be accomplished," he wrote in the *Advocate*, "and it is as idle to attempt any great reforms without that as it is to go to work without tools. Place the surplus mechanics on their own land in the west in Rural Townships with their large Public Square and Public Hall in the center of each, leaving full employment to those who remain in the cities." There was hardly a labor meeting at which he did not appear to present this plan, in complete disregard of the practical question of whether the workers, even if they could, would want suddenly to pull up stakes and take up farming in the distant West.

The climax of Evans's activities was the establishment of the National Reform Association in 1845. His earlier experience had led him to distrust third-party political action, and the purpose of the new organization was to demand support for his program from all candidates for public office as the condition for securing the workingmen's votes. Evans hoped to demonstrate that the agrarians meant business. "We, whose names are annexed, desirous of restoring to man his Natural Right to Land," the membership pledge of the National Reform Association stated, "do solemnly agree that we will not vote for any man, for any legislative office, who will not pledge himself, in writing, to use all the influence of his station, if elected, to prevent all further traffic in the Public Lands of the states and of the United States, and to cause them to be laid out in Farms and Lots for the free and exclusive use of actual settlers."

Although support for this program was by no means limited to the workingmen, their close ties with the National Reform Association were clearly revealed in the membership of the original central committee. It included four printers, two cordwainers, a chair maker, a carpenter, a blacksmith, a bookbinder, a machinist, a picture-frame maker, and a clothier. Associated with Evans, moreover, were such trade union leaders of the 1830s as John Commerford, who had been president of the General Trades' Union in New York, and John Ferral, leader of the Philadelphia Trades' Union. The new labor journals, reemerging after the panic of 1837, almost universally made land reform one of their basic demands.

The movement was strongly opposed by capitalists and employers in the eastern states. "By your policy you strike down our great manufacturing interests," one of their spokesmen declared in Congress, ". . . You turn thousands of our manufacturers and labourers out of employment. . . . You depreciate the value of real estate. You make a bid for our population, by holding out inducements for our productive labourers to leave their old homes, under the seductive promise of land for nothing, and railroads without taxes, thereby decreasing our population and consequently increasing the burden of those that remain in the old states." But farmers and other settlers in the West joined forces with the eastern workingmen in supporting the movement. With its alluring slogan of "Vote Yourself a Farm," the National Reform Association appeared to be making substantial headway.

The workingmen of the 1840s were not to profit from its program, and its relevance to their relief from industrial oppression may also be questioned. The movement instituted by Evans, however, was to lead directly to passage of the Homestead Act in 1862. While this measure did not provide for either inalienability or exemption from seizure for debt, it granted 160 acres of free land to all bona fide settlers.

Land reform was closer to the interests of the workingmen than many of the mid-century humanitarian movements, but the most immediately practical undertaking was the renewed drive for the ten-hour day. While it had been widely won for artisans and mechanics in the 1830s, factory employees, as we have seen, were not generally affected. The new movement was primarily for the relief of this new group of wage earners. Unlike the earlier drive, it did not take the form of trade union activity—the factory operatives were unorganized—but of political pressure upon state legislatures to establish a ceiling on hours in private industry. The National Reform Association even unbent sufficiently to make the demand for a ten-hour day one of its subsidiary planks, and it was taken up by many other workingmen's associations formed for this specific purpose.

The most protracted struggle took place in Massachusetts, where the development of the textile industry created both the greatest need for reform and the strongest opposition to it. A call for concerted action on the part of the workers, seeking to bring together various local associations, was first issued in 1844 and was responsible for formation of the New England Working Men's Association. Both Fourierites and land reformers tried to take control of this organization and for a time appeared to have succeeded in diverting attention from the ten-hour issue, but the agitation in favor of the latter reform nevertheless gained increasing headway. Almost swamped with petitions (one from Lowell being 130 feet long with some 4,500 signatures), the Massachusetts General Court felt compelled to make an official investigation.

Its committee reported that the average working day in the textile factories ranged from 11 hours and 24 minutes to 13 hours and 31 minutes, according to the season, and that there was no question but that shorter hours and more time for meals would benefit the workers. It also asserted the right and duty of the legislature to regulate hours whenever public morals or the well-being of society were menaced. In spite of such premises, however, it concluded, largely on the grounds that industry would be driven from the state, that no action should be taken. "The remedy is not with us," the committee stated, casually brushing aside legislative responsibility. "We look for it in the progressive improvement of art and science, in a higher appreciation of man's destiny, in a less love for money, and a more ardent love for social happiness and intellectual superiority."

The factory operatives attacked the report as clearly reflecting "a cringing servility to corporate monopolies" and renewed a struggle which now crossed state lines and aroused workers throughout the country. New arguments and counter-arguments were advanced. Labor did not emphasize, as it had in the 1830s, the need for more time for self-education and fulfillment of the duties of citizenship. It stressed instead the improvement in the quality of work which would result from shorter hours. The employers, however, were more concerned about production costs. In combating the workingmen's views, they stated that shorter hours would have to mean a lower day's wage. At the same time, they reasserted a paternalistic attitude toward workers' welfare. "The morals of the operatives will necessarily suffer," one of them stated, "if longer absent from the wholesome discipline of factory life, and leaving them thus to their will and liberty, without a warrant that this time will be well employed."

While the debate still raged over conditions in Massachusetts, the reformers succeeded in winning at least partial victories in a number of other states. New Hampshire passed the first state ten-hour law in the nation's history in 1847; Pennsylvania adopted a bill the next year providing that no person should work more than a ten-hour day or sixty-hour week "in cotton, woolen, silk, paper, bagging and flax factories." During the 1850s, Maine, Connecticut, Rhode Island, Ohio, California, and Georgia also fell into line with some sort of ten-hour laws. There was a catch, however, in almost every case. The ten-hour provision could be circumvented by "special contracts." The employer could virtually disregard the law, that is, by refusing to hire anyone unless he was willing to accept a longer working day, and, by combining with other employers, he could effectively blacklist any worker who attempted to stand up for his legal rights.

The inclusion of the special contract clause was defended by employers as necessary to protect the right of a citizen to sell his services as he himself saw fit. It was an argument to be advanced even more aggressively in later years when the Fourteenth Amendment was interpreted as specifically safeguarding individual freedom of contract from any infringement by state laws. Its speciousness, although he had originally opposed hour legislation, was exposed by Horace Greeley.

"To talk of the Freedom of Labor, the policy of leaving it to make its own bargains, etc." he wrote in the *Tribune* on September 18, 1847, "when the fact is that a man who has a family to support and a house hired for the year is told, 'If you will work thirteen hours per day, or as many as we think fit, you can stay; if not you can have your walking papers; and well you know no one else hereabout will hire you'—is it not most egregious flummery?"

The workers in Massachusetts undoubtedly thought so, and in continuing their struggle through a series of Ten-Hour Conventions, they insistently demanded effective legislation which would not mean simply a standardization of the working day but a real—and en-forceable—abridgment of the hours of labor. "We do declare, ex-plicitly and frankly," it was stated in 1852, "that our purpose, and our whole purpose, is, the enactment of a law which shall prohibit, in stringent and unmistakeable terms, and under adequate penalties, the corporations, chartered by the laws of the State, from employing any person in laboring more than ten hours in any one day. This is just the law—and all the law—we want on this subject."

This straightforward demand was not realized in Massachu-setts—nor in any other state. The inclusion of the special contract clause rendered such laws as were passed unenforceable, and factory workers remained subject to whatever conditions their employers chose to impose upon them. "The ten-hour law will not reduce the hours of labor," one newspaper emphatically stated in regard to the New Hampshire bill. "... Its authors did not intend any such result. It will also fail, we think, to humbug the working-men—the only ob-ject had in view by the demagogues who originated it."

A final effort to keep the ten-hour movement alive was undertaken through a series of industrial congresses, a further outgrowth of such organizations as the National Reform Association and the New England Working Men's Association. They were first set up on a na-tional basis, and then in the form of state or other local conventions. Instead of furthering practical labor aims, however, they proved to be somewhat vague and ambiguous assemblages, once again attracting reformers rather than trade union delegates. They tried to influence legislation in favor of free land and cooperation as well as the ten-hour day by promising political support to those who would advocate these reforms, but no real progress was made. Moreover, while it was again hoped to "eschew partyism of every description," as George Henry Evans had advocated for the National Reform Association, the politicans were soon successfully taking over. The Industrial Con-gress in New York, for example, originally sought to limit member-ship to delegates of labor organizations, but before long Tammany Hall was in almost complete control.

The old story of reformers dividing among themselves and profes-sional politicians preying on the idealistic repeated itself. James Gor-don Bennett predicted the fate of the New York Industrial Congress in 1850. "It will fall into the hands of a few wire-pullers, who will turn it to their own advantage and sell the trades to the highest bidder," he wrote prophetically in the *New York Herald*. "Then will be acted over

again the farces already played in this city, in which the trades have
been made the ladder of needy or ambitious politicians, who kicked
them away the moment they gained the summit of their aspirations."

Not until well into the 1850s did workers begin to rebuild essentially labor organizations. An improvement in economic conditions,
although interrupted by another brief depression in 1857, promoted
this shift. Once again the bargaining position of the workers was
strengthened and the way was opened to effective action through the
practical weapon of strikes. The unions of this period, however, were
to reveal in one important respect a somewhat different philosophy
from that held by the earlier societies of the 1830s. They were much
less concerned over the solidarity of labor and fastened their attention
far more narrowly on the needs of their own individual membership.
Little effort was to be made to form city centrals or any other labor
federations comparable to the general trades' unions.

The unions of both periods were primarily made up of artisans and
mechanics, that is, skilled craftsmen; they were largely concentrated
in the old established trades. But whereas those in the earlier period
were more sympathetic toward the organization of unskilled workers
and factory operatives, and prepared to cooperate with such societies
as they might form, there was less interest in these groups of workers
on the part of the trade unions of the 1850s. The division between
skilled and unskilled workers hardened as the former became reluc-
tant to link their fortunes to the latter.

The more limited scope of the labor movement in the 1850s
resulted partly from the difficulties of organizing the less skilled and
partly from the ethno-religious factors alluded to above. The bulk
of the skilled workers were American-born and Protestants, the unskilled overwhelmingly immigrants, Catholics, women and children.
This split between the two broad sectors of the working class was to
weaken the labor movement well into the twentieth century.

While the revived unions of the 1850s consequently stressed the
maintenance of apprenticeship rules, the closed shop, and higher
wages and shorter hours for their own members, they promoted the
labor movement as a whole with less vigor. They lacked the dynamic
drive of their predecessors. Still they recognized, as a resolution of
one society frankly stated, that under existing conditions "there exists
a perpetual antagonism between Labor and Capital . . . one striving to
sell their labor for as much, and the other striving to buy it for as little,

as they can." But their efforts to combat capital on these grounds were only partly successful.

The most interesting development of the time was the first real attempt to form national trade unions. The National Typographical Union, the National Molders' Union, and the Machinists' and Blacksmiths' National Union were organized, and a National Protective Association was founded by railway engineers with delegates representing fourteen states and fifty-five railways. Other embryonic national unions were also started by cordwainers, upholsterers, plumbers, stone cutters, and cotton mule spinners. None of these organizations was too successful, but they helped to pave the way for more effective activity in later years.

In other respects, the general organization of labor conformed to familiar patterns. The local unions still retained various benefit features, collected dues from their members, sought to maintain strike funds, engaged in collective bargaining with employers, and were prepared to call strikes when their legitimate demands were not met. At times strikes were widely prevalent. "Each spring," the *New York Tribune* declared on April 20, 1854, "witnesses a new struggle for enhanced wages in some if not most of the trades of this and other cities." Public opinion recognized that there was real reason for the restlessness of the workers in the already customary failure of wages to keep pace with advancing living costs, and the unions' demands often received sympathetic support in the press. "Men should always have a fair compensation for their labor," the *Trenton Daily State Gazette* stated on April 24, 1857, commenting on an agreement recently reached among master and journeymen carpenters in that city, "and we believe it is seldom that they demand more."

One strike toward the end of the period, which broke out early in February 1860, evoked widespread concern and was to prove the most extensive yet recorded in American history. It was called by the shoemakers of Natick and Lynn, Massachusetts, and spread throughout New England. With the formation of mechanics' associations in some twenty-five towns, close to 20,000 workers were ultimately reported to have turned out. In making the demand for higher wages responsible for this strike, the shoemakers declared that they were acting in the interests of the whole community "inasmuch as the wealth of the masses improves the value of real estate, increases the demand for manufactured goods, and promotes the moral wealth and intellectual growth of society." Their emphasis upon the purchasing power of wages did not, however, persuade their employers of the desirability of meeting their demands.

The strike was described in newspaper headlines as "Revolution in the North," "Rebellion Among the Workmen of New England," and "Beginning of Conflict between Capital and Labor." For almost the first time, the police and militia were called out in a labor disturbance. But there was no violence, and in many towns the workers had the sympathy and support of their fellow citizens. Many female employees took part in the strike and in their demonstrations and parades proved to be zealous advocates of the cause. "They assail the bosses," a reporter for the *New York Herald* wrote from Marblehead, "in a style which reminds one of the amiable females who participated in the first French Revolution."

Relatively early in the strike some employers began to meet the strikers' wage demands. But then, and more so subsequently as the strike dragged on into the early spring, shoe manufacturers fought the organized, collective strength of labor. Employers would not recognize unions or sign written agreements with them. Their strike was only partly successful; in the end, the strikers settled for increased wages but lost the union which they had struggled to build.

As the 1850s drew to a close, the slavery issue began to impinge on the labor movement as it did on every phase of economic or political activity throughout the country. Among northern workingmen, the same divisions of opinion were evident as among other elements of the population. In New England, there was strong abolitionist sentiment, especially among operatives in the cotton mills, but in other parts of the country there was little disposition to allow sympathy for the Afro-American to be carried so far as to favor a war to effect his freedom. It was felt in the growing industrial centers that the slavery of the white wage earner was often quite as degrading as the slavery of the black, and that reform might better begin at home. Even after Lincoln's election in 1860, many unions vigorously supported the various compromise proposals which were being put forward to reconcile northern and southern differences.

Thirty-four leading trade unionists, indeed, banded together for action early in 1861 and with the slogan "Concession not Secession," summoned a National Workingmen's Convention to protest against the government's course. "Under the leadership of political demagogues and traitors," they vehemently stated in the *Mechanics' Own*, ". . . the country is going to the devil as fast as it can, and unless the masses rise up in their might, and teach their representatives what to do, the good old ship will go to pieces." Their meeting was held in Philadelphia on February 22 with parades, speech-making, and resolutions upholding the Crittenden Compromise. It was not a very impressive affair, however, and it could not in any event exercise any appreciable influence on the forces that were so soon to plunge the country into war.

Once hostilities were declared, the workers enlisted in great numbers in response to President Lincoln's call for troops, and many of those who had been most strongly opposed to war were among the early volunteers. In a number of cases, the members of unions entered the service as a group. "It having been resolved to enlist with Uncle Sam for the war," read a typical resolution by one such organization, "this union stands adjourned until either the Union is safe or we are whipped."

Workers supported Lincoln and the Union because Republican ideology and principles appealed to them strongly. Republicans portrayed the civil conflict as a struggle between freedom and slavery, democracy and aristocracy, equality and privilege. Workers marched to war against the "slave power" under the democratic banner of free men and free soil. As Eric Foner, the historian, has shown, the Republicans, through their free-labor ideology, made northern workers a vital element in a new polticial coalition.

The war was to tax labor heavily. The workers were subject to the draft, while the wealthy could escape service by paying bounties or buying substitutes, and they suffered severely from an inflation that for manufacturers and tradesmen meant rising profits. There were rumblings of discontent as the issuance of greenbacks whirled the cost of living even higher. "What would it profit us as a nation," the workers asked, "were we to preserve our institutions, save our constitution, and sink the masses into hopeless poverty and crime?" They were prepared to play their full part in the war effort, but their resentment flared against profiteers and speculators.

By 1863 the situation in New York shockingly reflected what a good thing war could be for those in a position to make money out of it. The hotels, theaters, jewelry establishments, and other luxury stores were doing a phenomenal business. The "shoddy," as the profiteers were called, were spending fortunes with reckless, shameless extravagance. "The men button their waistcoats with diamonds of the first water," said Harper's, "and the women powder their faces with

gold and silver dust." The hard-hit workingmen earned no such profits, and strikes soon spread as they demanded that wages be kept in
some reasonable relation to rising prices.

The bricklayers in Chicago insisted on a raise; conductors and
horsecar drivers walked out in New York; union printers in St. Louis
struck for higher wages; carpenters, painters, and plumbers were
everywhere threatening to throw down their tools unless their
demands were met; the iron molders sought a 15 per cent advance;
shipwrights and longshoremen went on strike; and the locomotive
engineers called out their members.

In occasional instances, martial law was proclaimed to combat such
disturbances, with troops acting as strikebreakers. But labor had a
friend in the White House. Lincoln may not have fully understood the
implications of an organized labor movement, but his sympathies were
with the workers. With one possible exception, he would not support
strike intervention by the government. "Thank God we have a system
of labor where there can be a strike," he had declared prior to the war,
and he steadfastly maintained his faith in labor and respect for labor's
rights throughout the national emergency. The democracy which he
affirmed was predicated on his belief that "working-men are the basis
of all government." In his first Annual Message to Congress he had
declared that labor was prior to, and independent of, capital, which
would never have been created without labor's first existing. Meeting
a delegation from the New York Workingmen's Democratic Republic
Association in 1864, he reiterated these views: "Labor is the superior
of capital, and deserves much the higher consideration."

In these circumstances, the strength of labor increased during the
Civil War, and the trade unions took a fresh lease on life. Between
1863 and 1864, the number rose from seventy-nine to 270, and it was
estimated that the total of organized workers was over 200,000—more
than at any previous time. Moreover, there were among these unions
thirty-two organized on a national basis which showed far greater
stability than those of the 1850s. The most prominent among them
was the reorganized Iron Molders' International Union,[1] but the
Machinists and Blacksmiths, the Locomotive Engineers, the
American Miners' Association, and the Sons of Vulcan (iron pud-
dlers) were other strong organizations which also revealed the changing character of the labor movement.

---

[1]The international union, introduced by the Molders, was so-called because of the
inclusion of Canadian locals.

The wartime revival of unionism was accompanied by the reemergence of an influential labor press that began to put forward organized labor's views and advocate labor reform. *Fincher's Trades' Review*, the organ of the Machinists and Blacksmiths, was the most important of these papers and, with representation on its editorial board from other unions, it became a spokesman for the whole labor movement. Its editor, Jonathan Fincher, was an able and indefatigable reporter and a forthright commentator on labor issues. Other labor journals were a new *Working Man's Advocate*, published in Chicago; the New York *Trades' Advocate*; and the *Weekly Miner*.

A further advance was the establishment of new trades' assemblies, which resembled the old general trades' unions. The local unions of Rochester, New York, first revived this form of organization and within a short time almost every city had a trades' assembly. They became a source of very real strength and introduced a new labor weapon—the boycott—as a means of forcing employers to yield to union demands. "All the trades unite for this purpose," read a contemporary report of the boycott, "and when a case of oppression is made known a committee from the Trades' Assembly calls upon the offender and demands redress. If the demand is not complied with every trade is notified, and the members all cease trading at the obnoxious establishment." The trades' assemblies also sponsored picnics, balls, and other social activities, and in some instances maintained libraries and reading rooms.

Labor emerged from the Civil War on the offensive. It was prepared to move into fields of even broader national organization, to bring the new unions together in a unified movement which could meet more effectively the consolidated forces of capital.

VI

Toward National Organization

Between the Civil War and the end of the nineteenth century, the United States underwent phenomenal industrial expansion. The railroads flung out new networks of rails to span the continent and knit the country into an economic whole. The burning stacks of steel mills lighting the skies over Pittsburgh symbolized the growth of a gigantic industry made possible by the discovery of the incalculable iron resources of the Mesabi range in Minnesota. Oil gushed from wells in western Pennsylvania and Ohio. In the great slaughterhouses of Chicago, Cincinnati, and St. Louis, thousands of cattle and hogs were butchered daily. The textile mills of New England hummed with activity and a ready-made clothing industry grew up out of the sweatshops of New York and other eastern cities. Everywhere new factories and mills reflected the triumphs of the machine and the growth of mass production. As cities and manufacturing towns mushroomed along the Atlantic seaboard and in the Middle West, the face of America was transformed.

The basic factors behind these developments were the nation's great natural resources, its labor reserves, and an insatiable demand for the products of the new industries. But the immediate driving force of industrial expansion came from a group of visionary, ambitious and ruthless business leaders and financiers. Jay Gould,

E. H. Harriman, and James J. Hill fashioned an empire of railroads, Andrew Carnegie an empire of steel, John D. Rockefeller an empire of oil. The corporation became the accepted form of business organization and, under the leadership of such men, mergers and consolidations were effecting the further nationalizing of business. Gigantic combinations sprang up in scores of industries—in oil, steel, sugar, linseed oil, stoves, and fertilizers. Monopoly was the goal of the industrialist, and a complacent government and complacent courts, wedded to the economic doctrines of laissez faire, gave free rein to policies which rapidly created a concentration of economic wealth and power that the country had never known before.

The laboring forces were swept along on this tide of expansion. Although such development would have been wholly impossible without them, the course of economic growth sometimes stole from workers their skills, statuses, and customs. As onetime independent craftsmen were drawn into the factories, mills, and foundries where their special skills had little value, and where they were called upon to perform only single, automatic steps in the complicated processes of mass production, they lost the bargaining powers which they had previously enjoyed. Industry looked upon labor as a commodity, to be bought as cheaply as possible. Little more sense of responsibility was felt toward the workers than toward the raw materials of manufacture.

"Before this concentration began, while as yet commerce and industry were conducted by innumerable petty concerns with small capital, instead of a small number of great concerns with vast capital," Edward Bellamy was to write in *Looking Backward* (1888), his famous utopian romance, "the individual workman was relatively important and independent in his relations to the employer. Moreover, when a little capital or a new idea was enough to start a man in business for himself, workingmen were constantly becoming employers and there was no hard and fast line between the two classes. Labor unions were needless then and general strikes out of the question. But when the era of small concerns with small capital was succeeded by that of the great aggregations of capital, all this was changed. The individual laborer, who had been relatively important to the small employer, was reduced to insignificance and powerlessness over against the great corporation, while at the same time the way upward to the grade of employer was closed to him. Self-defense drove him to union with his fellows."

With the laws of supply and demand so completely determining wages, everything possible was done by industry to make certain that the supply of labor would be plentiful. During the Civil War, the business interests of the country had taken a first step in enlisting the support of Congress to make assurance doubly sure on this point. There was passed, in 1864, a contract-labor law which permitted the advance of passage money to prospective immigrants in return for a lien upon their wages. With such encouragement, the American Emigrant Company, capitalized at $1,000,000 and backed by such prominent figures as Chief Justice Samuel Chase, Secretary of the Navy Gideon Welles, Senator Charles Sumner and Henry Ward Beecher, undertook to meet the requirements of an expanding economy by building up the resources of available workers. Its announced program was "to import laborers, especially skilled laborers, from Great Britain, Belgium, France, Switzerland, Norway and Sweden, for the manufacturers, rail-road companies, and other employers of labor in America." Its advertisements declared that it was prepared to provide, at short notice and on reasonable terms, miners, puddlers, machinists, blacksmiths, molders and mechanics of every kind.

The agents of the American Emigrant Company, together with those of the railroads, steamship companies, and many industrial corporations, were soon drumming up trade in this new form of contract labor almost as had the "newlanders" two centuries before in their continental quest for indentured servants. "These men, when they arrive," stated an alarmed report to a labor convention, "as a general rule, have but little money; consequently they are compelled to work at starvation prices. . . . We stand no chance of competing with these men."

In fact, however, relatively few immigrant workers entered the United States as contract laborers. Moreover, the Civil War reduced the flow of immigration substantially, and it would not be until the decade of the 1880s that a truly mass movement resumed. But contract, or specially recruited, skilled workers did compete with craftsmen in such industries as the flint glass trade, and Asians immigrated in large numbers to the Pacific Coast.

In California, and in the construction of the first trans-continental railway, employers turned to Chinese labor. The Chinese also entered general construction, precious metal mining, cigar making, and such service trades as laundries and restaurants. When Congress enacted a law excluding Chinese immigrants, West Coast employers turned first to Japanese and then to Filipino immigrants. The abortive experiment was even made, although on a very small scale, of employing Chinese in the shoe industry in Massachusetts. "They are with us!" exclaimed the *Boston Commonwealth* in June 1870, "the 'Celestials'—with almond eyes, pigtails, rare industry, quick adaptation, high morality, and all—seventy-five of them—hard at work in the town of North Adams, making shoes."

As time went on, the number of European immigrants mounted steadily—almost half a million entered the country in 1880 and in the following decade over five million, or nearly twice the total for the previous ten years. Moreover, there was a gradual shift in the source of supply. The great bulk of the immigration no longer came from northwestern but from southeastern Europe. The steerage of the trans-Atlantic steamships was crowded with Italians, Poles, Czechs, Slovaks, Hungarians, Greeks, and Russians—displaced peasants and ambitious townspeople eager to seize the opportunities promised by the New World. They provided an apparently inexhaustible reserve of cheap labor for mines, mills, and factories.

Immigration had always impinged upon the efforts of American labor to raise living standards, but by the close of the century its massive proportions affected wages more than ever. Although European immigrants constantly augmented the supply of unskilled labor, their presence often benefited American-born and skilled workers, whose skills were scarce by contrast and who were now needed as foremen and supervisors.

It was not mass immigration alone that worked to the detriment of skilled labor. Rather, the growth of modern mass-production industry diluted many traditional skills; sometimes they even eliminated them and made craftsmen redundant. Those whose skills were now less needed labored under the shadow of pay cuts and unemployment. Moreover, as enterprises grew in scale and size, the chance for individual workers to become entrepreneurs diminished. Industrialization challenged the faith of many in the concept of the self-made man. "The hope that the workingmen may enter this circle," the *Working Man's Advocate* of Chicago declared as early as 1866, "is a glittering delusion held up before him to distract his attention from the real object of his interests."

The cruel paradox of "progress and poverty," which Henry George noted in his widely read book by that name (1879), was not even then anything new, and it became increasingly apparent as the years went by. Economic growth and expansion were undeniable facts, and so were the rise in the national income and the improvement in living standards for the country as a whole. Yet at the same time many millions lived in abject poverty in densely packed slums. They were all too often without the most simple comforts and conveniences which their own labor made possible for others. They struggled merely to maintain their families above the level of actual hunger and want. While circumstances were better for those who still retained special skills, the great majority worked such long hours for such little pay that their status was an anomaly in the light of the prosperity so generally enjoyed by business and industry.

As the introduction of machinery caused an increasing division of labor, permitting more and more of the work of manufacture to be done by the semiskilled or unskilled, employers were able to use "green hands" rather than the artisans and mechanics of an earlier day. Migratory workers threatened the jobs of local workers, and periodic unemployment undermined the onetime security of established craftsmen. As business became nationwide, moreover, the competition of different manufacturing areas meant that prices and wages were no longer determined by local conditions. They fluctuated as a consequence of economic changes wholly beyond the control of the employers or workers immediately concerned.

In this new national market, for example, the makers of stoves in Troy and Pittsburgh, Philadelphia or Detroit, had to meet the competition of manufacturers in Chicago and St. Louis. Wages scales in the East were linked with those in the West. If the iron molders in Troy or St. Louis wished to protect themselves from wage cuts in time of business recession, they had to look beyond merely local conditions and search out means to uphold the wages of comparable workers in other parts of the country.

It became increasingly clear in these new conditions that labor had to meet the challenge of nationwide industry by itself organizing on a nationwide basis. This meant, in the first instance, an attempt to build up national unions which would enable the workers in any trade to safeguard their wage scales against competition from whatever quarter, and, in the second instance, an effort to confront the community of interests growing up among all employers by a like community of interests among all workers. There was to be much talk of the solidarity of labor as a new group of leaders sought to bring the national unions, political labor parties, cooperatives, and other labor reform associations into what might be termed a united front to combat the rising power of organized capitalism.

In seeking to effect this broader national organization in the years immediately following the Civil War, labor was nevertheless still so confused by the new forces of industrialism as to be wholly uncertain as to what course it should follow. It was drawn into various political movements, beguiled by new promises of reform, and caught up in controversy over socialist theory and radical concepts of class struggle. There was continued debate over the relative benefits of political as against economic action, and the advantages of craft unions as opposed to more all-inclusive unions.

On many occasions, workers took matters into their own hands regardless of the fine-spun theories being discussed at labor conferences. Feeling themselves ground down more and more heavily under the heel of capitalists, they ignored a leadership which appeared to be out of touch with the actualities of economic circumstance and rose in spontaneous revolt to protect their rights. Before the Civil War, strikes had been local, short-lived and generally peaceful, but in the latter half of the century their character was to change drastically. The country was to experience widespread and violent industrial strife.

The initial step toward a national organization of labor was taken in 1866. A group of union leaders, wholly forgetful of similar moves in the 1830s, summoned what they called "the first National Labor Congress ever convened in the United States." It was held in Baltimore and attended by some seventy-seven delegates from various local unions, trades' assemblies, and national unions. The avowed purpose of the conference was to create a new unity within the ranks of labor as a whole. In organizing what was to become the National Labor Union, provision was made for the membership, not only of the skilled workers enrolled in existing trade unions, but also of unskilled workers and farmers. At last all those who toiled were "to rise in the majesty of their strength" and challenge the employing class to acknowledge their rights and privileges.

From the outset, the National Labor Union aimed primarily at reform through political action. It was the first broad attempt to bring all labor together on a common program which joined trade unionists, social reformers, and even feminists in an alliance to remake society in a more egalitarian manner. Like many antebellum and subsequent nineteenth-century labor movements, the NLU commited itself to abolition of the wage system.

The leaders of the NLU preferred to leave to the trade unions the achievement of such practical objectives as the immediate improvement of working conditions. They declared that the labor movement was dependent on trade unions and urged every workingman to join one. Meeting at Baltimore, however, they upheld political action as the most effective means of promoting the workers' interests, and they strongly deprecated resort to strikes. The advocates of economic rather than political action were able to defeat a motion for the immediate formation of a straight-out political labor party, but the conference nevertheless agreed that one should be set up "as soon as possible."

The general aims of the National Labor Union were set forth in an *Address to the Workingmen of the United States*. It primarily emphasized, as "the first and grand desideratum of the hour," a demand for the adoption of laws establishing eight hours as a legal day's work in every state in the Union. As we shall see, this represented a reform with deeper implications than the earlier drive for a ten-hour day, and for a time it appeared to dominate labor activity. The National Labor Union, however, also sought to promote both consumers' and producers' cooperatives, and, partly as a means to make capital more readily available for such enterprises, it was to become more and more absorbed in currency and banking reform. The abolition of convict labor; the restriction of immigration, particularly of Chinese to the West Coast, in order to safeguard the living standards of native workers; the disposal of public lands only to actual settlers; and the establishment by the national government of a Department of Labor were further objectives set forth in 1866.

These largely political goals were supplemented by appeals for the broader organization of working people. The interests of women in industry were recognized; the new union pledged individual and undivided support to "the sewing women, factory operatives, and daughters of toil," and the head of the Troy Laundry Workers, a union of female workers, was made one of the association's assistant secretaries. The organization of blacks was also encouraged, but in this first recognition of their possible role in the labor movement, they were urged to form their own unions rather than invited to join the National Labor Union.

This new organization for the first time created a national labor leadership, and among the men figuring most prominently in its activities, chosen its president in 1868, was William H. Sylvis. Commenting on the gathering of labor leaders which attended the convention that chose him president, the New York *Sun* bore witness to the prominence he had won throughout the country by declaring that his "name is familiar as a household word."

Sylvis was at this time a man of forty, medium-sized, and strongly built, with a florid complexion, light beard and mustache, and "a face and eyes beaming with intelligence." Few labor leaders have been more devoted to the cause, more willing to sacrifice every personal consideration for labor's interests, or commanded more loyalty and affection on the part of their fellow workers. He was very literally to wear himself out in their behalf. "I love this Union cause," he declared on one occasion. "I hold it more dear than I do my family or my life. I am willing to devote to it all that I am or have or hope for in this world."

Sylvis's views on the policies which labor should promote underwent marked shifts and changes. He was erratic and highly inconsistent in his thinking. But whatever his position at a particular moment, he defended it aggressively. He once assailed his critics as a "two-faced, snarling crew, who act the part of puerile wiffets." His most telling shafts were always reserved, however, for the new capitalistic class which he strongly felt was seeking only to exploit the workers—"a monied aristocracy—proud, imperious, and dishonest. . . blasting and withering everything it comes in contact with."

Sylvis was born the son of a wagon maker, in Annoph, Pennsylvania, in 1828, and as a boy worked in the local iron foundry. It was some time in the 1840s that he graduated from his apprenticeship and was duly invested with the "freedom suit" that marked his new status as a journeyman molder—a fine broadcloth coat, white shirt, woolen hose, calfskin boots, and high silk hat. Continuing to work at his trade in and about Philadelphia, he joined the local Stove and Hollow-Ware Molders' Union and at once became an active labor organizer. He was inspired with the idea of bringing all molders together in a single organization, and it was largely through his efforts that a convention was held in Philadelphia in 1859, at which forty-six delegates from eighteen locals established the National Molders' Union.

It collapsed with the outbreak of the Civil War, and Sylvis himself enlisted for a short period of army service. In 1863, however, he was again back at his chosen work and was elected president of the revived Iron Molders' International Union. His only interest was in building up this organization, and through his unflagging zeal he introduced new methods and techniques in labor organization. Traveling back and forth across the country, often begging a ride in the engineer's cab because he had no money for railway fare, he met with groups of local molders in city after city, helped them to organize locals, and admitted them to membership in the national union. Returning for the annual convention in 1864, he was able to boast that "from a mere pigmy, our union has in one short year grown to be a giant." With fifty-three locals and a total membership of 7,000 (soon to rise to 8,500), the Iron Molders' International Union had by 1865 become the strongest and most closely knit labor organization in the country.

Sylvis was to look back upon this period when he traveled so widely and came in such intimate contact with so many workingmen in New England, the seaboard states, the Midwest, and Canada as the happiest in his life. But he exhausted the slight capital at his disposal and was wholly dependent upon small funds given him by the molders. "He wore clothes until they became quite threadbare and he could wear them no longer," his brother wrote of these days. "...The shawl he wore to the day of his death...was filled with little holes burned there by the splashing of molten iron from the ladles of molders in strange cities, whom he was beseeching to organize."

Sylvis also proved himself to be as capable in administration as he was in organization. Control was effectively centralized in the national union, a per capita tax on all union members provided a revenue which built up a substantial strike fund, and the issuance of union cards and publication in the labor press of a "scab album" made possible general enforcement of a closed shop. Sylvis believed strongly in collective bargaining and did not encourage strikes, but when they proved to be the workers' only resource, he was ready to back them up to the hilt—"the results will depend on who can pound the hardest."

Until the winter of 1867–1868, the policies pursued by the Molders' Union were uniformly successful, but during that difficult season the National Stove Manufacturers' and Iron Founders' Association launched an all-out counterattack. Wages were cut and members of the union laid off. When the workers went out on strike, the employers were then in a strong enough position to lock them out.

The embattled molders fought back for months as best they could, but their strike funds became exhausted, internal dissensions eventually broke their united front, and they began to straggle back to work on the employers' terms. Sylvis was able to save the union from complete extinction, but with the failure of the strike it largely lost the strength and influence which it had once exerted.

Sylvis was so discouraged by this experience that he increasingly shifted his attention from trade unionists to more general labor reform and thus found in the new National Labor Union broader scope for his activities. He was ready to support, as vigorously as he had formerly supported union organization, the drive for the eight-hour day by legislative enactment, the formation of cooperatives, and currency reform. Reversing his earlier views, he threw all his influence behind the trend within the National Labor Union to promote these reforms by political action. "Let our cry be REFORM," he demanded in his first circular as its president. ". . . Down with a monied aristocracy and up with the people."

Meetings of the National Labor Union clearly revealed the growing absorption with political reform. Among the delegates at the convention in 1868 (whose "philosophic and statesmanlike views of the great industrial questions" were warmly commended by the *New York Herald*) were representatives of eight-hour leagues, land-reform associations, antimonopoly societies, and many other political causes. Conspicuous among them were two advocates of woman suffrage, Elizabeth Cady Stanton and Susan B. Anthony. While Sylvis and other leaders supported woman suffrage, their presence created something of a furor, for the delegates as a whole were not prepared to go this far. They agreed to seat the suffrage leaders only after making it plain that in so doing they were not endorsing their "peculiar ideas." The *Herald* nevertheless noted that Anthony was "delightfully insinuating and made no mean impression on the bearded delegates."

The National Labor Union took a step at this same convention which clearly foreshadowed its own transformtion into a third party. It encouraged the formation of labor reform parties in the several states and urged them to undertake direct political action. Its activities showed that in the 1860s and 1870s no clear division separated trade unionists from social reformers. The two types were interchangeable. Sylvis was the outstanding example of this trend, but other former trade unionists were by the close of the 1860s no less zealous partisans of reform and political activity.

The impetus given to the National Labor Union by the election of Sylvis as its president was to prove short-lived. On the eve of its annual convention in 1869, he suddenly died. The blow was a harsh one for the labor movement and "cast a veil of despondency upon the whole working class." There was scarcely a union which did not adopt laudatory resolutions, and the labor press published innumerable editorials upon the irreparable loss of a great leader in the zenith of his fame. "Sylvis! The National Calamity," one paper headed its comment upon his death; the *Working Man's Advocate* appeared with black borders.

From Europe came further condolences from the leaders of the International Workingmen's Association—the First International—with which Sylvis had sought to establish an alliance in the "war between poverty and wealth." A letter signed by Karl Marx, among others, declared that the world could ill afford the loss of "such tried champions in the bloom of life as him whose loss we mourn in common."

The contributions that Sylvis had made to the labor cause were the example and inspiration of his organizing zeal in building up the Molders' International Union and his stalwart support of the rights of the workers on the national stage. He had made himself a true spokesman for labor, and his words commanded attention and respect. Short as his life was, he stands out as the first truly national labor leader in the United States.

Whether the history of the National Labor Union would have been much different had he lived is problematical. It had already become largely political, and Sylvis had encouraged rather than sought to restrain the diversion of its energies to reform efforts. In any event its days were numbered. Richard F. Trevellick, a coworker with Sylvis and head of the International Union of Ship Carpenters and Caulkers, succeeded him as president. He, too, had moved toward mounting concern with politics. Under his presidency, the National Labor Union made the final plunge and, at its annual convention in 1872, transformed itself into the National Labor Reform Party. A program primarily emphasizing currency reform was adopted, and Judge David Davis of Illinois was nominated for the presidency. When Davis withdrew his name, the political movement largely collapsed. With that collapse, the National Labor Union ended its days.

Although the National Labor Union was both short-lived and unsuccessful, certain issues with which it was concerned deserve further consideration. The first of these was the campaign for a legislative eight-hour day which in 1866 was declared to be "the question of all others, which at present engrosses the attention of the American workingman." It was based upon theories that went much deeper than the old arguments which upheld a shorter working day in order to promote the health, the moral well-being, or the educational opportunity of workers. The eight-hour day, according to its advocates, was to transform the existing organization of society by raising both the wages and status of the workers and thereby gradually narrow the gap between employer and employee "until the capitalist and laborer are one."

The high priest of the eight-hour movement was Ira Steward, a Boston machinist and loyal union member, who was so deeply convinced that his ideas were the solution for all of labor's problems that he could not be swerved from his self-appointed task of promulgating them at all times and in all places. "Meet him any day as he steams along the street," wrote a contributor to the *American Workman*, ". . .and, although he will apologize and excuse himself if you talk to him of other affairs. . .if you only introduce the topic of 'hours of labor,' and show a willingness to listen, he will stop and plead with you till night-fall."

Steward addressed innumerable workingmen's audiences on the eight-hour day, testified before the Massachusetts legislature, wrote pamphlets and articles for the labor press, and organized first the Labor Reform Association and then the Grand Eight Hour League of Massachusetts. His ideas fired the imagination of the workers. Eight-hour leagues sprang up all over the country and, in making their program its own, the National Labor Union was reflecting a nationwide interest in the reduction of labor's working day.

Steward's basic theory clearly pointed to ideas and practices which in the twentieth century were to be even more widely accepted. In favoring the reduction of the working day to eight hours, he assumed that it would not mean any loss of wages. The workers would demand pay at least equal to what they had been receiving for ten and twelve hours work, and, since such a demand would be universal, the employers would have no valid ground for refusing it. Any resistance "would amount to the folly of a 'strike' by employers themselves, against the strongest power in the world, viz., the habits, customs and opinions of the masses." With their increased leisure, the workers would then be in a position to enjoy, and consequently would want to purchase, more of the products of industry. Maintaining that it was a "mechanical fact, that the cost of making an article depends almost entirely upon the number manufactured," Steward then asserted that the manufacturers would immediately profit from an expansion of their markets because onetime luxuries could be widely sold to the working population.

Steward's major point was that the reduction of working hours could be effected without any cut in wages, and this idea was popularized by a jingle attributed to his wife:

> Whether you work by the piece or work by the day
> Decreasing the hours increases the pay.

It was at least problematical whether employers would actually pay their old wages for an eight-hour day in the hope of building up purchasing power for their goods. The eight-hour leagues were highly successful, however, in promoting this optimistic view of a complete regeneration of capitalistic society. Both the national government and a number of states, moreover, were induced to take action to meet the workers' demands. The former established an eight-hour day for all its employees in 1868, and six states also made eight hours "a legal day's work."

As in the case of the earlier legislative drive for a ten-hour day, however, the action taken by the states was to prove illusory. The new laws were again subject to the reservation "where there is no special contract or agreement to the contrary," and there appeared to be no way to circumvent such limitations. A contemporary report to the National Labor Union was wholly discouraging. "Your committee wishes also further to state," it read, "that Eight Hour laws have been passed by six states, but for all practical purposes they might as well have never been placed on the statute books, and can only be described as frauds on the laboring class."

Faced with these actualities, the movement lost the support it had temporarily commanded. Maximum-hour laws were to remain an objective of social reformers. They were eventually to be adopted by the states without qualifying clauses, and in the 1930s Congress approved comparable legislation for all employees engaged in interstate trade. But during the last quarter of the nineteenth century, labor gave up the attempt to secure a shorter working day by political action and returned to economic pressure. The eight-hour movement of the 1880s and the 1890s found the unions making demands directly upon employers, as had the original trade societies, and seeking to enforce compliance through strikes.

As the maximum-hour drives of the 1860s subsided, a new enthusiasm for cooperation as the solution of labor's problems took its place and was in turn wholeheartedly supported by the National Labor Union. Again more was involved than in the comparable agitation of the 1840s. The latter-day sponsors of cooperation envisaged the complete reformation of society as had the proponents of the eight-hour day. Through the establishment of producers' cooperatives in every trade, the workingmen were to set up a system of self-employment which would ultimately do away with the wage system, provide practical means for an equitable distribution of the profits of industry, and free labor totally from its bondage to capital.

Sylvis had himself taken the lead in this movement with the establishment of cooperatives by the iron molders. Not only had their local unions set up foundries at Troy, Rochester, Chicago, Cleveland, Louisville, and other cities, but, after its disastrous strike experiences, the national union itself went directly into cooperation in 1868. Impulsively changing its name to the Iron Molders' International Cooperative and Protective Union, it embarked on an ambitious project, at a cost of $15,000, for a large foundry at Pittsburgh. So enthusiastic was Sylvis over this program that at one time in 1868 he appeared to be ready to give up everything else to promote it. "The time has come," he stated, "when we should abandon the whole system of strikes and make co-operation the foundation of our organization and the prime object of all our efforts."

Other unions followed the molders' example. The machinists set up a number of shops on a joint-stock basis; the shoemakers established both producers' and consumers' cooperatives; the coopers organized some eight shops in Minneapolis; and comparable projects were started by bakers, printers, hatter, carpenters, and shipwrights.

For a time some of these cooperatives appeared to be successful, but one by one they gradually failed. There was strong opposition to them on the part of the business community, which attacked such "Frenchy theories of communism," and they faced cut-throat competition. But the real trouble was in their own business operation. The union officials lacked managerial skill, and the cooperatives were run inefficiently, sometimes even dishonestly, with the result that they got into increasing difficulties. Moreover, there was a basic handicap, in a day when large outlays of capital had already become necessary for any productive enterprise, in the unions' lack of funds and the virtual impossibility of their obtaining credit.

The latter consideration, indeed, caused the National Labor Union to turn its attention to currency reform as a basic factor in any move by labor to help itself. On the surface, there was nothing more to this agitation, growing out of the proposed retirement of the greenbacks issued during the Civil War, than a demand for an inflationary policy to combat falling prices. It seemed to be a strange shift of emphasis from the days when the workers had favored hard money. The theories underlying Greenbackism, however, went deeper than any mere change in the price level. Labor aligned itself with the farmers on this issue because it promised radical reform of the whole financial, economic system. Like the eight-hour day and cooperation, currency reform also looked toward the creation of a producers' commonwealth to replace capitalism.

Taking their ideas in large part from the proposals for a new monetary system which had been advanced as early as 1848 by Edward Kellogg, the currency reformers urged the transformation of the public debt into bonds bearing 3 per cent interest and interconvertible at will with a legal tender currency based, not upon gold, but upon the physical wealth of the country. Such a program, it was believed, would break down the monopoly of "irresponsible banking associations," abolish the "robbery of interest rates," and free the economic system from that dependence upon gold whereby "the very heart's blood of the workingman was mortgaged from the cradle to the grave."

Here was a final panacea for assuring labor its natural rights. "It would effect," the National Labor Union declared in already familiar phrases, "the equitable distribution of the products of labor between non-producing capital and labor, giving to laborers a fair compensation for their products, and to capital a just reward for its uses, remove the necessity for excessive toil and afford the industrial classes the time and means necessary for social and intellectual culture."

Once again Sylvis, who had been swept along in turn by trade unionism, the eight-hour movement, and cooperation, eloquently preached this newest reform. Everything else was forgotten. "There are about three thousand trades' unions in the United States," he wrote. ". . . We must show them that when a just monetary system has been established, there will no longer exist any necessity for trade unions."

It was through adopting this program and allying itself with the political Greenback movement, however, that the National Labor Union lost the support of trade unionists and then collapsed after trying to run a political campaign in 1872. Still, currency revision had its impassioned devotees among both farmers and workers, and local Greenback-Labor parties were formed throughout the country in succeeding years to press the demand for legal-tender currency and interconvertible bonds. Eventually such parties coalesced to set up a national Greenback-Labor party, and in the mid-term elections of 1878 succeeded in polling over a million votes and sending fourteen representatives to Congress.

The pressure this party exerted helped to bring to a halt the further retirement of greenbacks, but the basic measures for which the currency reformers agitated were not enacted. The outstanding notes were made redeemable in gold in the Resumption Act of 1878. With the adoption of this measure, the Greenback-Labor party, which appeared to have temporarily aligned labor and agriculture on a common program, soon disappeared. Greenbackism had won the support of reformist-minded labor leaders, but it may well be doubted whether it had ever evoked very much enthusiasm among the rank and file of workers.

After the collapse of the National Labor Union in 1872, there were various efforts to set up some new organization which would eschew politics and get labor back on the straightforward path of trade unionism and economic action. A series of industrial congresses were held between 1873 and 1875 whose delegates declared that "the great desideratum of the hour" was no longer the eight-hour day, currency revision, or any other reform but "the organization, consolidation, and cooperative effort of the producing masses." Two secret societies were also formed—the Industrial Brotherhood and the Sovereigns of Industry—with the same general aims. These efforts, however, represented moves on the part of a few leaders to impose some sort of control over labor from the top down, and they did not have any really substantial backing. They provided little more than forums for discussion and debate.

Moreover, economic conditions at this time had once again cut the ground out from under the labor movement and created seemingly insuperable barriers to any effective activity. In 1873 the country was swept by a panic that ushered in an even more prolonged and severe depression than that of the 1830s. There was a repetition of the old story of falling prices, business stagnation, curtailed production, wage cuts, and unemployment. As mines, mills, and factories reduced operations or actually closed up, some three million persons were thrown out of work. Hard times not only brough an abrupt end to such nebulous strivings for labor unity as the National Labor Union and the industrial congresses, but again they almost completely shattered the existing national unions. They could no more survive the harsh impact of wage cuts and mounting unemployment than the promising unions forty years earlier had been able to survive the disrupting consequences of the Panic of 1837.

There were some thirty national unions when the crisis developed. The *Labor Standard* listed only nine in 1877 and the total strength of unionized labor was reported to have declined from 300,000 to perhaps 50,000. Union after union had the same experience. The Knights of St. Crispin was a remarkable organization of shoemakers which had been established on industrial lines, rapidly built up a membership of 50,000, and proved itself to be amazingly effective in enforcing the closed shop through a series of successful stirkes. But it collapsed as quickly as it had risen and had completely disappeared by 1878. The Machinists and Blacksmiths had lost two thirds of their members and the Coopers almost three fourths. Even the more stable National Typographical Union suffered a loss of half its members, while the newly organized Cigar Makers' National Union fell from almost 6,000 to little more than 1,000. Trade unionism was not entirely crushed, but with employers taking every advantage of hard times to combat it, and the workers unable to protect themselves, it was virtually forced underground.

In the decade since the Civil War, labor had failed to adjust itself to the new conditions of an industrialized society and had not yet attained the underlying strength to withstand depression. Its leaders advanced innumerable ideas and programs, but their shifting, changing attitude toward trade-union activity, reform, and politics did not command the popular support of the great mass of workers or inspire any real feeling of cohesion. For all the wordy talk at labor conventions, and the articles and appeals of the labor press, there appeared to be an increasingly wide gap between the handful of active participants in the labor movement and their nominal followers.

As far as there had been any definite philosophy behind the activities promoted by the National Labor Union, it was based upon the belief that the wage system should be abolished and that producers themselves should take over the economic system cooperatively. Those who led the labor movement had direct knowledge of a past substantially different from the present. They knew the history of the emerging industrial capitalistic order. Hence they refused to accept the permanence of wage-earning as a way of life. The eight-hour movement, Greenbackism, and cooperation sprang from a comprehension that the economy had once been organized in radically different ways and thus might be so reorganized again. The depression of the 1870s killed the organizational manifestations of such beliefs, but the ideas themselves remained alive to reemerge in the worker movements of the 1880s and 1890s.

VII

An Era of Upheaval

The depression of the 1870s ushered in one of the most confused periods in American labor history. Against the somber background of hard times, the workers rose to protest violently against what they considered to be their ruthless exploitation by employers. Demonstrations by the jobless were held in city after city, often calling out forceful intervention by the police; strikes among miners led to bloodshed and killing; and in 1877 a spontaneous uprising on the part of the railway workers caused such widespread rioting that the country seemed to be facing a general labor insurrection.

Even after these disturbances had subsided, the unrest and dissatisfaction of the workers continued to simmer dangerously below the surface and when, in the 1880s, the country again experienced depression, so many strikes broke out that the period has been called that of "the Great Upheaval." As never before, the nation came to realize the explosive force inherent in the great mass of industrial workers who were the product of its changing economy.

It was not surprising that the public, as well as conservative business interests, believed that the country was endangered by these disturbances. Among the immigrants entering the country were many continental European radicals, especially Marxists fleeing Bismarck's antisocialist code in Imperial Germany. These German immigrants were central participants in the founding of socialist organizations and parties in the United States (in the early 1870s they had joined in moving Karl Marx's International Working Men's Association—the First International—first to New York City and then to Philadelphia, where it expired in 1876). Their fascination with revolution and resort to violence-laden rhetoric frightened many moderate citizens, who associated anarchism and socialism with strikes and demonstrations by the unemployed. Such fears climaxed in the tragic Haymarket Square incident of 1886.

In their outcries against communism and anarchism, however, the conservatives were greatly exaggerating the radicalism of American labor. In spite of its left-wing elements and however discontented it may have been, labor presented no immediate danger to the existing system. The improvement of existing conditions rather than the over-throw of capitalism was still labor's goal. In holding foreign radicals responsible for the disturbed labor scene of the 1870s and 1880s, the newspapers of that era tended to disregard the underlying factors of low wages and unemployment which were basically responsible for the workingmen's discontent.

The violence that marked such a dramatic revolt as the great railway strike of 1877 must be set against the background of a long depression unrelieved by any public consideration of the plight of those whose wages were cut or who were unable to earn any wages whatsoever; the unfeeling attitude of such great employers as the railroads which were controlled by bankers and financiers interested only in profits; and the lack of any organization among the workers to direct their protests against injustice in effective form. The smoldering discontent among the railway workers did not need the spark of radical agitation to burst into open revolt; wage cut after wage cut drove the frustrated workers to strike back violently at those whom they identified as their ex-ploiters.

These years of labor strife were also to witness the slow growth of the Knights of Labor and of those national unions which in mounting rivalry with the Knights were later to band together in the American Federation of Labor. But these basically more important devel-opments were for a time overshadowed by the unorganized violence and radical agitation which reflected labor's growing pains in a capitalistic society where the human factor in industrial relations was still largely ignored.

As the effects of the Panic of 1873 deepened and widened, there were scenes of disorder in cities throughout the country. In New York, Chicago, Boston, Cincinnati, and Omaha, crowds of unemployed workers gathered in huge meetings to protest against the intolerable circumstances in which they found themselves with factories and workshops closed down. Unemployment in an industrialized society was far more serious than it had ever been in the less complex agrarian society of the first half of the nineteenth century. Homeless, hungry, and despairing, the workers refused to disperse when the police sought to break up their gatherings. They fought back in defense of what they considered their right of free assembly and challenged society to meet their demands.

The most noted of these outbursts was the Tompkins Square riot in New York on January 13, 1874. A meeting of the unemployed had been called to impress upon the city authorities the need for relief, and it was at first approved, the mayor himself promising to speak. Then, evidence that radical agitators were prepared to address the proposed gathering (members of the American section of the International Workingmen's Association had participated in the arrangements) caused a last-minute cancellation of the police permit. At the scheduled hour, Tompkins Square was nevertheless densely packed with working people who knew nothing about the change in the official attitude toward the meeting. Suddenly a squadron of mounted police appeared on the scene. Without warning, they charged into the crowd, indiscriminately swinging their clubs and hitting everyone within reach. Men, women, and children were ridden down as they fled in panic, and scores of innocent bystanders were severly injured.

The *New York Times* reported the next day that the police applied their clubs with "reasonable but not excessive severity" and that "the scrambles of the mob as the officers advanced were not unamusing." Ignoring the underlying causes for the workingmen's discontent, and whatever rights they had in seeking unemployment relief, the *New York Times* took the attitude that the demonstration was wholly the work of alien radicals. "The persons arrested yesterday," it editorialized, "seem all to have been foreigners—chiefly Germans or Irishmen. Communism is not a weed of native growth."

There was one young laboring man who took very much to heart the lesson that the Tompkins Square riot appeared to teach of the risks which trade unions ran in accepting radical leadership. The youthful Samuel Gompers was on hand when the mounted police charged the crowd. By jumping down a cellarway, he barely saved his own head from being cracked open.

"I saw how professions of radicalism and sensationalism," he wrote years later in his autobiography, "concentrated all the forces of society against a labor movement and nullified in advance normal, necessary activity. I saw that leadership in the labor movement could be safely entrusted only to those into whose hearts and minds had been woven the experience of earning their bread by daily labor. I saw that betterment for workingmen must come primarily through workingmen."

In the wake of such disturbances as the Tompkins Square riot and demonstrations in other cities, outbreaks of violence in the anthracite coal fields of eastern Pennsylvania next evoked public attention. The workers in this industry, following the lead of the soft-coal miners who had established the Miners' National Association, had formed a union of their own in the Miners' and Mine Laborers' Benevolent Association. It succeeded in reaching a trade agreement with the Anthracite Board of Trade, but in December 1874 the operators independently cut wages below the agreed upon minimum. The miners at once walked out of the pits and, in what became known as "the long strike," they tried to compel the operators to restore the wage cuts. As hunger and want began to exact their toll among the workers and compelled many of them to return to the pits, something like open war developed between the remaining strikers and the coal-and-iron police sent into the area by the operators to protect strikebreakers.

Into this troubled situation there was then projected another element whose exact role in the long strike it is still impossible to determine. At the time, however, sensational reports appeared in the press of the operations of a secret organization among the miners, the Ancient Order of Hibernians, more popularly known as the Molly Maguires, which was said to be terrorizing the coal fields and preventing those miners who wished to return to work from doing so. The members of this society were also charged with attempting to intimidate the coal operators—as they had once sought to intimidate Irish landlords under the leadership of a redoubtable widow named Molly Maguire, from whom they took their name—by violent threats against foremen and superintendents, sabotage and destruction of mine property, and outright murder and assassination. It has subsequently been revealed that the operators themselves instigated some of these attacks on the mines in order to provide an excuse for moving in, not only to crush the Molly Maguires, but also all union organization. This interpretation of the wave of violence that swept over eastern Pennsylvania would appear to be substantiated at least in part by the steps taken to suppress the disorders.

The bitterly antilabor head of the Philadelphia and Reading Railroad, which controlled many of the mines, took the initiative in this campaign. He hired a Pinkerton detective, one James McParlan, to obtain proof of the criminal activity of the Molly Maguires at any cost. Posing as a fugitive from justice, McParlan won his way into their confidence, and under circumstances not entirely clear,[1] finally succeeded in turning up evidence in the fall of 1875 which led the authorities to make a series of arrests. His testimony on the stand and that of other witnesses who turned state's evidence was in many instances suspect, but the trials resulted in the wholesale conviction of twenty-four of the Molly Maguires. Ten of them were hanged for murder, and the others were sentenced to jail for terms from two to seven years.

Peace and order were restored in the coal fields. Whatever the power and influence of the secret society had really been, it was shattered by this attack. But the operators had also succeeded in breaking the Miners' Benevolent Association and forcing the strikers back to work on their own terms. The long strike ended in complete failure for the workers and the virtual collapse of their union.

Unemployment riots and violence in the anthracite coal fields were but a prelude to the railroad strikes of 1877 which led to disorders and rioting that called for the intervention of federal troops before they could be suppressed. The workers at first commanded public sympathy. Their wages had been arbitrarily cut while high dividends were still being paid on watered stock, and the railways were in any event highly unpopular in the 1870s. "It is folly to blink at the fact," the *New York Tribune* reported, "that the manifestations of Public Opinion are almost everywhere in sympathy with the insurrection." But as

---

[1]A recent study of this confused episode is Wayne G. Broehl, Jr., *The Molly Maguires*, Cambridge, Mass., 1964.

the violence continued uncontrolled, the choice appeared to become one between civil law or chaos. Although not everyone agreed with the *Nation's* blunt statement that the strikers should have been confronted by "trained bodies of men sufficient to overawe or crush them at the first onset," it was recognized that the government could not evade its responsibility to restore public order.

The strikes, which broke out in early July 1877 in protest against the wage cuts, were spontaneous. The first one was on the Baltimore and Ohio, and it was at once followed by similar moves on the part of railway workers on the Pennsylvania, the New York Central, and the Erie. Within a brief time, all lines east of the Mississippi were affected, and the movement then spread to the Missouri Pacific, the St. Louis, Kansas and Northern, and other western lines. Railroad traffic throughout the country was interrupted and in sections completely paralyzed. As rioting flared up dangerously in Baltimore, Pittsburgh, Chicago, St. Louis and San Francisco, the country was confronted with its first national industrial outbreak. "It is wrong to call this a strike," the *St. Louis Republic* exclaimed, "it is labor revolution."

The strikers on the Baltimore and Ohio were the first to clash with authority; at Martinsburg, West Virginia, order was restored only after two hundred federal troops had been sent to the scene. Rioting on a much larger scale occurred in Baltimore. There the strikers stopped all trains, refused to allow them to move, and began to seize railroad property. When the militia, called out by the Governor of Maryland, marched from their armory to the railway station, a gathering crowd of workers and their sympathizers attacked them with brickbats, stones and clubs. The troops opened fire and broke for the station, but the rioters had had a taste of blood. They kept up the assault and set fire to the station. When police and firemen arrived, the mob for a time tried to prevent them from putting out the blaze, but finally gave way. Disturbances continued through a wild and riotous night, and only the arrival of federal troops the next morning brought any real return of order. By then the toll of victims had mounted to nine persons killed and more than a score (of whom three later died) gravely injured.

In the meantime, a still more serious outbreak took place in Pittsburgh, where the strikers also stopped trains and took possession of railway property. Here popular sympathy was wholly with the railway workers because of a deep seated resentment against the policies of the Pennsylvania Railroad. The local militia, openly fraternizing with the strikers, refused to take any action against them. The arrival of a force of 650 soldiers, dispatched from Philadelphia to protect railway property, consequently precipitated a pitched battle in which the troops opened fire and, after killing some twenty-five persons and wounding many more, took over possession of the roundhouse and machine shops.

The infuriated strikers, their ranks swelled by miners, mill hands, and factory workers, returned to the attack with arms seized from nearby gun shops and laid siege to the troops. As night fell, freight cars were set afire and pushed into the roundhouse until it, too, was blazing. The troops, surrounded by flames and nearly suffocated with smoke, fought their way out amid a hail of bullets and retreated across the Allegheny River.

An enraged crowd, swelled to between four and five thousand persons, now had the field to itself. Railway tracks were torn up, freight and passenger cars broken open, and what could not otherwise be destroyed, was set afire. Some two thousand cars, the machine shops, a grain elevator and two roundhouses with one hundred and twenty-five locomotives went up in flames. The Union Depot itself was burned down. As the rioting continued unchecked, the more unruly and desparately poor and criminal elements broke into the liquor stores and began to pillage at will. They carried off furniture, clothing, and provisions.

"Here a brawny woman could be seen hurrying away with pairs of white kid slippers under her arms," read one contemporary description; "another carrying an infant, would be rolling a barrel of flour along the sidewalk, using her feet as the propelling power; here a man pushing a wheelbarrow loaded with white lead. Boys hurried through the crowd with large-sized family Bibles as their share of the plunder, while scores of females utilized aprons and dresses to carry flours, eggs, dry goods, etc. Bundles of umbrellas, fancy parasols, hams, bacons, leaf lard, calico, blankets, laces and flour were mixed together in the arms of robust men, or carried on hastily constructed hand barrows."

It was not until after the angry poor and unemployed had spent a whole weekend seizing or despoiling an estimated five to seven million dollars of property that the police, reinforced by bands of armed citizens, began to restore some semblance of order. In the meantime, the entire state militia had been called out, and following an emergency cabinet meeting, President Rutherford B. Hayes ordered all federal troops in the Atlantic Department made available to cope with the emergency. Only when the regulars arrived in Pittsburgh did railway property finally receive full protection.

Headlines and editorials declared that communism was at the bottom of the strike and responsible for its violence. It was described as "an insurrection, a revolution, an attempt of communists and vagabonds to coerce society, an endeavour to undermine American institutions." The *New York Tribune* stated that only force could subdue this "ignorant rabble with hungry mouths"; the *New York Times* characterized the strikers as "hoodlums, rabble, bummers, looters, blacklegs, thieves, tramps, ruffians, incendiaries, enemies of society, brigands, rapscallions, riffraff, felons and idiots," and the *New York Herald* declared that the mob was "a wild beast and needs to be shot down." Reading such headlines as "Pittsburgh Sacked—The City Completely in the Power of a Howling Mob," and "Chicago in the Possession of Communists" caused many citizens to become hysterical.

As the federal troops reached the scene in city after city, however, the rioting subsided as quickly as it had flared up. The strikers not only made no further attempts to interfere with the railroads' operations, but gradually went back to work. They knew when they were beaten; they knew that they had no chance with the government upholding the railroads. By the end of July, the trains were generally running again and the strikes were over.

The outbreaks of violence brought vigorous enforcement of law and order, but in the suppression of the strikes the original grievances of the railway workers appeared to have been overlooked completely. The *New York Tribune*, which at first had admitted that public opinion was largely with the workers, took the position that they should have been willing to practice greater self-denial and economy until conditions had settled down. It was not impossible to sustain life on two dollars or even one dollar a day, it editorialized, and if the railway employees were unwilling to work for such wages, they had no right to prevent others from taking jobs they spurned; because of their attitude, "they deserve no sympathy, but only punishment."

This reflected a view widely held during these years of the need for workingmen to submit to whatever conditions prevailed in industry. "God intended the great to be great and the little to be little," the noted preacher, Henry Ward Beecher, once wrote. "...I do not say that a dollar a day is enough to support a working man. But it is enough to support a man! Not enough to support a man and five children if a man insists on smoking and drinking beer. . . . But the man who cannot live on bread and water is not fit to live."

The month of July 1877 had, in any event, been one of the most turbulent in American history, and the long-term consequences of its disorder and rioting were to be highly important. The business community was aroused as never before to the potential power of industrial workers and embarked on an aggressive program to suppress all labor activity. Businessmen revived the old conspiracy laws, sought to intimidate workers from joining unions, imposed the "iron clad" oath, and enlisted strikebreakers whenever trouble threatened. The lesson driven home for labor was the need for organization and authority that would prevent strikes from developing into uncontrolled mob action which inevitably invited suppression by state or federal troops. Capitalism had won this first round of industrial strife, but it was fearful of the future. Labor had lost, but it had a new realization of its latent strength.

The violence that marked both unemployment demonstrations and railway revolts in the 1870s had its counterpart in another round of strikes during the next decade, but the Haymarket Square riot in 1886 more than any other outbreak of these years served to arouse and alarm the public. Anarchists were held responsible for this affair, and, while only a tiny segment among the workers in Chicago were at all influenced by their violent "propaganda by the deed," the repercussions of the riot affected the entire labor movement. The foes of unionism made the most of this dramatic incident in trying to discredit organized labor and stigmatize it as radical, revolutionary, and un-American.

The left-wing groups within the labor movement were in this as in other periods constantly shifting their alignments and organizing new parties. The International Workingmen's Association had been dissolved in 1876, and the socialist forces in the United States had formed a new Working Men's party. It was not important; its small membership was largely drawn from German and other European-born immigrants; but it had been active during the railway strike in 1877 trying to foment a general strike.

Its ranks were soon split by further internal quarrels. There was embittered rivalry between the Marxian socialists, who sought to promote trade unionism as a base for the revolutionary activity that was eventually to overthrow the capitalistic state, and the Lassalleans, who urged direct political activity as a far more effective means of achieving the same end. In addition to these two groups, a third flirted with the far more radical doctrines of anarchism which were being preached in the United States by Johann Most, a big, black-bearded German immigrant who had formerly been a socialist, but, after he arrived in the United States in 1882, had become a fiery exponent of revolutionary violence. The radicals who espoused his brand of anarchism established an International Working People's Association, to become known as the Black International, which succeeded in winning control of the Central Labor Union in Chicago. It had some 2,000 members drawn from German and Polish metal workers, cabinet makers and packinghouse employees, and through the pages of its organ, the *Alarm*, it openly called for immediate revolution.

Anarchism itself had a long history in America and a tradition of suspicion of all government and authority, and was influenced by the moral philosophy of the Massachusetts writer, Henry David Thoreau. Hence it was not odd for an American-born worker like Albert Parsons to ally with the immigrant Johann Most to propose a combination of trade unionism and anarchism as the solution to labor's plight. These radicals, not all of whom favored violent deeds, built a real following among Chicago workers, if not elsewhere in the country. Thus the Chicago newspapers constantly stressed the danger of violence in every demonstration of labor militancy. "The Nihilistic character of the procession," read one report of a labor parade in which members of the Central Labor Union apparently participated, "was shown by the red badges and red flags which were thickly displayed throughout it."

When in 1886 a movement spread across the country for general strikes in favor of the eight-hour day, the Chicago anarchists were ready to take advantage of every opportunity to preach their own doctrines of revolution. The day set for the strike itself—May 1—passed off very quietly, but two days later a clash between strikers and strikebreakers at the McCormick Harvester plant in Chicago led to police intervention and the death of four men. Here was the sort of situation for which members of the Black International had been waiting. That night leaflets were circulated through the city calling upon the workers to avenge their slaughtered comrades.

"The masters sent out their bloodhounds—the police," this appeal read; "they killed six of your brothers at McCormick's this afternoon. They killed the poor wretches because they, like you, had the courage to disobey the supreme will of your bosses. . . . To arms we call you, to arms!''

A protest meeting was summoned for Haymarket Square the next evening, May 4, and some three thousand persons gathered to hear impassioned and inflammatory speeches by the anarchist leaders. But it was an entirely peaceful meeting in spite of all these alarms (the mayor himself attended it and left upon finding everything quiet), and, when a cold wind began to blow gusts of rain through the square, the crowd gradually melted away. The meeting had, in fact, virtually broken up when a police detachment of two hundred men arrived and their captain peremptorily ordered such workers as remained to disperse. Suddenly there was a sharp explosion. Someone had hurled a bomb into the ranks of the police, killing one outright. They at once opened fire, and there were answering shots from the workers. During the fray, seven police in all were either killed or fatally wounded, and some sixty-seven injured; four workers were killed and fifty or more injured.

Almost immediately the authorities and the press blamed the anarchists for the deaths and injuries. An outraged cry arose for the punishment of the perpetrators. The police combed the city for suspects, and finally eight known anarchist leaders were arrested and charged with murder. In a frenzied atmosphere compounded equally of fear and the desire for revenge, they were thereupon promptly found guilty—seven of them sentenced to death and the eighth to fifteen years' imprisonment. There was no evidence whatsoever connecting them with the bombing. They were condemned out of hand for their revolutionary views and the incitements to violence which supposedly caused the bombing. "Convict these men, make examples of them, hang them," urged the state's attorney, "and you save our institutions."

Two of the convicted men pleaded for executive clemency and were given life imprisonment. Six years later, Governor John Peter Altgeld pardoned them, together with the eighth man who had been sentenced to fifteen years' imprisonment, on the ground that they had not been granted a fair trial. So violent was the feeling against the anarchists, even at this late date, that Altgeld was assailed throughout the country for what has since been universally recognized as an act of simple justice.

Organized labor was in no way associated with the Haymarket Square bombing and had at once denied any sympathy whatsoever for the accused anarchists. The Knights of Labor were as violent in condemning them as the most conservative newspapers. "Let it be understood by all the world," their Chicago organ declared, "that the Knights of Labor have no affiliation, association, sympathy or respect for the band of cowardly murderers, cut-throats and robbers, known as anarchists." Wholly disregarding the complete failure of the prosecution to connect the accused men with the actual crime with which they were charged, the Knights clamored for their conviction. "Better that seven times seven men hang," it was declared, "than to have the millstone of odium around the standard of this Order in affiliating in any way with this element of destruction."

The reason for such an outburst was obvious. The capitalistic enemies of labor were seeking to hang upon the labor movement this "millstone of odium" by charging that the Knights of Labor and the unions, generally, were permeated by the spirit of anarchism and communism. It did not matter that few labor leaders and equally few ordinary workers were associated with anarchism or socialism. All labor was thrown on the defensive.

This whole episode was to have an important influence on the developing trend of trade unionism, but it has taken us beyond our account of the growth of the labor movement as a whole. As already noted, the rise of the Knights of Labor during the 1880s was far more significant than occasional outbreaks of violence or the role of what were then tiny and sectarian leftist organizations.

VIII

The Rise and Decline
of the Knights of Labor

It was seventeen years before the Haymarket Square riot and eight years before the great railway strike that the first step had been taken in the organization of what was to become the Noble and Holy Order of the Knights of Labor. Nevertheless, it was the years of labor unrest and industrial strife that intervened between these two events which saw its rise to an unprecedented pinnacle of power. Even though there was at the same time a slow revival of national unionism, and Samuel Gompers was stubbornly promoting the policies that were to come to fruition with the formation of the AFL, the future of American labor in the mid-1880s appeared to lie with the Knights of Labor. For the first time a labor association seemed strong enough to challenge industry on its own grounds. "It is an organization," one contemporary writer stated emphatically, "in whose hands now rests the destinies of the Republic. ...It has demonstrated the overmastering power of a national combination among workingmen."

The Knights were to be accused in the feverish atmosphere of these days of promoting the radical ideas being preached by foreign agitators, and the repercussions of the Haymarket Square riot contributed to a decline in their strength almost as rapid as had been their rise to power. But the Noble and Holy Order was in reality an indigenous response to American conditions and, much as had been the National Labor Union, a combination of trade union and general reform philosophy. Its leaders looked forward to the abolition of "wage slavery" and the construction of a "cooperative commonwealth." However hazy their goals may have been, they stressed organization, education, and political agitation as the best means to build a new society. The Knights insisted that the existing economic system could only be changed peaceably, and this often led them to oppose strikes.

More significantly, they sought to promote a unionism which would embrace all workers, skilled and unskilled, in a single labor organization. They recognized the vital importance of the role of industrial workers in the emerging capitalistic system and were convinced that trade unionism, as it had been known, had to give way to labor organization on a much broader basis. Their attitude in some measure foreshadowed the industrial unionism of a later day, but rather than being a federation or congress of individual unions, the Knights continually emphasized the solidarity of labor and looked toward a centralized association which would include the workers in all industries and occupations. Their ideal of a pervasive unity among workingmen everywhere—"an injury to one is an injury to all"—was a high-minded concept, but one never fully achieved in the United States or anywhere else. Thus their efforts to bring the unskilled workers within the fold of organized labor won only temporary success. However right in theory they may have been as to the importance of the organization of the unskilled, they were ahead of the times. The great mass of such workers, largely drawn from the ranks of the newly arrived immigrants, were separated by almost insuperable barriers of race, language, and religion. Employers were quick to take advantage of every opportunity to stir up the friction and animosities which blocked any real cooperation. Moreover, as the workers' ranks were constantly swelled by new arrivals, a tremendous reservoir of potential strikebreakers was always at hand to furnish cheap replacements for those who dared to take part in any union activity. The unskilled, industrial workers did not have in the 1880s either the cohesiveness or the bargaining power to make their inclusion in the organized labor movement easy. In the face of unrelenting employer opposition, it was not, indeed, until after the restriction of immigration in the 1920s and government support for labor organizations in the 1930s, that industrial unionism—with some few notable exceptions such as in coal mining—was successfully promoted.

The members of the traditional trade unions—the counterpart of the mechanics and artisans of an earlier day—realized this in the 1880s and became increasingly unwilling to link their fortunes with such weak allies as the unskilled workers proved to be. They felt compelled to create a more structured, stable, and successful alternative to the Knights of Labor, one that drew its strength from the quite real solidarity of skilled workers. As they increasingly distinguished themselves from the Knights, the trade unions in the AFL became the embodiment of a "new unionism" concerned primarily with the needs of craftsmen.

Nine inconspicuous tailors, meeting in Philadelphia in the hall of the American Hose Company, founded the Knights of Labor on December 9, 1869. Members of a local Garment Cutters' Association which had been forced to dissolve because of lack of funds to maintain its benefit program, they decided to form a new association which originally differed little from any other craft union, except that it was a secret society and its activities were centered about an elaborate ritual. But one of the group, Uriah S. Stephens, had a far broader vision of labor organization, and his fellow members were soon caught up by his idealistic enthusiasms. This was the concept of a new labor solidarity which would make it possible to include all the nation's workers in a single unified order, without regard to nationality, sex, creed, or color.

There was no idea of class struggle in the thinking of the founders of the Knights of Labor. They did not plan any attack upon the citadels of industry—"no conflict with legitimate enterprise, no antagonism to necessary capital." While they looked ultimately to "the complete emancipation of the wealth producers from the thralldom and loss of wage slavery," this was to be brought about gradually by mitigating the evils of the existing economic system and by establishing producers' cooperatives. In time a new industrial commonwealth would then be created in which moral worth, rather than material wealth, would be accepted as the true standard of individual and national greatness.

The leader of the nine tailors who met in Philadelphia, Stephens, was born in Cape May, New Jersey, in 1821 and educated for the Baptist ministry. Forced to abandon his studies after the Panic of 1837, he became apprenticed to a tailor, and the 1840s found him working at his trade in Philadelphia. Some time later he traveled extensively—to the West Indies, Mexico, and California—but on the eve of the Civil War he was back again in Philadelphia. He attended the workers' antiwar convention in 1861 and the next year helped to organize the Garment Cutters' Association. Never a trade unionist in any strict meaning of the term (he believed that unions were too narrow in their outlook and circumscribed in their operations), Stephens drew from his religious background that vision of the universality of labor which was symbolized in the mysticism of the Knights of Labor's secret ritual.

"Cultivate friendship among the great brotherhood of toil," he was to advise his followers; "learn to respect industry in the person of every intelligent worker; unmake the shams of life by deference to the humble but useful craftsman; beget concert of action by conciliation. ...The work to which this fraternity addresses itself is one of the greatest magnitude ever attempted in the history of the world. ...It builds upon the immutable basis of the Fatherhood of God, and the logical principle of the Brotherhood of Man."

This was the strain that ran through all Stephens's writing and addresses. In pursuing the ultimate goal of consolidating "all branches of labor into a compact whole," he dismissed the idea of organizing separate trades or callings and would have done away with both boycotts and strikes, whose benefits he felt were "partial and evanescent." His vision embraced all mankind. "Creed, party and nationality," he wrote, "are but outward garments and present no obstacle to the fusion of the hearts of worshippers of God, the Universal Father, and the workers for man, the universal brother."

Stephens's role in the foundation of the Knights of Labor was all-important, and he became the first Grand Master Workman when it was nationally organized. Nevertheless, he did not stay with it for very long. He turned to politics and, becoming interested in currency reform, ran unsuccessfully for Congress on the Greenback ticket in 1878. Resigning his post in the Knights, he then drifted away from the labor movement altogether and died in 1882 without witnessing the Order's rise to unprecedented prominence. Yet his influence lived on. "All through our rituals and laws," the *Journal of United Labor*, organ of the Knights, wrote upon announcement of his death, "will be found the impress of his brain, and inspiration of his keen insight into the great problems of the present hour."

In the meantime, the original Philadelphia assembly of the Knights of Labor grew very slowly. The secrecy which had been adopted to enhance the mystical appeal of ritual and ceremony, as well as to protect members from possible retaliation by employers, was rigidly maintained. A prospective new member would be invited to attend a meeting of the group without being told what it was, and only after having given satisfactory answers to various questions as to his opinion upon "the elevation of labor" would he be considered eligible for initiation. The ritual was passed on by word of mouth, and outsiders had no way of knowing the existence of the Order, let alone its purposes. In all public documents or notices, the name was designated by five asterisks.

Provision was made for expansion through the admission of "sojourners," workers in other crafts than that of tailoring, on the payment of an initiation fee of $1. When their number became sufficient, they could "swarm" and form an assembly of their own. But it was not until 1872 that a second assembly, made up of ship carpenters, was actually established. The pace of growth then speeded up. In the next two years, some eighty locals were formed in and about Philadelphia, and in 1874 the first assembly outside this immediate area was established in New York. These groups were all composed of workers in distinct crafts—garment cutters, ship carpenters, shawl weavers, masons, machinists and blacksmiths, house carpenters, tin plate and iron workers, stone cutters and gold beaters.

The next step in the evolution of the Knights was the formation of district assemblies made up of delegates from the local assemblies. The first of these units was established in Philadelphia in 1873. The next year, one was set up in Camden, New Jersey, and another in Pittsburgh—a first step toward invasion of the West. Soon there were district assemblies in Ohio, West Virginia, Indiana, and Illinois as well as Pennsylvania, New York, and New Jersey, with a membership which included unskilled and semiskilled workers in addition to craft workers.

As time went on, many local assemblies were established as mixed assemblies of workers in different trades. Miners, railway workers, and steel workers joined the Knights in increasing numbers, and wherever there were not enough members of a single trade to form a trade assembly, especially in small towns and rural areas, the mixed assembly became a general catchall. Eventually, the mixed assemblies outnumbered the trade assemblies and with their inclusion of unskilled workers gave the Knights their distinctive character. In all, some fourteen district assemblies, with a total membership of about nine thousand, had been formed when the leaders of the movement decided that the time had come to send out a call for a general convention to form a national body.

This meeting was held in Reading, Pennsylvania, in January 1878 with thirty-three delegates present. After long discussion, a constitution was adopted which established a General Assembly as the supreme authority of the Knights, with control over both the district and the local assemblies. In theory, the new organization was highly centralized, but the district assemblies had authority within their own jurisdictions and were never subject to control as rigid as the constitution theoretically contemplated. The Order became, however, a truly national organization in a sense never attained by its predecessors, and it further differed from them in that the membership remained on an individual basis rather than through affiliated unions. The workingman anxious to join simply applied for membership in a local assembly, was duly initiated, paid chapter dues, attended meetings, and so became an accredited Knight of Labor.

Membership was open to all wage earners and to all former wage earners (although the latter could not exceed one fourth of the membership in any local assembly), with the exception of lawyers, doctors, bankers, and those who sold or made their living through selling liquor—to which excluded group were later added stockbrokers and professional gamblers. "It gathers into one fold," stated a later provision in the constitution, "all branches of honorable toil."

The preamble to the constitution, taking over the general principles which had been put forward by the earlier Industrial Brotherhood, called attention to "the recent alarming development and aggression of aggregated wealth" and stated that, unless it were checked, it would inevitably lead "to the pauperization and hopeless degradation of the toiling masses." Only through unification could labor be assured of the fruits of its toil, the Knights declared, and to bring this about, "we have formed . . . with a view of securing the organization and direction, by cooperative effort, of the power of the industrial classes."

The constitution itself set forth many of the traditional demands of organized labor and also outlined certain new goals. It called for the establishment of cooperatives, the reservation of public lands for actual settlers, the eight-hour day, and a fiat currency in very much the same terms as had the National Labor Union. It demanded abolition of the contract system for prison labor, the prohibition of child labor, equal pay for the sexes, establishment of bureaus of labor statistics, and, by later amendment, government ownership of the railways and telegraphs, and adoption of a graduated income tax.

These provisions were largely reformist or political. Insofar as industrial action was concerned, the Knights of Labor supported boycotts, which were to become increasingly important, but they strongly favored arbitration rather than resort to strikes, which they at first wholly opposed. While a resistance fund was eventually set up for use in certain carefully defined contingencies, it was provided that only 30 per cent of the money collected could be directly used for strikes, with 60 per cent set aside for cooperatives and 10 per cent for education. The Knights had to recognize that strikes might sometimes be necessary, but they were unwilling to support them except when specifically approved by their Executive Board. "Strikes at best afford only temporary relief," the revised constitution of 1884 was to state, "and members should be educated to depend upon thorough education, cooperation and political action, and through these the abolition of the wage system."

This cautious attitude was in part due to the experience of the workers during the railway strikes of 1877. The lawlessness to which these strikes had led, with consequent intervention by federal troops, seemed to make such direct action a very dubious expedient in the minds of the leaders of the Knights of Labor. But they had no solution to the problem of how arbitration was to be enforced should employers refuse to deal with their representatives. The Knights consequently became involved in strikes in spite of themselves, and when the local assemblies were threatened by retaliatory measures on the part of industry, the Executive Board felt bound to come to their aid.

The ambiguities of its position on the strike issue might also seem to mark the stand of the Noble and Holy Order on political questions. The contemplated reforms in some respects went even beyond those put forward by the National Labor Union, and yet the Knights sought to remain primarily an industrial rather than a political organization. While they engaged in lobbying activities and in time entered more directly into politics, they made no attempt to set up a labor party. "Politics must be subordinated to industry," the General Assembly declared in 1884, and made it clear that "this Order is in no way bound by the political expression of its individual members."

The basic policies of the Knights of Labor, in short, remained somewhat vaguely idealistic and humanitarian, in the pattern originally set forth by Uriah Stephens, and they sometimes appeared to be highly contradictory. The Knights sought to emphasize their industrial character, and yet agitated for an all-inclusive program of social reform; they discouraged strikes and yet became deeply involved in them; they called for political action and denied that they had any direct concern with politics. Moreover, while the Order was theoretically highly centralized, leading to charges that its policies were dictatorially determined by a handful of leaders, its membership actually took things very much in their own hands and went their own way.

The first General Assembly set the stage for further expansion. A membership of 9,287 rose to 28,136 a year later, and then declined to 19,422 in 1881. The secrecy which had at first provided a protective screen safeguarding members from employer attack began to react upon the Order as a whole. It became associated in the public mind with such other secret societies as the Molly Maguires and aroused such suspicion on the part of the Roman Catholic Church that, in Canada, all Catholics were forbidden to join it. Measures were consequently taken to make the name of the Order public, remove the oath from the initiation proceedings, and eliminate all Scriptural passages from the ritual. Through the intercession of James Cardinal Gibbons, who was persuaded that there was nothing about the revised ritual offensive to religious doctrine, the Pope was then induced to withdraw his condemnation and uphold the propriety of Church approval. The membership rapidly recovered its losses after these moves to do away with secrecy. It had doubled in 1882 to a total of over 42,000, and within the next three years it rose to more than 100,000.

Upon Stephens's retirement in 1879, Terence V. Powderly was chosen as his successor in the exalted post of Grand Master Workman. This young labor agitator, only thirty at the time, had been born at Carbondale, Pennsylvania, in 1849. The son of Irish Catholic parents who had emigrated to the United States in the 1820s, he worked while a young boy as a switch tender in the local railway yards but soon decided that he wanted to become a machinist. When seventeen, he was apprenticed to this trade, and three years later got a journeyman's job in the shops of the Delaware and Western Railroad in Scranton.

In the next few years he successively joined the International Union of Machinists and Blacksmiths, became the Pennsylvania organizer for the Industrial Brotherhood, and, in 1874, was initiated into the Knights of Labor. After a brief period of "sojourning," he organized

and became Master Workman of Assembly No. 222 and corresponding secretary for District Assembly No. 5. His mounting interest in labor politics also led to participation in the activities of the
Greenback-Labor party and, in 1878, he was elected on its ticket as
the mayor of Scranton.

Powderly was to continue to hold this latter post until 1884, even
though he had in the meantime been elected Grand Master Workman
of the Knights. He always had many and varied interests. He studied
law and later practiced at the bar, served as a county health officer,
was part owner and manger of a grocery store, and became vice-
president of the Irish Land League. At one time he applied, unsuccessfully, for the post of head of the Bureau of Labor Statistics in
Washington, established largely through the efforts of the Knights.
After he lost the presidency of the Order in 1893, he obtained a
governmental post in the Bureau of Immigration. He lived until 1924,
when his stormy career as a labor leader was almost forgotten by a
generation far removed from the turbulent industrial strife of the
1880s.

Powderly did not look like a labor leader. Slender and under
average height, he had wavy light brown hair, a blond drooping
mustache, and mild bespectacled blue eyes. He dressed convention-
ally and well, his usual costume being a double-breasted broadcloth
coat, stand-up collar, plain tie, dark trousers, and small, narrow shoes.
His manners were formal and polite and gave every appearance of a
man of breeding and refinement. "English novelists take men of
Powderly's look," commented John Swinton, a labor journalist, "for
their poets, gondola scullers, philosophers and heroes crossed in love
but no one ever drew such a looking man as the leader of a million of
the horny-fisted sons of toil."

He was straitlaced, almost puritanical in his point of view. A convinced total abstainer, he warred incessantly against the saloon and
had little toleration for those who liked to drink. While he inspired
both affection and loyalty among his followers, he was never an easy
mixer or really at home in labor gatherings. He had his own sense of
humor, as is shown in his autobiographical writings, but there was no
natural give and take about the man.

On assuming his post as Grand Master Workman, Powderly did
yeoman work in building up the Knights of Labor's membership. He
was an eloquent and persuasive speaker and an indefatigable letter
writer. Yet even in these early days of enthusiasm, he never dedicated

himself to the labor movement with the wholehearted devotion of Sylvis. Powderly continually protested that his other interests did not allow him to give full time to his job as Grand Master Workman, and on occasion he petulantly complained that his health (which was never very good) was not equal to the heavy demands being made upon it. He not only resented the incessant requests for him to speak, but with a sense of his own importance which time did not diminish, he insisted that, when he did speak, it should be under circumstances suitable to his high office in the Order.

"I will talk at no picnics," he once wrote exasperatedly in the *Journal of United Labor*. "When I speak on the labor question I want the individual attention of my hearers and I want that attention for at least two hours and in that two hours I can only epitomize. At a picnic where. . . the girls as well as the boys swill beer I cannot talk at all. . . . If it comes to my ears that I am advertised to speak at picnics. . . . I will prefer charges against the offenders for holding the executive head of the Order up to ridicule."

For all his prima-donna attitude, or perhaps because of it, there was no gainsaying his skill as an organizer, while his able handling of the dispute with the Roman Catholic Church was largely responsible for Cardinal Gibbons' intercession with the Pope in the Knights' behalf. Powderly was also a master at labor politics and built up a personal machine which enabled him to keep close control over the General Assembly during its years of growth and expansion. There were times when he declared that there was nothing that he wanted more than to hand over his post to someone else, but this did not prevent him from vigorously combating any opposition to his policies, sharply assailing his opponents, and clinging firmly to office.

Powderly's ideas and theories were closely in accord with the underlying aims of the Knights of Labor as expressed in their original First Principles—and they had the same idealistic, broadly humanitarian, and often contradictory scope. He believed in education rather than direct economic action, but it was not always clear for what he was agitating. He was given to uttering vague generalities clothed in the most grandiloquent phrases.

"The Knights of Labor is higher and grander than party," he declared on one occasion. "There is a nobler future before it than that which clings to its existence amidst partisan rancor and strife. . . . We seek and intend to enlist the services of men from every society, of every party, every religion, and every nation in the crusade which we have inaugurated against these twin monsters, tyranny and monopoly; and in that crusade we have burned the bridges behind us; we have stricken from our vocabulary that word fail; we aim at establishing the complete rights of man throughout the world."

Cooperation was the means by which he apparently hoped to achieve these idealistic aims, but at times he seemed to be ready to place major emphasis on some other reform. "In my opinion," he told the General Assembly in 1882, "the main, all absorbing question of the hour is the land question. . . . Give me the land, and you may frame as many eight-hour laws as you please yet I can baffle them all and render them null and void." His zeal for temperance also led him to emphasize this issue. "Sometimes I think it is the main issue" he wrote while engaged in one of his periodic attacks on the "rum seller" and the "rum drinker." But sooner or later he would return to cooperation as the ultimate solution of labor's problems.

The Knights of Labor became very active in various ventures along these lines. Many of the district assemblies set up both consumers' and producers' cooperatives, some 135 in all, and the national organization itself purchased and for a time operated a coal mine at Cannelburg, Indiana. These undertakings, whether in mining, cooperage, shoe manufacturing, printing or other industries generally failed, however, for the same reasons as had most previous experiments along these lines. The Knights of Labor were no more successful than the National Labor Union in meeting the competition of private enterprise, securing the capital funds necessary for the expansion of their undertakings, or in providing them with efficient management.

Powderly nevertheless clung to his conviction that cooperatives represented the way in which labor could establish the self-employment that was its ultimate salvation. "It is to cooperation," he told the General Assembly in 1880, ". . . that the eyes of the workingmen and working women of the world should be directed, upon cooperation their hopes should be centered. . . . There is no good reason why labor cannot, through cooperation, own and operate mines, factories, and railroads. . . . By cooperation alone can a system of colonization be established in which men may band together for the purpose of securing the greatest good to the greatest number, and place the man who is willing to toil upon his own homestead." He likened the movement to the Revolution and long after it had been abandoned by the Knights; he continued to assert his faith in the ultimate creation of a cooperative commonwealth. "My belief that cooperation shall one day take the place of the wage system," he wrote years later in his autobiographical *The Path I Trod*, "remains unshaken."

Although these long-term aims were his real concern, as head of the Order he had to deal with such immediate and practical issues as shorter hours and higher wages—objectives in which the Knights themselves were far more interested. This raised the question of strikes. As an idealistic man of peace, Powderly opposed them. "The tendency of the times is to do away with strikes," he wrote in 1883; "that remedy has been proved by experience to be a very costly one for employer and employee." He was later to boast that "not once did I, during my fourteen years' incumbency of the office of General Master Workman, order a strike." But in his attitude on this vital issue of the 1880s, lay perhaps his greatest weakness. As the Knights of Labor repeatedly became involved in strikes, both with and without the approval of their governing body, the Grand Master Workman had a responsibility to support them which he could not avoid. There were times when Powderly did so courageously, in spite of his own inner conviction that they were futile; but in other instances he seemed to be so timid as to be ready to conclude any sort of settlement with employers. His vacillating attitude often led to confusion and broke down the united labor front that under more forthright leadership might have carried the strikes through to real success.

Powderly was at heart a humanitarian who thought in terms of the general elevation of the producing class to a higher level in society. "If I had the right to give myself a name," he later wrote in his autobiography, "I would call it equalizer." Nothing could have more clearly portrayed his impatience with the immediate, short-run objectives that most interested the great majority of workers in their growing acceptance of their status as wage earners.

"Just think of it!" he once wrote in self-pitying explanation of his position. "Opposing strikes and always striking. . . . Battling with my pen in the leading journals and magazines of the day for the great things we are educating the people on and fighting with might and main for the little things. Our Order has held me in my present position because of the reputation I have won in the nation at large by taking high ground on important national questions, yet the trade element in our Order has always kept me busy at the base of the breastworks throwing up earth which they trample down."

It was when hard times again hit the country in the 1880s, leading to widespread wage cuts and unemployment in the traditional pattern of the economic cycle, that the Knights of Labor became involved in the strikes that were first to promote their spectacular growth and then to precipitate their gradual decline. Powderly was to be tried and found wanting. But both the rise of the Noble and Holy Order and its ultimate collapse were in reality due to economic and social forces far beyond his control.

As restive workers sought to combat the exactions of employers trying to reduce operating costs, there were walkouts in 1883–1884 by glass workers, telegraph operators, and cotton spinners in Fall River, Massachusetts, shoemakers and carpet weavers in Philadelphia, miners in Pennsylvania and Ohio, iron molders in Troy, New York, and shopmen on the Union Pacific Railroad. Knights of Labor participated in each of these strikes and played a major role in four of them. What was most significant was that, while the other strikes were crushed by the employers, those in which the Knights most actively engaged resulted, with a single exception, in victories for the workers. The most important of these strikes was that of the railway shopmen, which succeeded in forcing the Union Pacific Railroad to restore wage cuts all along the line.

The victory of the workers in this strike was due in large part to the aggressive leadership of Joseph R. Buchanan, a militant labor agitator who had joined the Knights in 1882. A onetime prospector in Colorado, he typified the new West—a large, rough, domineering type of man. His success in leading the shopmen's strike was primarily due to the creation of a feeling of unity among the workers through organization of the Union Pacific Employes' Protective Association and the subsequent establishment of local assemblies of the Knights of Labor.

A year after the Union Pacific affair, another strike of railway shopmen broke out on the lines making up the so-called Southwest System—the Missouri Pacific; the Missouri, Kansas, and Texas; and the Wabash. It had no sooner got under way through spontaneous work stoppages than Buchanan hurried to the scene, as a representative of the Knights of Labor assemblies on the western railroads, and repeated his earlier success on the Union Pacific by organizing the disaffected workers of the Southwest System into local assemblies. With the support of the trainmen, the striking shop workers were able to put up such a strong front that again they won their demands.

These victories, so surprising in the light of the disastrous experience of the railway strikes in 1877, redounded to the credit of the Knights of Labor, and their prestige began to soar even though so far only local assemblies had been involved in the strikes. But an even more sensational success was won a little later, in 1885, when the Noble and Holy Order clashed directly, as a result of further disputes on the Wabash, with Jay Gould, the powerful, astute and unscrupulous financier who controlled the entire Southwest System. The Wabash had begun in April and May to lay off shopmen who were members of the Knights of Labor in what appeared to be a determined effort to break the local unions. The district assembly which had been organized the previous year in Moberley, Missouri, at once called a strike and appealed to national headquarters for help. The executive board was still seeking to maintain a general antistrike policy, but it was forced to recognize that the very existence of the Order was at stake in this challenge to the organization of railway workers. When the Wabash bluntly refused to halt its lay-offs, the board consequently felt driven to take action. All Knights of Labor still working on the Wabash were ordered out, and those on other railways in the Southwest System and on the Union Pacific were instructed not to handle any Wabash rolling stock. The workers responded enthusiastically. Trains were stopped and the cars uncoupled, engines were "killed," and widespread sabotage, in some cases leading to disorder and violence, spread throughout the Southwest.

The threat to his entire transportation system, which the Knights appeared to be strong enough to tie up completely, forced Gould to consider coming to terms. A series of conferences was held in New York, and the country was treated to the amazing spectacle of the management of one of the nation's greatest railway systems negotiating with the executive board of a nationwide labor organization. Nothing like it had ever before happened. Moreover, it resulted in an understanding between them. Gould agreed to end all discrimination against Knights of Labor on the lines which he controlled, reputedly saying that he had come to believe in labor unions and wished that all his railroad employees were organized. Powderly called off the strike and promised that no further work stoppages would be authorized until conferences had been held with the railway officials. "The Wabash victory is with the Knights," exclaimed the *St. Louis Chronicle* in astonishment. "No such victory has ever before been secured in this or any other country."

For the nation's workers generally, Gould's apparent capitulation was the signal for an overwhelming rush to join an organization which had proved itself to be so powerful. During the next few months, more local assemblies of the Knights of Labor were formed than in the previous sixteen years. It is not at all clear what sorts of workers now joined the organization. Some thought that the Knights had a special appeal for unskilled and semiskilled workers in such basic industries as coal, steel, and the railroads. The more rapid growth of mixed rather than trade (craft) assemblies seemed to confirm such an assumption. Indeed, even some farmers, shopkeepers, and petty producers joined. Moreover, female and black membership surged. But craftsmen remained the core and cadres in the Knights of Labor. As the organization attracted the skilled and unskilled, male and female, black and white between July 1, 1885, and June 30, 1886, the number of local assemblies rose from 1,610 to 5,892, and total membership shot up from around 100,000 to over 700,000. "Never in all history," exulted the editor of one labor paper, "has there been such a spectacle as the march of the Order of the Knights of Labor at the present time."

So great was the influx that harried organizers found themselves initiating new members so rapidly that they wholly lost control of the situation and were for a time compelled to suspend the formation of new assemblies. The Order was expanding much too rapidly. Powderly was later to state that "at least four hundred thousand came in from curiosity and caused more damage than good." Nevertheless, in the spring of 1886, the Knights of Labor appeared to have taken control of the entire labor movement and to be virtually all-powerful.

Wild rumors magnified even the astounding growth which had actually taken place. The membership was said to be almost 2,500,000 and the war chest some $12,000,000. The conservative press conjured up the frightening prospect of the Order wholly dominating the country. It was prophesied that it would name the next President, or even more fearfully that it would overthrow the whole social system.

"Five men in this country," an article in the New York *Sun* stated, "control the chief interests of five hundred thousand workingmen, and can at any moment take the means of livelihood from two and a half million souls. These men compose the executive board of the noble order of the Knights of Labor of America. . . They can stay the nimble touch of almost every telegraph operator; can shut up most of the mills and factories, and can disable the railroads. They can issue an edict against any manufactured goods so as to make their subjects cease buying them, and the tradesmen stop selling them. They can array labor against capital, putting labor on the offensive or the defensive, for quiet and stubborn self-protection, or for angry, organized assault as they will."

As the head of this powerful organization, Powderly was said to have become an absolute czar of labor, ruling his followers with "despotism and secrecy." Actually he was overwhelmed by the uncontrolled expansion of the Order and the tremendous responsibility suddenly thrust upon him. "The position I hold," he ruefully commented, "is too big for any ten men. It is certainly too big for me."

The Knights of Labor were at the peak of their astounding prestige. Everywhere workers were singing:

> Toiling millions now are waking—
>   See them marching on;
> All the tyrants now are shaking,
>   Ere their power's gone.

> *Chorus:*
> Storm the fort, ye Knights of Labor,
>   Battle for your cause;
> Equal rights for every neighbor—
>   Down with Tyrant laws!

The magnitude of the early victories, however, held the seeds of dissolution. Success produced its own problems. Despite warnings from the Knights' executive board and its official journal concerning precipitate strikes, many rank and filers felt their power to be unlimited. In an organization with relatively few full-time paid officials and without any real managerial structure, little discipline or restraint could be exercised over the membership. Hence the workers continued to press their demands upon employers and to count upon the Order to support them. Out of this situation were to come a succession of defeats, as discouraging for the Knights as their original triumphs had been stimulating.

An early setback resulted from another strike by the railway workers on the Southwest System. The employees of the Missouri Pacific and the Missouri, Kansas and Texas were still discontented. They had been ready to strike in support of the shopmen on the Wabash in 1885, and, with highly exaggerated ideas of the strength of the Knights of Labor, were seeking a pretext the following spring to walk out in demand for higher pay. When a Knights of Labor foreman on the Texas and Pacific Railway was fired, the Master Workman of District Assembly No. 1, a local leader named Martin Irons, promptly called a strike without awaiting any official authorization. It quickly spread from the Texas and Pacific to workers on the other lines.

"Tell the world that men of the Gould Southwest system are on strike," read one grandiloquent appeal. "We strike for justice to ourselves and our fellowmen everywhere. Fourteen thousand men are out. . . . Bring in all your grievances in one bundle at once, and come out to a man, and stay out until they are all settled to your entire satisfaction. Let us demand our rights and compel the exploiters to accede to our demands."

Such extravagant demands were all that Gould and the officials of the railways he controlled needed in order to convince them that the Knights of Labor should be crushed. Gould never really favored unionization in the slightest; he had retreated in 1885 only to gather force for a counterattack in 1886. Powderly, indeed, was later to charge that the management of the Texas and Pacific had instigated the new strike, actually coercing Irons into calling out the men against his will. However that may be, the Southwest railroads now fought the strikers with all the weapons at their command. When the workers again uncoupled cars and killed engines, management hired strike-breakers and Pinkerton guards and appealed to state governors for military protection. This time there were to be no concessions and no compromises.

Powderly felt himself to be in an impossible situation. He did not approve the strike and had had nothing to do with calling it, but he found himself accused by the railways of violating the pledge he had made not to authorize any work stoppage without previous conferences. He sought out Gould and tried to find a basis for settlement which the strikers could accept. But the railway magnate now had no intention of negotiating with the Knights, and the conversations were entirely fruitless.

In the meantime things were going badly for the workers. Only some 3,000 out of 48,000 employees on the Gould system were reported to have actually turned out, and in their battles with the scabs, they were being worsted. Respectable opinion was also against them. "They are, in fact," the *Nation* declared, "trying to introduce into modern society a new right—that is, the right to be employed by people who do not want you and who cannot afford to pay what you ask." Such voices condemned "the forcible resistance of the strikers, to the conduct of the business by anybody but themselves."

Finally, with the railroads refusing all concessions, a congressional committee investigating the strike, and opposition to the workers' cause gaining strength, Powderly in effect washed his hands of the whole affair. He recognized the importance of the controversy for the prestige of the Noble and Holy Order and was unwilling to capitulate to Gould, but he saw no way in which the strike could be carried through successfully. Left with the responsibility which the Grand Master Workman evaded, the executive council then gave way and ordered the men back to work. The Knights of Labor had suffered their first serious reverse, and their organization among the workers on the Gould system collapsed.

There were to be further defeats as other employers, following Gould's lead, marshaled their forces to crush every workers' uprising and permanently break the power of the Knights. During the latter half of 1886, some 100,000 wage earners were involved in labor disputes and the great majority of these strikes and lockouts were wholly unsuccessful.

The Knights suffered most severely from a strike in the Chicago stockyards in which the eight-hour day was the issue at stake. The associated meat packers not only refused to meet this demand but declared that they would no longer employ any members of the Order. The strike, nevertheless, tied up the packing houses completely; there seemed to be some chance of a compromise agreement when, suddenly and without warning, Powderly ordered the men back to work with the threat to take away their charters if they refused. He was to be accused both of selling out to the employers and of being unduly influenced by the intercession of a Roman Catholic priest in this maneuver. His own account of the episode states that the strikers were bound to be defeated and that he took such action as he did to prevent further suffering and possible bloodshed. In any event, the Knights lost control of the situation as a result of their leader's erratic attitude. With the collapse of the strike, their prestige suffered another irremediable blow.

It was clear that the tide had turned. The aggressive counterattack of industry, quick to take advantage of every opportunity, rolled back labor's earlier gains. As early as July 1886, John Swinton had declared that, while at the opening of the year the Golden Age appeared to be on hand, it already looked as if the workers "had been deceived by the will-o'-the-wisp." Now he was wholly convinced of it: "the money power had swept all before it and established its supremacy beyond challenge."

"Jay Gould, the enemy's generalissimo," Swinton continued, "had squelched the railroad strikes of the Southwest and this was followed by the failure of hundreds of other strikes. . . . The union men had been blacklisted right and left and a vast conspiracy against the Knights of Labor has shown itself in many localities. The laws had been distorted against boycotting. Pinkerton thugs had been consolidated into petty armies for the hire of capital. . . . The constitutional rights of citizens had been invaded, labor meetings broken up and labor papers threatened or suppressed."

The onslaughts of industry and consequent loss of strikes were not the only developments that now served to undermine the strength of the Knights of Labor. The organization's lack of an efficient administration led its leaders into numerous tactical errors. As Powderly led workers away from strikes and toward producers' cooperatives, many restive workers felt deserted. They saw an organization and a leader unwilling to support their legitimate demands upon employers.

An example of Powderly's tactical blunders was his response to the effort of the reviving national trade unions in 1886 to promote the general strike for the eight-hour day. Although the Knights of Labor strongly favored an eight-hour day, Powderly would not associate the Order with the strike call. "No assembly," he stated in a secret circular, "must strike for the eight-hour system on May 1st. under the impression they are obeying orders from headquarters, for such an order was not, and will not be given." Instead of such direct action, he suggested that the local assemblies have their members write short essays on the eight-hour day for simultaneous publication in the press on Washington's Birthday! Many of the district assemblies nevertheless adopted resolutions to support the general strike in spite of Powderly's attempt to dissuade them. When May 1 arrived, thousands of Knights took part in this first mass demonstration on the part of the nation's workers to impress their demands upon industry.

It was not a success. Some 340,000 workers were estimated to have participated in the eight-hour movement, and over half of this total actually went out on strike on May 1. But while 200,000 were said to have secured employer recognition of the eight-hour day, their gains proved to be short-lived. It was reported by the close of the year that employers had retracted for all but some 15,000 workers the concessions which they had temporarily felt compelled to grant. The anti-labor reaction which followed the Haymarket Square affair was perhaps largely responsible for this debacle, but the failure of the Knights of Labor to support the movement in the first instance was an important contributing factor.

When the Knights of Labor met for its convention in the fall of 1886, appearances still belied the inner weaknesses that were leading to dissolution. The National Assembly at Richmond, Virginia, was the most impressive labor gathering which the country had ever witnessed, and the seven hundred delegates were formally welcomed by the Governor of Virginia. But this strong showing was little more than a bright facade, and there was something empty in the impassioned eloquence of the assembly speakers who attacked "the lash of gold" that was falling upon "the backs of millions." The failure of so many strikes, the collapse of the eight-hour movement, the unhappy consequences of most of the cooperative ventures, and the after-effects of the Haymarket Square riot had started the Knights of Labor on a decline from which it would never recover.

Many of the local assemblies simply dissolved, and others made up of skilled craftsmen threw their support behind the movement that was leading to the formation of the American Federation of Labor. For the Knights were already deeply involved in that decisive struggle with the emerging forces of the new unionism that was to complete their downfall. A membership of 700,000 dropped to 200,000 within two years. By 1893, the Knights had fallen to 75,000. The conservative press rejoiced at the disintegration of an organization which had once been thought to hold the destinies of the republic in its power. "The only wonder," one editor commented with relief, "is that the madness lasted so long."

For a time the leaders of the Knights of Labor sought to combat this trend by turning toward political as opposed to industrial activity. Powderly urged the workingmen to protect their interests by making their concerted pressure felt "upon that day which of all days is important to the American citizen—ELECTION DAY." The support of the Order was thrown behind local labor candidates for political office in a dozen cities in the fall of 1886, and the Grand Master Workman himself campaigned energetically for Henry George and his single-tax program in the mayoralty election in New York. Although Powderly still did not believe in a third-party movement, his feeling of frustration over the failure of economic action led him more and more to politics as a last resort. In 1889, he was urging the Knights "to throw strikes, boycotts, lockouts and such nuisances to the winds and unite in one strike through the legislative weapon in such a way as to humble the power of the corporations who rule the United States today."

In the final stages of decline the political and reformist tendencies always powerful within the Knights of Labor became dominant. In 1893, James R. Sovereign of Iowa replaced Powderly as Grand Master Workman. A product of the trans-Mississippi West, where farmer-labor politics seemed both an actuality and a success, Sovereign concerned himself overwhelmingly with reform politics.

"It is not founded on the question of adjusting wages," Sovereign stated in 1894 in describing the functions of the Order, "but on the question of abolishing the wage system and the establishment of a cooperative industrial system. When its real mission is accomplished, poverty will be reduced to a minimum and the land dotted with peaceful happy homes."

The words had a familiar ring—Sylvis, Stephens, or Powderly himself might have uttered them—but Sovereign now spoke to a dying organization. As assembly after assembly drifted away, the Order reverted to something like the status of the old labor congresses. A handful of politically minded leaders occasionally met to urge measures which they were wholly unable to carry through.

In spite of its sorry end, the Noble and Holy Order had given a tremendous impetus to the organization of labor, and both its successes and failures were to be of continuing significance for the growth of the labor movement as a whole. For the Knights had, indeed, created a solidarity among the workers which had been but dimly felt before their advent, and they offered a challenge to the power of industry which revealed as never before the inherent strength of organization. After all, the growth within less than twenty five years from a little secret society of seven journeymen tailors to a nationwide organization of seven hundred thousand workers was in itself an almost incredible achievement.

Powderly well realized before his final retirement that the Order was in the throes of final dissolution, and he believed that, whatever the faults or virtues of its leadership, internal contradictions made its impending fate inevitable.

"Teacher of important and much-needed reforms," he wrote in 1893, "she had been obliged to practice differently from her teachings. Advocating arbitration and conciliation as first steps in labor disputes she had been forced to take upon her shoulders the responsibilities of the aggressor first and, when hope of arbitrating and conciliation failed, to beg of the opposing side to do what we should have applied for in the first instance. Advising against strikes, we have been in the midst of them. Urging important reforms we have been forced to yield our time and attention to petty disputes until we were placed in a position where we have frequently been misunderstood by the employee as well as the employer. While not a political party we have been forced into the attitude of taking political action."

The Knights of Labor had failed. But as one of its earliest historians, Norman J. Ware, wrote:

> The Order tried to teach the American wage-earner that he was a wage-earner first and a bricklayer, carpenter, miner, shoemaker, after, that he was a wage-earner first and a Catholic, Protestant, Jew, white, black, Democrat, Republican after. This meant that the Order was teaching something that was not so in the hope that sometime it would be. It failed, and its failure was perhaps a part of the general failure of democracy—or is it humanity?

IX

The American
Federation of Labor

QUESTION: You are seeking to improve home matters first?

ANSWER: Yes, Sir, I look first to the trade I represent...the interest of the men who employ me to represent their interests.

CHAIRMAN: I was only asking you in regard to your ultimate ends.

WITNESS: We have no ultimate ends. We are going on from day to day. We fight only for immediate objects—objects that can be realized in a few years.

In this often quoted testimony given by Adolph Strasser, president of the International Cigar Makers' Union before the Senate Committee on Education and Labor in 1885, we find the core of the philosophy which underlay the revival of trade unionism and was to inspire the formation of the American Federation of Labor. The new leaders of organized labor were as interested in winning higher wages and shorter hours for their followers as in seeking a total reformation of society. Although they retained the humanitarian, idealistic goals of their predecessors, they prided themselves above all else on being "practical men." As such, they defended the interests of their trade-union followers within the framework of the existing industrial system.

While the old national trade unions had been almost wholly broken up during the somber days of depression in the 1870s, the same years that witnessed the dramatic rise of the Knights of Labor found them slowly coming back to life. In some instances they were associated with the Knights, joining the Order as national trade assemblies; in other cases they stayed aloof and maintained a complete independence. Their role in the labor movement appeared in either event to be largely overshadowed by that of the Knights throughout the greater part of the 1880s. A public impressed with the apparent unity and strength of the Noble and Holy Order little realized that the future was to lie with the trade unions rather than with the inchoate masses of skilled and unskilled workers who were believed to be so completely at the beck and call of Terence V. Powderly.

The history of the national unions during these years conforms to no set pattern. Their revival after the 1870s was marked by rivalry, conflict, and all the intricate maneuvering of labor politics. But the "new unionism," which Strasser had in mind with his emphasis upon immediate and practical goals, gradually took shape and form as events demonstrated that the program of the Knights of Labor was failing.

This practical approach to labor problems was not of course entirely new. The original trade societies half a century earlier had stressed organization on a strictly craft basis, job protection, and such forthright objectives as higher wages and shorter hours. The national unions of the late 1860s and early 1870s had these same ends in view, and an immediate progenitor of the new program could be found in the Molders' International Union in the days before William Sylvis was converted from trade unionism to reform. Nevertheless, there was to be in many respects a fresh approach to the basic problem of the organization of labor born of the unhappy experience of the national unions during earlier periods of depression.

Among such unions one which had narrowly escaped complete extinction was the Cigar Makers' International Union. Its membership had dwindled to little more than a handful when its reorganization was undertaken by three militant leaders—Adolph Strasser, Ferdinand Laurrell and, most conspicuously, Samuel Gompers—who undertook to put it back on its feet with the adoption of sound, efficient practices. A New York local was established in 1875, Gompers taking over the presidency, and in 1877 Strasser was elected president of the international. A strike among the New York cigar makers in protest against the sweatshop system failed disastrously this latter year, but defeat merely strengthened the determination of the new union officials to carry their program through and give the cigar makers an organization which could protect their interests effectively. "Trade unionism," as Gompers wrote, "had to be put upon a business basis in order to develop power adequate to secure better working conditions."

Initiation fees and high dues, together with a system of sickness and death benefits, were adopted to insure the stability and permanence of the new union. The principle of equalization of funds, whereby a local in a strong financial position could be ordered to transfer some part of its reserves to any local in distress, was borrowed from the practice of British trade unions. A highly centralized control gave the international officers virtually complete authority over all local unions and guaranteed both strict discipline in the promotion of strikes and adequate support when they were officially authorized. The Cigar Makers laid paramount stress on responsibility and efficiency. While they were prepared to use the strike as the most effective weapon in enforcing a demand for trade agreements, it was to be employed only when the union commanded the resources to make it successful.

"With the administration of Strasser," Gompers wrote of these days in his autobiography, "there began a new era for the Cigar makers and for all trade unions—for the influence of our work was to extend far. There was the beginning of a period of growth, financial success, and sound development for the International Cigar Makers' Union of America, a period during which uniform regulations, high dues, union benefits, union label, better wages, and the shorter workday were established."

Other unions adopted these procedures, notably the Brotherhood of Carpenters and Joiners under the able leadership of Peter J. McGuire. But the cigar makers were the real pioneers, and they carried their reorganization through so successfully that they became the model for the new unionism. Their experience graphically illustrated what could be done on a firm foundation of financial stability and centralized authority. There was no nonsense about producers' self-employment, a cooperative commonwealth, or any other utopian goal. "Necessity has forced the labor movement to adopt the most practical methods," it was stated emphatically. "They are struggling for higher wages and shorter hours. . . . No financial scheme or plan of taxation will shorten the hours of labor."

This pragmatic approach during the last quarter of the nineteenth century did not signify the repudiation of more general reforms or the traditional search for emancipation from "wage slavery." Rather, it reflected the ability among the proponents of the "new unionism" to distinguish what was immediately attainable from what was ultimately desirable. It also flowed from their belief that ultimate ends could never be won in the absence of stable organizations which satisfied the urgent needs of their members. Many of the new-style unionists, including Gompers and especially McGuire, remained wedded to egalitarian, radical, and socialist ideals. Their philosophy was based on the notion that only through self-action could workers emancipate themselves, and that the craft union was essential to such action. For the present, they sought to win for wageworkers the greatest attainable benefits from the economic system. Its overthrow could be left to an undertermined future.

Hence the reorganized labor movement remained hospitable to radicals. The revolutionary element, which had had a part in the disorder of the 1870s and 1880s, found a place in the trade unions. The adherents of both Marxian and Lassallean socialism continued "to bore from within" in their attempts to swing labor into their respective camps, and they were to win converts among members of unions affiliated with the American Federation of Labor. Only after 1900 did most trade unions publicly repudiate socialism and become more conservative on many economic and social issues.

If the driving force behind the new unionism came largely from the International Cigar Makers, it was Samuel Gompers above all others who was its most able spokesman and the principle architect of the national organization that was to promote its basic principles. He was not only to become the first president of the American Federation of Labor, but, with the exception of a single year, he held that post until his death in 1924. The reorientation of the labor movement upon the decline of the Knights of Labor, and the success of the AFL in surviving the depression of the 1890s, were in large part the work of this stocky, matter-of-fact, stubborn labor leader whose character and philosophy were in such glaring contrast to the character and philosophy of Powderly.

Gompers was born in London's East End in 1850. His father, of Dutch-Jewish stock, was a cigar maker, and the young Samuel was apprenticed to this trade at the age of ten. When the family emigrated to the United States in 1863, he first helped his father to make cigars in their tenement home in New York's East Side, but he soon got a job of his own and joined a local union as early as 1864.

The cigar-making shops at this time were schools of political and social philosophy as well as factories, and there was no more avid student than the young immigrant from London already steeped in the background of British trade unionism. As he sat at his bench in the dark and dusty loft, dexterously fashioning cigars, he listened with eager attention to the talk of socialism and labor reform among his fellow workers. Most of them were European-born, and many of them were members of the International Workingmen's Association. They had the custom of having one of their number read the labor periodicals and other magazines aloud to them (they chipped in to make up the pay he would otherwise have lost), and Gompers was often given this assignment.

Gompers's thorough exposure to Marxian philosophy did not, however, make the young cigar maker a theorist. On the contrary, it appears to have confirmed his hard-headed, practical approach to the problems of labor. He was perhaps greatly influenced in maintaining this point of view by Ferdinand Laurrell, a tough-minded Swedish immigrant experienced in all phases of radicalism. Laurrell advised him to read Marx and Engels, but to be constantly on guard against being carried away by their theorizing. He warned him not to join the Socialist Labor party. "Study your union card, Sam," he told Gompers, "and if the idea does not square with that, it ain't true."

It was with such a background that Gompers plunged into the task, in cooperation with Strasser and Laurrell, of rebuilding the Cigar Makers' Union. Looking back upon the experiences of those days, Gompers was always to think of them as responsible, not only for his own career, but also for the future course of American labor. "From this little group," he wrote of the men with whom he had thrashed out his ideas in endless discussion, "came the purpose and initiative that finally resulted in the present American labor movement. . . . We did not create the American trade union—that is the product of forces and conditions. But we did create the technique and formulate the fundamentals that guided trade unions to constructive policies and achievements."

Gompers was twenty-nine when the International Cigar Makers' Union was reorganized. At this time in his life, he was both an advocate of stable business unionism and broad reforms, of working to get the most from the existing system and seeking ultimately to transform it. In 1887 he said, "I believe with the most advanced thinkers as to ultimate ends, including the abolition of the wage system." And almost simultaneously he declaimed that in America he saw "the arrogance of the rich ever mounting in proportion to the debasement of the poor." In the midst of the depression of the 1890s, Gompers snarled: "The ownership and control of the wealth, of the means of production, by private corporations which have no human sympathies or apparent responsibility, is the cause of the ills and wrongs borne by the human family." Finally, he made no bones about the class character of trade unionism. "Class conscious?" he asked in the early 1880s. "As a matter of fact there is no other organization of labor in the entire world that is so class conscious as are the trade unions."

He tried to synthesize the socialist ideals of his youth with the practical demands of union leadership and responsibility. He sought to protect the immediate interests of workers without sacrificing the chance to build a new and better future society. He concentrated on building the strength of the more highly skilled workers in the hope that their successes would redound to the benefit of all workers. While the organizations he led from the 1870s through the 1890s were small and weak, Gompers held a grand vision of labor's place in the social order. After 1897, as the AFL gained size and strength, Gompers's vision blurred and he lost sight of the cause of labor as a whole.

In promoting the interests of his own union and then of the American Federation of Labor, his zeal was reenforced by an apparently inexhaustible fund of energy. There were never to be any complaints of being unable to meet the demands made upon his time. As an organizer and administrator, Gompers was tireless, traveling all over the country to address labor meetings and conventions. Once known as "Stuttering Sam," he outgrew any hesitations in his speech and eloquently boomed forth the exhortatory platitudes that were so much his stock in trade. His speeches, it is true, were sometimes rather vague and confused, for he had no real gift for oral expression. His manner was often solemn and pontifical. But with a flair for the dramatic, he knew well how to hold the center of the stage.

Off the platform and outside the conference room, Gompers was friendly, easy-going and very much one of the boys. His nature was warm and open-hearted. He liked beer parlors, the theater, music halls, show girls, and the Atlantic City boardwalk. He completely shed his official character when he gathered with a group of friends for the evening, comfortably relaxed in the congenial atmosphere of the back room of a saloon, a big black cigar gripped in his teeth, and a foaming stein of beer on the table. His conviviality shocked his strait-laced, puritanical rival in the Knights of Labor. "The General Executive Board," stated a pamphlet issued by the Knights in the midst of their struggle with the American Federation of Labor, "has never had the pleasure of seeing Mr. Gompers sober." It was an unfair comment by an ardent temperance advocate, but there was no question that Gompers hugely enjoyed his beer.

In appearance, Gompers looked far more like a labor leader than the somewhat effete Powderly. Gompers's short, thick-set, sturdily built body—he was only five feet, four inches tall—seemed to justify his boast that "the Gompers are built of oak," and the strong jaw beneath a broad forehead revealed both the force and stubborness of his character. In the early 1880s he had dark, unruly hair and wore a drooping walrus mustache with a little tuft of hair on his chin. In later years, he was to be clean shaven with a glittering pince-nez shielding his dark, snapping eyes. He dressed well, was quite accustomed to a silk hat and Prince Albert coat on important occasions, and his manners were gracious. Business leaders somewhat patronizingly spoke of his being "very much a gentleman."

For all his later hobnobbing with the great, he never lost touch with the workers themselves and liked to refer to himself as "one who had not grown up from the ranks but still is proud to be in the ranks." He was intensely loyal and always ready to sacrifice his personal well-being and comfort for the cause for which he worked. Impeccably honest, he was to die a poor man and in the 1930s his widow had to accept work from a welfare agency of the federal government.

None of this is to say that Gompers was not ambitious. He felt himself born to leadership and clung tenaciously to the presidency of the American Federation of Labor. He built up both a powerful political machine and a closely knit labor bureaucracy. He was something of a dictator in pushing his policies and never one to give way before younger, more progressive leadership as time went on and he grew older. But his ambition for power and a public career did not lead him to seek either riches or political preferment. He was to remain wholly content with "serving his class" by making trade unionism and the AFL his life work.

"I look back over the years of work for my trade," he wrote in his autobiography, "and I rejoice in the conviction that the bona fide trade union movement is the one great agency of the toiling masses to secure for them a better and higher standard of life and work."

The first move toward the alliance of national and international unions that resulted in the American Federation of Labor occurred at a Pittsburgh meeting of labor leaders in 1881. Attended by delegates from both the trade unions and the Knights of Labor, the original purpose of the conference was to set up an association that might embrace all labor. "We have numberless trade unions, trades' assemblies or councils, Knights of Labor and other various local, national and international unions," the call for the meeting stated. "But great as has been the work done by these bodies, there is vastly more that can be done by a combination of all these organizations into a federation of trades." The growing rivalry between adherents of the new unionism and the leaders of the Knights of Labor, however, was to make achievement of such a goal impossible, and the Federation of Organized Trades and Labor Unions which grew out of the Pittsburgh meeting was to be short-lived.

Some of the national unions were affiliated with the Knights as trade assemblies, but they were becoming increasingly opposed to the doctrines of the Noble and Holy Order. More and more of them were breaking away altogether, and they naturally resented any attempted interference in their affairs or infringement on the territory which they believed to be within their jurisdiction. Their attitude was frankly expressed by McGuire of the Carpenters: "While there is a national or international union of a trade, the men of that trade should organize under it and. . .the Knights of Labor should not interfere."

The Knights nevertheless did interfere. Recognizing the importance of skilled workers belonging to the trade unions, and their strategic position in the labor world, the Order was anxious to hold their allegiance. Powderly, for example, promised the newly organized Amalgamated Association of Iron, Tin and Steel Workers—a craft union—that, if it would join the Knights, it could retain its separate identity and maintain its own system of government. But the skilled workers in this and other organizations saw themselves pulled down to the level of unskilled workers in submission to the Knights' control. They declared that they would maintain their autonomy against all outside pressure "to protect the skilled trades of America from being reduced to beggary."

Gompers attended the Pittsburgh meeting in 1881 as a delegate of the Cigar Makers and was chosen chairman of the committee on organization. Although he was actually a member of the Knights of Labor, having joined the Order in the 1870s, his opposition to its basic principles led him to make every effort to keep the proposed new federation a strictly trade-union affair. His proposals were defeated after vigorous debate. "There seems to be something singular about the manner in which we are changing base," one delegate stated on the floor. "This Congress was widely advertised as a labor congress and now we are talking about trades. Why not make the Knights of Labor the basis for the federation?" While this was not done, the new organization did not draw any line between skilled and unskilled workers and was theoretically to include all labor without distinction of creed, color, or nationality.

The Federation of Organized Trades and Labor Unions was in many ways a transitional stage in labor's swing toward the restricted program of the new unionism. While the ideal of solidarity was upheld, the Federation was primarily concerned with such immediate gains as the wage earners might be able to win rather than fundamental reforms in the economic system. Its legislative program, for whose support it asked all trade bodies to seek representation in the legislature, called for the legal incorporation of trade unions, the abolition of child labor, enforcement of the statutory eight-hour day, prohibition of contract labor, uniform apprentice laws, and repeal of the conspiracy laws.

The Federation did not, however, win any active support. The representatives of the Knights withdrew almost at once, and most of the national unions soon followed them. There were only nineteen delegates at the second annual convention and twenty-six at the third. Gompers was elected president in the latter year—1883—but he did not even attend the next meeting. Out of touch with the workers themselves, the new organization soon became, like the old National

Labor Union, little more than an annual conference. Its only significant action was its promotion of the eight-hour strike on May 1, 1886, but as we have seen, it was unable to succeed in this movement without the support of the Knights of Labor.

The Federation was, indeed, about to give up the ghost entirely in 1886. The leaders of the national unions had become convinced that it did not offer any hope of meeting their problems. In the face of the continued attacks being made on their form of organization by the Knights of Labor—who in the flush of victory were now stating that there was no place in the labor movement for independent trade unions—they decided to take a more forthright stand in their own defense. Another meeting of national unions was consequently called for May 18, 1886, in Philadelphia with the express purpose of seeking means "to protect our respective organizations from the malicious work of an element who openly boast that 'trades unions must be destroyed.'"

The ire of the trade unionists had been especially aroused by the interference of the Knights in the affairs of the Cigar Makers' International Union itself. As a result of internal dissensions in the New York local, involving the related issues of admitting unskilled workers and promoting socialism, a dissident faction had withdrawn from the parent body to form the Progressive Cigar Makers' Union. Strasser strongly condemned this move, refused to recognize the rebels in any way, and caustically described them as "tenement house scum." In the face of this situation, District Assembly 49 of the Knights of Labor jumped into the fray, aggressively supported the rebel union, and campaigned for its admission into the Order.

When the Philadelphia conference met, one more effort was made, at least in theory, to discover a common ground of understanding that might persuade the Knights to cease their hostility toward national unions. A "treaty" was proposed to reconcile the divergent aims of the two groups within the labor movement and end their feuding. The Knights were to agree that they would not initiate into the Order any trade union member without the permission of his union, or any other wage earner who worked for less than the prescribed wage scale of his craft, and they were also called upon to revoke the charter of any local assembly organized by workers in a trade where there was already a national union.

Was this actually a treaty? Its one-sided terms appeared rather a demand for the Knight's complete capitulation to the national unions.

Some of the delegates at Philadelphia may have considered it the statement of a position from which they would be willing to retreat if the Order proved to be conciliatory. There can be little question, however, that in the minds of the adherents of the new unionism, it was a declaration of war. Their real aim was to swing the support of the national unions behind still another federation which would break away from the Knights of Labor altogether and concentrate wholly upon protecting the interests of the skilled craft workers. Gompers had wished to do this five years earlier, but the time had not been ripe. Now the increasing hostility between the Knights and the national unions, emphasized by the struggle over dual unionism among the Cigar makers, provided the opportunity for decisive action.

The Noble and Holy Order played right into the hands of those who favored a complete break. In spite of some professions of willingness to explore means of reconciling the issues which were in dispute with the national unions, no official action whatsoever was taken in regard to the proposed treaty. Even though the failure of their strikes and the repercussions of the Haymarket Square affair were already weakening their position, the Knights were determined to adhere to their own program and saw no need to make any concessions. Powderly did not even submit the treaty for consideration at the Richmond assembly in October 1886. The national unions were defied by the establishment of new national trade districts; the Progressive Cigar Makers were formally admitted to the Order, and no gesture whatsoever was made toward settling other jurisdictional quarrels.

The answer of the national unions was to meet again, at Columbus, Ohio, on December 8, 1886, and at this conference they were joined by the handful of delegates still representing the almost defunct Federation of Organized Trades and Labor Unions. Altogether, there were present some forty-two representatives of twenty-five labor groups. Among the national unions participating were the Iron Molders, Miners and Mine Laborers, Typographers, Journeymen Tailors, Journeymen Bakers, Furniture Workers, Metal Workers, Granite Cutters, Carpenters, and Cigar Makers. Their total membership approximated 150,000. The sole concern of the delegates had now become the promotion of the interests of the crafts which they respectively represented, and, after due deliberation, they formed a new organization for this purpose and elected Samuel Gompers as its first president. Here at last was the American Federation of Labor. Its date of origin was subsequently to be pushed back to 1881, the year in which the Federation of Organized Trades and Labor Unions was established, but although the AFL took over the treasury and records of its predecessor, the two groups were quite distinct, and the history of the American Federation of Labor really begins in 1886.

A guiding principle of the new organization, growing out of the circumstances of its birth, was "strict recognition of the autonomy of each trade." The executive council set up to handle affairs on a national level was given no power whatsoever to interfere in those that fell within the jurisdiction of member unions. The unity of labor was to be promoted through education and moral suasion rather than through the centralized controls inherent in the structure of the Knights of Labor. Nevertheless, the executive council had important functions. It issued the charters for constituent unions, and, as a means for stamping out the dual unionsim which was felt to threaten the labor movement as a whole, was authorized to settle all jurisdictional disputes. A per capita tax was imposed on all member unions in order to build up the financial reserves which would enable the AFL to extend practical assistance in strikes and lockouts, and a legislative program drawn up in the approved fashion of all labor organizations. Finally, there were to be formed, under the general authority of the executive council, both city centrals and state federations to further the passage of labor legislation.

Major emphasis was placed upon economic or industrial action. The AFL was to support the national and international unions in winning recognition from employers, entering into collective bargaining agreements, and maintaining a position which would enable them to strike effectively when other measures failed. The legislative program, which included most of the objectives which had been sought by the old Federation of Organized Trades and Labor Unions, was subordinated to this basic line of attack in frank recognition of the inadequacy of the policy of its predecessor.

In its early years, the American Federation of Labor was almost entirely Samuel Gompers. He had loyal associates, but it was he who gave the new organization life and direction. "There was much work, little pay, and very little honor," he later wrote of these days, but such considerations did not daunt him. Setting up his headquarters in an eight-by-ten-foot office made available by the Cigar Makers, with little furniture other than a kitchen table, some crates for chairs, and a filing case made out of tomato boxes, he set about breathing vitality into the new organization with a zeal, devotion, and tireless energy that largely accounted for its survival. He wrote innumerable letters, always in his own hand, to labor leaders throughout the country; for a time he edited the *Trade Union Advocate* as a means of publicizing his campaign; he issued union charters, collected dues, handled all routine business, managed conventions, and went on speaking and organization tours, and slowly but persistently transformed the American Federation of Labor from a purely paper organization into a militant and powerful champion of labor's rights. He felt himself to be engaged in a holy cause, and from the day that the AFL came into being until his death thirty-eight years later, it was his entire life.

While the long-term struggle of the Federation was to be with the forces of industry, its early years were also marked by its continuing feud with the Knights of Labor. Further efforts were made in the late 1880s and early 1890s to draw the two organizations together, but these proved to be completely unsuccessful. The situation was not unlike that which would develop almost half a century later when the American Federation of Labor found itself in turn challenged by the dissident unions that were to form the Congress of Industrial Organizations. There were principles at stake, but they were often overshadowed by the political rivalries and ambitions of contesting leaders.

Powderly moved steadily toward complete scorn of national unions. "I will tell you frankly," he wrote an associate in 1889, "I don't care how quick the National Trade Assemblies go out. They hinder others from coming to us and I am strongly tempted to advise them all to go it alone on the outside and see how it will go to turn back the wheels of the organization for the benefit of a few men who want to be at the head of something." Gompers grew equally caustic in his opinion of the Knights of Labor, their aims and aspirations. "Talk of harmony with the Knights of Labor," he said in 1894, "is bosh. They are just as great enemies of trade unions as any employer can be, only more vindictive. It is no use trying to placate them or even to be friendly."

In such circumstances, the possibility of labor unity faded away, and the gradually dwindling strength of the Knights was counteracted by the slow growth of the American Federation of Labor. The latter was anything but spectacular. The original membership of 150,000 had increased to only 250,000 six years later. The violent counterattack of industry upon all unions during these years, the generally repressive attitude of the government and the courts, and, finally, the trying times of the depression that began in 1893 made it highly difficult to hold any labor organization together, let alone promote its growth and expansion. But Gompers stuck grimly to his task. He refused to allow the Federation to be drawn away from its immediate, practical aims, and, at the annual convention in 1893, he was able to look with pride upon what had already been accomplished.

"It is noteworthy," he told the assembled delegates, "that while in every previous industrial crisis the trade unions were literally mowed down and swept out of existence, the unions now in existence have manifested, not only the powers of resistance, but of stability and permanency."

The importance of the AFL in promoting the practical concepts of the new unionism should not obscure the fact that the national unions were the real basis for the revived labor movement—both at the close of the nineteenth century and in later years. They could exist without the AFL, but the AFL had no meaning without them. Their autonomy was complete, and it was they who controlled the local unions that made up the membership of the labor movement. Their functions were to direct the activities of the locals, extend union organization through the trade or industry over which they had jurisdiction, provide such assistance as they could in collective bargaining and strikes (for which per capita taxes were levied for a general defense fund), and participate in the more general program of the AFL.

With time the original craft unions were to extend greatly their jurisdiction and their names often reflect the history of this expansion. Many examples might be given, but one often cited as illustrating this trend is the International Association of Marble, Slate and Stone Polishers, Rubbers and Sawyers, Tile and Marble Setters Helpers and Terrazo Helpers. The introduction of new techniques and other economic changes, were to make the settlement of jurisdictional problems one of the major concerns of the AFL from the days of its foundation.

One important group of unions that did not affiliate with the AFL was the railway brotherhoods. The organization of railroad employees has followed its own course, and while based on craft lines has for reasons peculiar to itself differed considerably in other respects from that of other workers. The Locomotive Engineers organized as early as 1863, the Railway Conductors five years later, the Trainmen in

1873, and a decade later the Firemen. Although involved in the railway strikes of 1877, the four brotherhoods became increasingly conservative in subsequent years, and because of the hazardous nature of their members' work, the insurance and benefit features of their union programs have always been of primary importance. The permanent organization of other railway employees was to develop more slowly. After an attempt by Eugene V. Debs to form an all-inclusive American Railway Union in the 1890s, to which we shall return, separate unions of Shop Workers, Switchmen, Yardmasters, Signalmen, Telegraphers, and Railway and Steamship Clerks were formed as affiliates of the AFL despite the continuing independence of the four brotherhoods.

The fact that the international unions survived the depression of the 1890s did not mean that labor was beginning to have its own way or that even the most strongly organized unions were able to meet employers on anything approaching equal terms. Wages remained low and hours long for the skilled workers in the 1890s, while the great mass of unskilled existed on the barest subsistence level. Labor was still considered a commodity to be bought at the cheapest rate possible, and its right to organize and bargain collectively had by no means been accepted. As industry sought to break the power of the unions with blacklisting, iron-clad oaths, strikebreakers, and Pinkerton detectives, and in combating strikes was able to call upon state militia and federal troops in the name of law and order, the workers found themselves struggling against what were still overwhelming odds.

X

Homestead and Pullman

While the lasting significance of the 1890s in labor history is found in the final triumph of the American Federation of Labor over the Knights of Labor and the demonstrated strength of the new unionism, the decade was marked more dramatically by its great strikes. Never before had labor and capital been engaged in such organized private warfare as would develop at Homestead in 1892, nor had the public ever become more alarmed over the dangers of industrial strife than during the great Pullman strike two years later. These two outbreaks differed from the uprising of railway workers in 1877 primarily because they were organized strikes led by trade unions rather than leaderless and uncontrollable revolts; yet they were marked by almost comparable violence and bloodshed. The gravity of the labor problem as it existed in the 1890s could hardly have been underscored more heavily.

Moreover, the general discontent among industrial workers which was reflected in these strikes had its political repercussions as the depression of the 1890s deepened and urban unrest was linked with agrarian revolt in the rise of Populism. The alliance between farmers and workers never fully materialized because the two groups represented partly conflicting socioeconomic interests. Nevertheless,

157

during the late 1890s, conservatives feared that an election victory for the radical Populists would threaten capitalism.

In the early morning of July 6, 1892, two barges were being towed slowly up the Monongahela River toward Homestead, Pennsylvania. There had been trouble at the local plant of the Carnegie Steel Company. The skilled workers at Homestead, members of the Amalgamated Association of Iron, Steel and Tin Workers, had refused to accept new wage cuts and were supported in their stand by the rest of the labor force. The company's general manager, tough-minded, stubbornly antilabor Henry Clay Frick, thereupon peremptorily shut down the entire plant and refused any further negotiations with the union. Special deputy sheriffs had been sworn in to guard company property, which was enclosed by a high board fence topped with barbed wire, but the locked out workers had run them out of town in the conviction that these preparations foreshadowed the use of strikebreakers. It was a challenge to his authority which Frick was only too glad to accept. Here was his chance to crush the Amalgamated once and for all. Aboard the two barges being towed up the Monongahela were three hundred Pinkerton detectives armed with Winchester rifles.

As the steel company's private army drew alongside the Homestead mills and prepared to land, there was a sudden exchange of shots between the barges and the shore. The workers had entrenched themselves behind a barricade of steel billets and, as the Pinkertons tried to take possession of the plant, they were beaten back in a raging battle that swirled along the river front. All that day, from four in the morning until five in the afternoon, the fusillade of shots continued. The strikers set up a small brass cannon behind a breastwork of railroad ties and opened a direct fire on the barges. Failing to sink them, they poured barrels of oil into the river and set the oil afire. With three men already dead and many more wounded, the Pinkertons were trapped. Deserted by the tug which had towed them upstream and helplessly crowded into the barge which lay farthest from the shore, they finally ran up a white flag and agreed to surrender. In return for a guarantee of safe conduct out of the community, they gave up their arms and ammunition.

But feelings were running too high at Homestead, where the casualties had included seven killed, for any easy reestablishment of order. When the Pinkertons came ashore, they were again attacked and had to run the gauntlet of an infuriated mob of men and women armed with stones and clubs before they were safely entrained for Pittsburgh. An uneasy calm then settled over the little town as the Homestead workers, victorious in this first round, awaited the next moves by the company.

It was not until six days later that there was any further development. Then on July 12 the state militia, mobilized eight-thousand strong by the Governor of Pennsylvania upon Frick's appeal for aid, marched in quietly to take control of Homestead under martial law. With such protection, the Carnegie Company began bringing in scabs—the "blacksheep" whom the locked out workers knew were being hired to take their jobs—and proceeded to file charges of rioting and murder against the strike leaders for the attack on the Pinkertons. The plant was then reopened with militia protection, and nonunion men were given the Amalgamated members' jobs. When the strike was officially called off in November, two thousand strikebreakers had been brought in and only some eight hundred of the original Homestead working force of nearly four thousand were reinstated.

In the aftermath of the original battle another act of violence had occurred. On July 23, a Russian-born anarchist, Alexander Berkman, who had no connection whatsoever with the strikers but who had been aroused by the Carnegie Company's employment of Pinkerton operatives, forced his way into Frick's office in Pittsburgh and tried to assassinate him. Although shot and stabbed, the steel executive was not fatally injured, and his assailant was captured. The assault had been planned by Berkman and his woman companion, Emma Goldman, a no less ardent advocate of "propaganda by deed," and only lack of funds to make the trip to Pittsburgh, as she later revealed in her autobiography, had prevented her from accompanying Berkman on his mission. He was sentenced to twenty-one years in prison for assault with intent to kill. Released after thirteen years of his term, he was later deported, together with Emma Goldman, to Soviet Russia.

These events aroused the country in some ways even more than had the Great Upheaval of the 1880s or the railway strikes a decade earlier. For the Homestead affair was not a spontaneous uprising on the part of unorganized workers. It was war between one of the most powerful of the great modern corporations and what was then one of the strongest unions in the country. Each party to the dispute had taken the law into its own hands. The *Chicago Tribune* gave over its entire front page on July 7 to a vivid account of what was described as "a battle which for bloodthirstiness and boldness was not excelled in actual warfare."

Until the Homestead strike, relations between the Carnegie Company and the union had been uniformly friendly, and working conditions had been governed by a three-year contract for the skilled workers which provided for a sliding-wage scale based on the price of steel billets. Carnegie had professed himself to be wholly in favor of unions, stating in an article for the *Forum* some years earlier that the right of workingmen to combine was no less sacred than that of manufacturers. Moreover, he had expressed real sympathy for workers threatened by the loss of jobs through the use of strike-breakers. "To expect that one dependent upon his daily wage for the necessaries of life," he had written, "will stand by peacefully and see a new man employed in his stead is to expect too much." But when the old union contract at Homestead expired in 1892, Carnegie opportunely removed himself to Scotland and left negotiations wholly to Frick.

Although Carnegie had expressed sympathy in print for workers and unions, it is unlikely that his presence would have changed the course of events. He had in fact given Frick a free hand and was aware of the latter's intention to crush the union. Indeed, he told a reporter in the course of the strike that "the handling of the case on the part of the company had my full approval," and, in a letter to William E. Gladstone, the British statesman, he declared that his firm had offered the workers generous terms and "they went as far as I could have wished." If Carnegie differed from Frick, it was in Carnegie's preference to starve the men rather than to beat them into submission. A committed pacifist, he had an aversion to bloodshed, and in the same letter to Gladstone noted, "The Works are not worth one drop of human blood."

Frick, however, was in control, and his intention in bringing in strikebreakers and Pinkerton guards, for which arrangements had been made even before the failure of the wage negotiations, was clearly to smash the union. And he succeeded: it collapsed completely at Homestead and was greatly weakened in other steel mills in the Pittsburgh area where sympathetic strikes led to sharp reprisals. The Amalgamated was to make some further effort to organize the steel workers, but in the face of continued opposition by the Carnegie Company and its successor, the United States Steel Corporation, it steadily lost ground. An effective steel workers' union would not be established until some forty years later.

The Amalgamated was affiliated with the American Federation of Labor, and Gompers strongly expressed his sympathy for the strikers and aided in raising funds for the defense of those charged with responsibility for the attack on the Pinkertons. But the Federation was not in a position to offer any effective assistance, and Gompers' grandiloquent phrases must have been cold comfort for the strikers.

"You Homestead steel workers," Gompers was quoted as saying in the *Pittsburgh Leader*, "if there is a rose bush blooming it is your work; if there is anything under the sun which shines upon you, which makes Homestead valuable, it is your work. You refused to bow down to this wonderful autocrat, and the first answer he gave you was to send that band of hirelings into this peaceful community to force you to bow down to him, and ultimately drive you from your peaceful homes. I know not who fired the first shot on that memorable morning of the 6th of July, but I do know the hearts of the American people beat in unison and sympathy with the brave men of Homestead. I am a man of peace and I love peace, but I am like that great man, Patrick Henry, I stand as an American citizen and, 'give me liberty or give me death.'"

Homestead was to take its place in the annals of labor history as one of the great battles for workers' rights, and its immediate repercussions were nationwide. There was agitated discussion in Congress over what such industrial warfare meant for the nation. Senator John M. Palmer of Illinois declared that the Pinkerton army had become as distinctly recognized as the regular army—"the commander in chief of this army, like the barons of the Middle Ages, has a force to be increased at pleasure for the service of those who would pay him or them"—and he maintained that the workers had the right to resist its attack in defense of their jobs and homes. "The owners of these properties," he further stated in reference to such corporations as the Carnegie Company, "must hereafter be regarded as holding their property subject to the correlative rights of those without whose services the property would be utterly valueless."

Outside the ranks of labor itself, however, such ideas found little support. Politics governed many expressions of opinion. Democratic newspapers opposed to a protective tariff seized the opportunity to show that, for all the claims made for high duties as safeguarding the wages of the American workingmen, the steel industry was nevertheless reducing wages and exploiting its employees. They condemned the use of Pinkerton mercenaries and expressed sympathy for the locked-out workers. Some Republican papers, resenting the injection of the tariff issue, urged the Carnegie Company to follow a more conciliatory course to refute Democratic charges. But, more generally, the press took the stand that, even though the Homestead employees did not want to work for the wages offered them, there was no justification for their seeking to prevent others from accepting such terms. "Men talk like anarchists or lunatics," the *Independent* stated, "when they insist that the workmen at Homestead have done right." The steel company was upheld in asserting its power to provide protection for whomever it chose to employ.

"If civilization and government are worth anything," the *Cleveland Leader* declared, "the right of every man to work for whom he pleases must and will be maintained." In an article in the *North American Review*, George Ticknor Curtis further developed this theory. "The first duty of the legislative power," he stated, "is to emancipate the individual workman from the tyranny of his class. The individual workman should not be permitted to commit moral suicide by surrendering his liberty to the control of his fellow-workmen." To protect an illusory right to decide the terms on which he could individually sell his services, the workingman's right to associate with others in collective bargaining was denied. The antiunion attitude of conservative employers could not have been more clearly expressed.

There were a number of other violent strikes during these dark days when the forces of the new industrialism were riding roughshod over the right of workers to organize and protect their interests. Metal miners at Coeur d'Alene, Idaho; switchmen in Buffalo, New York; and coal miners in Tennessee walked out in defiance of their employers, and in each instance their strikes were forcibly broken through the intervention of the state militia. As depression settled ominously over the land and the army of unemployed swelled to some three million, labor disputes reached a peak involving even more workers—some 750,000—than the strikes in 1886. Of all these conflicts, however, the Pullman strike of 1894 stood out most vividly.

The employees of the Pullman Palace Car Company were in one respect in a quite different situation from the great mass of industrial workers. They had the privilege of living in a model town. The head of the company, George M. Pullman, had established for his employees a community with neat brick houses grouped about a little square, where bright flower beds alternated with green stretches of lawn. The whole was "shaded with trees, dotted with parks, and pretty water vistas and glimpses here and there of artistic sweeps of landscape gardening." In the exuberant enthusiasm of the company's press agent, Pullman was "a town, in a word, where all that is ugly and discordant and demoralizing is eliminated and all that which inspires self-respect is generously provided."

But were these happy attributes of life in Pullman actually so "generously provided?" The employees had no choice but to live within this feudal domain, rent their homes or apartments from the company, buy their water and gas from the company, pay the company for such other services as garbage removal and the daily watering of streets, buy supplies from the company store, and subscribe to the company's rental library. And rents for apartments in the model town, which in most instances had no bathtubs and one water faucet for every five families, were some 25 per cent higher than in nearby communities. A high premium was also charged for public utility services. "Oh, Hell!" the forthright Mark Hanna was quoted as commenting on his brother industrialist's baronial domain. "Model ———. Go and live in Pullman and find out how much Pullman gets selling city water and gas 10 per cent higher to those poor fools!"

With the depression of 1893, the Pullman Company was for a time hard hit and after laying off more than 3,000 of its 5,800 employees, it cut the wages of those kept on from 25 to 40 per cent without any corresponding reduction in rents for the company houses. The consequences were disastrous. A worker seldom earned as much as six dollars a week after the company had made its deductions. In one instance, an employee found that, after payment for the rent was taken out, his paycheck came to 2 cents. "He never cashed it," the Reverend W. H. Carwardine, of the Pullman Methodist Episcopal Church reported. "He has it framed." And yet at the same time such things were happening, the Pullman Company kept on paying dividends. Even after business began to improve, enabling the company to take back some 2,000 of its employees, no steps were taken to restore the wage cuts or to reduce rents.

Finally, in May 1894, a committee of employees asked for some consideration of their grievances. Pullman flatly refused to consider any wage adjustments on the ground that the company was still losing money, and he would take no action in regard to rents. There was no relationship whatsoever, he declared, between the company's dual functions as employer and landlord. Almost immediately after the interview, in spite of definite assurances that there would be no discrimination against the grievance committee, three of its members were summarily discharged.

During this year of hardship and suffering, the Pullman workers had been extensively organized in locals of the American Railway Union. This new association, independent of all other labor federations, had been formed only the year before by Eugene V. Debs as an industrial union open to all white employees of the railroads. Upon the dismissal of the three members of the grievance committee, who were also members of the American Railway Union, the Pullman locals called a strike. When the company countered by laying off all workers and closing the plant, an appeal was made to the national convention for assistance. Attempts were made to submit the issues in dispute to arbitration, but when Pullman met these overtures with the uncompromising statement: "there is nothing to arbitrate," the American Railway Union prepared for action. On June 21 it adopted a resolution that if arbitration was not accepted within five days, its members would be ordered not to handle any Pullman cars.

When this boycott, which involved not only the Pullman Company but railroads using its cars, went into effect, the challenge of the union was promptly taken up by the General Managers' Association, a group composed of executives of twenty-four railways entering Chicago which altogether controlled some forty thousand miles of track. It ordered the discharge of any worker "cutting out" a Pullman car from any train. But the membership of the American Railway Union was not so easily frightened. Every time a man was fired for refusing to handle a Pullman car, the entire train crew would quit. By the end of July, the strike had become so general that nearly every railroad in the Middle West was affected, and the nation's entire transportation system was seriously threatened.

"The struggle," Debs declared in a ringing appeal to the railway workers, ". . . has developed into a contest between the producing classes and the money power of the country. We stand upon the ground that the workingmen are entitled to a just proportion of the proceeds of their labor." But while there was sympathy for the strikers in some quarters, Mark Hanna again privately expressing his scorn for Pullman's refusal to arbitrate, the conservative press solidly supported the General Managers' Association. "The necessity is on the railroads to defeat the strike," the *Chicago Herald* declared, while the New York *World* stated that it was "war against the government and against society."

As leader of the railway workers, Debs sprang overnight into nationwide fame. The American Railway Union was only a year old and yet, under his shrewd and capable leadership, it had already gained a membership—some 150,000—which was greater than that of the four railway brotherhoods and rivaled both the declining Knights of Labor and the slowly emerging American Federation of Labor. Both management and the trade unions feared that should Debs carry the ARU to success in this contest with the railroads, the principle of industrial unionism which it embodied might win a victory which would set the pattern for future labor organization.

Debs was the son of French-Alsatian immigrants who had settled in Terre Haute, Indiana, where his father kept a grocery store. Born in 1855, he had gone to work in the railway yards at the age of fourteen and had become an engineer at sixteen. For a time he left the yards to work as a grocery clerk and play about with politics, but in 1878 he turned to the labor movement and, two years later, at the age of twenty-five, was elected both national secretary-treasurer of the Brotherhood of Locomotive Firemen and editor of the *Locomotive Firemen's Magazine*. It was largely through his efforts that this union was built up during the next dozen years into a flourishing and financially sound organization.

However, Debs grew increasingly concerned over the exclusive attitude maintained by the brotherhood and the complete lack of cooperation between its members and other railway employees. He became convinced that only through the union of all workers on the nation's railroads in a single association could the interests of this important branch of labor be successfully promoted. In 1892 he suddenly resigned his well-paid post in the Brotherhood of Locomotive Firemen and undertook almost single-handedly to form the American Railway Union.

Debs was an able organizer, shrewd and practical; he was an eloquent and forceful speaker, and he was also an idealist prepared to make any sacrifice for a cause in which he believed. Throughout his life, he commanded an amazing measure of respect and loyalty. During the Pullman strike, he was to be villified and abused as few men have been. He was attacked as a labor dictator, a criminal, an anarchist, a lunatic, and a madman, but with time even those who continued to denounce the things for which he stood could not help but honor the man. There could be no doubting his unflinching honesty and sincerity, whether in the 1890s as an aggressive labor leader or in later years as the spokesman of American socialism. No one ever identified himself more closely with the struggling masses in American national life or was a more passionate defender of the underprivileged.

"While there is a lower class I am in it," Debs once said in a much-quoted statement. "While there is a criminal element I am of it; while there is a soul in prison I am not free."

Tall and gaunt, nearly bald even at the time of the Pullman strike when he was thirty-nine, with high forehead and candid eyes, his manner was quiet and modest. Something about him inspired not only confidence but also affection. "There may have lived some time, somewhere," Clarence Darrow, the Chicago labor lawyer, was to write, "a kindlier, gentler, more generous man than Eugene Debs, but I have not known him."

Debs had not desired the strike that was forced upon the American Railway Union by the appeal of the Pullman workers. Even though it had already won a surprising strike victory on the Great Northern Railway, he knew that his young organization was not yet strong enough for such a formidable encounter with the united railway corporations. But when Pullman refused to arbitrate, he felt that the union could not stand aside without betraying the Pullman employees. Forced to back them up, Debs consistently counseled moderation and restraint. He ordered the strikers to remain wholly passive and in no way to injure railroad property, and during the first phase of the strike these orders were rigidly obeyed.

The General Managers' Association, however, could not afford a peaceful strike. It was soon importing strikebreakers from Canada, secretly instructing them to attach mail cars to Pullman cars so that when the strikers cut out the latter, they could be accused of interfering with the mails. Conjuring up a still nonexistent danger of violence, it induced Attorney General Richard Olney, avowed friend of the railroads, to have 3,400 men, who were actually hired by the railroads and paid by the railroads, sworn in as special deputies to help keep the trains running. These tactics were successful. There were clashes between strikers and deputies; rioting broke out, and railway property was destroyed. Promptly asserting that such violence had already become uncontrollable, the Managers' Association thereupon appealed to President Grover Cleveland to send federal troops to restore order, safeguard the mails, and protect interstate commerce. Four companies of the Fifteenth Infantry were sent to Chicago.

Governor Altgeld of Illinois immediately protested against this move. The situation was not out of hand, he wired the President, and local officials were entirely capable of handling it. "The Federal Government," he stated, "has been applied to by men who had political and selfish motives for wanting to ignore the State government. . . .At present some of our railroads are paralyzed, not by reason of obstruction, but because they cannot get men to operate their trains. . . .As Governor of the State of Illinois, I ask the immediate withdrawal of Federal troops from active duty in this State." But Altgeld's protest went unheeded. He had recently pardoned the anarchists involved in the Haymarket Square affair, and the newspapers fiercely attacked him as the "friend and champion of disorder." Even though Cleveland had in an earlier message to Congress called for the investigation and arbitration of wage disputes, he looked no further on this occasion than to the maintenance of order. He stoutly maintained the position he had assumed and justified the use of federal troops, in spite of charges of usurping the functions of the state, on the ground that it was his constitutional duty to keep the mail trains operating. "If it takes every dollar in the Treasury and every soldier in the United States to deliver a postal card in Chicago," he was reported as saying, "that postal card should be delivered."

Still the ranks of the strikers held firm and in spite of strikebreakers, special deputies and the army, three fourths of the railroads running into Chicago were almost at a standstill. Moreover, the strike was spreading. Sympathetic walkouts by engineers, firemen, repairmen, signalmen, yardmasters, and other workers occurred on many lines in both the East and Far West. At the same time, violence was also increasing. As the struggle became intensified, the strikers could no longer be held in check by Debs' peaceful persuasions. When trains began to move under the protection of the troops, angry mobs sought to stop them. Railway stores were looted, freight and passenger cars burned, and damage inflicted on other property.

As disorder spread, newspapers and magazines declared the danger to society in what the *New York Tribune* called "the greatest battle between labor and capital that has ever been inaugurated in the United States." It was almost universally insisted that "this rebellion must be put down" regardless of every other consideration. The attempt was made to draw a line between the railway workers and strike agitators. The former were said to be "the victims of selfish, cruel and insolent leaders," and all honest workingmen were called upon to free themselves from such "insufferable tyranny." The *New York Times* attacked Debs as "a lawbreaker at large, an enemy of the human race," and the *Chicago Herald* asserted that "short work should be made of this reckless, ranting, contumacious, impudent braggadocio."

News stories carried alarming accounts of mob action and battles with the police and troops. With such a newspaper as the *Washington Post* screaming in its headlines that "Chicago Is at the Mercy of the Incendiary's Torch," the general impression given was that the entire city was in the throes of revolution and anarchy. However, a correspondent for the *New York Herald,* somehow keeping his balance amid such exaggerated fears and alarms, reported to his paper on July 9 that business was going on as usual; the stores were crowded with shoppers; and "there is no sign of mob or riot or strike, even, about the main part of the city."

But the railroads had already played their trump card. They had persuaded Attorney General Olney to intervene directly and, on July 2, a blanket injunction was obtained from Judge Peter J. Grosscup, of the federal district court, forbidding any person to interfere with the operation of the mails or other railroad transportation in interstate commerce and to seek to induce any employees of the railroads to refuse to perform their normal services. With the whole force of government and the courts thrown against him, Debs was desperate. For a time he hoped to win labor support for a general strike, only to be rebuffed by the American Federation of Labor. Gompers felt constrained to call a labor conference to consider the issue, but he was entirely opposed to a strike. It was, indeed, hardly surprising that a weak, struggling organization would have reservations about supporting the American Railway Union against the massed strength of the railroads and the federal government.

"We declare it to be the sense of this conference," a statement issued by Gompers on July 13 read, "that a general strike at this time is inexpedient, unwise and contrary to the best interests of the working people. We further recommend that all connected with the American Federation of Labor now out on sympathetic strikes return to work, and those who contemplate going out on sympathetic strike are advised to remain at their usual vocations."

Without help from any quarter, Debs then offered to call off the strike and boycott if the Pullman Company would agree to reinstate all workers without discrimination. With the courts swinging into action, the railroads had no further cause for concern. They bluntly rejected Debs's peaceful overtures; there would be "no recognition of anarchism."

Judge Grosscup now summoned a special jury to hear charges that the strike leaders were guilty of conspiracy in obstructing the mails, and, under instructions from the court, Debs and three of his aides were promptly indicted. Arrested on this count, they were released on bail, but within a week were rearrested for contempt of court for disobeying the original injunction. This time they went to jail. Other injunctions were enforced against individual strikers and nearly 200 were arrested on federal charges in addition to the several hundred jailed by local police. Deprived of all leadership and direction and completely demoralized, the railroad workers gave up what had become a futile struggle and gradually drifted back to work. The troops were withdrawn on July 20. Government by injunction had won its first victory.

After some delay, the contempt charges brought against Debs were sustained in the circuit court on the ground that, under the terms of the recently enacted Sherman Antitrust Act, the strike leaders had engaged in a conspiracy to restrain interstate commerce. The following spring the Supreme Court, while not expressly ruling on the applicability of the Sherman Act, upheld the lower court. The federal government was declared to have inherent authority to intervene to protect any obstruction to interstate commerce or the transportation of the mails.

Debs went to jail in Woodstock, Illinois, for six months. The action of the courts had made him a martyr and, on returning to Chicago after expiration of his sentence, he was wildly acclaimed by a crowd of over 100,000 sympathizers. At a gigantic mass meeting he was hailed by the Chicago reformer and publicist, Henry Demarest Lloyd, as "the most popular man among the real people today. . . the victim of judicial lynch law."

Imprisonment radicalized Debs. Once simply a Democrat and a trade unionist, he left prison a Populist, soon to declare himself a socialist. The strike of 1894 and its aftermath convinced him that labor could not receive justice under capitalism. From this time forward, he dedicated his life to struggle against a system which enabled employers, as he repeatedly declared, to call upon government to enforce their dictate, "work for what we want to give you, or starve."

Until his death in 1926, Debs campaigned ceaselessly for labor's rights under the Socialist banner and was five times the candidate of his party for the presidency.

Labor and its sympathizers bitterly denounced the intervention of federal troops and use of the injunction in the Pullman strike, but the policy of the government was vigorously upheld in other quarters. Both the Senate and the House adopted resolutions supporting Cleveland. There were innumerable statements from public leaders praising his handling of the situation, and the conservative press hailed him as a national hero for so vigorously suppressing what was universally called the "Debs Rebellion." The power of government had been asserted in no doubtful fashion. "To Cleveland and to Olney," the historian James Ford Rhodes wrote, "we in this country of reverence for just decisions, owe a precedent of incalculable value."

Perhaps the most important consequence of the Pullman strike was its revelation of the power that the injunction placed in the hands of industry in combating the demands of labor. What chance had wage earners when their employers could so easily go into court and obtain injunctions against both strikes and boycotts; when government was ready to throw all its force against labor regardless of right or wrong in the issues under dispute? The workers' hands appeared to be completely tied. The campaign for abolition of government by injunction that at once got under way was taken up by the American Federation of Labor in spite of its reluctance to run any risks in supporting the American Railway Union. That campaign became from that day on one of labor's primary concerns.

The forceful suppression of such strikes as those at Homestead and Pullman fanned the mounting discontent of the workers, but unemployment created even greater discouragement and despair. Throughout the country "industrial armies" took to the road and began to march on Washington to demand relief. The most famous of them was Coxey's Army, which actually reached the capital only to be dispersed after its leader was arrested for trespassing on the White House lawn. But there were other groups of ragged, down-at-heel workers on the march. Throughout the country, local authorities were called upon to break up these demonstrations and maintain law and order in the face of a constant danger of mob action.

In the meantime, the growing unrest among the nation's farmers, who also found themselves increasingly hard-pressed in a period of falling prices that cut the value of agricultural products almost in half, was fanning the sparks of agrarian revolt. Populism swept through the cotton and tobacco states from Texas to North Carolina and the trans-Mississippi wheat states. But it also appealed to coal miners, gold, silver, and copper miners, machinists, and railroad workers. In such western states as Montana, Idaho, Colorado, and Washington, Populism was as much a workers' as a farmers' movement. For Populism challenged the whole concept of government by organized wealth. It strove to recover for the common people the political power that was felt to have been usurped by the business community.

The People's, or Populist party, formally organized in 1892, accepted as its basic premise the idea that wealth belonged to those who produced it, and called for a union of all the laboring elements in the nation to uphold their rights. Every effort was made to win the adherence of industrial workers. While the demand for the free and unlimited coinage of silver was a reflection of agrarian discontent, other demands put forward were wholly industrial in character.

"The urban workmen," the Populist platform stated, "are denied the right to organize for self-protection, imported pauperized labor beats down their wages, a hireling standing army, unrecognized by our laws, is established to shoot them down, and they are rapidly degenerating into European conditions." To combat this situation, the Populists supplemented their program for currency and other general reforms by taking over many of the demands traditionally pressed by the National Labor Union, the Knights of Labor and even the AFL. They called for restrictions on immigration, enforcement of the anticontract labor law and of the eight-hour day on government projects, an end to the use of injunctions in labor disputes, and the outlawing of the "army of mercenaries known as the Pinkerton system."

The Knights of Labor were ready to throw their enfeebled strength behind the Populists. The groups which supported Henry George in his campaign for the single tax and Edward Bellamy in the formation of Nationalist clubs dedicated to socialist reform, formally allied themselves with the People's party. Eugene V. Debs, while brooding over the failure of the Pullman strike, wholeheartedly backed a program which he believed provided ground for the common people to unite against the money power. Only the American Federation of Labor, once again reflecting the influence of Samuel Gompers, officially held aloof.

A determined effort on the part of socialists within the Federation to swing it in favor of a labor third party on a platform demanding "collective ownership by the people of all means of production and distribution" had been defeated only a short time before. Gompers won out, but in the process had been defeated in 1894 for the AFL presidency. John McBride, of the United Mine Workers, was elected to this post, and the headquarters of the Federation was moved to Indianapolis. Gompers's eclipse, however, was only temporary. At the next convention he was not only restored to the presidency, but the stand he had taken against socialism was emphatically reaffirmed. When the demand was voiced for the AFL to take a partisan position in support of Populism, its re-elected president was all the more determined to steer clear of any direct participation in politics. The American Federation of Labor was not prepared to endorse the party of inflation. "These Middle Class issues," Gompers declared in reemphasizing the importance for wage earners of concentrating all their energies upon the problems of unionism, "simply divert attention from their own interest."

When the Democrats took over the Populist program in 1896 and challenged not only the Republicans but the conservatives within their own party, they nevertheless commanded widespread support among industrial workers. Both parties fully recognized the importance of the labor vote. William Jennings Bryan, the Democratic candidate, went so far as to state in one speech that if elected President, he was prepared to make Gompers a member of his cabinet—a gesture that failed to move the AFL chieftain. The Republican high command, with Mark Hanna astutely managing William McKinley's campaign from the wings, tried a different tack. Workers were warned by notices in their pay enevelopes that a Democratic victory would mean the further closing of factories and the loss of jobs. Every effort was made to keep them in line by dire prophesies of economic disaster should "the socialistic and revolutionary forces" led by Bryan, Altgeld, and Debs win the election.

The organized forces of capitalism, represented by the Republican party, were able to hurl back the onslaught of farmers and workers campaigning under Democratic banners. McKinley was elected. The alliance had not been powerful enough, or strongly welded enough, to create a farmer-labor party which could carry through successfully a program of economic and social reform. The American Federation of Labor under Gompers practiced a cautious yet opportunistic nonpartisanship. The Republicans of 1896 astutely appealed to the labor vote, stressing the protective tariff and business confidence as the prescription for full employment and prosperity. In the slogan of the campaign, Republicans promised workers "a full dinner pail." If the triumphant Republicans feared militant labor and defended government by injunction, they also identified themselves as the party of high wages and positive government.

As the excitement of the campaign of 1896 subsided, labor had reason for discouragement in taking stock of the situation in which it found itself. The gains that had been made in wages prior to the depression had been largely wiped out. The average annual earnings for manufacturing employees were estimated at no more than $406. Except in a few of the highly skilled trades, working time was far longer than the eight-hour day for which labor had been struggling so long. It generally ranged between fifty-four and sixty-three hours a week—and even more in steel mills, textile factories, and the tenement sweatshops where women and children in the garment industry toiled endless hours for a pittance. Nowhere was there any real economic security for the industrial worker.

While there was a beginning of labor legislation, little progress had been made in attaining the goals first put forward in the late 1860s by the National Labor Union. A Bureau of Labor Statistics had been set up by the federal government, and there were comparable bureaus in thirty-two states; an Alien Contract Labor Law had been enacted; the Chinese Exclusion Acts were on the statute books; and in 1898 President McKinley was to recommend the creation of an Industrial Commission to investigate the causes of industrial violence. There were also various state laws regulating certain phases of industrial activity and looking toward the improvement of working conditions in mines and factories. But these were only moderate gains in the face of the weakened position of the unions in general. The old conspiracy laws had, in effect, been revived through the application to unions of the Sherman Act's ban on combinations in restraint of trade and the use of the injunction in suppressing strikes and boycotts.

Moreover, the number of organized workers had declined from the peak figures of the 1880s. A total of approximately a million had fallen to little more than a third of this figure. Even though Gompers had been able to boast in 1893 that the national unions had for the first time withstood depression, the American Federation of Labor had only some 250,000 members in 1897, and there were perhaps another 100,000 workers in the Railway Brotherhoods and other unaffiliated unions. This was a more compact and effectively organized nucleus than in earlier years, but in total union strength it was not very much greater than organized labor had claimed in either the early 1830s or the late 1860s.

The great mass of unskilled industrial workers remained unorganized. With their employers able to draw upon limitless replacements from the continuing stream of immigrant labor and to obtain support for strikebreaking from the government and the courts, they had few defenses against long hours, low wages and arbitrary dismissal. The crushing defeat of both the Homestead and Pullman strikes had been a bitter lesson in the overwhelming power that could be mustered to smash the efforts of industrial employees to organize in protection of their rights. The best prospect of any promise for labor appeared to be the further strengthening of the old-line trade unions brought together within the protective fold of the AFL.

XI

The Progressive Era

            The Progressive era, which extended from Theodore Roosevelt's accession to the presidency in 1901 to American entry into the First World War sixteen years later, was a time of vast changes in the United States, especially those affecting the place of workers and unions in society. Within both major political parties and in a myriad of voluntary reform associations, individuals grappled with the issues raised by the growing concentration of industry and the increasingly urban character of life.

  One group of reformers sought social justice by curtailing corporate influence in government and ending special privilege in whatever form; others tried to prove that large corporations could simultaneously serve the interests of their stockholders, employees, and the community. One group favored laws and programs to regulate the hours of work, wages, sanitary factory conditions, unemployment, and retirement; others looked forward to achieving the same goals through voluntary corporate action. Moreover, some advocates of what became known as "welfare capitalism" even conceded to the government a role in those areas of policy beyond the effective reach of corporate programs. It was the emergence of this rudimentary combination of "welfare statism" and "welfare capitalism" which gave the years between the Spanish-American War and the First World War its distinctive character and the appellation, "an age of reform."

The federal government actively promoted corporate responsibility, regulated the railroads, reformed the monetary system, and lowered tariffs. State governments regulated the working conditions of women and children, enacted protective laws for men laboring in dangerous occupations, established systems of workmen's compensation, and initiated programs of housing reform. Private corporations instituted job-safety programs, sanitary work environments, profit-sharing, and health-accident-retirement benefits for their employees. Everywhere, it seemed, people were accepting the need for collective public and private action to meet the problems raised by industrialization and urban growth. As the economy expanded, productivity increased, and living standards improved, many people felt a renewed faith and confidence in "democratic capitalism." They looked forward to the new century in a mood of buoyant optimism.

Although labor participated in the reform ferment of the era and benefited from federal and state legislation, such gains as it achieved were unevenly distributed. The material conditions of the great bulk of working people did not keep pace with the enormous growth in national wealth. The real income of workers in fact grew less rapidly than that of professionals, stock- and bondholders, and property owners in general. Moreover, the increasing introduction of labor-saving machinery on the one hand, and the rising tide of immigration on the other, combined to maintain a constant surplus of labor. Not only did this situation hold down wages; it also heightened the feeling of insecurity among workers over whom hung always the dread shadow of unemployment.

And in spite of the new legislation, actual working conditions for the great majority of wage earners were slow in showing any real change. The factory codes were still inadequate and all too often ineffectively enforced. In the coal mines, steel mills, and packing houses; in the textile factories still exploiting women and children, and in the sweatshops of the urban clothing industry, the harsh circumstances of life were a sad commentary on the prosperity enjoyed by the country as a whole.

As far as labor organization itself was concerned, the gains of these years were uneven and somewhat equivocal. For a time a new era of industrial relations appeared to have opened with bright promise of labor peace, but as the unions grew in strength, industrial counterattack soon led to further strife and sharp setbacks for labor in the courts and on the picket line. Only toward the end of the period was this early advance renewed with substantial gains in union membership and enhanced bargaining power.

The organized labor movement was almost wholly dominated by the American Federation of Labor, and its concern was still the well-being and status of its affiliated unions whose membership was principally made up of skilled workers. This was to remain a basically important consideration in forthcoming years. While the AFL unions in coal mining, the garment industry, and textiles were industrial in character, and others included some less skilled workers, the overwhelming number of employees in the great mass production industries—largely newcomers of peasant origins from the east and south of Europe—remained outside union ranks. During the progressive period, less than 10 per cent of the nation's wage earners were directly involved in the course of organized labor.

At the end of what Secretary of State John Hay called our "splendid little war" with Spain, the favorable turn in relations between national unions and employers was so pronounced that the years from 1898 to 1904 have been called "the honeymoon period of capital and labor." Strikes occasionally disrupted such harmony, but at least in comparison with the turbulent industrial strife of the 1890s, there was great improvement. In many industries, employers and wage earners alike seemed determined to seek out peaceful solutions to their problems. Many labor leaders had become convinced of the certainty of failure in such struggles as those epitomized by the Pullman strike, and many industrialists had come to realize the dangerous economic and political implications of strikes even when they were successfully suppressed. The country had been sobered by past experience, and increasingly demanded some way of dealing with industrial disputes which would safeguard the public interest.

This new approach to labor problems was best represented by the National Civic Federation. It had been first set up in Chicago in 1898, but at the turn of the century was operating on a nationwide basis with the avowed object of bringing capital, labor, and the public together in a joint campaign to maintain industrial peace. In sharp contrast to the prevailing corporate attitude in the 1890s that tended to identify all labor agitation with anarchy, it was founded on the premise that "organized labor cannot be destroyed without debasement of the masses." Antiunion employers were declared to be as great foes to national stability as radical or socialistic labor leaders. The National Civic Federation accepted unionization and trade agreements as basic principles and was prepared to offer its services "in establishing right relations between employers and workers" whenever both parties were willing to submit their disputes to its arbitration.

The leaders in the National Civic Federation were Mark Hanna and Samuel Gompers, and associated with them were a group of outstanding public figures. Grover Cleveland, President Charles W. Eliot of Harvard, and Archbishop John Ireland were among the representatives of the public; John D. Rockefeller, Jr., Charles M. Schwab, and August Belmont were included in the employer group; and John Mitchell of the United Mine Workers, James O'Connell of the Machinists, and James Duncan of the Granite Cutters were among the spokesman for labor. The membership list was an impressive one, and for a time the influence exercised by the National Civic Federation appeared to be a highly hopeful augury for labor-capital cooperation.[1]

Several important employer groups came to terms with the unions on the basis of mutually acceptable trade agreements. Pacts were concluded between the National Founders' Association and the International Association of Machinists. The Newspaper Publishers' Association and the International Typographical Union entered upon a series of agreements. Railroad operators recognized and negotiated with the railway brotherhoods. There were of course exceptions to this apparent progress toward industrial peace and the acceptance of collective bargaining. A final attempt on the part of the Amalgamated Iron and Steel Workers to organize the steel industry, for example, failed completely when the United States Steel Corporation, whose board of directors had secretly adopted a resolution stating its unalterable opposition to any extension of union labor, crushed a hard-fought strike in 1901. This was an important and highly significant defeat, but the growing number of trade agreements that were

---

[1]At a meeting in 1902, Charles Francis Adams read an interesting paper in the light of present-day labor laws, "Investigation and Publicity as Opposed to 'Compulsory Arbitration,'" in which he proposed legislation to set up a commission to investigate and report to Congress whenever a labor dispute threatened to disrupt interstate commerce. It was to be without coercive powers.

the fruit of the AFL's program and policies seemed to indicate a change in general employer attitudes that greatly encouraged labor. "It was the harvest," Gompers happily declared, "of the years of organization which were beginning to bear fruit."

The unions flourished under these circumstances and in many parts of the country attained a new position of importance. They were strongest, and showed the greatest gains, in those trades which had the longest history of labor activity. The Miners, Printers, Cigar Makers, Carpenters, Molders, Longshoremen, Brewers, and Machinists stood in the forefront of international unions affiliated with the American Federation of Labor, and in each instance they showed substantial gains in membership.

The exposures of the muckrakers, who delved during these years into every phase of industrial life, aroused a certain measure of popular sympathy for labor's efforts to improve its bargaining position. "Capital must make up its mind to get along with organized labor," the *Springfield Republican* declared in 1902. "Such labor is here to stay, and the law is more likely to compel the unionization of labor than it is to outlaw the labor union. The sooner this fact is recognized, the sooner will the country be placed on the way toward attaining a permanent industrial peace." Several years later, as spokesman of the new progressivism, Herbert Croly was equally emphatic in upholding labor organization. "Labor unions," he wrote in *The Promise of American Life*, "deserve to be favored because they are the most effective machinery which has yet been forged for the economic and social amelioration of the laboring classes."

Also indicative of changing popular attitudes was the role that government assumed in the most important strike of these years. For when the anthracite coal miners became locked in a bitter struggle with the operators in 1902, President Roosevelt exercised his influence not to crush the strikers, as had President Cleveland when he sent federal troops to Chicago in 1894, but to enforce arbitration. While his primary concern was to avert a possible coal famine, it did not blind him to the legitimate grievances of labor.

Since the 1870s, the turbulent days of the Long Strike, and the Molly Maguires, there had been periodic outbreaks in the coal fields as the miners struggled to improve working conditions. But not until the organization of the United Mine Workers in 1890 were they able to present a solid front against the combined strength of the

operators. This new union succeeded in organizing the workers in the bituminous mines of Pennsylvania, Ohio, Indiana, and Illinois[2] and won full
recognition in 1898 from the operators in an agreement governing both
wages and hours. Fresh from this victory, it then moved upon the anthracite area of eastern Pennsylvania.

Its task here was more difficult. The operators were organized in a
virtual trust under railroad domination and could hardly have been
more opposed to union recognition, while there was such a large element of Poles, Hungarians, Slovaks, Italians, and other newly arrived
immigrants among the workers that they lacked all cohesive unity.
Moreover, the operators made the most of this lack of homogeneity
by doing everything possible to stir up mutual animosities and fric-
tions.

The United Mine Workers made slow progress in the face of such
handicaps, but while their membership in the anthracite area was still less
than 10,000, ten times this number responded to a first strike call in
1900. The operators were ready to meet this attack, but Mark Hanna intervened and persuaded them to avert a prolonged conflict. His motive
was wholly political. The Republicans were campaigning in 1900 on a
platform of prosperity symbolized by the full dinner pail, and a coal strike
would have sounded an unfortunate note of discord in the theme song of
party orators. The operators reluctantly concluded an unwritten understanding with the miners which did not mean recognition of their union
but partially met their immediate demands through a 10 per cent wage
increase.

This was a truce, however, and not a settlement. The strikers had
not won their real objectives, and the operators regretted even the
slight concessions they had been forced to make. With no real improvement in conditions, the United Mine Workers consequently put
forward further demands in 1902 and this time the operators, resolved
not to let any further political pressure postpone a showdown, bluntly
refused to consider the miners' new proposals or to deal in any way
with the union. Another strike call was issued and 150,000 workers
now walked out of the mines.

Their grievances were very real. The pay was low by any standard, the
ten hours of work a day were hard and dangerous, and frequent lay-offs
cut down average earnings to less than $300 a year. Accidents

---

[2]The Central Competitive Field (CCF) included the four above-named states.

were common, with a death toll of 441 in 1901, and the mine owners did nothing whatsoever either to insure greater safety or to compensate their employees for injuries. But even more galling to the workers than low wages and poor working conditions was the rigid feudal system maintained by the operators through their control over the company towns. The workers, Samuel Gompers later wrote, "were brought into the world by the company doctor, lived in a company house or hut, were nurtured by the company store...laid away in the company graveyard."

With the outbreak of the strike on May 9, 1902, the operators at once threw 3,000 coal-and-iron police into the area, together with 1,000 other special deputies, and began moving in strikebreakers. They trumped up charges of violence, sabotage, and rioting against the workers and demanded the further protection of the state militia. The strike was to be fought as another anarchistic, revolutionary uprising against property rights and public order.

In spite of such provocation, there was relatively little resort to violence. It was on the whole a more orderly strike than the coal fields had perhaps ever experienced. The workers simply stayed away from the pits and maintained a completely passive attitude. Their ranks held firm in spite of all the suffering and hardship which the strike entailed for their families. If it was to be a fight to the finish, they were ready for it; they would not mine coal until their demands were met.

Many of the miners in the anthracite region belonged to diverse and insular ethnic cultures; before the great strike, this had acted as a source of divisiveness, but it now served to bind them more tightly to the union cause. For these miners of southern and eastern European extraction, the battle became more than a workers' or union struggle. For them, it was also a matter of community pride in the face of the companies which dominated their lives; any miner who shirked the fight appeared to be a traitor to his ethnic group. This ethnic context provided the anthracite miners with the resiliency and solidarity to wage a peaceful and orderly strike.

They also benefited from astute leadership by the president of the United Mine Workers. Since 1898, this post has been held by John Mitchell. He had started work in the mines as a boy of twelve, thrown in his lot with the union during its darkest days, and risen to leadership while still only twenty-eight, in large part through his skill in organizing the many nationalities who worked in the mines. Slight and wiry, with brown eyes, and a swarthy face, he had a modest—

almost diffident—manner. His strength was in his patience, his conciliatory attitude both in union politics and in employer relations, and his willingness to compromise on anything but what he thought were major issues.

No labor leader of the period was more conservative in his social and political attitudes, more willing to accept arbitration, or more disapproving of radicalism and violence. No trade unionist had proved more adept at using contacts with capitalists and public officials to enrich himself. He had originally opposed the strike in 1902, consistently refused to call out the bituminous miners in support of those in the anthracite fields because the former had signed a contract with the operators, and was ready at any time to submit the issues in dispute to settlement by any impartial body. He suggested a committee of five to be appointed by the National Civic Federation, or one composed of Archbishop Ireland, Bishop Henry C. Potter of New York, and any third person they might choose.

"If they decide that the average annual wages received by the anthracite miners," he stated, "are sufficient to enable them to live, maintain and educate their families in a manner conformable to established American standards and consistent with American citizenship, we agree to withdraw our claims for higher wages and more equitable conditions of employment, providing that the anthracite mine operators agree to comply with any recommendations the above committee may make affecting the earnings and conditions of labor of their employees."

In contrast to the moderation displayed by Mitchell was the truculent attitude of George F. Baer, the tough, hard-boiled spokesman of the operators. His reply to Mitchell's proposals was that "anthracite mining is a business and not a religious, sentimental or academic proposition." He was out to break the union at whatever cost. There was to be no submission of the dispute, as he never hesitated to make clear, to any outside group, let alone direct negotiations with the union. He believed wholeheartedly in the paternalistic controls maintained by the operators. Answering an appeal that he should seek to bring the strike to an end as his Christian duty, he stated his position in terms which seemed even to the *New York Times* to "verge very close upon unconscious blasphemy."

"I beg you not to be discouraged," Baer wrote his correspondent. "The rights and interests of the laboring man will be protected and cared for—not by the labor agitators, but by the Christian men to whom God in His infinite wisdom has given the control of the property interests of this country."

As the strike dragged on, a growing scarcity of coal, reflected in steadily rising prices, began to create mounting public concern and a popular demand for settlement. Whereas popular sympathy had originally been with the miners, the conservative press now felt free to blame them for the continued halt in production, and whenever any disorders were reported in the coal fields, it made the most of them. The New York *Journal of Commerce* declared in a familiar vein that what was taking place was "insurrection, not a strike," and the New York *Evening Post* called for "stern measures of suppression."

With the continued failure of the operators to make a single conciliatory gesture, however, public support soon began to swing back in the miners' favor. Editorials and cartoons singled out Baer for strong condemnation after his assertion of "divine right" with rising criticism in many quarters for his stubborn obduracy. But the primary interest of the country was not in either the workers or the operators. It simply wanted coal. Perhaps public opinion was more aptly reflected in a cartoon in the *New York Herald* depicting the public stretched on a rack with the operators pulling at one end, the miners at the other. Its caption read: "The victim is not particular which quits first."

President Roosevelt felt the force of this demand for peace in the coal fields. His own position on labor issues was somewhat equivocal but his concern now was in getting the mines open. He felt compelled to act to protect the public interest and, as his correspondence reveals, because he feared the political repercussions of a coal famine. His program was not to crush the strike, although the operators were demanding an injunction against the United Mine Workers as a conspiracy in restraint of trade under the Sherman Act, but to compel arbitration. To that end, he summoned a conference of both operators and strike leaders which was held at the White House on October 3.

While Mitchell declared himself willing to accept the findings of any commission appointed by the President, Baer once again bluntly refused to have anything to do with arbitration. His intransigent stand, as contrasted with the conciliatory attitude of the miners' leader, infuriated Roosevelt. Baer not only attacked the strikers but angrily rebuked the President for seeking to negotiate "with the fomenters of . . . anarchy and insolent defiance of the law." The conference was stormy. "If it wasn't for the high office I hold," Roosevelt is reputed to have said of Baer, "I would have taken him by the seat of the breeches and the nape of the neck and chucked him out of that window."

Still, almost no coal was being mined. Although 10,000 state troops were thrown into the territory to protect the strikebreakers, the men would not go back to work. The public grew more and more restive. Even conservative newspapers now stated that the operators had forfeited their claim to popular support and should settle the strike on the basis of negotiations with the United Mine Workers. "And the public," the *Chicago Evening Post* declared, "will not wait very long either."

Roosevelt decided to intervene even more directly. He secretly drew up a plan to put the army in the field with orders to its commanding general to dispossess the operators and run the mines as a receiver, and dispatched Secretary of War Elihu Root to inform J. P. Morgan, as the real power behind the operators, that this was his alternative if arbitration was still refused. Under such direct governmental pressure, the mine owners were finally induced to capitulate. They requested the President to set up an arbitration commission. Even at this point, however, they still balked at going the whole way and declared that they would not accept a labor member on the commission. The prospect of negotiations again hung in the balance until Roosevelt overcame this last obstacle by the appointment of the Grand Chief of the Railway Conductors, not as a labor representative but as "an eminent sociologist"! On October 23, after more than five months in which their lines had held almost without a break, the miners went back to work.

The award of the President's commission, announced in March 1903, granted a 10 per cent wage increase, reduced the working day to eight and nine hours for different classes of workers, and set up a special board to settle disputes arising during the three years in which the award was to remain in force. The miners had not won recognition of their union. They had failed to achieve their full aims and accepted the award reluctantly. But in the face of the operators' stubborn opposition, they had made real and important gains which greatly strengthened the position of the United Mine Workers in the anthracite area.

For all the advances made in the opening years of the century (total union membership increased from 868,500 in 1900 to over 2,000,000 in 1904), and in spite of the more generally sympathetic public attitude shown during the coal strike, there was trouble ahead for organized labor. Employers who had for a time seemed willing to recognize unions now became alarmed at their growing power. Largely abandoning the program for industrial peace originally sponsored by the National Civic Federation, they were beginning by 1903 to join forces in a vigorous campaign to block any further labor gains.

They encouraged the use of "yellow-dog" contracts which obligated employees to agree that they would not join any union. They played upon the natural rivalries of immigrant groups to discourage any cooperative action, employed labor spies to inform on labor agitators who would then be summarily fired, and exchanged blacklists of workers charged with radical views. The great employing corporations were ruthless in this renewed antiunion drive and were able, moreover, to bolster its force by successfully calling upon the courts for support in conspiracy indictments and injunctions.

The earlier accords in the machinery and metal trades broke down as employer associations in both instances reverted to their original anitlabor attitudes. Following the action of United States Steel in bluntly refusing to deal with union labor under any circumstances, there was open warfare in the structural iron industry, with the workers resorting to violence and dynamite. The packinghouses suppressed a strike in which their employees sought collective bargaining; delivery firms in Chicago joined forces to crush completely a teamsters' strike for recognition. Organized labor seemed to have been set back in almost every area; employers who had appeared willing to bargain with workers a few years earlier now refused to do so.

There was a change of heart on the part of the National Civic Federation itself. In the face of the increasing breakdown of trade agreements, it appeared to lose its early enthusiasm for unionization. The employer members still professed their friendship for labor but directed their energies primarily toward combating socialism and the closed shop. Gompers continued to work with them, being no less opposed to socialism, but in spite of his defense of the National Civic Federations's activities, labor lost confidence in its impartiality in industrial disputes.

Openly opposed to all labor organization were the Industrial Alliances which met in national convention in 1903 to form the Citizens' Industrial Association. Their lobbying and propaganda were highly successful in swinging public opinion against labor. After a meeting in 1906 which brought together some 468 delegates, representing almost as many employers' associations, President C. W. Post reported enthusiastically on the progress that he felt was being made. "Two years ago the press and pulpit," he declared, "were delivering platitudes about the oppression of the workingmen. Now all this has been changed since it has been discovered that the enormous Labor Trust is the heaviest oppressor of the independent workingman as well as the common American Citizen. The people have become aroused and are now acting."

The antiunion campaign was at the same time carried forward even more conspicuously by the National Association of Manufacturers, organized in 1895 but embarking on its first real attacks on organized labor about 1903. Its slogan and war cry was "the open shop," a guarantee of the right to work regardless of union affiliation. This appeal in the name of individual freedom, however, thinly disguised an all-out drive against both union recognition and collective bargaining. The NAM stood for industry's sole and exclusive right to determine both wages and the conditions of employment.

"Since the principles and demands of organized labor are absolutely untenable to those believing in the individualistic social order," delegates at the annual convention in 1903 were told by President David M. Parry, "an attitude of conciliation would mean an attitude of compromise with regard to fundamental convictions. ...The greatest danger lies in the recognition of the union." And one of the early pamphlets of the NAM, widely distributed in a propaganda campaign reaching out to the schools and churches as well as to the press and industrial organs, flatly stated that "our government cannot stand, nor its free institutions endure if the Gompers-Debs ideals of liberty and freedom of speech and press are allowed to dominate."

The principle of the open shop, often sustained with a conviction that went beyond all purely economic considerations, was used to justify or condone the most drastic measures in seeking to crush unions. This was perhaps most graphically illustrated in the suppression of the strike of employees of the Colorado Fuel and Iron Company and other coal companies in Colorado in 1913. The real issue at stake in this dispute was recognition of the United Mine Workers, who had sent their organizers into the territory. Rather than make this concession, the companies fiercely fought the strikers with hired detectives, special deputies, and the state militia.

Open warfare continued for months in the Colorado mine fields and finally reached a bloody climax when the militia attacked a colony of the strikers at Ludlow. After several rounds of indiscriminate machinegun fire, the tents in which the workers' families were living were soaked in oil and put to the torch. Women and children huddled in pits to escape the raging flames, and in one of them eleven children and two women were later found burned or suffocated to death. The nation was horrified by this massacre, but still the coal companies refused to consider negotiations with the union to end the strike.

The Colorado Fuel and Iron Company was controlled by the Rockefeller interests, and in an investigation of the strike by the House Committee on Mines and Mining, John D. Rockefeller, Jr., was called to the witness stand. In reply to questions as to whether he did not feel that "the killing of people and shooting of children" should not have led to efforts to reestablish labor peace, he implied that rather than give in to the miners, his company was prepared to go to whatever lengths were necessary. The only way that the strike could be settled, he stated, was through unionization of all the mines, which could not be accepted because "our interest in labor is so profound and we believe so sincerely that that interest demands that the camps shall be open camps, that we expect to stand by the officers at any cost." He resented particularly the idea that outside organizers should seek to stir up men who were "thoroughly satisfied with their labor conditions." There could be no surrender. "It was upon a similar principle that the war of the Revolution was carried on," Rockefeller declared. "It is a great national issue of the most vital kind."

This was not an isolated instance of uncompromising opposition to unionization, and the courts generally sustained employers in making nonmembership in a union a condition of employment.

In 1898, Congress had passed a law, the Erdman Act, which prohibited any discrimination against workers by the interstate railways because of union membership. Ten years later, in *Adair* v. *the United States*, the Supreme Court held this provision of the Erdman Act unconstitutional as an invasion of both personal liberty and the rights of property. A comparable state statute was outlawed in *Coppage* v. *Kansas* in 1915, and the Supreme Court then proceeded to uphold an injunction granted at the request of the Hitchman Coal and Coke Company, in West Virginia, which prohibited the United Mine

Workers from seeking to organize company employees who had been compelled to agree not to join the union under yellow-dog contracts.

These legal obstacles to unionization did not pass uncriticized even in the Supreme Court. Justice Oliver Wendell Holmes strongly dissented. "In present conditions," he argued in the Coppage case, "a workman not unnaturally may believe that only by belonging to a union can he secure a contract that shall be fair to him. ...If that belief may be held by a reasonable man, it seems to me that it may be enforced by law in order to establish equality of position between the parties in which liberty of contract begins. Whether in the long run it is wise for the workingmen to enact legislation of this sort is not my concern, but I am strongly of the opinion that there is nothing in the Constitution of the United States to prevent it." His brethren on the Supreme Court were not convinced, however. The decisions upholding and enforcing yellow-dog contracts stood until passage of the Norris-La Guardia Act in 1932 finally reversed public policy.

The courts also sustained the employers in their counterattack upon union boycotts. The American Federation of Labor had found this weapon highly effective in promoting union recognition. By persuading its members to refrain from buying any goods which did not bear a union label, many recalcitrant employers were brought into line. To meet this situation, the American Anti-Boycott Association was established to aid employers in going to court on the ground that such boycotts were conspiracies in restraint of trade and subject to injunction as "malicious" interference with the "probable expectancies" of property rights. Two important cases involving these issues dragged through the courts between 1902 and 1916, and in each instance resulted in a decisive defeat for the AFL.

In 1902 the United Hatters declared a nationwide boycott of the hats of D. E. Loewe & Company, of Danbury, Connecticut, in support of a strike by a local union to win recognition. The company at once instituted a suit charging the United Hatters with conspiring to restrain trade in violation of the Sherman Act and claimed triple damages from the individual members of the local union who had gone on strike. After a long period of legal wrangling, the company was upheld in 1916 and allowed total damages and costs assessed at $252,000. The bank accounts of the union members were attached and foreclosure proceedings introduced against their homes, but the fines were eventually paid through contributions from the national union and the AFL.

The Danbury Hatters' case particularly awoke the resentment of labor because of its effect in bringing secondary boycotts under the ban of the Sherman Act and subjecting individual members to damage suits. But even while it was making its tortuous way through the courts, the American Federation of Labor itself became involved in another dispute which had even wider repercussions. In 1906 the metal polishers employed by the Buck's Stove and Range Company of St. Louis went on strike for the nine-hour day and appealed for aid. The AFL responded by placing the company on its "We Don't Patronize" list in the *American Federationist* and advising all union members to boycott its products. J. W. Van Cleave, president both of the Buck's Stove and Range Company and of the National Association of Manufacturers, promptly secured an injunction not only restraining the officers and members of the AFL from placing his firm on the "We Don't Patronize" list, but also from in any way calling attention to the metal polishers' strike either in writing or orally.

The AFL refused to heed this sweeping court order. While the offending company was taken off its unfair list, Gompers continued to state that union men could not be coerced into buying Buck stoves and ranges. He was thereupon found in contempt of court and sentenced to a year's imprisonment; two other officers of the Federation were also adjudged guilty and given somewhat lighter sentences. Gompers was never to serve this sentence. Court proceedings continued even after the death of Van Cleave and withdrawal of the original injunction, but the case was finally dismissed by the Supreme Court. Although the AFL leaders consequently escaped jail, their conviction was nevertheless a shock which aroused labor even more against injunction law than its earlier defeats on this score. Gompers could not be reconciled to the position in which he found himself—a conservative, the friend of employers, the arch foe of labor radicalism, attacked by the courts as though he were a revolutionary or an anarchist.

The effect of these decisions, and others in which injunctions were freely granted to employers, appeared to labor to represent a revival of the old conspiracy laws against which it had so often fought. The principles at stake closely paralleled those set forth in the legal cases of the early nineteenth century. Labor felt itself to be fighting again for the basic right to organize and strike against courts which had wholly gone over to the employers' camp in banning union activity as being in restraint of trade. The formerly accepted theory that possible injury to property rights through strikes or boycotts was only incidental to their legitimate purpose of seeking to improve working conditions was being denied under conditions which seemed to threaten the very existence of unions.

The American Federation of Labor considered it imperative to seek legislative relief from such restrictions. Yet Gompers and his allies on the executive council still firmly rejected the labor left's (socialists composed about one third of total AFL membership) pleas for independent political action and public ownership and control of the means of production. Gompers declared to the Socialists in 1903, "economically, you are unsound; socially you are wrong; industrially you are an impossibility"—and was upheld by a vote of 11,282 to 2,147. But somehow the unions had to be freed from the disabilities under which they were suffering. Protection for the right to organize, to bargain collectively, to strike, to boycott, and to picket had become of immediate and vital concern. This meant that the American Federation of Labor and the trade unions had to become more active politically, a reality which by the First World War brought them into a working alliance with the Democratic party.

A first step in trying to exercise more effective political pressure in support of such aims came in 1906, when the AFL submitted a Bill of Grievances to the President and to Congress. It included most of the traditional demands that labor had been voicing since the Civil War and approved most of the more general measures being promoted by progressives throughout the country. Most important, however, were the demands for exemption of labor unions from the Sherman Act and relief from injunctions which were said to represent a judicial usurpation of power which properly belonged to the legislature. "We have waited long and patiently and in vain for redress," the Bill of Grievances concluded. ". . . Labor now appeals to you, and we trust it may not be in vain. But if perchance you may not heed us, we shall appeal to the conscience and support of our fellow citizens."

Congress did not heed labor's spokesmen. The bills which labor sought to introduce were sidetracked or pushed aside, and the AFL entered actively into the congressional campaign of 1906. It not only called for the support of all congressional candidates friendly to labor's aspirations, but where neither party had named an acceptable candidate, it advised the nomination of a trade unionist. Two years later, Gompers appealed to both party conventions for support. The

Democrats adopted an anti-injunction plank in their platform, but the Republicans completely ignored him and nominated William Howard Taft, who had built a reputation as a notorious antilabor injunction judge while serving on the federal bench. The *American Federationist* openly opposed Taft and came out defiantly in favor of William Jennings Bryan. When Taft was elected and the Republicans continued to pass over labor's demands, further support for the Democrats appeared to be forthcoming. Thus, in the election of 1912, the AFL worked for Wilson's election, even cooperating with the Democratic National Committee in scheduling trade-union campaign speakers.

These political tactics were stoutly defended by Gompers as in no sense departing from the AFL's traditional nonpartisan stand of rewarding labor's friends and punishing its enemies. Legislation was needed to free the unions from existing restrictions, according to his thesis, and the Democrats had shown themselves to be more open-minded and sympathetic than the Republicans. "In performing a solemn duty at this time in support of a political party," the AFL chieftain declared in 1908, "labor does not become partisan to a political party but partisan to a principle."

How successful such political activities were before the Wilson administration was highly dubious. State legislatures adopted a number of measures which materially improved conditions for industrial workers, with special reference to women and children, but as has been suggested already, they were a response to the awakened sense of social responsibility which typified the whole progressive era rather than the result of political pressures exerted by organized labor. They had grown out of a humanitarian feeling which was not so much concerned over labor's rights—union recognition and collective bargaining—as with the more general aspects of an industrial society that harbored so much poverty, disease, and crime.

While labor supported these reforms, moreover, they were not of primary consideration according to the philosophy of the AFL and Samuel Gompers. Suspicious of the state, Gompers was unwilling to rely upon government for the protection of labor's interests. He favored laws to safeguard women and children in industry, but did not want laws to govern either hours or wages for union members. The only effective means for improving general working conditions, in his opinion, was the economic pressure of organized labor. All that he asked of the state were guarantees of the right to exercise such pressure.

Gompers and the American Federation of Labor's antipathy to public regulation of social and economic conditions—what today is known as welfare-state practices—flowed from their commitment to the principle of "voluntarism." Voluntarism served the trade unions and their leaders in several ways. First, it cemented rank-and-file loyalty to an institution which alone protected workers against unemployment, injury, illness, and indigent old age. Second, it shielded unions and their leaders from any form of public intervention and regulation. Third, it served as an ideological shield between unions and agencies of the state, especially courts, which were perceived as enemies of the working class. Fourth, it resonated with the traditional American stress on voluntary associations, self-help, and private initiative. For skilled workers organized in stable trade unions, voluntarism made sense and provided protection.

In an editorial in the *American Federationist* in 1915, Gompers offered the fullest explication of his organization's commitment to voluntarism. "Whither are we drifting?" he asked. ". . . If there is no market for cotton those interests demand a law. If wages are low, a law or commission is the remedy proposed. What can be the result of this tendency but the softening of the moral fibre of the people? Where there is unwillingness to accept responsibility for one's life and for making the most of it, there is a loss of strong, red-blooded, rugged independence and will power. . . . We do not want to place more power in the hands of the government to investigate and regulate the lives, the conduct and the freedom of America's workers."

The economic and social reforms enacted during the progressive era were nevertheless important, and directly or indirectly they greatly benefited all working people. Child-labor laws, which placed restrictions on the age at which children might be employed, limited their hours of work, and otherwise safeguarded health and safety had been adopted by some thirty-eight states by 1912, and protection was afforded women in industry through legislation in twenty-eight states setting maximum hours. More important was the widespread adoption—in at least thirty-five states by 1915—of workmen's compensation laws providing for compulsory benefit payments for industrial accidents. These latter measures were often inadequate and not always effectively enforced, but they demonstrated significant progress toward insuring employer responsibility for the health and safety of workers in mines and factories.

A beginning was also made in the passage of general maximum-hour laws. The demand for such legislation by the states, which had been pressed so vigorously in the 1840s and again in the 1860s, was not taken up by labor as it had been in these earlier periods. Collective bargaining rather than legal limitation were the means on which the unions principally relied to reduce the working day. As a result of progressive rather than special labor agitation, however, some twenty-five states enacted laws during this era which in the interests of public health and safety limited hours of work for men as well as women. They differed sharply from the earlier maximum-hour legislation in that the old clause exempting "special contracts" was finally eliminated. For the first time, state hours laws were enforceable.

The courts had originally blocked the passage of much of this labor legislation, taking the stand that exercise of the state's police power could not be carried so far as to interfere with either the property rights of the employer or the individual freedom of the worker to conclude whatever contract he desired. In *Lochner* v. *New York,* a case in which a maximum-hour law for bakery workers was declared unconstitutional in 1905, the Supreme Court stated that such legislation was barred by the guarantees of liberty in the due process clause of the Fourteenth Amendment. However, the court gradually swung over to a more liberal interpretation of constitutional safeguards, and it finally upheld the maximum-hour laws for both men and women and also accepted the new workmen's compensation laws. When the further attempt was made to enact minimum-wage laws, however, the Supreme Court divided evenly on their constitutionality, and the validity of such legislation, as passed in seven states, remained in doubt. The issue did not again come up for determination until 1923, and the Supreme Court then ruled, in *Adkins* v. *Children's Hospital,* that wage restrictions could not be reconciled with liberty of contract. This decision was to stand until 1937, when the Supreme Court finally acknowledged that, under existing conditions of employment, liberty of contract was a fiction which in no way preserved the individual worker's freedom in determining either his hours of work or his wages.

In general, state legislation in behalf of industrial workers, while still lagging far behind contemporary European experiments with both old-age pensions and unemployment insurance, had substantial achievements to its credit during the Roosevelt and Taft administrations. On the national stage, as has been said, there was far less cause for satisfaction. The Bill of Grievances submitted by the AFL in 1906 appeared to have been permanently tabled by hostile committees in both the House and the Senate. No progress whatsoever was being made in enacting its general provisions for union security. As action in so many cases demonstrated, the injunction and union prosecutions under the Sherman Act became increasingly powerful weapons in the hands of labor's foes. The attitude of the Democratic House elected in 1910 was an early sign of a more favorable attitude toward labor. An effective eight-hour day for workers on public contracts was finally passed, an Industrial Relations Commission was set up "to discover the underlying causes of dissatisfaction in the industrial situation," and provision made for a Department of Labor particularly designed to promote the wage earners' welfare. But it was not until the election of 1912 and the inauguration of the Democratic President, Woodrow Wilson, in 1913 that a real turning point was reached so far as broader legislation by the national government was concerned.

Wilson had attacked what he called "the antiquated and impossible" laws currently governing the relations of employers and employees during the campaign of 1912. His inaugural further emphasized the need for legislation that would not only safeguard the workers' lives, improve conditions under which they worked, and provide rational and tolerable hours of labor, but also give them "freedom to act in their own interest." He denied that such laws could be considered class legislation and asserted that they were in the interests of all the people. Labor rejoiced in such a defense of its position and confidently looked forward to the remedial legislation in respect to injunctions and conspiracy prosecutions for which it had striven so long and unsuccessfully. "We are no longer journeying in the wilderness," Gompers proclaimed. "We are no longer in the season of mere planting. We are in the harvest time."

The results appeared for a time to bear out this optimism. In 1914 Congress passed the Clayton Act which both strengthened earlier antitrust legislation and incorporated important clauses affecting the rights of labor. Specifically declaring that "the labor of a human being is not a commodity or article of commerce," the new law stated that nothing in the antitrust laws should be construed to forbid the existence of unions, prevent them from "lawfully" carrying out their legitimate objects, or hold them to be illegal combinations or conspiracies in restraint of trade. Furthermore, it outlawed the use of injunctions in all disputes between employers and employees "unless necessary to prevent irreparable injury to property, or to a property right...for which injury there is no adequate remedy at law."

Gompers hailed this statute as the "Magna Carta" of labor—a final guarantee of the workers' right to organize, to bargain collectively, to strike, to boycott, and to picket. Other opinion varied as to the real meaning of the new law. Althought the *Wall Street Journal* described Congress as "a huddled mob of frightened cowards...watching for the labor boss to turn down his thumb," many newspaper editorials, political leaders, and even some labor spokesmen pointed out that the cautious phraseology of the Clayton Act showed that labor had really won no new rights and that injunctions had not actually been outlawed. Gompers chose to ignore all such practical considerations as he spread the glad tidings of what he insisted was a great labor victory. Perhaps in order to justify the policies he had followed and to build up the prestige of the AFL, he admitted no doubts as to the full freedom which the unions had theoretically won.

The skeptics were soon shown to have been justified. The guarantees of the Clayton Act proved to be largely illusory once they were subjected to interpretation by the courts. Loopholes were discovered in the supposed exemption of unions from the antitrust laws; the provisions in regard to the use of injunctions were so interpreted as to provide no real relief. The statement of principle that labor was not a commodity remained, and it had a real significance as marking a change in public attitudes, but it had no practical effect on employer-employee relationships.

Yet there were substantial gains for labor during the Wilson administration and, in spite of disappointment over the later interpretation of the Clayton Act, these years were to find organized labor driving ahead on many fronts. It won legislative support on three important issues. Passage of the La Follette Seamen's Act in 1915 remedied many of the most glaring abuses in the employment of sailors and immeasurably improved conditions in the forecastles of American merchant vessels. A demand by railway workers for shorter hours was met the next year when the Adamson Act established an eight-hour day, with time and a half for overtime, for all employees of interstate railways. And congressional enactment of a literacy test for all European immigrants in 1917 was a first step toward the policy of immigration restriction which the AFL had so long demanded.

The growth of labor unions during the first decade of the new century had been temporarily halted by the industrial counterattack launched about 1904. The membership of the American Federation of Labor actually declined in 1905 and for the next five years remained almost stationary. It was only 1,562,000 in 1910 in comparison with 1,676,000 six years earlier. Between 1910 and 1917, however, the AFL gained some 800,000 new members, and trade-union enrollment as a whole rose to over 3,000,000. It was almost four times what it had been at the opening of the century.

The urge to join a union, in these years as in other periods, came not only from the expectation of economic gain through collective action. The hope that the worker would attain greater security—a square deal and protection from arbitrary discipline—was always highly important, but there was also an often unconscious desire on the part of the individual wage earner to strengthen his feeling of individual worth and significance in an industrialized society. Machinery was, more and more, making the worker an automatic cog in a process over which he had no influence or control. The complete impersonality of corporate business, with management far removed from any direct contact with employees, further accentuated this loss of individual status. The wage earner could find satisfaction in membership in such a meaningful social organization as a labor union that was denied him as one among many thousands of depersonalized employees. The desire to take part in some group activity was, indeed, particularly strong during the progressive era. It was a period marked by the rapid growth of social clubs, lodges, and fraternal and professional associations. The unions, which often used some of the ritual of the fraternal lodges, met a very real need entirely apart from the support which they provided for collective bargaining.

The expansion in union ranks by 1917, in any event, was brought about both by the increase in membership in old unions and the establishment of new ones. The United Mine Workers had built up a membership of 334,000, by far the strongest union in the country; the building trades—carpenters, painters, masons, and bricklayers—had over 300,000 workers in their various unions; and important additions to the organized labor movement were the unions among garment workers.

Activity in this industry had received dramatic impetus from the "uprising of the twenty thousand" among the shirtwaist makers in New York. This strike in the fall of 1909 sensationally dramatized the plight of young immigrant female workers, mostly Jewish and Italian, who worked long hours for low wages. More important, it demonstrated the will and the ability of semiskilled female workers to act collectively in order to gain their aims. The women withstood strikebreakers, police brutality, and harsh winter weather until they won higher wages, better conditions, and partial union recognition. Their courage enabled the International Ladies' Garment Workers' Union (ILGWU) the organization to which they belonged, to transform itself from bankruptcy to vigor.

Only a year later, in the summer of 1910, the ILGWU led a general walkout by 60,000 cloak and suit makers in New York City, the center of the women's garment industry. These strikers, mostly immigrant men representing the more skilled, better-paid sector of the trade, showed equal solidarity. They walked the picket lines for over four months, until an outside mediator, Louis D. Brandeis, soon to be appointed an associate justice of the Supreme Court by Woodrow Wilson, brought the union and employers together in a compromise settlement. Brandeis devised the famous "Protocol of Peace," which awarded workers higher wages, reduced hours, the preferential union shop (union members to be given preference over nonunion members in employment), and established grievance-arbitration machinery as a substitute for strikes. These victories transformed the ILGWU from a feeble organization into one of the nations's larger, more militant unions.

A similar set of events occurred among workers in the men's clothing industry. The American Federation of Labor union in that trade, the United Garment Workers of America, was larger and more successful than the ILGWU before the upheaval of 1909–10. But the United Garment Workers had neglected the workers in the most rapidly growing sector of the industry—the men's ready-made suit and coat branch. New York, Chicago, Baltimore, and Cleveland, immigrant tailors of Jewish, Italian, and Lithuanian extraction, among a large variety of other ethnic groups, found themselves ill-served by the United Garment Workers. Again and again the union negotiated strike settlements which betrayed the immigrant workers. Unable to make their voices heard effectively or to reform the United Garment Workers from within, the Jewish and Italian tailors rebelled. They walked out of the 1914 United Garment Workers' convention and a year later founded their own organization, the Amalgamated Clothing Workers of American (ACWA).

From its founding in 1915 until 1934, the ACWA existed outside the American Federation of Labor, which treated it as a dual union.[3] Yet it succeeded in organizing the bulk of the immigrant men's clothing workers, women as well as men, and leading them to victory in a series of strikes. By the First World War, the ACWA had also grown to become a large and militant union.

The successes and growth of the ILGWU and the ACWA were significant for many reasons. The experiences of these unions proved, contrary to much American Federation of Labor rhetoric, that new immigrant workers could be organized. They also proved that women as well as men could be organized, if unions made a real effort to attract women and to offer them a role in the union. This was especially important at a time when the number of women in the wage labor force continued its steady growth and when female workers dominated such industries as clothing. The ILGWU and the ACWA, moreover, organized all workers in an industry, regardless of specific skill or job description, into one organization. They showed that industrial, or horizontal unionism, could work as well as more conventional craft unionism. Not only that, the garment unions also preached and practiced socialism, and they did so without impairing their success at collective bargaining. Indeed, it can be argued that their socialism, militancy, and concern for their membership's general welfare strengthened the two unions—so much so that many contemporary commentators could not shower too much praise on the "new unionism" of the ILGWU and ACWA, which many heralded as the wave of the future.

If the ILGWU, ACWA, and perhaps the United Mine Workers were industrial organizations and practiced the "new unionism," they remained exceptions to the general rule of labor unionism. There were no unions of any significance in steel, automobiles, agricultural machinery, electrical manufactures, public utilities, tobacco manufacture, or meat packing. The very industries that were becoming most important in the economic development of the country, and employed an increasing proportion of industrial workers, were unaffected by the labor activity of these years because the corporations

---

[3]After being admitted to the American Federation of Labor in 1934, it was suspended only two years later for its role in the formation of the CIO. See Chapter XVI.

controlling them were so stubbornly antiunion and so powerful that every effort to organize their employees was doomed to failure.

It was the continued low wages and long hours for workers in these mass-production industries that largely accounted for the unevenness of the gains that may be attributed to labor during the progressive era. The social legislation of the period, wage advances for skilled workers banded together in the unions comprising the AFL, and changing public attitudes and public policy toward unionization were counteracted by the depressed circumstances of the great hordes of unorganized industrial workers who still accounted for approximately 90 per cent of the total labor force.

XII

Thunder on the Left

While the wage earners in the national
and international unions were generally willing to accept an economic
system under which they appeared to be making slow but definite
gains, disturbing currents of a deeper discontent developed during
the progressive era among the workers who were outside the bounds
of existing trade unionism. New demands were voiced for organization on industrial lines or for the all-inclusive union structure abandoned after the collapse of the Knights of Labor; the adherents of
socialism grew in strength and redoubled their efforts to build up an
effective political party; and there was radical agitation among the
unorganized workers for direct action to secure their share of the
benefits made available by an expanding economy.

"The labor men are very ugly and no one can tell how far such
discontent will spread," Theodore Roosevelt was somewhat fearfully
writing Senator Henry Cabot Lodge of Massachusetts as early as
1906. "There has been during the last six or eight years a growth of
socialistic and radical spirit among workingmen and the leaders are
obliged to play to this or they lose their leadership."

The upsurge of radicalism may have appeared somehow out of
place in a period in which the spirit of the country was one of buoyant
confidence and such general advance appeared to be under way for

the people as a whole. It was a direct reflection, however, of the extent to which the interests of the unskilled workers were being ignored. As the American Federation of Labor continued to neglect the bulk of new immigrant mass-production workers and become itself less receptive to radical influences, the embers of discontent flared into flame. Fertile ground was provided for a revival of revolutionary activity whose aim was the immediate abolition of the wage system and the complete overthrow of capitalism. For a brief time the radicals threatened to transform the entire labor movement. Their spearhead was the Industrial Workers of the World (IWW).

Miners, loggers, and migratory harvest hands in the West joined with socialists among the unorganized industrial workers of the East in the formation of this new association. The "Wobblies," as they came to be called in the West, denied that there was anything in common between the working class and the employing class. The IWW called upon the workers to take over themselves possession of the machinery of production.

"Instead of the conservative motto, 'A fair day's wage for a fair day's work,'" their ringing manifesto declared, "we must inscribe on our banner the revolutionary watchword, 'Abolition of the wage system.' It is the historic mission of the working class to do away with capitalism."

The IWW grew out of a secret meeting in Chicago in 1905 which drew together all the radical and dissident elements in the labor movement. These militant western miners, socialists of various persuasions, advocates of industrial unionism and anarchistic exponents of direct action closed their ranks for a unified and direct attack upon capitalism. Events were to prove that they agreed upon little else than their mutual scorn for the program and tactics of the AFL. Accepting the thesis of class struggle as their common starting point, however, they set up an economic organization whose aim was to work on both the political and industrial fronts for the final emancipation of labor.

The most important group behind the organization of the IWW was the Western Federation of Miners. It had once been affiliated with the AFL but let its membership lapse in 1897 as a result of the Federation's coolness to the interests of workers in the mountain states. Hardened by a series of violent strikes, which they had fought with the mine owners of Idaho, Montana, and especially Colorado between 1894 and 1904, the leaders of the hard-rock miners became

militant socialists. Dynamitings, train wrecks, strikebreakers, private detectives, murders, and the imposition of martial law taught these western
workers harsh lessons in social reality. Daily life, not Marxist treatises, exposed for them the reality of class conflict. When in 1903–1904 the full
weight of the State of Colorado was used to crush their strike in the Cripple Creek district, the Western Federation of Miners' leaders decided that
they needed radical allies.

They had previously formed the Western Labor Union (1897) and then
the American Labor Union (1902) in an effort to bring together all workers in the western states in a single industrial organization, and the Federations's leaders were now ready to welcome any move toward even broader
organization. They hopefully answered the call for the Chicago convention that was to result in formation of the IWW. Their delegates numbered only five out of a total of some two hundred at this meeting, but,
with 27,000 members, the western miners were far and away the strongest union represented.

Socialists were the other principal group represented at the convention of 1905. But they were divided into two competing factions. One,
under the domineering leadership of Daniel De Leon, a brilliant orator
and pamphleteer known as the "socialist Pope," had long waged open
war against the AFL. De Leon called the Federation "a cross between a
windbag and a rope of sand," while Gompers was intermittently a "labor faker," "an entrapped swindler," and "a greasy tool of Wall
Street." The other faction included men and women who had chafed
at De Leon's iron party discipline and his version of revolutionary
practice. Friendlier to the trade unions and more willing to seek immediate reforms, these insurgents coalesced in 1901 to form the Socialist
Party of America (SPA). With Eugene V. Debs as its presidential candidate five times, the SPA was from its founding until 1920 the most successful national radical political party in twentieth-century America.
Although the SPA declined to send an official delegation to the Chicago convention, Debs and other prominent party members attended
individually. At odds since the 1890s, Debs and De Leon promised in
1905 to shake hands "over the bloody chasm of the past."

While other independent radical unions were officially represented,
including the American Labor Union, the United Metal Workers, and
the United Brotherhood of Railway Employees, individuals rather than
organizations were primarily responsible for the establishment of

the IWW, and the convention was enlivened by the clash of their divergent personalities. In addition to De Leon and Debs, other delegates were William D. Haywood, of the Western Federation of Miners; Father T. J. Hagerty, a big, black-bearded Catholic priest who was the editor of the American Labor Union's official organ and a militant advocate of industrial unionism; A. M. Simons, the socialist intellectual and editor of the *International Socialist Review*; Charles O. Sherman, the general secretary of the United Metal Workers; William E. Trautmann, a radical leader of the United Brewery Workers and editor of its German-language paper; and "Mother" Jones, a fiery, intrepid woman of seventy-five, with curly white hair and kindly gray eyes, whose zeal as an agitator kept her in the front lines of labor's fighting for almost half a century.

Among these varied and colorful figures, the most arresting was Haywood. A rugged hulk of a man, he had a tough, almost sinister appearance. "Big Bill" Haywood was a powerful and aggressive embodiment of the spirit of the militant western worker. Forced to leave school as a young adolescent, Haywood worked at odd jobs on the streets of Salt Lake City until going down into the mines at the age of fifteen. He soon became a skilled miner and, at the end of the 1890s, was a leader in the Silver City, Idaho, WFM local. In 1900 he left the mines permanently, becoming a secretary treasurer of the WFM. For the remainder of his life, "Big Bill" acted as a labor radical. Nowhere did he play that role better than at the founding convention of the IWW, of which he was chairperson. He addressed it as "the Continental Congress of the working class" and from the onset clearly revealed that his real interest was in organizing the forgotten unskilled workers and especially the migratory laborers of the West—the "bums" and "red-blooded working stiffs." "We are going down in the gutter," Haywood shouted, "to get at the mass of workers and bring them up to a decent plane of living."

Except for Haywood, none of these convention delegates had more than a corporal's guard of followers to bring into the IWW. They spoke for themselves, and their individualistic attitudes on labor policy appeared to be irreconcilable in the excitement of convention debate. After giving full vent to their opposition to what they derisively called "the American Separation of Labor," they nevertheless agreed upon a general program for the IWW.

Gompers had nothing but scorn for these leftist maneuvers and the attempt to revive a form of labor organization which he roundly condemned as "fallacious, injurious, reactionary." He struck out particularly at his old foe, De Leon, whose adherence to the IWW he hoped would "bring unction to the soul" of its other promoters. "So the trade union smashers and the rammers from without and the 'borers from within,'" he wrote, "are again joining hands; a pleasant sight of the 'pirates' and the 'kangaroos' hugging each other in glee over their prospective prey."

Gompers's belief that such strange bedfellows could not long work together soon appeared to be substantiated. Faction and controversy split the ranks of the IWW almost immediately. At the convention of 1906 a conflict between the more moderate elements, primarily represented by the Socialist party, and the outright proponents of revolution led to wholesale desertions by reformists. The next year, the Western Federation of Miners itself withdrew, reducing the actual membership of the IWW to less than 6,000, and then in 1908 a final struggle broke out over the basic issue of political or economic action. The group favoring the former policy was led by De Leon and the latter by Trautmann, but the decisive element at the convention was a delegation of western rebels—"the Overalls Brigade"—which beat its way to Chicago on freight trains and had scant interest in doctrinaire squabbling.

The majority ousted De Leon's followers—who promptly held a rival convention to form a new organization—and then proceeded to amend the Chicago constitution to their liking. The amended constitution eliminated political action and party affiliation as means to achieve a workers' revolution. IWW members instead sought to overthrow capitalism by direct economic action. Openly revolutionary in theory and practice, the IWW pledged never to make peace with capitalists, nor to sign binding time contracts with employers. It promised to gain its cooperative and harmonious utopia one day through the general strike—the ultimate weapon of working-class power.

Only through "One Big Union," breaking through all craft lines, it was now declared, could the workers present an effective united front in the class struggle. The AFL had betrayed labor and fallen under the complete domination of employers.

"Tie 'Em Up," sang the Wobblies:

We have no fight with brothers of the old A.F. of L.
But we ask you use your reason with the facts we have to tell.
Your craft is but protection for a form of property,
The skill that you are losing, don't you see.
Improvements on machinery take your skill and tools away,
And you'll be among the common slaves upon some fateful day.
Now the things of which we're talking we are mighty sure about.—
So what's the use to strike the way you can't win out?

Tie 'em up! tie 'em up; that's the way to win.
Don't notify the bosses till hostilities begin.
Don't furnish chance for gunmen, scabs and all their like;
What you need is One Big Union and One Big Strike.

Refusing to abandon the right to strike at any time or on any occasion, the IWW viewed everyday struggles for wages and hours as only the first line of attack; the decks had to be kept clear for the final assault. Industrial unions were to provide the "structure of the new society within the shell of the old," and a workers' government would replace what in a capitalistic society was "simply a committee employed to police the interests of the employing class."

The IWW made its greatest appeal to western miners, construction gangs, loggers, and migratory harvest hands who were not interested in political action since they seldom had the vote. Ill-paid, homeless, often unmarried; drifting from job to job, largely cut off from the usual ties of society, they considered themselves victims of an economic system designed solely to exploit them. They were ready to strike, not for the nebulous dream of "pie in the sky," but for down-to-earth ownership of the means of production. Converts were also won among the immigrant workers of steel mills, packing plants, and textile mills whom the IWW was prepared at all times to aid. More stable and settled than the western workers and also more firmly integrated into ethnic communities, the eastern factory workers found direct action to be an appealing doctrine and the Wobblies to be firm allies.

Membership in the IWW never became very great—probably no more than sixty thousand at its peak. Several hundred thousand union cards were issued, but migratory workers did not remain very long in the ranks. The significance of the IWW as has been suggested, was its revolutionary leadership. The Wobblies became commonly but unjustly associated with violence. "Hanging is none too good for them," the *San Diego Tribune* exploded on one occasion in 1912. "They would be much better dead, for they are absolutely useless in the human economy; they are the waste material of creation and should be drained off into the sewer of oblivion there to rot in cold obstruction like any other excrement." Yet without this class of workers, however obstreperous, the West would hardly have developed so rapidly. Wobblies did the rough and heavy work: cut the timber, harvested the crops, dug out the minerals. And however hopeless their struggle against society, they had courage and militancy which were colorful and exciting.

Their spirit found expression in the IWW songs sung at their union meetings, in harvest camps, and on the picket line: "Are you a Wobbly?" "Dump the Bosses Off Your Back," "Paint 'Er Red," "What We Want," "The Red Flag," and "Hallelujah! I'm a Bum!"

> O! I like my boss,
>   He's a good friend of mine,
> And that's why I'm starving
>   Out on the picket-line!
> Hallelujah! I'm a bum!
>   Hallelujah! Bum again!
> Hallelujah! Give us a hand-out
>   To revive us again!

There were IWW strikes in the mining fields, on lumbering projects, in the construction camps of the Northwest; in Pacific Coast canneries, eastern textile mills, midwestern steel and meat packing plants, and among streetcar workers, window cleaners, and longshoremen. The IWW leaders, and notably "Big Bill" Haywood, who had stayed with the IWW in spite of the withdrawal of the Western Federation of Miners, were ready to back up the unorganized workers—anywhere, anytime. They directed strike activity, manned picket lines, provided relief for the workers' families, and agitated and organized with a reckless ardor that made the tactics of the AFL seem pale and insipid.

When local authorities tried to suppress the IWW and threw its organizers into jail, "free-speech" fights broke out from Walla Walla, Washington, to New Bedford, Massachusetts. There was no sooner news of arrests in some particular town than the Wobblies would arrive upon the scene by the scores to exercise their constitutional rights and defy the police. When the first contingents were jailed, others took their place until the harassed authorities found the burden upon the community so great that they had no alternative but to set their prisoners free. The Wobblies would pour from the jail triumphant, ready again to agitate, to picket, to battle for their rights.

The West was the scene of the most spectacular strikes and free-speech fights waged by the Wobblies, but one of their greatest victories was won in a struggle of textile workers in Lawrence, Massachusetts, in 1912. In spite of eastern fears of an intrusion of frontier violence, however, this strike was marked by rigid discipline. The IWW realized, as always, that violence only provided the occasion for repression, and so they did everything possible to maintain order. They also realized that revolutionary rhetoric did not fill empty stomachs. Without any support from other unions, which were jealous of their invasion of an eastern factory town, the IWW leaders in Lawrence directed all their energies toward maintaining the united front among the strikers which ultimately forced the employers' submission.

A reduction in wages for the 30,000 workers in the Lawrence textile mills, about half of whom were employed by the American Woolen Company, brought on the strike. The earnings of the mill hands, largely Italians, Poles, Lithuanians, and Russians, averaged less than $9 a week—when the mills were running full time. Moreover, in addition to insufficient wages and long hours, a premium system had been introduced to speed up the work under conditions which imposed terrific pressure and tension. The pay cuts were the last straw. The angry workers spontaneously began to walk out on January 12, 1912, as the bells of the city hall rang a general alarm, in a concerted protest which soon involved some 20,000 men and women.

There were some union members in the mills. A few belonged to the United Textile Workers, an AFL affiliate, and something like a thousand to the IWW. The rest were unorganized. Foreseeing the strike, the IWW members had already sent to headquarters for help, and Joseph J. Ettor, a member of the general executive board, hurried to Lawrence and was soon joined by another IWW leader, Arturo Giovannitti. These two men at once took over virtual control of the strike, organized it on a realistic basis, and imposed strict discipline. Ettor arranged great mass meetings to keep the strikers united, established picket lines, and saw that relief was given to the needy and suffering families whose sole sources of income had been abruptly cut off. Relief was, indeed, his greatest problem because over half of the city's population of 85,000 were either strikers or their dependents. General committees were formed for each separate national group to distribute supplies, maintain soup kitchens, and provide other aid.

The first suggestion of lawlessness was the discovery, announced in scare headlines in the press, of dynamite planted in various parts of the city. The IWW was at once accused of importing its terroristic methods, and such sympathy as had at first been aroused for the strikers turned to angry resentment. "When the strikers use or prepare to use dynamite," the *New York Times* declared editorially, "they display a fiendish lack of humanity which ought to place them beyond the comfort of religion until they have repented."

The strikers protested at once that the dynamite planting was none of their doing. Events were to vindicate them. Before the strike was over, it was proved that a local undertaker had planted the dynamite, in an obvious effort to discredit the strikers and particularly the IWW, and that the plot had been contrived by persons closely associated with the mill owners themselves. With the arrest of the head of the American Woolen Company on the charge of being implicated in this scheme, even the most conservative newspapers strongly assailed the strategy of trying to involve the workers in pretended bombing plots. The *Iron Age* spoke of "betrayal of the cause of employers generally," and the New York *Evening Post* condemned "an offense on the part of capitalism which passes the worst acts ever committed by labor unions."

In the meantime the American Woolen Company, still refusing even to consider the workers' demands, tried to reopen the mills. This move caused a violent clash between strikers and police, and during the struggle an Italian woman was shot and killed. The authorities promptly declared martial law, twenty-two militia companies were called out to patrol the streets in order to prevent any public meetings or talks, and Ettor and Giovannitti were arrested as accessories to murder.

Neither the strike committee nor the IWW allowed these developments to drive them into unwarranted counterviolence or to lessen their determination to see the strike through. "Big Bill" Haywood took charge after the arrest of Ettor and Giovannitti, and in spite of his own and the IWW's revolutionary policies, he continued to insist upon an attitude of passive resistance. With such control, the workers held firm. The protection offered by the militia to employees desiring to return to their jobs did not encourage any defections from the ranks. "In the spinning room every belt was in motion, the whir of machinery sounded on every side," wrote a newspaper reporter visiting one of the mills, "yet not a single operative was at work and not a single machine carried a spool of yarn."

The problem of feeding the strikers became increasingly difficult, however, and early in February the committee evolved a plan which had the double objective of helping to meet immediate needs and dramatically calling public attention to them. Labor sympathizers in other cities were asked to provide temporary homes for the children of the strikers. The response was immediate, and several hundred children were sent to other communties. Alarmed at the effect of this move, which the head of the United Textile Workers took the lead in denouncing as made solely "to keep up the agitation and further the propaganda of the Industrial Workers of the World," the Lawrence authorities stated that no more children would be allowed to leave the city. When the strike committee undertook to send another group away, the police forcibly interfered under circumstances which were more successful in creating sympathy for the strikers than anything else could possibly have been.

"The station itself," read a report of the Women's Committee of Philadelphia, which was to take care of the children, "was surrounded by police and militia. . . . When the time approached to depart the children, arranged in a long line, two by two, in orderly procession, with their parents near at hand, were about to make their way to the train when the police, who had by that time stationed themselves along both sides of the door, closed in on us with their clubs, beating right and left, with no thought of the children, who were in the most desperate danger of being trampled to death. The mothers and children were thus hurled in a mass and bodily dragged to a military truck, and even then clubbed, irrespective of the cries of the panic-striken women and children."

This was perhaps the turning point in the strike. Neither the Lawrence authorities nor the mill owners could withstand the flood of protests from every part of the country. There were to be further at-tacks on the strikers and further arrests—the latter totaled 296 during the two months of the strike—but with the picket lines holding firm, the American Woolen Company finally admitted defeat and on March 12 offered terms which virtually met all the workers' demands. Wages were to be increased from 5 to 25 per cent, with time and a quarter for overtime; the premium system was equitably adjusted; and there was to be no discrimination in rehiring the strikers. At a great mass meeting on the Lawrence Common, Haywood advised acceptance of this offer, and the mill operatives agreed to return to their jobs.

A final episode was the trial of Ettor and Giovannitti. For a time it appeared that they would not be given a fair hearing and were likely to be convicted in spite of the lack of any evidence directly implicating them in the murder with which they were charged. The IWW organized a defense committee which collected $60,000, and the workers in Lawrence, declaring that unless the authorities opened the jail doors they would close the mill doors, went on a twenty-four-hour protest strike—15,000 strong. In the final outcome, both men were found innocent and on being released were wildly greeted by crowds who held them in no small part responsible for the victory which the Lawrence textile employees had won under their direction.

Before the trial ended, the two accused men made speeches to the jury setting forth their position in which they frankly avowed the revolutionary aims of the IWW and their refusal to be intimidated by the police. That of Giovannitti, a poet in his own right, whose revolutionary verses are to be found in many anthologies, was eloquent and moving.

"Let me tell you," he declared, "that the first strike that breaks again in this Commonwealth or any other place in America where the work and help and the intelligence of Joseph J. Ettor and Arturo Giovannitti will be needed and necessary, there we shall go again, regardless of any fear or of any threat. We shall return again to our humble efforts, obscure, unknown, misunderstood soldiers of this mighty army of the working class of the world, which, out of the shadows and darkness of the past, is striving towards the destined goal, which is the emancipation of human kind, which is the establishment of love and brotherhood and justice for every man and every woman on this earth."

The IWW had won an astounding triumph in Lawrence. Its membership among the textile workers jumped almost overnight to 18,000, and this renewed vitality appeared to promise still further

growth. Alarm was created within the AFL as to the future development of its aggressive strike tactics, while even greater fears were
aroused in the business community over the possible spread of radical
doctrines among American workers. "Are we to expect," an article in
the *Survey* asked, "that instead of playing the game respectably, or
else frankly breaking out into lawless riot which we know well enough
how to deal with, the laborers are to listen to a subtle anarchistic
philosophy which challenges the fundamental idea of law and order,
inculcating such strange doctrines as those of 'direct action,' 'syn-
dicalism,' 'the general strike,' and 'violence'? . . . We think that our
whole current morality as to the sacredness of property and even of
life is involved in it."

These fears soon proved to be groundless. Lawrence represented
the high point of the IWW's success among immigrant industrial
workers, not the beginning of a revolutionary groundswell. The aftermath of Lawrence also disclosed how much more powerful employers
were than unions. With the textile industry deep in recession by 1913,
Lawrence employers shifted production from union to nonunion
mills, discharged union militants, and showered promotions and
favors on the ethnic groups most resistant to the IWW, mostly Irish
and French Canadian. As the IWW seemed unable to protect
Lawrence's workers against employer tactics, most of its members
drifted away and sought comfort and security in their families and
ethnic associations.

The next important strike in which the IWW participated was a har-
binger of its decline. Trouble developed in 1913 in the silk mills of
Paterson, New Jersey, and among other leaders of the Wobblies,
Haywood and Ettor were again on hand. This strike was a prolonged
and embittered struggle. The Paterson authorities were determned to
crush the revolutionary menace of the IWW, and it in turn felt that
too much depended on a victory in this strike to give in. The brutality
of the police in arresting strikers on any pretense, clubbing them into
insensibility when they resisted, and breaking up their picket lines,
was notorious. Yet the strike went on. Among others who were won to
sympathy for the silk workers was John Reed, the young Harvard-
educated revolutionary who was to write *Ten Days that Shook the
World* and be buried in the walls of the Kremlin. Describing the scene
at Paterson, he said that he could never forget "the exultant men who
had blithely defied the lawless brutality of the city and gone to prison
laughing and singing." But after five grueling months, the exhaustion

of their funds and the growing need of their families forced the strikers to surrender. The IWW had to admit defeat.

Succeeding years saw the Wobblies engaged in scores of minor strikes, while their membership greatly fluctuated as local unions broke up and the migratory construction workers and harvest hands drifted in and out of the organization. There were clashes with authority in many instances and, in the western states, a mounting tendency to suppress strikes by any means and at any cost. A free-speech fight at Everett, Washington, for example, resulted in seven deaths when deputized sheriffs opened fire on a boatload of Wobblies landing in the harbor.

Upon the outbreak of the European conflict in 1914, the IWW took a decisive stand against war. "We, as members of the industrial army," read a resolution adopted at its convention that year, "will refuse to fight for any purpose except for the realization of industrial freedom." When the United States entered the war in April 1917, the IWW deemphasized its anitwar rhetoric yet declined to end class conflict and temporarily suspend the right to strike. The interests of the workers in their continuing struggle against capitalism were held equal to those of the country as defined by a government which the IWW considered no more than a committee of the ruling class. Hence in the summer of 1917 the Wobblies led strikes by western copper miners and northwestern timber workers. Employers and public officials asserted that the strikes were sabotaging vital war industries. Wobblies retorted that as soon as hours were reduced, wages increased, and working conditions improved, the strikes would end.

The public reaction was to condemn the IWW as unpatriotic, pro-German, and treasonable. In the frenzied atmosphere of war, popular feeling was everywhere whipped up to fever pitch against "Imperial Wilhelm's Warriors." And employers, seeing their chance to smash the IWW once and for all, did everything possible to add fuel to these blazing embers of hatred with the enthusiastic cooperation of much of the press. "The outrageous eruption of the IWW in the far West," the *Chicago Tribune* declared, ". . . is nothing less than rebellion." "While the country is at war," echoed the *Cleveland News*, "the only room it can afford IWW's . . . is behind the walls of penitentiaries."

Such sentiments found concrete expression. Washington acted under the provisions of the Espionage Act of 1917. In September 1917 federal agents raided IWW headquarters nationwide and seized everything they could lay their hands on. They also arrested all the organization's leaders, several hundred in all. Beginning in 1918, federal authorities held a series of mass trials of Wobblies, who were charged with obstructing the war effort. The largest such trial was held in Chicago, where Haywood and a hundred other Wobblies were found guilty of sedition and conspiracy and sentenced to up to twenty years in prison. Other, if smaller, federal trials were held in Sacramento, California, and Wichita, Kansas, with similar results. The evidence in all the trials proved flimsy and contradictory. Rarely did the prosecution link a Wobbly defendent to an overt criminal act. Speech and writings, most antedating the entry of the United States into the war, formed the bulk of the government's evidence. But in the frenzied atmosphere of war, patriotic jurors did not seek or require substantial evidence of wrongdoing. Radical intent sufficed to convict the Wobblies.

When the authorities did not act promptly enough, loyalty leagues and local vigilantes often took the law into their own hands. Brutal clubbings, horse-whippings, and tar-and-featherings took place in many communities; in at least two instances, IWW members were lynched by lawless mobs. In July 1917, some 1,200 striking miners at Bisbee, Arizona, of whom less than half were actually IWW members, were forcibly deported from the town by a posse deputized by the sheriff at the instance of a local loyalty league. They were put into cattle cars, taken across the state line, and abandoned in the desert. After thirty-six hours without food or water, they were rescued by federal authorities and taken to a detention camp in Columbus, New Mexico.

The energies of the IWW were largely absorbed during these war years in trying to defend what it insisted were its "class war prisoners." Unable to do so successfully, it soon found itself without leaders. Haywood himself eventually skipped bail and fled to Soviet Russia. The organization did not break up—it later experienced recovery of a sort—but it never regained its militant prewar strength.

Changing economic conditions in the West, marked by the increased use of farm machinery and developing automobile transportation, depleted the ranks of the migratory workers who were such an important element in the membership. The Communist Party of America, organized as a branch of the Third International in 1919, drew away many of the radical socialists. Finally, what was left of the IWW became far less aggressive with the loss of its old leadership. Emphasis was placed upon preparations for administering control of the means of production rather than upon revolutionary action to seize such control. "The 'Wobblies' . . . said nothing of revolution or class consciousness, of exploitation . . . or of the necessary overthrow of the capitalist system," a reporter for the New York *World* wrote of an unemployment conference after the war. "They talked instead of 'uninterrupted production,' 'the coordination of industrial processes.'" By the mid-1920s, the old fighting IWW had already become a legend.

The impact of the IWW on the labor movement was more important than either its membership or its erratic strike activity would suggest. Apart from such direct results as may have been obtained in improving working conditions in western mines, lumber camps, harvest fields, and occasionally in eastern factories, this revolutionary movement spectacularly centered attention on the desperate needs of vast numbers of unskilled workers and gave a new impetus to industrial unionism which even the AFL could not entirely ignore. The radical doctrine of class struggle badly shook, for a time at least, the complacency of conservative labor leaders who refused to look beyond the confines of traditional trade unionism.

In its time the IWW surely failed to achieve its avowed goals. It neither abolished the wage system nor destroyed capitalism. Perhaps it generated more fear and hostility among employers and public officials than respect and loyalty among workers. The AFL continued to dominate the labor movement and to preach its brand of "business unionism." But many of the ideas and actions associated with the IWW resonated elsewhere in the labor movement. Direct action and industrial unionism found echoes in the United Mine Workers, the Ladies' Garment Workers, and the Amalgamated Clothing Workers—all advocates of the "new unionism" with a social conscience. Moreover, as long as millions of workers earned too little, worked too long, lacked job security, and had no union representation, the IWW cause lived on. In 1965, when the IWW was unknown to most Americans or was only a faded romantic memory to a tiny minority, one among a small handful of remaining IWW loyalists told a *New York Times* reporter: "The things we set out to do in 1905 remain to be done and because they remain to be done we have a future."

The working women of Lynn, Mass., protest, early 1840s. *Wayne State University, the Archives of Labor and Urban Affairs*

Top: William H. Sylvis, 1828–1869. *Wayne State University, the Archives of Labor and Urban Affairs* Bottom: Terence V. Powderly, leader of the Knights of Labor, 1879–1893. *Ohio Historical Society* Opposite top: A typical late nineteenth-century protest march, Union Square, N.Y. Bottom: Coal miners and their wives harassing strikebreakers, late nineteenth century. *Wayne State University, the Archives of Labor and Urban Affairs*

Top: A typical labor leaders' portrait, late nineteenth century. *Wayne State University, the Archives of Labor and Urban Affairs* Bottom: United Mine Workers of America membership certificate. Opposite: The Battle of Homestead, 1892. *Wayne State University, the Archives of Labor and Urban Affairs*

Virginia, tenth annual convention of the Knights of Labor, at Richmond. Frank J. Farrell, "Colored Delegate of District Assembly No. 19," introducing General Master Workman Powderly to the Convention. *Wayne State University, the Archives of Labor and Urban Affairs*

Top: Eugene V. Debs, Pullman Strike leader and martyr. Five times Socialist Party candidate for president. *Wayne State University, the Archives of Labor and Urban Affairs* Bottom: Joseph Ettor, the Brooklyn-born IWW organizer and agitator who was prominent in the Lawrence strike, with fellow workers, 1912.

Top: An IWW gallery: William D. "Big Bill" Haywood, far right; Elizabeth Gurley Flynn, center; Carlo Tresca, to her left—Paterson, N.J., 1913. Bottom: Elizabeth Gurley Flynn speaking to striking silk workers near Paterson, N.J., 1913. *Wayne State University, the Archives of Labor and Urban Affairs*

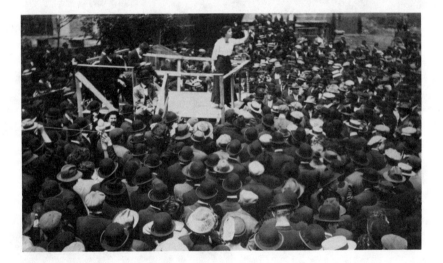

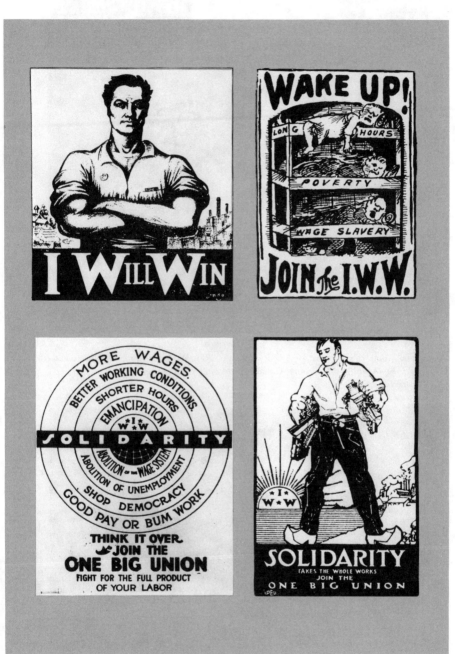

A sample of IWW propaganda stickers. *Personal collection*

Top: Samuel Gompers, spokesman for American labor, c. 1923. *Wayne State University, the Archives of Labor and Urban Affairs* Bottom: Samuel Gompers in a World War I propaganda picture, 1917–1918. *Ohio Historical Society*

Top: Mother Jones, the "coal miners' angel," on the right. Next to her, William Z. Foster, trade union and Communist party leader, c. 1922. Bottom: The Flint Sit-Down Strike, January-February, 1937, and the Women's Emergency Brigade. *Wayne State University, the Archives of Labor and Urban Affairs*

Top: The CIO's founders, John L. Lewis, Sidney Hillman, Philip Murray, at first convention, November 1938. Bottom: Sidney Hillman, president of the ACWA and Franklin D. Roosevelt's wartime adviser. *Wayne State University, the Archives of Labor and Urban Affairs*

Top: Black women railroad workers, World War II. *Photo courtesy of the National Archives* Bottom: American labor supports the war effort. Philip Murray (left), William Green, president of the AFL, 1925–1953 (right). *Ohio Historical Society*

John L. Lewis at site of Illinois coal mine disaster, 1950s. *State Historical Society of Wisconsin* Opposite: George Meany (left) and Walter Reuther (right) clasping hands at merger of AFL-CIO, 1955. *Wayne State University, the Archives of Labor and Urban Affairs*

Opposite top: Jimmy Hoffa (right) and Frank Fitzsimmons (left), both standing. *Wayne State University, the Archives of Labor and Urban Affairs* Bottom: Cesar Chavez, leader of Chicano farm workers in California, 1970. *Dave Evans/Stockton Record* Above: Dolores Huerta signaling to scabs in fields near Delano, September 24, 1965. *Harvey Richards*

Top: Solidarity Day march in Washington, D.C., September 19, 1981. Bottom: Lane Kirkland, president of the AFL-CIO, at Dartmouth College, 1982. *Courtesy of the AFL-CIO*

Striking air traffic controllers on the picket line at O'Hare International Airport in 1981. *UPI/Bettmann Newsphotos*

Striking workers at Hygrade Food Products picket in support of the striking Hormel workers, Livonia, Michigan, 1986. *UPI/Bettmann Newsphotos* Opposite: The Pittston Coal Miners strike in Kentucky, 1989. *Wide World Photos*

American worker training in Japan to work in America on a Toyota—GM joint effort. Her T-shirt says, "Doryoku," Japanese for "effort." *Wide World Photos*

The American Toyota plant in Fremont, California. *New United Motor Manufacturing, Inc.*

Joyce Miller, Vice President and Director of Social Services of ACTWU, and first woman on executive council of AFL-CIO. *Photo courtesy office of Joyce Miller*

XIII

The First World War— and After

As the shadow of impending war fell over the United States and events rapidly drove the country toward participation in the European struggle, American labor was confronted with a grave problem. Was the conflict one in which workingmen had anything at stake? Should the war effort be supported or should labor take advantage of the national crisis to promote its own class interests? The IWW had made its choice in 1914 and stuck to it. The socialists were divided, but, true to his convictions, Eugene V. Debs continued to attack what he declared to be a wholly capitalistic war—and went to jail. The American Federation of Labor, however, carrying with it the great majority of the nation's wage earners, declared and maintained complete loyalty to the government and its entire war program. As the outstanding spokesman for labor, no public figure was more exuberantly patriotic than Samuel Gompers and no one proved himself to be a more faithful adherent of the Wilson administration.

On the eve of hostilities, organized labor was stronger than it had ever been before and had won for the first time what was in effect official recognition of its role in the national economy. The report of the Commission on Industrial Relations (1915), ascribed much labor discontent to denial of the right to organize and definitely upheld trade unionism as an essential institution for the settlement of industrial disputes. The Clayton Act apparently exempted unions from prosecution under the anit-trust laws, and President Wilson had demonstrated his friendliness on many occasions and declared that no future President would ever be able to ignore the organized labor movement.

Moreover, the victory won by labor in 1916 when Congress passed the Adamson Act marked an important extension of governmental authority in the field of labor relations. It was true that Congress had acted under the imminent threat of a railway strike which would have paralyzed the national defense program, and there was widespread resentment against the tactics employed by the railway brotherhoods. But the acceptance of an obligation to safeguard the interests of the workers was nonetheless highly significant.

It was with a new sense of both power and responsibility that the spokesmen of some three million wage earners undertook to define the attitude of labor toward war. The issue was first taken up at a conference held on March 1, 1917—almost a month before hostilities, but at a time when war already appeared imminent—which was attended by representatives of seventy-nine international unions, the railway brotherhoods, and the AFL executive council. At its conclusion the conferees issued a public statement on "American Labor's Position in Peace or in War." It pledged the full support of all labor organizations should the country become directly involved in conflict with Germany.

It was not an unconditional pledge. Organized labor was determined that such gains as had been made in recent years should be protected in the event of war, and, in pledging support to the Wilson administration, insisted on full recognition of its newly attained status. The unions were to be the medium through which government would operate to seek the cooperation of wage earners, and they were to be given representation on all boards dealing with national defense. Labor was to be free to exercise the right to organize, and, while prepared to use all possible restraint, did not agree nor intend to surrender the weapon of the strike. These conditions for labor cooperation were said to be necessary because of the very nature of the aims for which the country was prepared to go to war.

"Wrapped up with the safety of this Republic," the labor leaders asserted, "are ideals of democracy, a heritage which the masses of the people received from our forefathers, who fought that liberty might live in this country—a heritage that is to be maintained and handed down to each generation with undiminished power and usefulness."

The administration was prepared to work with labor on this basis and, after American entry into the war, tried to pursue a policy in respect to industrial relations which would forestall strikes. Agreements with the American Federation of Labor specifically provided for the enforcement of trade-union standards in all government contracts; labor representatives were appointed to all appropriate government agencies, and Gompers was made a member of the Advisory Commission of the National Council of Defense. "While we are fighting for freedom," President Wilson told the AFL convention in November 1917, "we must see among other things that labor is free."

But industrial peace was not to be so easily maintained during 1917. As prices rose under the stimulus of wartime purchasing without a corresponding increase in wages, there was discontent among the workers and general demands for increases in pay. When such demands were not met, strikes broke out on a scale which exceeded even prewar years. Before 1917 ended, they reached a total of 4,450 and involved over a million workers.

Many of these strikes were instigated by the IWW. Under its radical leadership, there were threatening outbreaks in the lumber camps of the Northwest, among shipyard workers on the Pacific Coast, and in the copper mines of Arizona. Labor unrest was by no means limited, however, to workers who fell within the radical fringe of the labor movement. Many of the conservative and patriotic unions affiliated with the AFL felt justified in making wartime demands and backing them up with strikes that seriously interrupted production in defense industries.

By the beginning of 1918 this situation threatened to block the flow of military supplies overseas. While efforts were constantly being made to resolve labor disputes through special wage adjustment boards and a Mediation Commission which had been set up by President Wilson in August 1917, the government felt obliged to intervene still further in order to assure essential industrial output. Both the friendliness of the administration toward organized labor and simple expediency dictated a policy which would win the workers' support rather than one of suppressing strikes by force. Representatives of labor and management were consequently appointed to a War Labor

Conference Board, and, after it had unanimously agreed upon a set of principles to govern future labor relations, the President appointed, upon its recommendation in April 1918, a National War Labor Board to serve as a final court of appeal to settle all industrial disputes which could not be resolved through other means. It was composed of five representatives of labor and five of management, with two joint chairmen representative of the public: former President Taft and Frank P. Walsh, who had been chairman of the Commission on Industrial Relations.

The general principles upon which the National War Labor Board operated were immensely significant as a reflection of new governmental attitudes toward labor and also foreshadowed those later to be incorporated in the labor legislation of the New Deal. In return for a general pledge that there would be no further strikes or lockouts for the duration of the war, the Wilson administration was prepared to accord labor full support for virtually all its traditional demands. The right to organize and bargain collectively through "chosen representatives" was definitely recognized and was not in any way to be abridged or denied by employers; all existing agreements in respect to union or open shops were to be upheld on their prewar basis; the eight-hour day was to be applied as far as possible; women entering industry were to be given equal pay for equal work; and there was complete acceptance of "the right of all workers, including common laborers, to a living wage. . . which will ensure the subsistence of the worker and his family in health and reasonable comfort."

Federal labor policies succeeded in curbing resentment among workers and in satisfying the demands of most AFL trade unions. As a result of the tight labor market and organized labor's greater status, more workers than ever before won the eight-hour day, and trade unions grew enormously. Because few industrial disputes paralyzed war production, no such drastic measures as a manpower draft, compulsory arbitration, or antistrike laws were enacted. In those few cases, however, in which strikes interfered with the war effort—most notably among loggers in the Pacific Northwest and munitions workers in Bridgeport, Connecticut—stronger action resulted, including in the former case the use of troops as workers. But, overall, the AFL upheld its side of the bargain into which it had tacitly entered, and Secretary of War Newton D. Baker declared on one occasion that it had proved to be "more willing to keep in step than capital."

As the principal spokesman for labor, Gompers continued to support the war effort in every possible way and succeeded in completely identifying the AFL with American foreign policy. He vociferously attacked all pacifist or suspected pro-German groups, promoted the American Alliance for Labor and Democracy as a counter move to socialist propaganda for peace, and staunchly upheld Americanism. "I want to express my admiration," was President Wilson's warm tribute, "of his patriotic courage, his large vision, and his statesman-like sense of what had to be done." In the fall of 1918, Gompers went abroad to attend an interallied labor conference, and he was in Paris during the peace conference as a member of the Commission on International Labor Legislation.

Labor policy was reflected in the wartime gains of the workers and the growth of unionism. Wages gradually rose until average earnings in manufacturing, transportation, and coal mining topped the $1,000 mark, and the unions in 1919 had over a million more members than in 1916—a total of 4,125,000. When the government took control of the railways, the recognition previously granted only to the railway brotherhoods was extended to shopmen, yardmen, maintenance-of-way workers, railway clerks, and telegraphers. In other industries where unionization had had hard going, there were important advances—among packinghouse employees, seamen and longshoremen, electrical workers, and machinists. The war had opened up great opportunities, and American labor had made the most of them.

The war emergency also led to substantial, if sometimes temporary, changes in the compensation of the American labor force. Eastern and southern European immigrants, who had once formed the mud-sill of the industrial labor force, improved their skills and jobs. Employers substituted them for more skilled or better-paid American-born workers who volunteered for military service or had been drafted. Many immigrant workers who before the war considered their American experience a temporary sojourn now began to think of themselves more commonly as Americans. Wartime job promotions and governmental and corporate Americanization campaigns transformed large numbers of recent immigrants into citizens, who now demanded their due in the factory as well as in the public arena.

Employers turned to other new sources of labor to fill empty factory places. Migration of southern blacks to the North, which had been a small stream from the end of Reconstruction to 1914, reached large proportions after American entry into the war. Between 200,000 and 300,000 southern blacks migrated to regions associated with heavy industries and the production of primary metal products—Pittsburgh-Youngstown, Cleveland-Akron, Chicago-Gary, St. Louis-East St. Louis. Black, native-born Americans, for half a century outdistanced in the job market by white European immigrants, were suddenly wanted, if not preferred. The same could be said of another group—Americans of Mexican origin and also Mexican citizens in the United States. They, too, helped to fill the ranks of new workers in northern centers of heavy industry and war production.

Women formed a third new element in the wartime work force. Once confined primarily to low-paying secondary jobs in domestic and retail service, they now found employment in foundries, steel mills, public transit, the railroads, indeed anywhere labor was needed. Not only did women who were already in the work force move from secondary to primary labor market jobs, but hundreds of thousands of women also left the household to take wage-labor jobs for the first time.

All in all, hitherto socially and economically marginal individuals and groups, people whose main prewar function had been to form a reserve labor army, now became citizen-workers, essential elements in the national war machine.

The conclusion of hostilities at once created a new situation. As wartime restraints were removed and government surrendered such controls as had been exercised by the National War Labor Board, both labor and industry prepared for the inevitable renewal of their historic contest. The precarious wartime truce expired. Labor was militantly determined not only to maintain the gains which it had made during the war but also to win further recognition of its rights, and industry was no less bound to free itself from all governmental control, check any further advance of unionization, and reassert its power. No holds were barred by either antagonist as industrial strife broke out in 1919 on a scale greater than the country had experienced ever before. The strikes that year were to be nationwide in their scope and would directly and dangerously affect the whole process of reconversion to peace.

Wages were an immediate cause for many of these disputes. The wartime price rises continued unchecked in 1919—the cost of living would ultimately reach twice the prewar level—and workers began to feel the pinch despite the high pay they were still able to command.

But the basic issue of union security was far less easily settled than wage adjustments. Many employers were willing to grant wage demands or at least compromise on them, but saw in any extension of collective bargaining a threat to their management of their own business. They refused to recognize union spokesmen, and concessions which had been made under the pressure of war were widely withdrawn.

The vital importance of this issue of union recognition was brought out in the one attempt which the Wilson administration made in postwar years to reconcile the differences between management and labor. The various agencies for handling labor disputes had been promptly scrapped after the Armistice, but, as the number of strikes increased, the President summoned a National Industrial Conference, this time composed of representatives of labor, industry and the public, in the hope that some basis could be found for labor peace. Fundamental disagreements at once developed over the nature of collective bargaining and the obligation of an employer to deal with men or groups of men who were not his own employees. The labor representatives insisted on the right "to organize without discrimination" as the only means of assuring recognition of national unions, and the conference collapsed when the public representatives, a group somehow including John D. Rockefeller, Jr., and Elbert H. Gary, chairman of the United States Steel Corporation, upheld those of industry in refusing to grant this concession.

While the conferees met in Washington, workers acted for themselves in the streets and factories of America. Before the year ended, over 4,000,000 workers participated in more than 3,500 strikes. A general strike paralyzed Seattle for four days; Boston police walked off the job, and in the fall steelworkers and coal miners engaged in nationwide strikes. Events in Europe gave the American strikes a foreboding character. The Bolshevik Revolution in Russia and the ensuing Russian civil war, a revolution in Bavaria, street fighting in Berlin, a Communist seizure of power in Hungary, and Italian workers' occupation of factories in Turin seemed to turn the world upside down. Many employers, governmental officials, and worried citizens saw the American strikes as the cutting edge of domestic revolution, not as an expression of justified, if long dormant, workers' grievances.

Employers and their governmental allies lost no time in identifying strikers as "Reds" or in suggesting that the strikes were ordered by

Bolsheviks in the Kremlin. The Communist International (Comintern) indeed preached world revolution and had American adherents in the two Communist parties which left-wing rebels from the SPA founded in 1919. But domestic Communists, whether American- or foreign-born, had little influence or visibility in the mainstream labor movement. Simultaneously, the IWW by 1919 acted largely as a legal defense organization.

Ironically, the employers and public officials who linked strikers to Bolsheviks found an unwitting ally in Gompers. In his own eagerness to dissociate trade unionists from Bolsheviks and to establish labor's respectability, Gompers acted as a strident red-baiter. His persistent attacks on Bolshevism magnified the extent of domestic radicalism and led some to suspect that there might in fact be "red rats" in American labor's woodpile. Thus the AFL leader inadvertently assisted employers in their efforts to associate strikers with Bolshevism. His warnings about radical influences also lent credence to demands from employers and influential citizens for forceful suppression of the strike wave in 1919.

The more sympathetic feelings about organized labor which had arisen between 1912 and 1918 evaporated as a reaction swelled against Woodrow Wilson's foreign and domestic policies. Snide observers spoke sarcastically of factory employees riding to work in their cars and buying silk shirts for themselves and silk stockings for their wives—at the very time that they were demanding higher wages. The strikes awoke "unstinted condemnation from almost every walk of life," one newspaper stated; another declared that the only One Big Union the nation would tolerate was "the one whose symbol is the Stars and Stripes."

The advocates of economic and social stability demanded a national antistrike policy. By the end of 1919, as strike after strike was collapsing, the *Literary Digest* pointed out that sentiment had strongly and definitely crystallized in favor of federal, state, and local police intervention in support of the employers and against the workers.

A strike which aroused anxiety in the postwar period was the so-called general strike which broke out in Seattle in February 1919. It was not actually to prove very important, but the background of violence out of which it grew and the very effort to call out all workers created national concern and evoked what were already becoming the inevitable charges of Bolshevism.

The incident which set off this strike was a demand on the part of shipyard workers in Seattle for higher wages. When it was bluntly rejected by their employers, the men walked out. The Central Labor Committee in Seattle at this time was controlled by James A. Duncan, a member of the Machinists Union who had risen to power amid the embittered industrial strife promoted throughout the Northwest by the IWW. He was an outspoken opponent of the conservative labor policies followed by the AFL, had strongly opposed entry into the war, and was sympathetic toward Soviet Russia. Seizing the opportunity to show labor solidarity, he called a general strike of all workers in Seattle. Some 60,000 responded, and for five hectic days the industrial life of the city was almost paralyzed although a union committee insured that all citizens received essential health and welfare services.

The general strike engendered considerable local and national resistance to labor's demands. Unable to coerce their adversaries to surrender, indeed unsure of their ultimate objectives, the local Seattle unions began to withdraw their support from the Central Labor Committee, and the strike completely collapsed. In the meantime, however, Mayor Ole Hanson had burst into the nation's headlines with sensational statements that the whole thing had been a Bolshevist plot which was crushed only by his own heroic measures.

Even more disturbing was the strike some months later of the Boston police. Discontented with low wages and other aspects of their jobs which they considered unfair, the police had formed a union, which was called the Boston Social Club, and applied to the American Federation of Labor for a charter. The Boston police commissioner promptly stated that no members of the force would be allowed to join a union, suspended nineteen of the men who had done so, and began to recruit volunteers to take over should any union activity continue. Outraged at what they considered such unwarranted and arbitrary action, the police took matters in their own hands and, on September 9, suddenly went on strike. Boston found itself without police protection that night, and its nervous citizens hardly knew what outbreaks of crime and violence to expect. There was a good deal of rowdyism by bands of hoodlums, but no such general lawlessness as had been feared. The next day volunteers and state guards took over the duties of police, and complete order was restored.

Settlement of the highly involved issues at stake was not so easy.

Charges and counter charges flew back and forth over responsibility for the strike and the failure to place on duty immediately the volunteer force which had supposedly been trained for just such an emergency. The police commissioner and the mayor were at odds. While the former refused to consider the grievances which had led to the strike or to reinstate any of the men who had taken part in it, the latter showed a good deal more sympathy for the strikers and charged that the whole affair had been miserably mishandled. From AFL officials came accusations that the police commissioner was more interested in trying to discredit labor than in solving the controversy, and that he had virtually goaded the police on to strike. Ethnic conflict between a city administration and police force largely Irish, Roman Catholic, and Democratic in character and a police commissioner and state government essentially Protestant and Republican exacerbated the issues in dispute.

Whatever was brought out in support of the police, however, influential citizens generally condemned them for deserting their posts and upheld the police commmissioner in his refusal to reemploy them. A "crime against civilization" was President Wilson's sharp comment on the strike, and a future President won nationwide fame by an even more positive statement. Calvin Coolidge, then Governor of Massachusetts, was requested by Gompers to remove the police commissioner and reinstate the strikers. He refused. "There is no right to strike against the public safety," read his terse telegram, "by anybody, anywhere, anytime." The public resoundingly cheered such sentiments; the Boston police were not reinstated; and Coolidge was started on the road to the White House.

Although the Seattle general strike and the Boston police strike attracted the attention of the entire country, they were local affairs. A great deal more significant in their national, industry-wide implications were strikes in steel and coal. They were defeated under the conditions prevailing in 1919, but they foreshadowed a new pattern of industrial conflict that was to be greatly accentuated after the Second World War. The steel strike was especially important. If the steel workers had been successful, the whole labor history of the 1920s might have followed a completely different course. Defeat of the strike, however, postponed effective organization of the workers in this basic industry for another eighteen years.

Conditions in the steel mills fostered universal discontent and underscored what labor leaders declared was an imperative need for unionization. Wages remained low in spite of wartime advances and were steadily falling further behind the continued rise in living costs. A twelve-hour day, six days a week, was still in effect for something over half the labor force, and the average working week was just under sixty-nine hours. Among the highly diversified immigrant groups which made up the majority of employees, living conditions were a bitter travesty upon the promise of a more abundant life which had drawn them to the Land of Opportunity.

Organizational progress on other sectors of the labor front had no parallel in the steel industry. Since suppression of the strikes of the old Amalgamated Association of Iron, Steel and Tin Workers in 1901 and 1910, no further efforts had been made toward unionization. While the Amalgamated was still in existence, it was a small craft union that did not touch the interests of the great mass of unskilled workers.

The first step leading toward the strike was the formation, in the summer of 1918, of an organizing committee made up of representatives of twenty-four unions having jurisdiction in the steel industry. Its objective was not only improvement of conditions in the mills but also the conquest of this key industry by union labor. The guiding spirit was William Z. Foster, a radical exponent of direct economic action whose early experience in industrial conflict was won in the ranks of the IWW and who later was to become a leading Communist. His organizational skill was outstanding and, as secretary-treasurer of the associated union committee, he was put in charge of this "one mighty drive to organize the steel plants of America." When Foster's organizing campaign began, several federal officials, most notably Frank Walsh, cochairperson of the War Labor Board, assisted it.

Within a year the number of organized workers in the steel mills jumped to 100,000, and an attempt was made to open negotiations with Chairman Gary of the United States Steel Corporation for a trade agreement. When he completely disregarded this request, a strike vote was taken and, in behalf of the steel workers, the union committee demanded collective bargaining, the eight-hour day, and an increase in wages. Gary's reply to further overtures for the discussion of these demands was blunt and unequivocal. "Our corporation and subsidiaries, although they do not combat labor unions as such," he stated, "decline to discuss business with them." The strike was then officially set for September 22, and by the end of the month nearly 350,000 men had quit work in nine states.

The steel industry was ready to meet this challenge and in its determined efforts to break the strike received the full cooperation of local, state, and even federal authorities. Thousands of strikebreakers were brought in, particularly large numbers of blacks; labor spies were hired to do everything possible to stir up animosity and antagonism among the different ethnic groups in the mills; and deputized guards, local police and state constabularies smashed picket lines and broke up strike meetings with little regard for civil liberties. Violence was held down by the enforcement of martial law in many localities, federal troops being dispatched to Gary, Indiana, under Major General Leonard Wood, but some twenty persons were killed—eighteen of them workers—before the strike was over.

The steel companies also opened up a terrific barrage through newspaper advertisements to discourage the strikers and convince public opinion that the whole thing was a plot hatched in Moscow for the overthrow of American Capitalism. The strike was not between the workers and their employers, the steel companies proclaimed, but between revolutionists and America. It could not win because the United States would "never stand for the 'red' rule of Bolshevism, I.W.W.ism or any other 'ism' that seeks to tear down the Constitution." Rumors were even circulated "that the Huns had a hand in fomenting the strike, hoping to retard industrial progress."

So great were the excitement and controversy stirred up under these circumstances that a commission of inquiry was set up by the Inter-church World Movement, an organization of Protestant churches, to investigate the strike. It could find no evidence whatsoever of the sinister intrigues which the steel companies alleged they had uncovered, and it stated that it was far more profitable to consider the workers' uprising in the light of industrial history than "in the glare of baseless excitement over Bolshevism." The repeated emphasis upon the radical, anarchistic, communist aspects of the strike, however, and Foster's left-wing views, served their purposes in spite of uncontradicted disclosures of the harsh conditions in the mills. Bolshevism became an issue. The very fact that so many of the steel workers were "hunkies," "dagoes" and "wops," was taken as convincing evidence that they were un-American, revolutionary and controlled by Moscow.

The strike committee could find no way to combat this propaganda successfully. There were withdrawals of support on the part of the sponsoring unions and discouragement spread through the ranks of the strikers themselves. Late in November the union committee consequently asked the Interchurch Commission to mediate and agreed to accept whatever plan it might suggest for ending the dispute. Gary refused to listen to any peace proposals. The strikers sought "the closed shop, Soviets, and the forcible distribution of property," he declared: ". . . there is absolutely no issue." The strike dragged on but the disheartened men now began to drift back to work. In January 1920, the leaders gave up. The strike was called off and such men as had not in the meantime been black-listed returned without having won a single concession.

"The United States Steel Corporation," the Interchurch Commission declared in a final report, "was too big to be beaten by 300,000 workingmen. It had too large a cash surplus, too many allies among other businesses, too much support from government officers, local and national, too strong influence with social institutions such as the press and the pulpit, it spread over too much of the earth—still retaining absolutely centralized control—to be defeated by widely scattered workers of many minds, many fears, varying states of pocketbook and under a comparatively improvised leadership."

The organization of steel was decisive if labor was to unionize other mass-production industries from which it had so far been barred. The business and financial community fully recognized the significance of the strike of 1919 as a showdown between the open shop and industrial unionism. The United States Steel Corporation was backed to the hilt. J. P. Morgan assured Gary of his full approval of the stand he had taken in refusing to deal with the unions. Every effort was made—and made successfully—to hold out the bogey of Bolshevism as a justification for refusing even to consider the demands of the workers. The results of the strike were not only a return to the twelve-hour day, but a return to uncontrolled paternalism and antiunionism in the country's most important industry.

Even before the end of the steel strike, conflict in the bituminous coal fields came to a head. The United Mine Workers had concluded a contract with the operators covering the war period, and with the higher prices of 1919 asked for an adjustment in wages which had not been raised since 1917. They proposed a 60 per cent increase in pay and adoption of the thirty-hour week in order to combat the unemployment resulting from the falling off of wartime need for fuel. The operators not only refused to consider the miners' demands, admittedly great, but they also insisted that the old contract was still in effect because the war was not yet technically over. A strike that was to involve 425,000 miners was then called for November 1.

The danger to the national economy of any prolonged stoppage in the mining of coal, as on other occasions both before and since 1919, was a matter of grave public concern. The government had already warned that a strike would be illegal under wartime legislation governing the coal industry. To the consternation not only of the United Mine Workers but of American labor generally, the formerly friendly Wilson administration now took the drastic step of securing an injunction, granted by Judge Albert B. Anderson of the federal district court in Indianapolis, which prohibited any further strike activity by union officials and called upon them to cancel the strike order.

Intervention by the government, in the face of what had been taken by labor as a pledge not to use its wartime authority to suppress strikes, aroused a storm of protest. The American Federation of Labor condemned the injunction as "an outrageous proceeding . . . which strikes at the very foundation of justice and freedom." It called upon the miners not to give in to governmental pressure and promised them full support in continuing their struggle.

The acting president of the United Mine Workers in 1919, John L. Lewis, was a forty-year-old labor leader who during the war years had been the union's chief statistician and who was not well-known outside union circles. But Lewis was to step at once into the popular limelight. He did so by calling off the strike. Aware that Justice Department officials were tapping his phones, that unnaturalized immigrant strikers and union officers were subject to peremptory deportation, and that Washington was prepared to use force to break a national coal strike, Lewis refused to heed the AFL's advice to stand firm. Instead of risking his own imprisonment and the destruction of his union, he advised retreat. First criticizing Wilson and government by injunction, Lewis then declared publicly: "We are Americans. We cannot fight our government."

The miners themselves, as Lewis expected, refused to follow his orders. They stayed away from the pits in spite of the cancellation of the strike order. Before they could be induced to return, further conferences were held in Washington, and an understanding was reached whereby the operators granted an immediate 14 per cent wage increase and agreed to leave final settlement of wage demands and other issues in dispute to a special Bituminous Coal Commission. The final award raised the wage increase to 27 per cent, almost half of what the miners had originally asked, but ignored altogether the demand for a thirty-hour week.

The strike had been ended by government action. Even though the miners won considerable gains, the important aspect of the controversy was the application of injunction law. A vital precedent had been established. In his decision to comply with the government's orders, Lewis showed a keen realization of how far the government was prepared to go to suppress strikes. The resentment that had been displayed in the case of the steel strike was even more intensified when the coal miners threatened the nation with a fuel famine just as winter drew on.

President Wilson declared the coal strike to be "wrong both morally and legally." Congress endorsed his position, and editorials throughout the country applauded the use of the injunction. "Neither the miners nor any other organized minority," the *Chambersburg* [Pa.] *Public-Opinion* commented, "has the right to plunge the country into economic and social chaos . . . A labor autocracy is as dangerous as a capital autocracy." "When enormous combinations of workingmen," the *Philadelphia Public Ledger* said, "deliberately enter upon a country-wide plan to take the country by the throat and compel the employers in that particular field of industry to yield to the demands of the men, they are engaged in an unlawful conspiracy." And the *Chicago Daily News* bluntly stated: "The public is weary of industrial strife. It is determined to protect itself."

The issue of Bolshevism was of course raised again. Senator Miles Poindexter of the State of Washington said that the strike was the penalty paid for an over-lenient governmental policy towards "anarchists and murderous communists." After its settlement, the *New York Tribune* declared that the firm policy finally adopted by the administration was both an example and a warning: "Tell this in Russia, proclaim it on the streets of Moscow, sear it into the mind of all domestic disintegrators."

Although the strikes of 1919 resulted in a sharp setback for labor and there was a feeling of embittered disillusionment with what was regarded as betrayal at the hands of the Wilson administration, the wartime advance in unionism was not yet halted. Labor was still militant in spite of defeats. In many important areas it succeeded in winning the wage increases for which it fought, and there was continued expansion in union membership. Among the 110 unions now affiliated with the AFL, machinists, nonoperating railway workers, textile operatives, and seamen showed especially important gains, and in such industries as food and clothing both unskilled and semiskilled workers were being organized.

The AFL, nevertheless, found itself in an increasingly difficult position. The government support on which it had counted in pursuing its program of business unionism had given way to a revival of injunction law, and consequently there was strong pressure to adopt more aggressive tactics. The Federation leadership still refused, however, to be drawn into political action and, in the face of new suggestions for a labor party, expressly reaffirmed the traditional nonpolitical objectives which had always governed AFL policy. At a conference in December 1919, a new "Labor's Bill of Rights" was proclaimed which called for union recognition, a living wage, and restrictions on the use of injunctions, but beyond this the Federation would not go.

Circumstances soon made such a program more difficult than ever. Before the end of 1920, a sudden, sharp depression struck the country. The collapse of the inflationary postwar boom led to tumbling prices all along the line, business failures, industrial stagnation, universal wage cuts, and unemployment on a large scale. By midsummer 1921, an estimated five million workers had lost their jobs. Industry took quick advantage of these circumstances to intesify its antiunion campaign. Injunctions and arrests broke a strike of the seamen's union, and subsequent blacklisting reduced it to less than a fifth of its wartime strength. The packinghouse employees were so badly defeated that the industry reverted to the open shop. And in 1922 the railway shopmen, under fire from all sides, suffered an even more significant reverse.

The latter strike broke out when the Railway Labor Board, set up to govern employee relations after the railroads had been returned to private ownership in 1920, abrogated agreements which had been negotiated during the war, abolished overtime, and authorized wage cuts totaling $60,000,000. The railway brotherhoods were not affected by these pay reductions and the maintenance-of-way workers agreed to arbitration, but the members of the six shop craft unions were incensed at the board's apparent submission to employer pressure. A strike was called and, on July 1, 1922, the shopmen walked out, 400,000 strong.

From the very first, they found the going hard. With the Railway Labor Board declaring their action an outlaw strike, the brotherhoods cooperating with management to keep the trains running, and President Warren G. Harding warning against any interference with the mails, the balance of power was almost entirely against the shopmen. Reality was perhaps most graphically revealed by the fact that among the strikebreakers brought in under the protection of deputized guards and militia, were hundreds of college boys. But this was not all. On September 1, 1922, as the strike appeared about to collapse in any event, the government stepped in to deliver the coup de grace. Attorney General Harry M. Daugherty obtained from Judge James H. Wilkerson, of the federal district court in Chicago, what has often been described as "the most sweeping injunction ever issued in a labor dispute."

It prohibited picketing of all sorts, strike meetings, statements to the public, the expenditure of union funds to carry on the strike, and the use of any means of communications by the leaders to direct it. No one was permitted to aid the strikers "by letters, telegrams, telephones, word of mouth," or to persuade anyone to stop work by "jeers, entreaties, arguments, persuasion, rewards or otherwise." Daugherty intended to break the strike at any cost. "So long and to the extent that I can speak for the government of the United States," he told the press, "I will use the power of the government within my control to prevent the labor unions of the country from destroying the open shop."

This drastic move caused vehement debate throughout the country. Not only those newspapers sympathetic to labor but many others, perhaps influenced by partisan considerations in a good many cases, assailed the injunction as wholly unwarranted and a denial of freedom of speech. The New York *Evening Post* declared that it had been watching the impending defeat of the strike with a sense that it was well deserved, but that this was "a blow below the belt." The *Newark Evening News* referred to the injunction as "gag law" and the New York *World* criticized it severely as "a clumsy step." On the other hand, conservative Republican papers tried to defend administration policy. The *New York Tribune*, the *Philadelphia Inquirer*, the *Boston Transcript*, and the *Chicago Daily News* agreed that, however broad the injunction, it was no broader than the lawlessness of the shopmen in threatening to paralyze all railroad transportation. The last word on the part of labor's enemies was perhaps spoken by the *Manufacturers'*

Record. The injunction, it declared, merely commanded the workers "to cease their adulterous intercourse with lawlessness."

For the railway shopmen, governmental intervention was the final straw. They eagerly seized upon a proposal by President Daniel Willard of the Baltimore and Ohio for separate settlements with individual roads and came to terms as best they could. The more friendly attitude of some lines enabled them to retain their organization for some 225,000 workers, but 175,00 were forced into company unions. Governmental intervention had swung the scales in favor of the employers, and railway labor had suffered a disastrous blow.

The whole labor movement continued to lose ground during the depression of 1921–1922 and, under the demoralizing influence of unemployment, was unable to command the strength to defend itself as the capitalistic counterattack, reinforced by injunction law, gathered steady momentum. Some unions were completely crushed; others suffered heavy losses. Labor had come out of the war strongly organized, determined to extend its gains, and confident that with friendly governmental protection it would be able to raise the standard of living for all American workers. Between 1920 and 1923, however, union membership as a whole fell from its peak figure of a little over 5,000,000 to approximately 3,500,000.

XIV

Labor in Retreat

The seven years from 1922 through 1929 were a period of expanding production, further concentration of economic power, rising national income, and probusiness government, which acted on the principles of prewar progressivism and economic efficiency, not antiquated nineteenth-century notions of laissez faire. It would not be incorrect to say that business dominated government. Such presidents as Warren G. Harding, Calvin Coolidge, and especially Herbert Hoover saw the world much as enlightened capitalists did. Private businessmen and public officials shared a common belief that a new cooperative capitalism with a conscience could simultaneously provide workers with steady employment at high wages, consumers with quality goods at stable prices, and stockholders with dividends adequate to stimulate greater investment. No one doubted him when Herbert Hoover proclaimed in his acceptance speech in 1928 that "we in America are nearer to the final triumph over poverty than ever before in the history of any land."

Enough truth underlay such images of a prosperous, poverty-free United States in the 1920s to sweep up most working-class families in a great consumption craze. Those workers who had steady jobs at good wages could for the first time buy now and pay later for washing machines, refrigerators, vacuum cleaners, radios, and sometimes even automobiles. Current savings provided cash for down payments; future earnings covered the monthly installment debt. The national economy floated ever higher on a tidal wave of mass consumption in which working-class families played a part. If few workers actually participated in that decade's feverish stock market speculation, that reality did not stop the Wall Street investment firm of Halsey, Stuart and Company from sponsoring a radio broadcast by AFL president William Green on "The Worker and his Money."

The image of America as the world's first mass-consumption society led the French writer, André Siegfried, to comment in 1927: "A workman is far better paid in America than anywhere else in the world and his standard of living is enormously higher. This difference, which was noticeable before the War, has been greatly accentuated since, and is now the chief contrast between the old and the new continents." And it led domestic observers to proclaim for perhaps the first, but certainly not the last time, that American workers had been absorbed into the middle class. All Americans, it was alleged, now took Sunday drives in their Fords and "Chevvies," watched the same movies, listened to the same radio programs, wore look-alike factory-made clothing, and danced the Charleston. If the sons and daughters of the working class did not go to Ivy League colleges, they did enter the state and municipal colleges. Clearly, then, the United States had become a classless society.

Not only classless but also more homogeneous. First, temporarily in 1921, and then permanently in 1924, Congress ended the era of mass immigration. It did so on a basis that discriminated against immigrants from southern and eastern Europe and excluded those from Asia. Meantime the prewar immigrants experienced the process of Americanization while their children and grandchildren absorbed it. Ethno-religious factors still divided the working class, but much less so than in the past.

One reason why society seemed more homogeneous and the working class itself less segmented was that racist and sexist thinking dominated national culture. The millions of blacks and Hispanic people who worked for a living remained in second-class citizenship, some might even say in the status of excluded castes. And women, who now worked for wages in greater numbers than ever before, still carried the stigma of temporary employees. Women, it was widely believed, worked outside the home only between leaving school and marriage, or, if married, merely for "pin money" (that is, to make possible frivolous or incidental purchases). No matter how much evidence appeared that women, as men, worked mostly to sustain themselves and their families, the image of the female as temporary employee proved resistant to the truth.

But the concept that workers were just like everyone else—a part of the great middle class—also conflicted with reality. One of the greatest books in American social-science literature, Robert and Helen Lynd's *Middletown* (1929), dissected the social structure of Muncie, Indiana, in the mid-1920s. The Lynds found that middle-sized, mid-American industrial city to be sharply divided between a laboring class (75–80 per cent of the population) and a business class (20–25 per cent) in all aspects of life and behavior—from how they earned their livings to what part of town they lived in, to when they retired and arose, to what they ate, and even where and how they prayed. Most important, laboring people and business people looked at the world and the future differently. Businessmen expected each new year to be better than the preceding one, to rise in their careers and income over time, and to be in full control of their community and their future. Workers, in contrast, looked from one year to the next with foreboding, expected advancing age to rob them of work and wages, and felt themselves powerless to shape their communities and futures.

Yet not a hint of class consciousness or rebelliousness stirred among Muncie's workers. However much their lives and behavior differed from those of the business class, local workers shared similar values and drives and measured success mostly in terms of money; they thought that the promise of wealth was open to all and valued education for its income-producing potential.

Other complexities and contradictions marked American society in the 1920s. Many segments of labor did not appear to have been invited to the feast of plenty that was provided by economic expansion, and even those groups of workers who profited most from the upward trend of wages could still feel that their share of the awards of prosperity were by no means commensurate with the far greater profits being made by businessmen.

More important, unemployment was by no means banished from the land and in some areas was unusually high. Technological advance, which was constantly enabling industry to produce more goods with fewer workers, led to declines in factory payrolls in many basic

industries. New machinery and labor-saving devices in road construction, textiles, the rubber industry, and electrical equipment, to cite a
few instances, cut the necessary labor for given output anywhere from
25 to 60 per cent. It was estimated that in manufacturing, railroads,
and coal mining, the labor of 3,272,000 fewer workers was necessary
to maintain old rates of production, and that increased economic activity called for the addition of only 2,269,000. This left a net decline
in employment in these industries of over 1,000,000. New opportunities in trade and service industries helped to offset this situation,
but there was nevertheless persistent unemployment throughout the
1920s which was estimated to have ranged in terms of man-years from
10 to 13 per cent of the total labor supply. At least two million persons were out of work even in 1928.

The insecurity of the industrial worker in respect to his job which
resulted from such conditions could never be wholly compensated by
high wages while he was at work. The Lynds found that the fear of being laid off was a constant obsession among the working-class families
whom they interviewed, even though Muncie was a prosperous community. The job was the thing in which they were interested, much
more than wages or hours. Whatever the general statistics of employment, the individual out of work faced the always bleak prospect of
trying to find something else to do before his meager savings melted
away altogether.

As for the status of organized labor—rather than that of wage
earners in general—conditions in the 1920s had a paradoxical effect.
In flat contradiction of what had been its record in every previous
period of national prosperity, the labor movement lost ground. Not
only was no further progress made in organizing the unskilled workers
in the mass production industries, but existing trade unions steadily
declined in membership. We have seen that, under the impact of the
depression in 1921, the total enrollment in American unions fell from
over 5,000,000 to approximately 3,600,000. What was far more
significant, however, was the failure during succeeding years to make
up any of these losses. At the peak of prosperity in 1929, total union
membership was 3,443,000—less than it had been in any year since
1917.

In the happy light of continued good times and generally rising
wages for those who had work, this did not seem to matter. While job
insecurity may have deterred some employees from joining unions in
the face of employer opposition, many of them apparently believed

that unions were no longer as necessary as they had formerly believed them to be. What point was there in strikes or other agitation for collective bargaining when the pay envelope was automatically growing fatter and a more abundant life seemed to be assured with the rapid approach to the final triumph over poverty?

There was no way for the workers to foresee in the halcyon atmosphere of these days that just over the horizon was another depression, a more devastating, long-lived depression than even those of the 1830s, the 1870s, or the 1890s, when fifteen million helpless workers would find themselves thrown on the streets, selling apples at corner stands, queueing up before soup kitchens, and crowding the breadlines. But the Great Depression's gathering shadows were soon to extinguish the "golden glow" of the 1920s and startlingly reveal the inherent weakness of labor's position. While the entire country was to suffer grievously from the sudden collapse of the New Economic Order, the impact of depression was once again to fall most heavily upon wage earners.

The economic recovery which succeeded the brief depression of 1921 found industry determined to prevent organized labor from recapturing the position it had attained during the war. The antiunion campaign which had been revived in 1919 was intensified, and a new emphasis was placed upon upholding the open shop. Theoretically, the open shop still implied nothing more than the right of the employer to hire whomever he chose, regardless of membership or nonmembership in a union. But, as in the early 1900s, it actually meant not only a policy whereby union members were almost invariably subject to discrimination, but also refusal to recognize the union even if a majority of the employees belonged to it. The open shop thus became more than ever a recognized technique to deny the whole process of collective bargaining.

To promote the drive against unions, open shop associations were formed throughout the country in the 1920s, as they had been during earlier periods of industrial counterattack. Fifty such employer groups were set up in New York, eighteen in Massachusetts, twenty in Connecticut, forty-six in Illinois, seventeen in Ohio, and twenty-three in Michigan. Local chambers of commerce, manufacturers' associations, and citizens' alliances further supported the campaign, and behind them stood the National Association of Manufacturers, the National Metal Trades Association, and the League for Industrial

Rights. With an inspiration born of the heightened nationalism of these postwar years, a conference of these various associations, which met in Chicago in 1921, formally named the open shop the "American Plan." The traditional values of rugged individualism were set against the subversive, foreign concepts of collectivism. "Every man to work out his own salvation," the proponents of the American Plan proclaimed, "and not to be bound by the shackles of organization to his own detriment."

Full advantage was also taken of every indication of corrupt union leadership and racketeering to convince both workers and the public that they were being duped by the supposed advantages of collective bargaining. And both corruption and racketeering could be found in some unions during the 1920s. Unlawful collusion between union leaders and employers, extortion by labor bosses, and outright graft were exposed in the building trades and service industries of such cities as New York, Chicago, and San Francisco. In some instances, gangsters, sensing an opportunity for even greater profit than bootleg-ging, moved in on the unions and fleeced both employers and employees by intimidation and violence. The conservatives' attack upon labor unions, however, made no distinction between these occa-sional examples of corrupt and antisocial policies and the overall pic-ture of responsible leadership in the great majority of unions. When labor leaders were not luridly depicted as Bolsheviks plotting revolu-tion, they were described as conscienceless spoilsmen, taking advan-tage of union members in every possible way to build up their own power and wealth.

"The palatial temples of labor," John E. Edgerton, president of the NAM grandiloquently declared in 1925, "whose golden domes rise in exultant splendor throughout the nation, the millions of dollars ex-tracted annually by the jewelled hand of greed from the pockets of wage earners and paid out in lucrative salaries, tell the pitiful story of a slavery such as this country never knew before." The employers of the nation were summoned to fulfill their duty "to break the shackles that have been forged upon the wrists of those who labor" and to free their employees from "the false leadership of designing pirates who parade in the guise of the workingmen's friend."

Nor was propaganda the only weapon employed to fight unionism and promote the open shop. Many employers continued to force yellow-dog contracts upon employees, to plant labor spies in their plants, to exchange blacklists of undesirable union members, and openly to follow the most discriminatory practices in hiring workers. It was the old story of intimidation and coercion, and when trouble developed in spite of all such precautions, strong-arm guards were often employed to beat up the troublemakers, while incipient strikes were crushed by bringing in strikebreakers under the protection of local authorities.

In the coal fields, for example, unionism found itself particularly hardpressed, with factionalism and conflict within labor's own ranks making it highly vulnerable to employer attacks. Coal was a sick industry, failing to share in the country's general prosperity as a result of competition from new sources of power, and the mine owners were doubly determined to meet the problem of cutting production costs by beating down labor. They sought to undermine wage agreements already signed with the miners, and, even more dangerously for unionism, began to shift production from the central bituminous field to nonunion mines in West Virginia, Kentucky, Tennessee, and Alabama, where they could operate without union restraints upon wages and hours.

The United Mine Workers were confronted with a hard dilemma. When strikes broke out in the nonunion fields, there were insistent demands for help. Should the union violate its contracts in the central bituminous field by declaring a sympathetic strike, or should it stand by passively and allow conditions to deteriorate in the nonunion mines and ultimately drag down the entire industry? John L. Lewis insisted upon maintaining contractual agreements. He refused assistance to all strikes not authorized by the union and proposed to meet the problem of the nonunion mines by organizing the workers in the South and bringing them under disciplined control.

His program failed. The United Mine Workers steadily lost ground in the unionized fields, even though it concluded and maintained further agreements with operators, and organization in the nonunion mines made no headway. The union agents were received in a manner somewhat at variance with traditional southern hospitality. They were tarred and feathered, ridden out of the company-controlled mining towns on rails, beaten up by armed guards, and sometimes murdered. Increasing strikes and disorder led, in some mining communities, to virtual civil war with an ugly record of violence, shootings, and assassination.

The more radical elements among the United Mine Workers bitterly resented the failure of Lewis to call a general strike in support of the nonunion miners. They helped to stir up discontent against a policy which was said to be both betraying the unorganized workers and destroying the union itself. There was rebellion among his own lieutenants and outlaw strikes even within union ranks. When Lewis countered by violently attacking his opponents as Communists, insisting upon complete submission to his authority, and expelling local leaders who countenanced unauthorized walk-outs, there was widespread dissatisfaction among the rank and file who saw in his maintenance of contracts only surrender to antiunion operators.

Lewis managed during these difficult days to retain control of the union, but it was badly split and in no position to maintain the influence which it had formerly exercised in the mine fields. The operators were able to whittle away the gains won through earlier national strikes, and the demoralization that marked the nonunion mines spread into the organized areas of the central bituminous field. In 1922, the United Mine Workers had attained a strength of 500,000—some 70 per cent of all coal miners. The story of decline is perhaps most graphically revealed in a membership that had shrunk ten years later to 150,000 or less.

In seeking to combat the antiunion campaign of employers, whether in the coal fields or elsewhere, labor could not look for any aid or support from government or the courts. The validity of yellow-dog contracts, so widely enforced in the southern coal mines, was still upheld; there was no legal redress for discrimination against union members, and successive court decisions wholly invalidated the supposed safeguards of the Clayton Act against injunction law.

Early in 1921, the Supreme Court stated in *Duplex Printing Press* v. *Deering* that nothing in the act legalized secondary boycotts or protected unions from injunctions which might be brought against them for conspiring to restrain trade. Later that same year, in the notable case of *Truax* v. *Corrigan*, any hope of legal relief for labor was even more effectively killed. Arizona had passed a law that sought to do away altogether with injunctions in labor disputes. The Supreme Court in effect declared it to be unconstitutional. In preventing an employer from obtaining an injunction, it was decreed, the state took away his means of securing protection and thereby deprived him of property without due process of law. With such encouragement, employers resorted to injunctions even more frequently than in the days before passage of the Clayton Act. In 1928, the American

Federation of Labor submitted a list of 389 injunctions which had been granted by either federal or state courts in the preceding decade, and this was obviously far from complete because of the large number unrecorded in the lower courts.

Perhaps the most revealing of all court decisions in this period was that in the previously noted case of *Adkins* v. *Children's Hospital,* which was handed down in 1923. In invalidating a minimum-wage law as a violation of constitutional safeguards of liberty of contract, it marked an abrupt reversal of the earlier trend toward sustaining such legislation, but it was even more significant because of a reassertion of the old concept that labor was a commodity. While the Supreme Court conceded "the ethical right of every worker, man or woman, to a living wage," it declared that the employer was not bound to furnish such a wage and that there was no warrant for the state to seek to establish it by legislation. Since in principle "there can be no difference between the case of selling labor and the case of selling goods," the court said, any attempt to compel the employer to pay a stated wage "is so clearly the product of a naked, arbitrary power that it cannot be allowed to stand under the Constitution of the United States."

Even Chief Justice Taft—the "injunction judge"—protested against this conclusion and pointed out that individual employees were not on a level of equality in contracting with employers and were "peculiarly subject to the overreaching of the harsh and greedy employer." Associate Justice Holmes also dissented, with sharp criticism of the court's one-sided support of "the dogma Liberty of Contract."

Although both government and courts theoretically recognized the desirability of labor unions (President Harding declared that the right of workers to organize was "not one whit less absolute" than that of management and capital), they were consistently restricting the activity for which unions were formed. The one exception to such repressive policies during the 1920s was the passage and approval of the Railway Labor Act of 1926. This measure provided for the formation of unions among railway workers "without interference, influence or coercion," and set up special machinery for the settlement of all railway labor disputes. In upholding this law, the Supreme Court declared that the legality of collective action on the part of employees would be "a mockery if representation were made futile by interferences with freedom of choice." But rights upheld for railway workers were not extended to other classes of employees until the 1930s.

Yellow-dog contracts and injunctions were not the only barriers in the path of unionization. The labor movement was also being killed by kindness. Industry complemented its aggressive enforcement of the open shop with a developing program of welfare capitalism. It sought to discourage trade unionism by making working conditions so favorable that the workers would no longer consider unions of any value, at the same time increasing production and industrial efficiency through closer labor-management cooperation.

Industry had long since tried to promote greater production per worker, to reduce labor turnover, and generally to improve technical standards through a process of "rationalization" in industrial management. During the progressive era, a program developed by Frederick W. Taylor had begun to be widely adopted. Time and motion studies, the development of piece work, increased productivity on the assembly line, and "scientific" adjustment of employee relations were the subject of universal experimentation. In the postwar era, "Taylorism" won even wider attention in the constant search to reduce manufacturing costs. Trade unionism had no place in this program of industrial efficiency, but employers recognized the need for some substitute to help to create the idea of "one big family" working cooperatively in the mutual interests of industry and labor. They thought that they had found it in shop councils, employee representation plans, and most specifically, company unions.

An early move along such lines was a program adopted by the Colorado Fuel and Iron Company after the strike that had culminated in the bloody massacre at Ludlow in 1914. The Rockefeller interests had refused to recognize the United Mine Workers and instead instituted a company union which was to provide "industrial democracy" without the dangerous implications of any association with the organized labor movement. The Rockefeller experiment was followed by many other corporations (125 set up company unions in one form or another during the war), and the open-shop campaign of postwar years led to still further emphasis upon this trend toward employer-controlled substitutes for outside unions. By 1926, the number of company unions had increased to over 400, with a membership of some 1,369,000, or about half the membership of unions affiliated with the AFL.

As personnel managers made further studies of the labor problem (almost three thousand books on the subject were published in the first five years after the war) other measures were adopted to strengthen the role of the company unions and win employee allegiance. Scores and then hundreds of corporations set up profit-sharing schemes, paid out bonuses in company stock, or otherwise sought to give the workers a direct financial interest in corporate activities. It was estimated in 1928 that over a million employees owned or had subscribed for over a billion dollars worth of stock in the companies which employed them. Group insurance policies, which were forfeited should the employee change his job, were also introduced, and some five million industrial workers were insured under such plans by 1926. At the same time, various old-age pension programs were established, free clinics were set up to help maintain health standards, and employee cafeterias and lunchroms were installed. Under the direction of personnel departments or company unions, picnics, glee clubs, dances, sports events, and other recreational activities were also sponsored for plant employees, while hundreds of company magazines proclaimed the goodwill and friendly human contracts between labor and management.

The amplifications of welfare capitalism knew no limits, and it succeeded to a very considerable extent in improving working conditions and indirectly increasing employee income. Its immediate benefits for the worker were quite real. Yet the entire program remained subject to the control of the corporation sponsor, and there was no reality to employee representation under such conditions. It was not without significance that those corporations which most generously provided for the workers' welfare were also those which were most strongly antiunion in their basic policies. How quickly welfare capitalism might collapse—and especially its stock-distribution program—should prosperity give way to depression was hardly realized at the time. Few of the members of company unions understood how dependent they had become upon their employers for the favors they were receiving in lieu of union recognition and the advantages of genuine collective bargaining.

This lesson would be learned after 1929, but in the meantime welfare capitalism won many victories. "The assertion may be boldly made," S. B. Peck, chairman of the Open Shop Committee of the National Association of Manufacturers, declared, "that the decreasing membership in most of the unions and the great difficulty they are experiencing in holding their members together, is due to the fact that

the employers—notably the once so-called 'soulless corporations'—are doing more for the welfare of the workers than the unions
themselves." The Committee on Education and Labor of the
Seventy-Sixth Congress reported, in 1926, that the NAM had done its
work in combating unionism so well that it was able to settle back "to
the quiet enjoyment of the fruits of their efforts during the years of
prosperity."

The consequences of the double-edged program of seeking to suppress bona fide labor unions and building up employee allegiance
through the benefits of company unions and welfare capitalism were
seen, not only in declining membership for the AFL, but also in a
greater measure of industrial peace than the country had enjoyed for
many years. This does not mean there were no strikes. Those on the
part of the depressed textile workers, for example, were persistent,
hard-fought, and marked by violence and bloodshed. In such southern
mill towns as Gastonia and Marion, North Carolina, and Elizabeth-
ton, Tennessee, open clashes between strikers and state troopers led
to heavy death tolls. The overall record, however, was one of a steadily declining number of labor disputes. During the war period, the
total number of strikes had averaged over 3,000 a year and involved
well over a million workers annually. By the mid-1920s, such figures
had been halved. At the end of the decade, the annual number of
strikes was around 800 and engaged only some 300,000 workers, or
slightly more than 1 per cent of the aggregate labor force.

The new capitalism of the 1920s provided the nation's workers with
a greater rise in wages during that decade than in any comparable
previous period. Annual earnings, indeed, rose between 1921 and
1928 from an average of $1,171 to $1,408. In terms of actual purchasing power, for there was no comparable rise in living costs, this has
been estimated to represent a gain of more than 20 per cent.

Both actual wages and their rate of increase were nevertheless very
uneven. The hourly rate for bricklayers in New York rose between
1920 and 1928 from $1.06 to $1.87 and that of newspaper com-
positors from 92 cents to $1.20, but in the case of bituminous miners
there was a decline in the hourly rate from 83 cents to 73 cents, and for
mule spinners in the cotton mills a drop from 83 cents to 63 cents. The
gains of the 1920s went primarily to the skilled workers and trade union
members. Millions of working-class families still had incomes of less
than $1,000 a year even in 1929.

As for hours of work, the general picture shows substantial improvement. The eight-hour day generally prevailed, and it was estimated that, since 1901, the working week for wage earners had been cut from 15 to 30 per cent. But wide discrepancies appear when available statistics are broken down. While a 43.5-hour work week was the average in the building trades, for instance, a 60-hour week was still being maintained for blast-furnace workers in the steel mills.

Factors other than wages and hours also affected the well-being of the nation's workers in these as in other years. The speed-up in industrial processes added to the strain and nervous tension under which men operating machines and working on the assembly line constantly labored. For many factory employees, the substitution of wholly mechanical operations for the exercise of individual skills meant monotony and boredom were not always compensated by higher wages and shorter hours. While this was nothing new in the history of industrialization, it was more than ever true during the 1920s.

With the march of the machine also holding over the worker's head the constant threat of losing his job, the industrial workers of the country were consequently still far from attaining that security and well-being which was the goal of organized labor. The gains that had been made were more precarious than impersonal statistics might suggest, especially since those that might be attributed to welfare capitalism were unprotected by any contractual understanding. So far as organizational strength and aggressive trade unionism had been sacrificed in accepting labor-management cooperation in place of genuine collective bargaining, the wage earners had seriously undermined their hard-won capacity to protect their own interests. They were almost wholly dependent on the continued willingness and ability of employers to treat them fairly.

But before 1929, few doubted the willingness and ability of employers to treat workers fairly. As David Brody has written, welfare capitalism was the idea "that management accepted an obligation for the well-being of its employees. . . . That promise. . . constituted the essence of welfare captialism. What made the promise credible was the performance of American capitalism in the 1920s."

Against the successes of American capitalism, 1920s-style, organized labor had few effective defenses or responses. Early in the decade, when employer antiunion impulses were most common, the

AFL and the railway brotherhoods began to feel that more direct political pressure would have to be exercised if it was to win any freedom of action in combating the employers' antiunion campaign. The drive for a labor party which had first developed in 1919 when "Labor's Bill of Rights" was drawn up gathered increasing force with further revelations of the Supreme Court's attitude.

This agitation had first come to a head in 1922, when a Chicago meeting of some 128 delegates from various farm, labor, and other liberal groups formed the Conference for Progressive Political Action. William H. Johnston of the powerful International Association of Machinists was a leading figure in this movement; the railway brotherhoods, smarting under the restrictions of the old Railway Labor Board and the revival of injunction law, backed it vigorously, and support was also forthcoming from twenty-eight national unions, eight state labor federations, several midwestern farmers' parties, the Women's Trade Union League, and the Socialists. When two years later both the Republicans and the Democrats nominated highly conservative candidates—Calvin Coolidge and John W. Davis—these progressives offered an independent nomination to Senator Robert La Follette of Wisconsin. On the condition that no attempt be made to run candidates for other offices than the presidency and vice-presidency (Senator Burton K. Wheeler of Montana was given the latter nomination), La Follette accepted this proposal, and the Conference for Progressive Political Action formally entered the campaign of 1924.

The platform, declaring that the principal issue before the country was the control of government and industry by private monopoly, was in large measure a carry-over of the progressive principles of prewar years. It called for public ownership of the nation's water power and railroads, the conservation of natural resources, aid for farmers, tax reduction on moderate incomes, downward tariff revision, and remedial labor legislation. "We favor abolition of the use of injunctions in labor disputes," it was stated, "and declare for complete protection of the right of farmers and industrial workers to organize, bargain collectively through representatives of their own choosing, and conduct without hindrance cooperative enterprises."

The American Federation of Labor was at first opposed to the Conference for Progressive Political Action, but when both major parties ignored labor's demands, it took the unprecedented step of endorsing the La Follette candidacy. The Republican and Democratic parties, declared the executive council, had "flouted the desires of labor" and were "in a condition of moral bankruptcy which constitutes a menace and a peril to our country and its institutions." In spite of this attack on the major parties, the AFL aligned itself with the Progressives of 1924 very cautiously. In keeping with his policy during the political flirtations of prewar years, Gompers tried to make it clear that the Federation made no commitments except to support La Follette as "a friend of labor" in this single campaign and was not countenancing a third party as such. While recognizing the need for legislation to free labor from the restrictions represented by injunction law, Gompers reaffirmed his faith in "voluntarism" by declaring that "we do not accept government as the solution of the problems of life."

Even with these qualifications and reservations, many AFL leaders refused to go along with the action of the executive council. John L. Lewis and William Hutcheson, of the Carpenters, gave their support to Coolidge, and George L. Berry, of the Printing Pressmen, at the last moment shifted over to the camp of John W. Davis. Although the AFL had so far departed from its traditional policy as to come out openly for a presidential candidate of a third party, its support was somewhat left-handed, and only $25,000 was raised as a campaign fund.

La Follette secured nearly five million votes—a substantial indication of popular discontent with both Republican and Democratic conservatism—but he carried only his home state of Wisconsin. The labor vote had not been delivered, and the Progressives' failure was widely interpreted as labor's failure. "The radical movement of this year," wrote the Washington correspondent of the *Seattle Times*, "represented the first attempt on the part of organized labor, through its governing bodies, to secure separate political action. The radical failure seems likely to end the possibility, for a good many years, of labor endorsement of a third-party presidential ticket." There was "no such thing as a labor vote," the *New York Herald Tribune* stated in analyzing the election returns, and the *Washington Star* agreed that "the workingmen of this country have not joined the insurgency against the established parties." More succinctly and colloquially, the *Philadelphia Bulletin* simply stated that "labor's incursion into politics was a dud."

The AFL apparently read very much the same meaning into the election. It promptly withdrew its support from the Conference for Progressive Political Action and reasserted its opposition to a third party. The entire movement collapsed. While in succeeding years labor continued to press for relief from injunctions, it made no further direct forays into politics. With even the Socialist vote falling off heavily, wage earners appeared ready to accept, with the rest of the country, the conservative political pattern which continued to characterize the national scene until the advent of the New Deal.

It was shortly after this unsuccessful campaign—in December, 1924—that the grand old man of the AFL, Samuel Gompers, died at the age of seventy-four. In his later years, it had become increasingly difficult for him to carry on his work. Nothing except death, however, could make him surrender the power he had held so securely ever since the Federation had been established forty years earlier. His control had momentarily appeared to be threatened in 1921 when Lewis entered the lists as a presidential candidate, but Gompers had put down this incipient rebellion as he had so many others. He was the acknowledged leader of organized labor, and there was no real rival to his preeminence in this field. Both the successes and the failures of the AFL largely reflected the application of the instrumental philosophy he so consistently upheld.

Labor mourned his death and so also did the business community. Newspaper editorials were an interesting commentary on the extent to which his moderate policies were applauded for forestalling more radical tendencies on the part of the nation's workers. Gompers was said to have held trade unionism to a straightforward, nonpolitical path by the sheer force of his personality, and he was generally praised for having consistently tried to bridge the gap between capital and labor. His death was termed a loss to America primarily because it opened up the possibility of a split within the AFL which might enable extremist elements to come into power.

When the choice of the Federation for its new president fell upon Willian Green, such fears died. For Green wanted no radical shift in labor policies; this assurance seemed to be made doubly sure by an immediate statement to the press that it would be his "steadfast purpose to adhere to those fundamental principles of trade-unionism so ably championed by Mr. Gompers." "Labor is safe under his leadership," the *Richmond Times-Dispatch* declared in a typical comment upon Green's election; "capital has nothing to fear, and the public is fortunate in having him as spokesman of a highly important group of citizens."

Green was born in Coshocton, Ohio, in 1873. Like so many labor leaders, he was a second-generation American, the son of Welsh immigrants, and as a boy had followed his father into the coal pits in Ohio. Joining the United Mine Workers, he was chosen a subdistrict union president in 1906 and started upon a gradual climb to the high councils of organized labor. As leader of the miners in Ohio, he was sent to the state legislature as a trade-union representative, and then elected secretary-treasurer of the United Mine Workers in reward for his faithful services. When in 1913 Gompers decided that the miners should be represented on the executive council of the AFL, he turned to Green and appointed him an eighth vice-president. As death one by one removed the higher officers, Green slowly rose in scale to third vice-president. It was from this post, with the backing of Lewis, that he was raised to the pinnacle of the AFL presidency.

Green appeared in 1924 a rather undistinguished figure without the forceful, dramatic characteristics which in different ways had marked Gompers, Mitchell, and Lewis. Sober and sedate—he had taught Sunday School as a young man and originally hoped to train for the ministry—he was not one to drink beer with the boys in the Gompers tradition. His teetotalism was rather a reminder of Terence Powderly. Secretary of Labor Frances Perkins was later to describe him as "the mildest and most polite of men," and his plump figure, round, humorless face, soft voice, and quiet manner did not add up to a very arresting personality. But Green was a great joiner (he belonged to the Elks, the Odd Fellows, and the Masons), and his pleasant, affable manner and general friendliness made him popular. He was also respected for his unquestioned integrity and conscientious, hardworking devotion to the concerns of union labor.

In 1917, Green had declared himself, as a result of his own experience with the United Mine Workers, to be completely in favor of industrial unionism, and this was one reason for the support which Lewis gave him. "The organization of men by industry rather than by craft," Green had stated, "brings about a more perfect organization, closer cooperation. . . . It is becoming more and more evident that if unskilled workers are forced to work long hours and for low wages, the interests of the skilled are constantly menaced thereby." But in his new office all this was forgotten. Craft unionism as opposed to industrial unionism was to remain the basic policy of the AFL, and no real attempts would be made during the 1920s to press for union recognition among the unskilled workers in mass-production industries.

In proving himself to be quite as cautious as Gompers had been,

Green appeared no more willing than his predecessor to recognize the possible need for changes in the AFL policy to meet changing circumstances. He continued to uphold the concept of voluntarism which Gompers had so stoutly defended with an emphasis upon "strong, redblooded, rugged independence" which might well have come from President Hoover himself. It was not until 1932, when the impact of the depression had undermined many AFL principles, that Green finally gave up his opposition to such forms of state intervention as old-age pensions and unemployment insurance.

Far from seeking to revive labor militancy, the American Federation of Labor made every effort to encourage labor-management cooperation. Green was destined to accept proudly in 1930 the gold medal of the Theodore Roosevelt Memorial Association for his outstanding services in allaying industrial strife. While the AFL could not countenance company unions, it passively acquiesced in many other aspects of welfare capitalism. Content with the gains that its own membership was making as wages rose in response to the demand for skilled workers, little effort was made to broaden the scope of union activity. At the close of the 1920s, the organized labor movement appeared to be accepting as complacently as any other element in the national economy the promise of assured economic advance.

This was the situation when depression gradually engulfed the country after the sudden collapse of the stock market in 1929. The story is a familiar one: the shock to national confidence as billions of dollars of security values melted away, the frantic assertions that conditions were fundamentally sound, and the slow strangulation of business as the cracks in the industrial system slowly widened and the whole structure seemed threatened with collapse. The depression was another historic turn in the economic cycle, but its impact on society was greater than that of any depression in the past.

Before it had run its course, farm prices fell to 40 per cent of their previous levels, the value of exports declined to a third of their former peak, industrial production was almost halved, and the balance sheet of corporate enterprise revealed a deficit of $5,650,000,000. In three years a national income estimated at $82,885,000,000 had dropped to $40,074,000,000. Even more significant—and far more devastating—unemployment rose to over seven million by the end of 1930, and then, in another two years, to something like fifteen million.

Statistics, however, give only an inadequate idea of the dire effects of the depression. They can hardly depict the scrimping and saving forced upon millions of middle-class families, the privations and hardships caused those in lower income groups, and the cruel suffering of the unemployed workers and their families. The bread lines, the tramp jungles so ironically called Hoovervilles which sprang up in the outskirts of countless cities, the army of young men and boys wandering back and forth across the country in hopeless search for jobs were a tragic commentary upon the glowing mirage of the era that was to abolish poverty.

The country's wage earners stood by helplessly as the depression cut into production, paralyzed normal trade, and caused many factories, mines, and workshops to shut down altogether. Early in 1930, a series of industrial conferences had been held in Washington at which employers promised to uphold wages and maintain employment. The workers accepted these pledges in good faith. Like the rest of the country, they could not believe that prosperity had so suddenly collapsed and were still hopeful that recovery was just around the corner. But there were no collective bargaining agreements in the mass-production industries—steel, automobiles, electrical equipment—to compel observance of wage scales. Pay checks were gradually cut and then all too often replaced by blunt notices of dismissal.

The whole program of welfare capitalism also went abruptly by the board as employers were forced to withdraw the benefits which in the piping days of prosperity had often been granted in the place of wage increases. Profit-sharing schemes, employee stock ownership, industrial pensions, and even workers' health and recreational projects were rapidly discarded. Circumstances forced retrenchment, but in some cases it was carried out at the expense of the workers while full dividends were still being paid on common stock. The company unions were powerless to protect their members' interests. Reliance upon welfare capitalism had proved to be a delusion.

Organized labor seemed to be completely demoralized. The national unions did not even try to exercise any direct pressure upon the government in favor of recovery measures, and their strength had been so sapped by the retreat before welfare capitalism that concerted action along economic lines was out of the question in the face of nationwide unemployment. Strike activity was at a minimum and in 1930 fell to a new low point when less than 200,000 workers were involved in all work stoppages. Continued declines in union membership were also the general rule. The total number of organized workers fell by 1933 to less than 3,000,000—or the approximate level of 1917.

In some ways, the most surprising phenomenon of the depression years was this apathetic attitude on the part of industrial workers while the unemployment figures steadily mounted and the bread lines lengthened. There was no suggestion of revolt against an economic system which had let them down so badly. There was no parallel of the railway strikes of 1877 or of the Pullman strike of 1894. In Park Avenue drawing rooms and the offices of Wall Street brokers, there was a great deal of talk of "the coming revolution," but the unemployed themselves were too discouraged and too spiritless to be interested.

Writing in *Harper's* in mid-summer 1932, the economist, George Soule, found that, while there was a distinct drift on the part of intellectuals into the radical camp, with rising interest in Communism, no such trend could be discovered in the ranks of labor. "The masses are in a desperate condition all right," he wrote, "but unfortunately there is no sign that they feel the slightest resentment. They just sit at home and blame prohibition. . . . Like the Republican administration, they are awaiting nothing more drastic than the return of prosperity." In another article in the same magazine, a journalist also commented with astonishment on "the quiet acceptance of the situation by men who have lost their jobs and everything else through the operation of the policies that were to abolish poverty."

There was one unexpected occasion when Green, addressing the AFL, "dropped his gentle manner," as described in the *Literary Digest,* "to let loose a verbal blast as thunderous as a crash of coal in the Ohio mine where he used to swing a pick." Unless a shorter work day and shorter work week were adopted to increase employment, he told a cheering audience, "we will secure it through force of some kind." Asked by eager reporters just what he meant by force, he quickly explained that he meant economic force. Even this vague hint of labor militancy, however, awoke concern. "Is this the time for industrial war?" asked the *Boston Transcript.* Any suggestion of trying "to coerce industry by the strike method" was deeply deplored by the *Washington Post.* The *New York Herald Tribune* felt that Green had suffered "an attack of nerves."

But this outburst was an exception to the generally cautious attitude of the American Federation of Labor. Maintaining until the end of 1932 its strong opposition to unemployment insurance, it urged nothing more concrete in the way of governmental action to promote recovery or relieve unemployment than "the stabilization of industry" through adoption of its program for increasing jobs by a shorter work week.

The press praised this attitude. "Today labor stands patient and hopeful," the *Cleveland Plain Dealer* wrote. ". . . Never has there been a period of depression so free from labor strife. Unemployment has harassed it. Closed factories have taken away its livelihood. But, in the face of enormous hardship, labor has showed its good citizenship and sturdy American stamina. Labor deserves a salute. "Whether the workers themselves were satisfied with this generous salute instead of jobs may be open to question. The *Philadelphia Record*, reflecting a more realistic attitude than that of the *Plain Dealer*, declared that the Federation's stand against unemployment insurance was a ghastly jest. "Liberty to starve?" it asked, "Is that what Mr. Green fights for?"

The consequences of government inaction and labor passivity were with every passing month more graphically reflected in the increasing number of jobless workers dependent upon state or private charity. The vaunted campaign to spread the work did not seem to have any effect other than to reduce workers' income and seldom opened any opportunities for those who had already been laid off.

Some of the states attempted to pass legislation to improve working conditions. New workingmen's compensation laws were adopted in a number of instances, fourteen states approved old-age pensions, and Wisconsin pioneered with a new Labor Bill of Rights and unemployment insurance. Early in March 1932, a highly significant victory for organized labor as a whole was won through the passage by Congress of the Norris–La Guardia Act. This measure at long last declared it to be public policy that labor should have full freedom of association, without interference by employers; outlawed yellow-dog contracts; and prohibited federal courts from issuing injunctions in labor disputes except under carefully defined conditions. Although at least one congressman rose to state that this bill represented a "long march in the direction of Moscow," it was overwhelmingly supported in both the House and Senate and received widespread popular approval. For all the importance of the Norris–La Guardia Act in pointing the way to the labor policies of the New Deal, it did not meet the immediate problem of the nation's wage earners—unemployment.

As conditions reached their nadir in the summer of 1932, the presidential campaign offered a practical opportunity for political protest against the failure of the Hoover administration to cope adequately with the depression. Franklin D. Roosevelt, as Democratic nominee, clearly demonstrated his sympathy for the working masses of the country and for "the forgotten man at the bottom of the economic pyramid." He repeatedly stressed the imperative need to provide direct relief and vigorously advocated unemployment insurance. Yet the American Federation of Labor declared its neutrality in the presidential campaign. Willing to endorse friends of labor among the congressional candidates, it refused to announce itself in favor of either Hoover or Roosevelt. Industrial workers helped to swell the great popular majority that Roosevelt won in 1932, but the AFL did not officially play any part in his election.

The campaign over, no further developments took place in respect to labor problems, and economic conditions continued to deteriorate. The American Federation of Labor urged a thirty-hour week and expanded public works; it finally came out in favor of unemployment insurance. But no positive action was taken to promote such measures. Labor was waiting, like the rest of the country, to see what the new President would do.

XV

The New Deal

"A host of unemployed citizens face the grim problem of existence, and an equally great number toil with little return. Only a foolish optimist can deny the dark realities of the moment. . . . Our greatest primary task is to put people to work."

When Franklin D. Roosevelt took office in March 1933, his stirring inaugural held out a promise of action to cope with the national emergency and created throughout the nation a new feeling of hope and confidence. The government was at long last prepared to accept the responsibility of extending that measure of direct aid to agriculture and labor, as well as industry, which alone could restore the disrupted balance of the national economy. As the President spiritedly declared that "the only thing we have to fear is fear itself," the country felt that it had found the leadership for want of which it had been floundering helplessly in the deepening morass of depression.

There was nothing in Roosevelt's immediate program that applied directly to labor except his promise to put people to work. Social security—with unemployment and old-age insurance—was already under consideration, but the labor provisions which were to be written into the National Recovery Administration codes, the Wagner

Act, and the Fair Labor Standards Act were not envisaged when he entered office. They evolved gradually out of the needs of the times. A basic understanding and sympathy for the rights of labor were nevertheless inherent in the emerging philosophy of the New Deal. For the first time in American history, a national administration was to make the welfare of industrial workers a direct concern of government and act on the principle that only organized labor could deal on equal terms with organized capital. Heretofore, labor unions had been tolerated; now they were to be encouraged.

The advent of the New Deal was thus to prove a momentous watershed in the history of the labor movement. Age-old traditions were smashed; new and dynamic forces were released. Never before had as much economic and political power seemed within the reach of organized labor. The struggles, hardships, and defeats of a century appeared to have culminated in the possibility of complete attainment of workers' historic objectives.

New Deal policy toward labor was based upon a premise which had already been set forth in the general recognition of the right to organize which was written into the Norris–La Guardia Act. A definite step toward implementing this right was taken in the famous—or infamous, as viewed in some quarters—Section 7(a) of the National Industrial Recovery Act, the Roosevelt administration's first experiment in overall economic control.

This important move was the end result of highly complex maneuvering. In March 1933, a bill was introduced into Congress by Senator Hugo Black of Alabama and Representative William P. Connery, Jr., of Massachusetts to establish the thirty-hour week which the AFL had been demanding to spread work and relieve unemployment. Roosevelt was very skeptical of its value unless it included some provision for maintaining wages. In behalf of the President, Secretary of Labor Frances Perkins consequently suggested amendments which would have combined a guarantee of minimum wages with the reduction in work hours. The theory underlying the new bill was not unlike the one that Ira Steward promoted in the 1860s—except that increasing pay by decreasing hours was secondary to wage stabilization. There was as yet no intention of going any further.

The idea of minimum wages provoked a storm of opposition from business interests and was not supported too enthusiastically by labor. In place of such a limited approach to the problems of depression, it was urged by both camps that the administration raise its sights and institute a far broader recovery program. The United States Chamber of Commerce proposed that business should be freed from the restrictions of the antitrust laws and encouraged to work out its own salvation. As a spokesman for labor, John L. Lewis advocated that the controls over production, prices, and wages which he had been demanding in coal mining should be extended to industry as a whole. As scores of such plans began to arouse increasing interest both in and out of Congress, several independent groups of presidential advisers began to try to work out specific measures. Little real progress was being made, however, and Roosevelt decided to intervene. Withdrawing administration support from the Black-Connery bill, in which his interest had been lukewarm, he called upon his advisers to get together on a common program—shutting themselves up in a locked room if necessary—until they could come to agreement.

The plan finally adopted and incorporated into the National Industrial Recovery Act was to allow industry to write its own codes of fair competition, but to compensate labor for granting industry such a free hand by providing special safeguards for its interests. Section 7(a) of the new measure, drawing in part from provisions of the Railway Labor Act of 1926, stipulated that the industrial codes should contain three important provisions: employees should have the right to organize and bargain collectively through representatives of their own choosing, free from interference, restraint, or coercion on the part of employers; no one seeking employment should be required to join a company union or to refrain from joining any labor organization of his own choosing; and employers should comply with maximum hours, minimum rates of pay, and other conditions of employment approved by the President. Thus, the ideas underlying the Chamber of Commerce's program, labor's traditional demand for union recognition, and certain modified provisions of the Black-Connery bill were brought together in a single omnibus measure, and to this overall plan was further added, under a separate title, a vast public-works program authorizing appropriations of $3,300,000,000.

The basic purpose of the National Industrial Recovery Act, as approved in June 1933, was, in the President's words, "to put people back to work." Its agency, the National Recovery Administration (NRA), was at once to insure reasonable profits for industry by preventing unfair competition and disastrous overproduction, and living wages for labor by spreading work through shorter hours.

Roosevelt termed the law "the most important and far-reaching legislation ever enacted by the American Congress."

The NRA virtually collapsed through internal stress and strain even before it was finally outlawed by the Supreme Court—a generally unlamented victim of early New Deal enthusiasm. Nevertheless, its implications for labor went far toward justifying Roosevelt's statement. The guarantee of collective bargaining and the establishment of wage and hour controls by congressional action, in spite of loopholes that were to develop in enforcement of the law, represented the most forward steps ever taken by government in the field of industrial relations. And these steps were not to be retraced even when other provisions of the NRA went by the board. The New Deal picked up the shattered fragments of Section 7(*a*) and put them together again, far more carefully, in the Wagner Act and the Fair Labor Standards Act. There was to be no retreat under Roosevelt from this advance in safeguarding the interest of industrial workers.

In June 1933, the NRA was hailed enthusiastically throughout the country. It is true that such a conservative organ as the *Manufacturer's Record,* looking with a jaundiced eye upon any concessions to labor whatsoever, was soon to state that "labor agitators...are trying to establish a labor dictatorship in this country," but this critical note was lost in the general chorus of excited approval for the new recovery program. In the bright dawn of its inception, the NRA started off under the dynamic direction of General Hugh Johnson amid a fanfare of patriotic oratory and popular demonstrations. As symbols of code acceptance, Blue Eagles were soon being proudly displayed the length and breadth of the land.

Labor joyfully acclaimed Section 7(*a*). "Millions of workers throughout the nation," William Green declared, "stood up for the first time in their lives to receive their charter of industrial freedom." Countless unions were aroused overnight from the doldrums of depression lethargy. Confident in the protection of the law, organizers set out to restore the depleted strength of moribund locals, form new ones, and invade territory from which they had formerly been barred. In the coal fields, placards at the mine pits announced "The President wants you to join the union." The UMW left it to individual miners to decide whether it was President Roosevelt or President Lewis. The workers themselves often did not wait for the official organizers, but set up their own locals and then applied for charters from the parent organization.

When the AFL met for its annual convention in October, President Green confidently announced that an unofficial count showed over 1,500,000 new recruits added to its ranks, recouping the losses of over a decade and bringing total membership to close upon four million.[1] He envisaged a goal of ten million, eventually twenty-five.

The greatest gains were in the so-called industrial unions, and particularly in those which had suffered most heavily during the depression. Within a few months, the United Mine Workers recouped 300,000 members and concluded new agreements in the formerly nonunion coal fields of Kentucky and Alabama; the International Ladies' Garment Workers added 100,000 to its rolls, recapturing lost territory in New York and runaway shops in other parts of the country and the Amalgamated Clothing Workers made up its earlier losses with some 50,000 recruits. But this was not all. Under the spur of Section 7(a), the AFL even appeared to be ready, with the new slogan of "Organize the Unorganized in the Mass Production Industries," to invade territory from which it had formerly held aloof. Nearly 100,000 workers were said to have been organized in the automobile industry, 90,000 in steel, 90,000 in lumber yards and sawmills, and 60,000 in rubber.

It was soon to develop, however, that this burst of activity among the unorganized workers had a very precarious foundation and that the proud boasts of President Green were not wholly justified. The traditional skepticism of the AFL toward industrial unionism, reinforced by the determination of old-line craft union leaders to retain control of the labor movement, retarded any campaign to organize the workers in mass production along industrial lines. The accepted technique was to form so-called federal unions, directly affiliated with the AFL itself, until jurisdictional problems could be worked out and the new union membership in steel, automobiles, rubber, and other industries could be gradually absorbed into existing unions. Between 1932 and 1934, the number of federal charters outstanding rose from 307 to 1,798. This was not the form of organization, however, that

---

[1]These figures were a broad estimate. It might be noted at this point, however, that all general statistics on union membership are only approximate because of widely different practices in reporting enrollment. Real exactitude is never possible. See Leo Wolman, *Ebb and Flow in Unionism* (National Bureau of Economic Research, Washington, 1936). For more recent and reliable statistics see Leo Troy, *Trade Union Memberhsip, 1897-1962* (National Bureau of Economic Research, New York, 1965) and Irving Bernstein, "The Growth of American Unions," *American Economic Review*, No. 44 (June 1954), pp. 301–318.

met the real need of unskilled workers, and very soon the initial flurry of activity in the mass-production industries began to subside.

Such evidence of failure gave rise to an insistent demand on the part of many leaders within the AFL for a change of tactics. They called for a more aggressive campaign to bring the unorganized workers into the fold and the immediate granting of industrial union charters in automobile and steel, in rubber, aluminum and radio. When the oligarchy in control of the AFL rejected these demands, a widening branch between adherents of craft unions and those who favored industrial unions led to what was to prove a critical split in the ranks of labor. Its unity was shattered at the moment of its greatest opportunity. Under circumstances to which we shall return, the labor insurgents set up their own Committee for Industrial Organization, and a new chapter was opened in labor history.

In the meantime, the older unions had also discovered that the high promise of their new charter of liberties was not to be realized without further struggles. Pending adoption of the NRA's industrial codes, all employers were asked to subscribe to the President's Re-Employment Agreement—a blanket code in which a forty-hour week was prescribed, miminum wages were set at either $15 a week or 40 cents an hour, and child labor was' abolished for all those under the age of sixteen. More permanent agreements were then to be drawn up by the trade associations, with the workers' interests supposedly protected by a labor advisory board in each industry. In the final analysis, however, the trade associations generally acted independently and employees had no real part in the formulation of the permanent codes. A majority of them established the forty-hour week, with minimum wages from $12 to $15 a week, but while some 95 per cent of the nation's industrial workers were ultimately given this protection, labor's rights in other respects were largely ignored. The safeguards for collective bargaining were either not definitely recognized or were gradually whittled away. The automobile manufacturers, for example, succeeded in having inserted in their code a clause which enabled them to select, retain, or advance their employees "on the basis of individual merit." In theory, such a right could hardly be disputed, but for antiunion employers it provided the means to discriminate against union members on any convenient pretext. President Roosevelt subsequently ordered that interpretations of Section 7(a) should not be included in any code. It did not interfere with the bona fide right of the employer to hire whom he chose, he asserted, but it clearly prohibited the exercise of this right as a device to keep employees from joining a union.

As industry began to recover and fearful employers crept cautiously out of the cyclone cellars into which they had been driven by the depression, further resentments developed over the concessions granted labor in return for management's freedom to control production and fix prices. The *Iron Age* warned of the dangers of what it chose to call "collective bludgeoning," and *Steel* stated that, with organized labor "baring its teeth," every effort should be made to retain the open shop. Viewing fearfully predictions of a membership of 10,000,000 in the AFL, the New York *Commercial and Financial Chronicle* declared that the country would then have "an organized body, or class within the State, more powerful than the State itself. That in itself would mean the extinction of freedom and independence. In the end oppression would prevail everywhere." Responding to such dire warnings, some employers bluntly refused to comply at all with the labor provisions of the codes, and other sought every possible means to evade the spirit if not the letter of the law.

One of the principal weapons used in combating the clear intent of Section 7(*a*) was the company union. Employees could not be required to join such an organization, but their employers were still free to exercise every possible kind of pressure to make it seem advisable. And this was done so effectively that enrollment in company unions rapidly rose from 1,250,000 to 2,500,000. The NRA not only tacitly approved such unions, stating that the government had not endorsed "any particular form of organization," but encouraged them by allowing proportional representation in collective bargaining. Even when a national union enrolled a majority of workers in a plant, it was not accepted as the spokesman for the whole labor force, and management could still deal with any other employee group. Such an interpretation of the law was attacked by labor as completely nullifying the whole principle of collective bargaining. The NRA was bitterly assailed as the National Run Around, and the Blue Eagle was said to have changed into a vulture.

As the old lines of industrial strife were again tightened, the NRA thus found itself caught between two fires: the recalcitrant attitude of many employers and the militant demands of labor. First a National Labor Board, then special boards in certain industries, and finally in July 1934, a National Labor Relations Board were set up to handle the growing volume of industrial disputes. These boards failed to win the confidence of either management or of labor and often appeared to be working at cross purposes with the NRA itself. The National Labor Relations Board stood for important principles. Its support for majority representation, secret elections, and bona fide collective bargaining, together with its refusal to acknowledge company-dominated unions, were to provide a basis for the policies of the later board with the same name. The original NLRB, however, was hampered and restricted under the operation of the National Recovery Administration and had no power to enforce its decisions.

To defend their interests, the workers felt more and more driven to strikes. The number of industrial disputes rose precipitately in the latter half of 1933—almost as many in this six-month period as in all of 1932—and the next year saw the total rise to 1,856. Almost 1,500,000 workers—more than 7 per cent of the total labor force—were involved. In steel, automobiles, and textiles, among the longshoremen of the Pacific Coast and the lumber workers of the Northwest, in scores of other industries, strikes were either threatened or broke out on a scale comparable to that of 1919. Many of these strikes were for wage increases, but a great number of them, at least a third, were for union recognition.

Fearful that strikes, especially in such basic industries as automobiles and steel, would irreparably damage its economic recovery program, the Roosevelt administration did its best to avert such conflicts. In automobiles and steel, where unions had few durable traditions and the AFL officials were loath to stimulate rank-and-file militancy, Washington deferred to the demands of employers. Roosevelt's lieutenants arranged settlements in the spring of 1934 which averted threatened strikes but left the AFL federal locals crippled. In coal and clothing, however, where the unions had long traditions of militancy and exercised real power, the federal government served as midwife to prounion settlements.

But the eruption of working-class militancy in 1934 was not easily contained, especially where it emerged under the leadership of non-AFL labor radicals. Three conflicts in the spring and summer of 1934 showed the potentialities and possibilities of militant labor action. A dispute in Toledo, Ohio, between workers at Electric Auto-Lite and their employers ultimately involved the entire local labor community. Led by A. J. Muste and other non-AFL radicals, the Toledo strikers united with the city's unemployed to fight Ohio's National Guard for control of the streets. Militancy there produced a worker victory.

Next, in San Francisco in May–June 1934, a violent dispute along the waterfront, which involved maritime workers and eventually tied up the whole Pacific Coast, led to a citywide general strike similar to the one which had paralyzed Seattle in 1919. In San Francisco, too, employers, public officials, and even officers of the AFL's International Longshoremen's Association accused the strikers of Bolshevism. Under the leadership of Harry Bridges, who was indeed sympathetic to Communism, the strikers refused to surrender. Forming their own non-AFL union, the International Longshoremen and Warehousemen's Union, the West Coast workers won a settlement far beyond anything yet achieved by waterfront workers on the East and Gulf coasts. Finally, in late July 1934, a violent strike among teamsters in Minneapolis–St. Paul caused the Governor of Minnesota, Floyd B. Olson, to place the Twin Cities under modified martial law. Once again radicals, this time former Wobblies and Communists, who now called themselves Trotskyites, led the strikers. Again militancy, and even violence, brought a union victory.

Each of these strikes proved that workers were willing, even eager, to act forcefully. They also disclosed that struggle rather than accommodation—the AFL's preferred strategy—produced gains. Moreover, they hinted at a new radicalism which was emerging among some workers and their leaders.

While militant workers and radical leaders were writing an important chapter in American labor history, the AFL unions suffered from a paralysis of will. This was suggested by events in automobiles and steel, where Federation leaders accepted federal mediation in preference to calling strikes, only to see unions dissolve as a result. It was revealed even more graphically in the outcome of the largest single strike in 1934 (the largest in American history to that time): the general textile-workers strike, which spread from Maine to northern Alabama and involved between 400,000 and 500,000 men and women.

Demanding a thirty-hour week without reduction in the minimum $13 wage, abolition of the stretch-out, and recognition of the United Textile Workers, the mill employees walked out in mass during August 1934—110,000 in Massachusetts, 50,000 in Rhode Island, 60,000 in Georgia, 28,000 in Alabama. In the South, where "flying squadrons" rushed from one mill town to another to call out the workers and set up picket lines, there were inevitable clashes with the police and special deputies. At the height of the struggle, some

11,000 national guardsmen in eight states were under arms to preserve order.

On September 7, 1934, after President Roosevelt had intervened and promised the appointment of a new Textile Labor Relations Board to study conditions in the industry, the union leaders called off the strike. As it turned out, employers continued to discriminate against union members, returning strikers were often barred from mills in southern towns, and demoralization spread further throughout the workers' ranks. The great textile strike had ended in disaster.

The gains which labor had made in the early days of the NRA seemed to be fading away. The attitude of employers unwilling to accept code provisions or carry out bona fide collective bargaining, the failure of the government to safeguard the workers in strike settlements, and the inability or reluctance of the AFL to give the mass-production workers the support which might have enabled them to organize effectively combined to dash labor's high hopes. Although union membership in 1935 was a million greater than it had been two years earlier, it was below the four million mark which Green had so proudly announced for the AFL alone at the close of 1933. Hundreds of thousands of new recruits had fallen by the wayside, and some six hundred federal unions were disbanded. The organized strength of the automobile workers dwindled to 10,000; the burst of activity in steel subsided with a residue of only 8,600 members in the Amalgamated Association of Iron, Tin and Steel Workers; and of the several hundred thousand who had joined the United Textile Workers during the textile strike, only 80,000 remained with the union. The dramatic movement touched off with the adoption of Section 7(*a*) had lost its momentum.

By the beginning of 1935, the failure of the NRA, not only to solve the problem of labor relations but also to stimulate recovery, could no longer be disguised. It was being openly attacked on all fronts in sad contrast to the exuberant fervor of the parades and flag waving with which it had first been greeted. An original impetus had been given to recovery, but the psychological effect of that shot in the arm had worn off. Big business was generally in revolt against the labor provisions of the codes. Little business felt itself squeezed to the wall both by the revival of monopoly and by union demands. Labor was convinced that it had been betrayed. With the whole program bogging down because of inner contradictions, the country was no longer willing to support a system of economic controls which could not be successfully administered and appeared to place the burden most heavily on the consumer. It was with relief rather than regret that the nation accepted the announcement in May 1935 that the Supreme Court had delivered the coup de grace to the entire set-up by declaring, in A. L. A. *Schecter* v. *the United States,* that the National Industrial Recovery Act was unconstitutional.

This development completely swept away such safeguards for labor as had been written into Section 7(*a*). However, an amendment to the Railway Labor Act had definitely extended them to railroad employees, and a drive to secure them on a firmer basis for all other workers had already been launched. In March 1934, Senator Robert F. Wagner of New York had introduced a bill to close the loopholes which enabled industry to cripple labor's strength by setting up company unions and refusing to bargain collectively with any other group. Wagner had temporarily withdrawn this measure on the President's plea for a further trial period under existing legislation, but he reintroduced it early in 1935. Just eleven days before the NRA was declared unconstitutional, it passed the Senate.

The Wagner bill had strong support from labor, and the collapse of the NRA naturally intensified the demand for its immediate acceptance by the House. "I do not mind telling you," an unusually militant Green testified before one congressional committee, "that the spirit of the workers in America had been aroused. They are going to find a way to bargain collectively. . . . Labor must have its place in the sun. We cannot and will not continue to urge workers to have patience, unless the Wagner bill is made law and unless it is enforced once it becomes law."

Roosevelt had no part in developing this new measure, and, according to both Secretary Perkins and Raymond Moley, one of Roosevelt's chief advisers, he did not particularly like it when it was described to him. It was Senator Wagner's work. But with the NRA out of the picture, Moley has reported, the President "flung his arms open" and suddenly embraced it. Labor could not be completely let down, and here was the means to reenact a stronger Section 7(*a*) so far as collective bargaining was concerned. With administration support, the measure now promptly passed the House. Roosevelt signed it on July 5.

Although the general policy of the Wagner Act—or the National Labor Relations Act as it was officially called—had been foreshadowed by Section 7(*a*) of the National Industrial Recovery Act, the new law heavily underscored the basic change in governmental attitude toward labor. Not only were old ideas of a laissez-faire attitude in industrial relations again ignored; the Roosevelt administration now upheld the right of wage earners to organize without making any such corresponding concessions to management as had been incorporated in the NIRA. It was prepared to strengthen the bargaining position of the workers, and consequently their ability to obtain a larger share of the national income, over against whatever claims might be put forward by industry. The justification for this position was that only through government support could labor meet management on anything like equal terms in an industrialized society, and that the time had come when the scales, always so heavily weighted in favor of industry, should be redressed in favor of the workers. Every unfair labor practice banned by the Wagner Act applied to employers, and it imposed no restraints whatsoever on the unions.

Roosevelt declared the purpose of the law to be the creation of a better relationship between labor and management, but he tactitly acknowledged its one-sidedness. "By preventing practices which tend to destroy the independence of labor," he stated, "it seeks, for every worker within its scope, that freedom of choice and action which is justly his."

To assure such freedom, labor's right to organize was not only expressly reaffirmed, but all employer interference was explicitly forbidden. It was to be an unfair labor practice for an employer to restrain or coerce his employees from exercising their rights, to try to dominate or even contribute financially to the support of any labor organization, to encourage or discourage union membership by discrimination in hiring and firing, or to refuse to bargain collectively. Moreover, representatives designated for collective bargaining by a majority of the employees in an appropriate unit, whether it was an employer, craft, or plant unit, were to have exclusive bargaining rights for all employees. The Wagner Act also outlawed company unions.

The administration of the Wagner Act was placed in the hands of a new National Labor Relations Board, made up of three members, with sole authority to determine the appropriate bargaining unit and to supervise the elections wherein employees chose their exclusive representatives for dealing with employers. The board could also hear complaints of unfair labor practices, issue "cease and desist" orders where they were found to be justified, and petition the courts for enforcement of its orders. The NLRB was not concerned with the substance of disputes over wages and hours, or any other issues affecting conditions of work, but solely with the practical encouragement and facilitation of collective bargaining.

"It should be clearly understood," President Roosevelt said in explaining the quasi-judicial functions of this administrative agency, "that it will not act as mediator or conciliator in labor disputes. The function of mediation remains, under this Act, the duty of the Secretary of Labor and of the Conciliation Service of the Department of Labor. . . . It is important that the judicial function and the mediation function should not be confused. Compromise, the essence of mediation, has no place in the interpretation and enforcement of the law."

At the time of its passage, the Wagner Act had widespread support. Most of the business community criticized the one-sidedness of the law, freely predicted union irresponsibility under its provisions, and were generally alarmed at what they considered the dangers to management's control. But public opinion polls repeatedly emphasized popular sympathy for labor's aspirations and revealed a general feeling that the workers were fully entitled to governmental protection.

Whatever the pros and cons of the new legislation, its implications were tremendous. At long last, the general expressions upholding labor's right to organize—in the Clayton Act, the Norris–La Guardia Act, and the National Industrial Recovery Act—were given substance. Labor had for over a century fought for freedom from legal restraints which hampered its activity. It had struggled against conspiracy laws, enforcement of yellow-dog contracts, judicial interpretations of liberty that actually nullified the individual worker's freedom, and against the arbitrary use of injunctions. The Wagner Act not only removed past obstructions to union activity but also erected substantial barriers to any interference on the part of the employers to the full mobilization of labor's economic strength.

The battle to realize the full benefits of the new law, however, had still to be fought. While some employers were ready to accept its provisions and bargain collectively with their employees in good faith, more were implacably opposed to unionization and were determined to continue their resistance to it at all cost. In many quarters, labor had to push its campaign for organization against as fierce opposition as it had ever faced. The workers again fell back on strikes to win the union recognition which many companies withheld in spite of all governmental guarantees.

The excuse often advanced for refusing to meet the new legal requirements of collective bargaining was that the Wagner Act was unconstitutional. Advised by their lawyers that the Supreme Court would almost certainly invalidate it as going beyond the power of Congress over interstate commerce, on which its provisions were based, antiunion employers did not hesitate to violate the law and obtained scores of injunctions to prevent the National Labor Relations Board from enforcing it. They launched an attack on labor which was aimed especially at unionization in steel, automobiles, rubber, and other mass-production industries. They still tried to maintain their control over company unions. Labor spies, stool pigeons, and agents provocateurs were hired to ferret out any evidence of union activity, sow seeds of distrust and suspicion among the workers themselves, and furnish the information which would enable the employers to get rid of all those who might be classed as agitators. Strong-arm squads were maintained in some instances to discourage union membership by more forcible methods, and outside organizers were beaten up, run out of town, and threatened with further violence should they ever show up again.

The report of the La Follette Civil Liberties Committee (headed by Senator Robert M. La Follette of Wisconsin) was a shocking revelation of the disregard of legal and constitutional rights which widely characterized industrial relations between 1933 and 1937. A first installment, made public in December 1937, disclosed that some 2,500 corporations (the list read "like a bluebook of American industry") had long followed the practice of hiring labor spies from agencies which specialized in industrial espionage. The records of such firms as the Pinkerton and Burns agencies, the Railway and Audit Inspection Company, and the Corporations Auxiliary Company showed that they had furnished in the three-year period under review, a total of 3,871 agents to report on union activities, stir up discontent among employees, and generally block labor organization. In carrying out their secret activities, individual operatives had become affiliated with ninety-three unions, and a third of the Pinkerton detectives had actually succeeded in becoming union officials. It was further stated that a selected list of companies, representative but not inclusive, had spent from 1933 to 1936 a total of $9,440,000 for spies, strikebreakers, and munitions, the General Motors Corporation alone footing a bill of $830,000.

"The public cannot afford to let this challenge presented by industrial espionage go unnoticed," the La Follette committee concluded. "Through it private corporations dominate their employees, deny them their constitutional rights, promote disorder and disharmony, and even set at naught the powers of the government itself."

When this same committee investigated the "Little Steel" strike of 1937, disclosures of the weapons which had been accumulated for industrial war were even more startling than those of industrial espionage. The Youngstown Sheet and Tube Company had on hand eight machine guns, 369 rifles, 190 shotguns and 450 revolvers, with 6,000 rounds of ball ammunition and 3,950 rounds of shot ammunition, and also 109 gas guns with over 3,000 rounds of gas ammunition. The Republic Steel Corporation had comparable equipment, and with the purchases of tear and sickening gas amounting to $79,000, was described as the largest buyer of such supplies—not excepting law enforcement bodies—in the United States. La Follette declared that the arsenals of these two steel companies "would be adequate equipment for a small war."

There was also brought to light one especially notorious example of industrial techniques in combating unionism, first developed by the Remington Rand Company and then widely publicized by the National Association of Manufacturers under the name of the Mohawk Valley formula. This formula blueprinted a systematic campaign to denounce all union organizers as dangerous agitators, align the community in support of employers in the name of law and order, intimidate strikers by mobilizing the local police to break up meetings, instigate "back to work" movements by secretly organizing "loyal employees," and set up vigilance committees for protection in getting a struck plant again in operation. The underlying purpose behind the Mohawk Valley formula was to win public support by branding union leaders as subversive and threatening to remove the affected industry from the community if local business interests stood by and allowed radical agitators to win control over workers otherwise ready and anxious to cooperate with their employers.

The evidence made public by the La Follette Committee unveiled previously hidden aspects of industrial warfare. Even the most conservative newspapers, while suggesting that the committee's investigation had been one-sided and its report undoubtedly exaggerated, recognized a state of affairs that could not be condoned and came to the defense of labor's civil liberties.

Labor was in the meantime combating this antiunion campaign

with its own militant tactics. Widespread industrial unrest continued throughout the whole period in which the basic principles underlying the Wagner Act were at stake. In 1937, strikes rose to a peak even higher than that of 1934. They totaled 4,720 and engaged almost two million workers.

The constitutionality of the Wagner Act was still undetermined as this new wave of unrest rose to a dramatic climax in the sit-down strikes[2] of General Motors automobile workers, but the Supreme Court finally acted on April 12, 1937. In a series of decisions, of which the most important was that rendered in the case of *National Labor Relations Board v. Jones and Laughlin Steel Company*, the law was sustained. This was a spectacular victory for the New Deal and for organized labor and reflected the change in the attitude of the court which dramatically punctuated the struggle over its reorganization initiated earlier in 1937 by President Roosevelt. The regulation of labor relations as they might affect interstate commerce was declared to be clearly within the province of Congress under the commerce clause, and the contention that the rights of either employer or employee were invaded by the provisions of the act was flatly rejected.

"Employees have as clear a right to organize and select their representatives for lawful purposes," Chief Justice Charles Evans Hughes stated in the five-to-four decision, "as the respondent has to organize its business and select its own officers and agents. Discrimination and coercion to prevent the free exercise of the right of employees to self-organization and representation is a proper subject for condemnation by competent legislative authority. Long ago we stated the reason for labor organizations. We said that they were organized out of the necessities of the situation; that a single employee was helpless in dealing with an employer; that he was dependent ordinarily on his daily wage for the maintenance of himself and his family; that if the employer refused to pay him the wages he thought fair, he was nevertheless unable to leave the employ and resist arbitrary and unfair treatment; that union was essential to give laborers opportunity to deal on an equality with their employer."

Its authority now established, the National Labor Relations Board was finally in a position to apply the law effectively. It interpreted broadly the provision that it was an unfair labor practice for an employer to interfere with, restrain, or coerce employees in the exer-

---

[2]About these, see pp. 291–296.

cise of their rights. Not only were such old practices as yellow-dog contracts, blacklisting, and other overt forms of discrimination outlawed, but the employment of labor spies and antiunion propaganda were also prohibited. Company-dominated unions were disestablished, both union shops and closed shops upheld, and interference with peaceful picketing was forbidden.

The majority of cases coming before the board in regard to unfair labor practices were actually handled without prejudice to the interests of industry. It of course remained true that wholly unjustified charges might often be brought up, and that management could not counter with any complaints of unfair practices on the part of the unions. The overall record of the NLRB was, nevertheless, quite a different one from that presented by a generally hostile press which lost no occasion to attack the board for its supposed partiality to labor.

Between 1935 and 1945, a total of 36,000 cases involving charges of unfair labor practices and 38,000 concerned with employee representation were handled. Considering them as a whole, 25.9 per cent were withdrawn without any action being taken, 11.9 per cent were dismissed by regional directors, 46.3 per cent were settled by informal procedures leading to mutual agreement, and only 15.9 per cent required official hearings. The latter cases led to the disestablishment of some 2,000 company unions and the reinstatement of 300,000 employees, with back pay aggregating $9,000,000, where employers were found guilty of discrimination against bona fide union members.

In addition to hearing cases of unfair labor practices and issuing cease and desist orders when it found them justified, the National Labor Relations Board during this period from 1935 to 1945 also held some 24,000 elections, in which 6,000,000 workers participated, to determine collective bargaining units. The CIO won 40 per cent of these elections, the AFL 33.4 per cent, independent unions 10.5 per cent, and in 16.1 per cent no bargaining unit was chosen. It should be remembered that the board had nothing whatsoever to do with disputes over wages and hours, but in respect to the issues which it was authorized to handle, its activities greatly helped to stabilize industrial relations.

The protection given labor's right to organize and bargain collectively was the most important phase of the prolabor policy that was generally followed under the New Deal. Once embarked on its course, the Roosevelt administration went far beyond any previous administration in encouraging the growth of unions and accepting the basic role which they played in the development of the national economy. But the Wagner Act was not the only New Deal measure which aided labor or contributed to the improved status of industrial workers.

From his earliest days in office, Roosevelt's insistence upon the obligation of government to cope directly with the fundamental problems of unemployment and relief clearly demonstrated a sympathetic understanding of the needs of the nation's wage-earners. The public-works program included in the National Industrial Recovery Act was principally intended as a means to prime the pump of industry, but both the Civilian Conservation Corps and the Federal Emergency Relief Administration had as their direct objectives relief for the great army of unemployed. They represented an approach to the vital problem of human needs which differed sharply from that of President Hoover, who had long held out against direct relief as undermining individual initiative and self-respect. The Roosevelt administration was to be much more realistic in recognizing the plight of the unemployed and the necessity of governmental aid until industry revived and could provide normal opportunities for employment.

This was further borne out in the program which culminated in the Works Progress Administration. This agency was set up in 1935, not only to aid the unemployed, but also to provide them with jobs which would enable them to retain their self-respect. The slow pace of recovery, and the recession that developed in 1937, were to involve the government far more deeply in this undertaking than had been originally contemplated. The wellbeing of industrial workers was nevertheless considered more important than possible economies, and the administration held to its course in spite of all criticism of the expense involved.

A much more far-reaching measure, considered by Roosevelt "the cornerstone of his administration," was the Social Security Act of 1935 with its comprehensive provision for unemployment insurance, old-age insurance, and other aid for the needy. The principles underlying this law had been opposed by the American Federation of Labor, as we have seen, until the reversal of its traditional policy on unemployment insurance at its convention in 1932. The AFL then came out in support of governmental action.

Roosevelt instituted studies on the best method of providing for social security early in 1933, talked continually with his advisers about what he termed "cradle-to-the-grave" insurance long before the phrase became current in England, and appointed a Committee on Economic Security to reconcile differing views on how the whole program should be handled. A proposed bill was placed upon his "must list" in 1934 and when Congress failed to act that year, he renewed his insistence upon its adoption at the next session. Final action was then taken, and, in August 1935, the Social Security Act was overwhelmingly approved.

The new law had three major parts. First, unemployment compensation was to be handled by the states through remission of 90 per cent of a national payroll tax to every state adopting an insurance program which met federal specifications. Second, old-age pensions were to be administered directly by the federal government from funds secured through equal taxes upon employers and employees which were to start at 1 per cent of the latter's wages and gradually rise to 3 per cent. Third, other assistance for the needy was to be provided through grants to the states for the aged, the blind, dependent children, and the crippled and disabled, while federal funds were allocated for maternal and child health services, child welfare work, the rehabilitation of the disabled, and general public health.

This social-security program was limited in its scope because of the exclusion of several categories of employees; its benefit payments were not over-generous by any standards, and it fell far short of the "cradle-to-grave" insurance about which Roosevelt liked to talk. The United States still lagged behind other countries which had long since developed more comprehensive plans. The new law was nevertheless another epochal development in the history of a nation so long wedded to concepts of the limited role of government in economic and social matters. That social security now won wide support was a highly significant indication of how the stress of economic circumstances had changed popular attitudes since the depression.

"The experience of these years," William Green wrote, "showed that the very disaster of the crisis compelled the government to assume responsibilities and discharge functions within the field of private endeavour which had been regarded as outside its scope. The national government, acting in behalf of all the people, was compelled to care for the needy and unemployed."

In addition to direct relief for the unemployed and social security, the New Deal was also committed to the improvement of working conditions first attempted in the wage and hour provisions of the NRA codes. Other means to attain this goal were at once sought when the National Industrial Recovery Act was declared unconstitutional. A first step was passage of the Walsh-Healey Public Contracts Act, which established the forty-hour week and minimum wages for all employees of contractors making supplies for the government. But this measure was obviously limited in its scope, and the real question was how a more general measure could overcome the constitutional objections which had been brought not only against the NRA but also against minimum-wage legislation by the states. Secretary Perkins explored the possibilities of a new approach to the problem, but the attitude of the Supreme Court seemed an insuperable barrier.

Minimum-wage legislation was an issue in the campaign of 1936. The Republicans came out in favor of minimum-wage legislation through state laws or interstate compacts, but the Democrats declared that they would continue to seek national legislation "within the Constitution." It was not until the Supreme Court battle had been fought out early in 1937, however, that Roosevelt gave the go-ahead signal for the introduction of a bill providing for maximum hours, minimum wages, and, as an almost last-minute addition, the abolition of child labor which had first been sought in the NRA codes.

The Fair Labor Standards bill, as it came to be known, met vigorous opposition, reflecting in part the political animosities growing out of the court struggle, and it was at first given only equivocal support even by labor. Many of the conservatives in the AFL were still opposed to wage legislation in principle, fearing that minimum wages would become maximum wages, and William Green took an unyielding stand against what he considered important shortcomings in the administration's proposals. With spokesmen for the American Federation of Labor and the National Association of Manufacturers in dubious alliance, few New Deal measures faced harder sledding.

Roosevelt repeatedly and emphatically stressed the importance of the bill both in messages to Congress and in "fireside chats" (radio addresses) to the country. "A self-supporting and self-respecting democracy," he declared in May 1937, "can plead no justification for the existence of child labor, no economic reason for chiseling workers' wages or stretching workers' hours." But entirely apart from justice to the wage earners themselves, the provisions of the proposed bill were supported as an essential means to sustain and build up national purchasing power.

The importance of high wages from this point of view was of course no new idea. Labor had always maintained that only when the workers were paid enough to enable them to buy the products of their own industry could the economic system function successfully. The assertion of this principle goes back at least as far as the statement of the Mechanics' Union of Trade Associations in 1827 on wages, consumption and manufacturing output. But the argument made slow headway and in the early 1930s was only gradually beginning to gain the acceptance that is today almost commonplace. The purchasing-power theory in support of high wages had been traditionally over-shadowed by the counter argument that, by increasing costs of production, high wages actually narrowed the market for manufactured goods and consequently slowed down production.

When Congress failed to act on the Fair Labor Standards bill in the summer of 1937, Roosevelt returned to the attack on this broad front and, after calling a special session in November, again demanded prompt passage. "I believe that the country as a whole," he stated, "recognizes the need for congressional action if we are to maintain wage increases and the purchasing power of the nation against recessive factors in the general industrial situation. The exploitation òf child labor and the undercutting of wages and the stretching of the hours of the poorest paid workers in periods of business recession had a serious effect on buying power. ...What does the country ultimately gain if we encourage businessmen to enlarge the capacity of American industry to produce unless we see to it that the income of our working population actually expands sufficiently to create markets to absorb that increased production?"

After successive delays, redrafts of the original bill to meet labor's objections, and the exercise of strong administration pressure, the opposition finally gave way. The Fair Labor Standards bill was passed in June 1938. It established a minimum wage of 25 cents an hour to rise to 40 cents an hour in seven years and a forty-four-hour week to be reduced to forty hours in three years, and it prohibited the labor of children under sixteen in industries whose products entered into interstate commerce. A movement whose origins may be traced back to the demands for a legislative ten-hour day voiced by labor over a century earlier had come to fruition. The state had entered more directly and comprehensively into the control of wages and hours than would have been believed even remotely possible prior to the depression. In its way, it was a development as far-reaching as the government's new support for collective bargaining.

Government had swung over to the support of the interests of labor, and so had the courts. The series of cases in which the Wagner Act, the Social Security Act, and the Fair Labor Standards Act were upheld marked a judicial reversal of earlier decisions and gave the final stamp of approval to New Deal policies. The view that laws which affected union membership or prescribed minimum wages violated constitutional guarantees of liberty of contract was abandoned when the Supreme Court stated that "regulation which is reasonable in relation to its subject and is adopted in the interests of the community" could not be construed to violate the due-process clause of either the Fifth or Fourteenth amendments.

Moreover, the courts now went on wholly to exempt unions from prosecution under the antitrust laws and to reverse other restrictive policies by generally upholding the right to strike, to boycott, and to picket. Whereas even during the progressive era labor found supposedly guaranteed privileges repeatedly curtailed by the Supreme Court, its position was now being constantly bolstered by favorable decisions. For example, in one notable case, *Thornhill* v. *Alabama,* peaceful picketing was declared to be a legitimate exercise of free speech, as guaranteed by the Constitution.

The New Deal revolution in labor law found a generally receptive response in the mid-1930s. Repeated public-opinion polls revealed strong support for each of the successive labor measures adopted by Congress between 1933 and 1938. President Roosevelt was undoubtedly justified at this time in asserting his belief that a majority of the people were glad "that we are slowly working out for labor greater privileges and at the same time greater responsibilities."

The continued strikes of these years, and particularly those of 1937, clearly showed that no final solution had been found for industrial relations, and a pronounced reaction to the prolabor policies of the New Deal was soon to set in. In spite of both labor disturbances and a growing demand for modification of the Wagner Act, however, Roosevelt remained convinced that the increased strength of unionism would in time lead to greater industrial stability. He believed thoroughly in the principle of collective bargaining. "It must remain," he declared, "as the foundation of industrial relations for all time." He was prepared not only to help labor to maintain its gains but to advance them still further.

"Only in free lands," he stated in an important address to the convention of the International Brotherhood of Teamsters in 1940, "have free labor unions survived. When union workers assemble with freedom and independence in a convention like this, it is a proof that American democracy has remained unimpaired; it is a symbol of our determination to keep it free."

Labor was still suffering from growing pains, in his opinion, and more responsible leadership was bound to emerge and make possible a larger degree of cooperation with equally responsible management. When warned on one occasion that the unions might become too powerful, he was quoted as replying, "Too powerful for what?" His attitude was that their power should prove an antidote for that of big business.

The basic importance of the New Deal program did not lie in immediate gains or losses for labor but in its recongition that this whole matter of working conditions was no longer the concern of employee and employer alone, but of society as a whole. Democratic capitalism could hardly hope to survive unless the great army of workers could obtain, through concerted effort, the freedom and the security which as individuals they were powerless to defend in an industrialized society. The New Deal's policy was prolabor, but it was prolabor in order to stablize an unbalanced economy. It looked to the well-being of workers in the conviction that upon their contentment and security rested the future stability of American capitalism and democracy.

XVI

The Rise of the
Congress of Industrial
Organizations

At the same time that the New Deal reforms in labor law promoted an upsurge in trade unionism, a dispute about the best way for organized labor to respond to the new situation shattered the ranks of the AFL. The split within the Federation led to the establishment of the Committee for Industrial Organization (CIO) and a trade-union civil war which persisted spasmodically until 1955.

On the surface, the dispute within the AFL was between craft unionism and industrial unionism. Should union organization be pursued principally in the interests of the skilled workers, or should it aim to include more effectively the great mass of unskilled workers? Ever since the decline of the Knights of Labor in the late 1880s, a few exceptions notwithstanding, the craft union structure had prevailed. For half a century, the great mass of semiskilled factory operatives concentrated in the mass-production industries lacked the economic ability and opportunity to form stable unions. The New Deal, however, promised to change that situation. The labor upheaval of 1933–1934 had already demonstrated mass-production workers' ripeness for organization. Yet the cautious leaders of the AFL, especially its dominant craft-union faction, had wasted that opportunity. And the failure to unionize the mass-production workers had weakened the whole labor movement. By 1935, with the passage of the Wagner Act, a second opportunity to build a mass labor movement came. The question for labor leaders now became, not whether to organize workers in craft or industrial unions, but whether to expend the funds, personnel, and energy to organize on a mass basis. As the leader of the insurgent faction within the AFL, John L. Lewis, argued again and again, the immediate issue was unionization of the unorganized on whatever structural basis they preferred. Questions about jurisdiction and whether to assign workers to craft or industrial unions must be postponed, Lewis asserted, until after workers were actually organized. In other words, the struggle that split labor's ranks in the 1930s was fundamentally over the will to act, about whether or not the AFL would seize an unprecedented opportunity to organize millions of mass-production workers.

Unfortunately the substantive issue involved in the labor split became entangled in a bitter, invective-filled personal dispute between the leaders of the two factions. William Green of the AFL and John L. Lewis of the CIO, once close associates and fellow leaders in the UMW, hurled charges and countercharges back and forth at each other.

"In the midst of our common effort to better the welfare of all workers," Green was to write, "came forth a man who sought other ends. Consumed with personal ambition, he gave the lie to the democratic process after it had rejected his leadership. He raised the voice of dualism and disunity, a voice which while pretending to unite sought to disrupt; a voice which while declaiming democratic ideals sought dictatorship."

Lewis struck back savagely at what he considered the obstructive attitude of the AFL, and the blind conservatism of its leadership. The organizing efforts of the Federation were said to represent "twenty-five years of unbroken failure," and its president was charged with being unable either to understand what was happening to the national economy or to rise to the opportunities of the hour. "Alas, poor Green," Lewis told reporters as the verbal brickbats were flying back and forth in 1936, "I knew him well. He wishes me to join him in fluttering procrastination, the while intoning O *tempora, O mores!*"

In taking over command of the campaign for industrial unionism and directly defying the oligarchy in control of the AFL, Lewis soon revealed himself to be the most aggressive and colorful figure that American labor had ever known. His spectacular success in reviving the United Mine Workers during the early days of the New Deal (he increased its membership from 150,000 to 400,000) attracted nation-wide attention. The magazine *Fortune* wryly commented that "he made a noise like the whole labor movement," and in time the noise was to rise to a deafening roar. It was characteristic of popular attitudes toward Lewis in this period that he was invariably described, whether by friend or foe, in gaudy superlatives. He was either an unexampled hero or an unspeakable villain.

Philip Murray, destined to succeed him as president of the CIO, declared that Lewis was "without a peer in the realm of America"; in the days of the united front with Communism, Earl Browder, Chairman of the Communist Party of America, hailed him not merely as the greatest of American trade union leaders but "as a leader of world democracy," and Senator Huey Long of Louisiana could pay him no higher compliment that to single him out as "the Huey Long of labor." The chorus of condemnation, on the other hand, reached its peak during the days of war. When *Fortune* held a poll in 1943 on the most harmful individuals in the United States, 70 per cent of the ballots bore the name of John L. Lewis.

Both Lewis's family origins and early life were typical of British immigrants to industrial America. Of Welsh stock, his parents came from mixed agrarian and laboring background and, like many Welsh immigrants, fled a native land being relentlessly transformed by capitalism and industrialism. John's father took a circuitous route to the place of his son's birth in 1880—the coal-mining town of Cleveland, Iowa. In that Welsh immigrant community in south central Iowa, the elder Lewis worked in the coal mines. For much of John's childhood, his family, like so many working-class families in late nineteenth-century America, moved from town to town in the Hawkeye State. The father tried his hand at farming and even city police work as well as mining. By the late 1890s, the Lewis family was back in the Cleveland-Lucas area, where the father and three sons, John included, combined farm work and coal mining. At this time, John first evinced an interest in unionism, becoming a member of the UMW in 1900. But he was a restless and ambitious young man and in 1901 left home for five years during which he roamed the Rocky Mountain area working at various odd jobs. When he returned to Lucas, Iowa, in 1906, John L. Lewis still lacked a vocation or a chosen career. He tried his hand at the feed and grain trade, only to be wiped out in the panic and recession of 1907–1908. Then for reasons still unclear, Lewis chose a "career" in trade unionism. In 1908 he moved with his entire family (a new wife, his parents, and his brothers and sisters) to the small town of Panama in the rapidly growing Illinois coal fields. There the Lewises built a family-based union political machine, which took John L. in rapid succession from the presidency of the Panama local to a position as an organizer for the AFL (1910–1916) and then to chief statistician, vice-president, acting president, and president of the UMW (1916–1920).

Lewis's early career as a union president was filled as much with failure as success. During the 1920s, he defeated all his opponents inside the UMW and became the union's unchallenged leader; some said dictator. Externally, however, the miners' union reeled from defeat to defeat. Taking over a union with more than 500,000 members in 1919–1920, Lewis presided over one with fewer than 100,000 dues-paying members by 1932. Yet it was his prompt seizure of the chance presented by the New Deal to recoup his union's fortunes that first demonstrated the shrewd tactical sense and astute opportunism, reinforced by great courage, which were to make him a national leader.

No public figure other than President Roosevelt was more familiar to the American people as he pursued his stormy, turbulent career after 1933—militantly challenging the world of industry ("They are striking me hip and thigh. . . right merrily shall I return their blows"), vilifying his enemies within the labor movement, making and breaking alliances as he shifted the grounds of his attack, and challenging the government in pursuit of his and the coal miners' interests. Innumerable articles attempted to find the answer to the question which he once asked: "What makes me tick? Is it power I am after, or am I a Saint Francis in disguise, or what?" An elemental force, a consummate actor, a consecrated leader, a self-willed opportunist—what was John L. Lewis? If the answer was indeed a Saint Francis, the disguise could hardly have been more complete. Cartoonists had a happy field day drawing the jutting jaw, the glowering scowl, and the bushy eyebrows of this mighty protagonist of labor.

No consistent philosophy could be discerned in the tortuous windings of Lewis's career. He paid eloquent tribute at one time to Herbert Hoover's "genius for constructive industrial statesmanship"; eagerly embraced the New Deal and threw the full weight of his influence behind Roosevelt in 1936; dramatically broke with the President four years later to stake retention of his office in the CIO on the election of Wendell Willkie. In politics and within the labor movement, it was "off ag'in, on ag'in, gone ag'in—Finnigin" for this union leader who defied American Presidents as well as fellow labor barons. Observers could never decide whether Lewis was devoted more to promoting his own self-interest or to advancing the cause of the American working class. Whatever his real motives (Lewis once responded to an inquisitive reporter: "Questions as to motive will be purely speculative. Some philosopher has said that the pursuit of motives is the most elusive task in the world."), Lewis proved himself the most constructive and creative labor leader of the 1930s.[1]

To the interviewers who flocked to discuss national problems with him in 1936 and 1937, Lewis talked pompously of industrial democracy but completely failed to clarify what the term meant. Like Franklin D. Roosevelt, he sought to preserve what he valued as the positive aspects of democratic capitalism, yet he believed that they could be preserved only through dramatic reforms and a redistribution of social and economic power. Lacking a long-range program or an ultimate goal, in may ways he also resembled Samuel Gompers. Equally opportunistic, he used the New Deal to rebuild the labor movement inherited from Gompers on a new foundation but never to seek an American revolution. As Gompers built an informal political alliance between labor and the Wilsonian Democrats, Lewis constructed a more formal one between workers and the Roosevelt Democrats. Yet when asked about the future of labor, his answers were lost in hazy and verbose platitudes. "It would be unwisdom to paint a picture that would only alarm our adversaries of tomorrow," he told one inquiring reporter. "Neither can I bond the purity of motive or the administrative rectitude of the labor movement of tomorrow."

On the platform, in public meetings and over the radio, Lewis showed a flare for the dramatic that inevitably arrested public attention. He well knew his ability as an actor ("My life is but a stage," he said on one occasion) and he would alternately cajole, denounce,

---

[1]About his own character, Lewis once said, on receiving a portrait of himself presented by coal-mine operators: "I value the portrait although I am going to have a hard time reading all the facets of his character."

threaten, and pontificate with equal self-assurance. His sense of his own importance was magnificent.

He performed prodigies of valor in building up the United Mine Workers and in organizing the CIO. Labor was to owe him an immense debt. But his domineering personality kept labor divided, and his defiance of the government during the Second World War was a highly important factor in alienating the public sympathy that labor had enjoyed in the early days of the New Deal. Whatever the losses he suffered in either public or labor support, however, Lewis could never be relegated to the background. With his miners standing firmly behind him and accepting his dictatorial control of their union because he got results, he continued to play an important role in labor politics.

The discontent with the fumbling policies of the AFL which was to give Lewis his chance to lead the movement for industrial unionism came to a head at the annual convention of the Federation in San Francisco in 1934. With union members in textiles, steel, automobiles, and rubber drifting away, the demand for industrial charters to replace federal charters became increasingly vocal. The leaders of industrial unions within the AFL attacked the policy which required new unions to be subordinated to the jurisdictional claims of existing craft unions. They vigorously reasserted their conviction that only the organization of all workers—the skilled and the unskilled—in single industry-wide unions could meet the needs of workers engaged in mass production.

The old-line craft union leaders were not convinced. The very fact that in previous years the membership in existing industrial unions had increased 130 per cent, while that of craft unions had gained only 10 per cent, simply emphasized for them the dangers of granting the new industrial charters which the insurgents demanded. They insisted that such a departure from traditional practice would destroy the foundations upon which the AFL had been built. Wage earners could not be successfully organized, it was reiterated, except by bringing them into "the respective national and international unions where jurisdiction has been established."

The controversy was temporarily resolved at San Francisco by a compromise engineered by moderates on both sides. It was agreed that charters would be granted for unions in automobiles, rubber, cement, radio, and aluminum, and an intensive drive initiated to organize the steel industry, but that the rights of existing craft unions would be fully protected and that all jurisdictional disputes would be submitted to an executive council enlarged to include representatives of the industrial unions.

This was at least a partial success for the insurgents, but the succeeding year saw little or nothing done to carry out the agreement. The AFL leadership had not in reality been aroused from its complacent conservatism. The craft-union leaders, and especially those of the building trades, had not been persuaded of the need for aggressive organizing. They still saw only dangers to their own hold on power in any broadening of the bases of the labor movement. They continued to postpone and delay any action along the lines to which they had supposedly agreed. The next convention of the Federation, held at Atlantic City in 1935, met against a background of growing union demoralization in the mass-production industries and an executive council report that "we did not deem it advisable to launch an organizing campaign for the steel industry."

Lewis came to Atlantic City demanding action. The situation in steel was for him one of particular concern. He had succeeded in organizing the workers in the captive coal mines belonging to that industry and was convinced that this new union redoubt could not be held unless the steel workers were also organized. This time he was determined, together with other leaders favoring industrial unionism, to compel the executive council to live up to its promises—or else.

The issue was placed fairly before the convention in majority and minority reports submitted by its resolutions committee. The former declared that, since it was a primary obligation of the AFL "to protect the jurisdictional rights of all trade unions organized upon craft lines," industrial charters would violate the agreements which had always existed between the Federation and its craft affiliates. The latter insisted that in any industry where the work performed by a majority of the workers fell within the jurisdictional claim of more than one craft union, industrial organization was "the only form that will be acceptable to the workers or adequately meet their needs."

On the one side in this embittered controversy were William Green, cautiously following the policies bequeathed to him by Samuel Gompers in spite of earlier advocacy of industrial unionism; the hard-boiled and hard-hitting head of all carpenters, William L. Hutcheson, firmly resolved to keep all workers in wood or its substitutes within the comfortable fold of his own union; Daniel J. Tobin, the pugnacious leader of the teamsters, who scornfully characterized the unskilled workers in the mass-production industries as "rubbish"; Matthew Woll, of the photoengravers, whose conservatism was exemplified by his role as acting president of the old and moribund National Civic Federation; and the dignified scholarly John P. Frey, head of the Metal Trades Department of the AFL. This was the Old Guard, ready to fight mass-production unionism with all the weapons at its command.

Lewis led the insurgents and had the support of some of the most forceful labor leaders of the day. Among them were Charles P. Howard, the calm, persuasive head of the Typographical Union and the actual author of the minority report; Philip Murray, the somewhat retiring and soft spoken, but extremely able, alter ego of Lewis in the United Mine Workers; Sidney Hillman, the Lithuanian-born needle-trades leader, who harbored a fund of nervous energy and ambition beneath his quiet manner and who had just brought the formerly independent Amalgamated Clothing Workers into the AFL; and David Dubinsky, one of the shrewdest of trade unionists and president of the International Ladies' Garment Workers.

The debate among these chieftains over AFL policy continued for several days, the issue sharpened by attack and counterattack on the floor of the convention. Its peak was reached when Lewis excoriated tactics that resulted in the new unions "dying like the grass withering before the autumn sun" and vehemently assailed what he regarded as the betrayal of the promises made at the preceding convention.

"At San Francisco, they seduced me with fair words," he thundered, "Now, of course, having learned that I was seduced, I am enraged and I am ready to rend my seducers limb from limb, including delegate Woll. In that sense, of course, I speak figuratively." He called upon the convention delegates to make a contribution to the welfare of their less fortunate brethren, to heed their cry from Macedonia, to organize the unorganized and make the Federation into the greatest instrument that had ever been forged to befriend the cause of humanity. And he solemnly warned that, if they let slip this opportunity, the enemies of labor would be encouraged "and high wassail will prevail at the banquet tables of the mighty."

But for all his eloquence, his appeals and his warnings, Lewis was unable to make the delegates see why they should modify traditional policies. The majority were unmoved by the threat of being rent limb from limb, even figuratively. Their ears were closed to all cries from Macedonia. They were not disturbed by the picture of high wassail at the banquets of the mighty. When the final vote was taken, the program for industrial unionism went down to defeat through a vote of 18,024 to 10,933 in favor of the majority report of the resolutions committee favoring craft unions.

Shortly afterward an incident occurred which appeared to symbolize the break that this crucial vote meant. In the course of further wrangling over procedure, Hutcheson so far departed from parliamentary decorum as to call Lewis a term which bystanders identified as "bastard." The rejoinder of the miner's chieftain was an uppercut, with all the force of some 225 pounds behind it, which caught the equally burly czar of the carpenters squarely on the jaw. The assailants were separated and the danger of a free-for-all happily averted, but the altercation hardly served to placate feelings, already so touchy, in the two camps into which labor had been divided. A rank-and-file carpenter promptly wired Lewis: "Sock him again!"

Immediately after the AFL convention, the advocates of industrial unionism met to consider further action. They were unwilling to accept a decision which once again put off any effective organizational work in the mass-production industries and, on November 9, 1935, took the first steps to set up their own Committee for Industrial Organization. As originally constituted, it was made up of Lewis, Howard, Hillman, and Dubinsky, together with Max Zaritsky, of the Cap and Millinery Department of the United Hatters; Thomas F. McMahon of the United Textile Workers; Thomas H. Brown of the Mine, Mill and Smelter Workers; and Harvey C. Fremming of the Oil Field, Gas Well and Refining Workers. It was the declared intent of this committee to work within the framework of the AFL rather than to establish an independent organization. Its functions were to be "educational and advisory" in an effort to promote the recognition and acceptance of "modern collective bargaining" in the mass-production industries. In spite of such statements, the leaders of the CIO were at once accused by Green of going against the majority decision of the AFL convention. Their sole motive, he repeatedly declared, was to force acceptance of their own views. The answer of Lewis was to bid further defiance to the executive council. "Dear Sir and Brother," he wrote to Green on November 23, 1935: "Effective this date I resign as vice-president of the American Federation of Labor."

The CIO at once began to lay plans for its own organizing campaign and, early in January 1936, submitted to the executive council of the AFL for a final time the old demand for industrial charters in steel, automobiles, rubber, and radio. But there was no break in the ranks of the "old guard." More fearful than ever of what the aggressive tactics of the new committee might mean to the established position of craft unions in the AFL, the members of the executive council now countered with an order for the immediate dissolution of the CIO. They charged that it was fomenting insurrection and that it was a dual organization created only to serve the interests of "a few self-seeking individuals."

Throughout the next few months, angry controversy raged between the leaders of the AFL and those of the CIO, and the cleavage in labor's ranks steadily widened. Green alternately pleaded and threatened in trying to bring the rebels back into the fold. Lewis adamantly went his own way. Finally, in late summer, the AFL executive council suspended the ten unions which had in the meantime affiliated with the CIO. Far from submitting to such discipline, Lewis declared that the council had acted without authority. "I fear his threats," was his answer to Green's charges on one occasion, "as much as I believe his promises." When the Federation met for its 1936 convention at Tampa, Florida, delegates from the CIO unions were conspicuously absent. The countermove of the AFL was to vote by an overwhelming but meaningless majority that their suspension should remain in effect until "the breach be healed and adjusted under such terms and conditions as the Executive Committee may deem best."

The CIO marched ahead with its own organizing program. New unions in steel, automobiles, glass, rubber, and radio joined the original members. In increasing alarm, the AFL again denounced the movement as threatening to destroy the whole basis of labor federation and assailed its leaders for betraying the union cause. In March 1937, amid the nationwide excitement caused by organizational drives in both steel and automobiles, the executive council made the decisive move of ordering all CIO unions expelled from state and city federations of the AFL.

Toward the end of 1937, again under the influence of moderate leaders in both camps, belated efforts were made to find some basis for peace. They were foredoomed to failure. The AFL proposed the return of the original CIO unions and the merger of its new ones with existing AFL unions. The CIO demanded admittance of its entire membership, now grown to some thirty-two unions, with full voting power. Each organization was looking toward domination in any proposed merger, and neither AFL nor CIO leaders were willing to make the concessions that might have enabled them to work together.

Never a simple dispute between craft and industrial unionists, the labor conflict intertwined issues of principle, power, and personality. The insurgents refused to concede to the "old guard" either power or antiquated labor traditions. The old guard feared that the "new" mass-production unionism would not only dilute their power but also misdirect trade unionism away from its tried and true path. And Green and Lewis developed a deep, visceral personal dislike of each other. However, the failure of the AFL and CIO leaders to reconcile their differences actually benefited workers and the labor movement. Competition between the two union federations led to more vigorous organizing efforts and to an enormous increase in the size of organized labor. By the end of 1937, the CIO claimed 3,700,000 members[2] and the AFL 3,400,000 for a total more than twice as great as in 1932–1933.

After the failure of these peace negotiations in the autumn of 1937, the AFL confirmed the action of its executive council in expelling all CIO members, except for the Ladies' Garment Workers, who were soon to return to the fold. Then, in May 1938, Lewis and his lieutenants took the final steps to transform what had originally been only an organizing committee into a permanent Congress of Industrial Organizations. These moves, however, were only formalities. The rift in the house of labor was already complete.

If in some respects the CIO seemed much like the AFL, in others it differed fundamentally. Like AFL affiliates, the CIO unions basically sought to advance the interests of workers through collective bargaining within a democratic capitalist system. Like their counterparts in the AFL old guard, such CIO leaders as Lewis, Hillman, and Murray preferred to act as labor generals who led their troops in battle, not as temporarily elected representatives who reflected the wishes of the ranks. Yet unlike typical AFL unions, the CIO unions promoted racial solidarity (they even established union civil-rights units), more

---

[2]Since many of the CIO members did not pay dues, it is hard to estimate the organization's real stable membership. One reason why some CIO leaders took a dim view of unity negotiations was their realization that they would still be only a minority in a reunited labor federation.

aggressively advanced the interests of workers of new immigrant stock, and proved more receptive to the demands of women workers. The CIO also was much more active politically, linking its success and future directly to that of Roosevelt and other New Deal Democrats. A major reason for the CIO's more radical position on many issues was that many of the organization's secondary leaders and cadres came out of the Socialist and Communist parties. Thus it was not surprising that many contemporaries saw the CIO as a new kind of labor movement, one akin to continental European social democratic movements, one that held much promise and peril for the future of the American nation.

The CIO wasted little time in building institutions to compete with the AFL for the loyalty of the American worker. It established state and city industrial councils as counterparts to the AFL's state federations and city centrals. It invited all new industrial unions to join, and it formed its own special organizing committees in steel, meat packing, and textiles. Also unlike the AFL, the CIO leaders claimed more power over their affiliates and, especially in the cases of the new unions and organizing committees, intervened more often and forcefully than had been the practice in the AFL.

The response to the CIO's vigorous campaign for industrial unionism, set in motion soon after its revolt against the dilatory and delaying tactics of the AFL in 1935, was immediate and nationwide. Here was what the great body of workers in mass-production industries had been waiting for, and they flocked to join unions that really met their needs and freed them from the discriminatory controls of federal unions. As organizers went out from the new CIO headquarters, supported by funds made available through contributions from the miners, needle workers, and other sympathetic unions, they were greeted with enthusiasm. With the energetic, skillful leadership of Lewis and Murray, Hillman and Dubinsky, progress was phenomenal.

The key drive of the CIO among the nation's steel workers was launched in June 1936 with the establishment of the Steel Workers' Organizing Committee. Under Murray's direction, it took over the nearly defunct Amalgamated Association of Iron, Steel and Tin Workers, set up district headquarters in Pittsburgh, Chicago, and Birmingham, and soon had some four hundred organizers distributing union literature, holding mass meetings, and canvassing from house to house in the steel towns of Pennsylvania, Ohio, Illinois, and

Alabama. With average annual wages among the workers as low as $560, compared with a minimum $1,500 standard-of-living budget, they found fertile ground for effective union propaganda. The steel industry, whose obdurate antiunionism could be traced from Homestead through the great steel strike of 1919, was prepared to meet this new challenge with full recognition of its significance. Full-page advertisements were inserted in papers throughout the country by the Iron and Steel Institute which declared that the companies' own employee representation plans fully met the needs of the workers, that the CIO was trying to intimidate and coerce them into joining the union, and that radical and Communist influences were again at work.

Lewis took to the radio in a nationwide broadcast to counteract this propaganda barrage and warned not only the steel operators but all industry that the drive sponsored by the CIO to unionize the industrial workers could not be withstood. "Let him who will, be he economic tyrant or sordid mercenary," he shouted into the microphone, "pit his strength against this mighty upsurge of human sentiment now being crystallized in the hearts of thirty million workers who clamor for the establishment of industrial democracy and for participation in its tangible fruits. He is a madman or a fool who believes that this river of human sentiment . . . can be dammed or impounded by the erection of arbitrary barriers of restraint."

But while the SWOC prepared to confront the steel industry, an even more dramatic and significant event in labor history occurred in the automobile industry. There had been seething unrest among its workers since the advent of the NRA and the failure of the incipient strikes of 1934. In spite of high hourly rates, seasonal lay-offs held down annual wages to an average of less than $1,000, while another widely held grievance was the speed-up on the assembly line. For the worker whose sole task was to stand by a conveyor belt and put a wheel on a passing chassis, set a fender, or simply tighten a bolt, the tense strain of working under increasing pressure sometimes became almost unbearable. But every attempt to secure modification of such conditions by concerted protest was beaten down by management. The automobile industry had developed its spy system so extensively that union activity appeared to be blocked before it could get started.

Nevertheless, unionization was not given up. The United Automobile Workers had been established through a merger of the federal unions originally set up by the AFL, and its organizers were actively at work. Still, progress was slow. Growing discontented with the meager support of the Federation, the new union thereupon broke away from the AFL in 1936 and threw in its lot with the CIO. Homer S. Martin was elected as president and preparations were made for a revitalized organizational campaign that was eventually to make the United Automobile, Aircraft and Agricultural Implement Workers the largest industrial union in the country.

Martin was young and idealistic, with little experience as either a worker or union member. After graduating from a small Missouri college, he had entered the Baptist ministry and in 1932 become pastor of a small church in a suburb of Kansas City. His outspoken sympathy for the workers soon led to his losing his position, and he took a job in a Chevrolet factory, where he began to preach unionism with evangelical zeal. Fired as a trouble maker, he devoted all his time to union work and rose to be vice-president of the struggling UAW. Described in appearance and manner as an almost typical YMCA secretary—friendly, quiet, bespectacled—Martin took control of the union after his election to the presidency and infused it with a new spirit. What he lacked in experience, he made up in energy. Under the impact of his inspirational appeals, which turned union meetings into something very much like old-fashioned revivals, the automobile workers joined up in rapidly increasing numbers.

There were some scattered strikes during the summer of 1936, and by late fall the United Automobile Workers—some 300,000 strong—was coming out into the open, prepared to demand recognition from the giants of the industry—General Motors, Chrysler, and Ford. "We don't want to be driven; we don't want to be spied on," was the workers' new refrain. But the companies, defying the provisions of the Wagner Act, were not yet willing to make any concessions. When Martin asked the officers of General Motors for a conference on collective bargaining, William S. Knudsen, vice-president, merely suggested that if the workers had any grievances they should take them up with local plant managers. Before the national UAW or CIO leaders could respond, union militants in Flint, Michigan, a General Motors stronghold, took matters into their own hands. This small militant minority, composed mostly of union radicals, seized the day. On the evening of December 30, 1936, without warning, they and a small group of loyal followers closed down the Chevrolet No. 1 factory in Flint. Thus began the "Great Sit-Down Strike," which, before it ended on February 11, 1937, paralyzed production throughout the General Motors empire and affected 112,000 of the company's 150,000 workers.

This strike proved the first full-scale use of a new labor tactic—the sit-down strike. There had been some earlier use of this radical technique, notably among the rubber workers at Akron and elsewhere, but this was to be the tactic's most vital test. The automobile workers refused to leave the plant; they just sat at their work benches. It was not an act of violence but one of passive resistance, doubly effective in that such a strike could be broken only by the forcible removal of the workers from company premises.

Excitement ran high in Flint and neighboring Detroit. General Motors management and the Flint Alliance, a company-sponsored association supposedly made up of loyal employees, assailed the sit-down as an unlawful invasion of property rights and called for the immediate ejection of the strikers. Martin countered with charges that General Motors proposed to invade the property rights of the workers.

"What more sacred property right is there in the world today," he demanded, "than the right of a man to his job? This property right involves the right to support his family, feed his children and keep starvation away from the door. This . . . is the very foundation stone of American homes . . . the most sacred, most fundamental property right in America."

Although Lewis was then deeply involved in the steel organizing drive, he and his CIO associates did not hesitate to offer the Flint strikers their total support. "You men are undoubtedly carrying on through one of the most heroic battles that has ever been undertaken by strikers in an industrial dispute," Lewis declared. "The attention of the entire American public is focussed upon you."

The latter part of his statement was unquestionably true and became even more so as violence broke out in Flint and the strikers showed their stubborn determination not to be dislodged from the occupied plants. The cutting off of all heat—even though it was the dead of winter—made no difference. When the police tried to rush Fisher Body Plant No. 2, they were met by a hail of missiles—coffee mugs, pop bottles, iron bolts, and heavy automobile door hinges. When the police then returned to the attack with tear-gas bombs, the strikers retaliated by turning streams of water on them from the plant fire hoses. The forces of law and order were finally compelled to make a hasty retreat in what the exultant workers promptly termed the "Battle of the Running Bulls."

The strike dragged on from week to week as the General Motors employees continued to sit it out with food and other supplies brought in to them through the picket lines. Discipline was rigid. "Brilliantly lighted," reads a contemporary description by a union organizer, "this vast plant was heavily guarded inside and outside—to keep strikebreakers and other interlopers from entering and to protect the building and its contents. Especially did these strikers guard the company's dies. No liquor was permitted on the premises, and smoking was prohibited on all production floors. Forty-five men were assigned to police patrol duty inside. Their word was law."

Both the company and the Flint Alliance now demanded that the state militia be mobilized to clear the plants since the police had failed to do so. But Governor Frank Murphy of Michigan, sympathetic with the automobile workers and fearful of the bloodshed that would certainly result, refused to take this step. Finally, however, General Motors obtained a court order setting 3:00 P.M. on February 3 as the deadline for evacuation of the plants under penalty of imprisonment and fines. The strikers were undismayed. "We the workers," they wired the governor, ". . . have carried on a stay-in strike over a month to make General Motors Corporation obey the law and engage in collective bargaining. . . . Unarmed as we are, the introduction of the militia, sheriffs or police with murderous weapons will mean a blood-bath of unarmed workers. . . . We have decided to stay in the plant."

Realizing that the strikers meant what they said, Murphy cooly summoned a peace conference. John L. Lewis rushed to Detroit ("Let there be no moaning at the bar when I put out to sea," he cryptically told reporters as he entrained in Washington) and began negotiations with Vice-President Knudsen, whom Governor Murphy had prevailed upon to meet him. But the morning of February 3 arrived without any settlement having been reached. The sit-downers were barricaded in the factories, armed with iron bolts and door hinges and protected against the expected tear and vomiting gas with slight cheesecloth masks. Outside the besieged plants, thousands of sympathetic workers and members of women's emergency brigades milled about as sound trucks blared forth the slogan of "Solidarity Forever."

The zero hour approached—and passed. Murphy refused to order the national guardsmen to enforce the court order. In spite of mounting popular pressure, he remained unwilling to make a move which would have precipitated violence on an unpredictable scale.

The next day President Roosevelt added his request for a continuation of negotiations to that of Governor Murphy, and the Lewis-Knudsen talks (with other representatives of both General Motors and the strikers present) were resumed. For a full week, while the sit-downers grimly held the fort, the conference proceeded until at long last, the weary, haggard governor was able to announce that agreement had been reached. General Motors undertook to recognize the United Automobile Workers as the bargaining agent for its members, to drop injunction proceedings against the strikers, not to discriminate in any way against union members, and to take up such grievances as the speed-up and other matters.

It was not a complete victory for the union. The UAW did not achieve exclusive representation rights, although General Motors did promise not to bargain with any other organization of its employees during the term of the agreement. Nor did the temporary settlement provide any form of union security. Yet it achieved important objectives for labor. For the first time, the CIO had defeated and wrested an agreement from a basic open-shop industry, in this case the largest, multinational business enterprise in the world. It proved to be only the first step in the ultimately total unionization of the auto industry. More important, its impact rippled throughout the economy and spread a wave of unionism and strikes across the nation.

Steel was among the first sectors of the economy to react to the news from Flint. By the end of 1936, SWOC claimed over 150 union lodges with a membership in excess of 100,000. It appeared strong enough to demand recognition and a contract, militant enough to threaten a national strike should steel reject its demands.

In this situation the chief executive officer of U.S. Steel, Myron C. Taylor, acted with the skill of a diplomat. Having seen the militancy of the auto workers and, more decisively, the refusal of state and federal officials to evict the sit-downers, Taylor decided not to risk a strike in steel. Instead, in February he began a series of secret meetings with John L. Lewis. On March 2, 1937, only three weeks after the UAW-General Motors settlement, Philip Murray, representing the SWOC and Benjamin Fairless, U.S. Steel, signed a union-management contract. The agreement recognized SWOC as the bargaining agent for its members, granted a 10 per cent wage increase, and conceded an eight-hour day, forty-hour week. Although U.S. Steel still proclaimed its commitment to the open-shop principle, it had for the first time since its formation in 1901 bargained honestly with a labor union and signed a contract—all this without even a strike. Over a hundred other independent steel companies followed U.S. Steel's lead, and by May 1937, the SWOC claimed over 300,000 members.

The CIO's successive victories over General Motors and U.S. Steel had no parallel in the history of the American labor movement. The nation's two greatest open-shop citadels had fallen before the onslaught of an awakened labor movement. The whole traditional pattern of labor relations in the mass-production industries seemed to be unraveling. What the AFL had failed to accomplish in half a century, the CIO had achieved in three weeks. Having conquered autos and steel, in March 1937 the CIO's future seemed unlimited. Lewis himself told other CIO leaders on March 9: "As years go by, this period will be marked as epoch in life of labor organizations—and economic, social, political history of America." And a contemporary journalist added that Lewis's leadership had made the CIO "the most progressive and vital force in American life today."

At first such claims seemed more than true, as sit-down strikes and union victories infected all parts of the nation. The workers of the Chrysler Corporation were among the first to join the strike wave. After a relatively brief sit-down, they succeeded in winning recognition for the union and a collective bargaining agreement comparable to that exacted from General Motors. Indeed, only Ford continued to hold out among the automobile companies, successfully resisting all attempts of the United Automobile Workers to organize its plants for another four years.

Other industries also felt the impact of labor's new weapon. Between September 1936, and June 1937, almost 500,000 workers were involved in sit-down strikes. Rubber workers, glass workers, and textile workers sat at their benches; striking Woolworth clerks stayed behind their counters but would not wait on customers; pie bakers, opticians, dress-makers and apartment-house janitors sat down. The longest strike of this kind was that of some 1,800 electrical workers in Philadelphia. Two bridegrooms sat out their honeymoons, and the wives of six other married strikers greeted their returning husbands with newly born babies.

As workers throughout the country eagerly took up this militant strategy to force antiunion employers into line, they enthusiastically sang their song of revolt:

> When they tie the can to a union man,
>   Sit down! Sit down!
> When they give him the sack, they'll take him back,
>   Sit down! Sit down!
> When the speed-up comes, just twiddle your thumbs,
>   Sit down! Sit down!
> When the boss won't talk, don't take a walk,
>   Sit down! Sit down!

These strikes aroused increasing popular resentment. Conservative newspapers grew hysterical in condemning such a flagrant invasion of property rights, and there was little support for the sit-downs from any quarter. While Upton Sinclair wrote from California that "for seventy-five years big business has been sitting down on the American people, and now I am delighted to see the process reversed," even among labor sympathizers there were few to echo this sentiment. The AFL explicitly disavowed the sit-down, and, while the CIO had supported the automobile workers, official approval was never given to its general use. After lively and acrimonious debate, the Senate resolved that such strikes were "illegal and contrary to public policy," and the courts eventually outlawed them as constituting trespass on private property.

For all the excitement which it occasioned during the first half of 1937, the sit-down strike in fact proved to be a temporary phenomenon and was abandoned almost as quickly as it had been adopted. It had been the quick and ready response of new and impatient union members fighting for recognition in the strongholds of antiunionism and embittered by the refusal of employers to comply with the provisions of the Wagner Act. When the law was sustained and the NLRB empowered to hold elections for collective bargaining units, the sit-downs were given up.

The immediate consequences of the CIO's activity throughout 1937 were, in any event, immense gains for all affiliated unions. If the dramatic victories won in steel and automobiles were the most important fruits of the general assault upon the mass-production industries, there were other developments that played their part in revolutionizing the labor scene. Organized drives among the rubber workers, radio and electrical workers, lumbermen, and longshoremen, among others, served to build up strong and powerful unions. The campaign of a new Textile Workers' Organizing Committee, under the skillful management of Sidney Hillman, was particularly significant in that it succeeded in organizing many southern mills where the AFL had failed to make any appreciable headway. Thousands of new converts for unionism were won in company towns where labor organizers had never before dared to show themselves, and within a year the union had signed hundreds of collective bargaining agreements throughout the industry.

More important than the actual strength of CIO unions at the close of 1937—600,000 mine workers, 400,000 automobile workers, 375,000 steel workers, 300,000 textile workers, 250,000 ladies' garment workers, 177,000 clothing workers, 100,000 agricultural and packing workers—was the broader base for organized labor as a whole that its campaign had finally achieved. The CIO had successfully organized the unskilled workers into industrial unions and broken through the narrow lines of craft unionism fostered by the AFL. It had welcomed, as the Federation had never done, immigrants, blacks, and women, without regard to race, sex, or nationality.

The CIO influence, moreover, extended to the entire labor front. The AFL, as has been suggested previously, soon found that it could not ignore the unskilled workers while its rival made such giant strides in organizing them. The AFL had, of course, never done so altogether. The lines between skilled, semiskilled and unskilled workers had, indeed, become so blurred with the advance of the machine and the assembly line that many AFL unions included all types. There had also always been industrial unions in the Federation, as we have seen in tracing the growth of organization among coal miners and workers in the garment industry. But the example of what had been done in steel, automobiles, and other mass-production industries aroused the AFL to the need of expanding its own organization to prevent the CIO from monopolizing the new opportunities for unionization. Thousands of workers whose skill was no greater than that of the rank and file of the industrial unions were drawn into such multiple-craft or semi-industrial AFL unions as the machinists, the boilermakers, the meat cutters, the restaurant employees, the hod carriers (who carried supplies to skilled workers in the building trades) and common laborers, and the teamsters. Galvanized into more strenuous activity than ever before, the Federation admitted new recruits wherever it could find them, and though its development was not as dramatic as that of the CIO, there were large gains in membership. Even with the defection of the unions which went over to the rival organization, the AFL's enrollment at the end of 1937, as we have seen, was about a million greater than in 1933.

The AFL and the CIO continued to strive to build up their strength in jealous competition. The former reached out to set up new industrial unions, the latter did not hesitate to charter craft unions. As labor leaders increasingly realized that there was no one formula for organization and that different working conditions demanded different approaches to union problems, debate over the old issues which had led to the split in the labor movement became wholly academic. While the CIO had a majority of industrial unions in the mass-production industries and the AFL included by far the larger proportion of what might still be called craft unions, old distinctions were largely broken down, and both organizations, becoming more and more alike, were prepared to welcome all comers.

The unhappy byproduct of these developments was the spread of jurisdictional quarrels between competing unions. The AFL carpenters fought the CIO woodworkers, the CIO automobile workers fought the AFL machinists, and AFL and CIO longshoremen, textile workers, electrical workers, packinghouse workers, and retail clerks battled indiscriminately. The heavens rang with charges of union raiding, scabbing, and mutual betrayal. The bitterness of these family squabbles often exceeded that of labor-capital disputes. The recriminatory attacks of the two organizations upon one another, and sometimes union battles within either the AFL or CIO were on occasion more violent than labor attacks upon industry.

In their efforts to win recognition for their respective unions, the AFL and the CIO embroiled the National Labor Relations Board in their feud. The NLRB, set up under the Wagner Act to defend labor's rights against antiunion employers, from 1936 to 1939 found itself under as much attack from the AFL as from industry. AFL leaders accused it of favoring the CIO and of sheltering Communists. Such charges coming from a labor federation lent credence to employers' accusations that the board exceeded its authority and acted in a biased manner. Before long, several AFL officials joined with leading industrialists to seek congressional restraints on the NLRB's power. Labor's civil war thus diluted the authority of a governmental agency created to foster union recognition.

Even more serious setbacks thwarted the labor movement's growth beginning in the spring of 1937. The first sign of weakness on the part of CIO came during a clash with the so-called "Little Steel" companies. Republic, Youngstown Sheet and Tube, Inland Steel, and Bethlehem refused to come to terms with the SWOC and began to mobilize their forces to resist any further union pressure. Under the leadership of Tom M. Girdler, the tough, reactionary, virulently anti-labor president of Republic, the battle lines were drawn.

The reply of the leaders of the SWOC was a strike call, and, during May, some 75,000 workers in the plants of "Little Steel" walked out in a concerted move to compel recognition of their union. The companies fought back and, through their strong control over the steel towns, did so successfully. Citizens' committees were formed to support a campaign of intimidation and violent coercion; back-to-work movements were organized with the protection of local police and special deputies; and attacks upon the picket lines, tear gassing of union headquarters, arrests of strike leaders, and the use of militia to protect strikebreakers gradually broke down the morale of the workers.

Violence flared up in a score of steel towns and reached a peak in a bloody clash near the South Chicago works of Republic Steel. On May 30, Chicago city police sought to disperse a peaceful holiday picnic crowd of steel strikers and their families. Whatever their actual reason or cause, the police opened fire on the gathering, which had refused orders to disperse. The unarmed workers broke ranks and frantically fled for safety from the hail of bullets, but they left ten of their number dead on the street and over a hundred injured. While some twenty-two of the police were also wounded in the affray, not a single one suffered any critical injury.

The "Memorial Day Massacre," as it was at once called by union labor, did nothing to bolster the strikers' cause. Later investigations, including careful study of moving-picture films, clearly revealed that they had not provoked the attack. But the sentiment in the steel towns themselves still remained strongly antiunion, and, with such support, the companies were too well entrenched for the workers to hold out. Propaganda, force, and terrorism broke the strike, and the CIO suffered a major defeat. Equally important, neither state nor federal officials interceded to protect labor's right to organize. Indeed in the state of Ohio, the Democratic governor, unlike Frank Murphy of Michigan, used police power to help break the strike.

Even worse fortune was to befall the CIO in 1937. The rapid and real economic recovery of 1936 prompted President Roosevelt to seek to balance the federal budget. He began to cut expenditures and public works programs. Instead of bringing a balanced budget, the President's cuts precipitated a deep economic decline in 1937–1938, sometimes called the "Roosevelt depression," and deeper federal deficits. The new economic collapse also increased unemployment and employer resistance to unions, especially in the sectors of the economy in which CIO was concentrated. As a result, CIO membership plummeted; its income from dues, never as large as its expenses, fell even more, and Lewis wielded a meat-ax in discharging national staff. By late 1937, retrenchment became the norm for CIO and organizing drives a memory of better days.

In contrast, the AFL seemed to thrive under the altered circumstances. Having many more old, stable unions than the CIO and a steadier dues-paying membership, as well as being more broadly spread across the nation, the AFL used its fuller treasury to organize aggressively, as it had rarely done before. AFL affiliates also seemed an attractive alternative to employers fearful of the radical CIO. By the end of 1937, the AFL had many more dues-paying members than the CIO, was growing more rapidly, and was more secure in its power. It had now learned that the workers whom Dan Tobin had previously dismissed as the "rubbish at labor's door" made good union members.

In this situation, one in which the policies and power of government were much more vital to organized labor than ever before, workers acted as a core element in the New Deal political coalition.

XVII

Labor and Politics

The role of labor in politics took on a new significance with the New Deal. With governmental intervention in industrial relations on such a broad scale, the maintenance in office of a national administration and Congress sympathetic toward labor's aspirations became of more vital import than ever before. The limited objectives sought by the lobbying activities of the AFL in the days when Samuel Gompers opposed minimum wages, old-age pensions, and unemployment insurance as "softening the moral fibre of the people" no longer met the needs of the nation's workers. The new industrial unions were especially dependent upon the protection afforded them by New Deal legislation and were consequently ready to do everything in their power to assure the continuance of a pro-labor administration in Washington.

The pronounced swing toward more extensive participation in politics was not, however, entirely due to this desire for effective enforcement of the new labor laws. There was a growing awareness of the larger issues involved in the Roosevelt program. The New Deal became a rallying point for all the progressive and leftist elements in the labor movement. For former Socialists, Roosevelt's policies promised the achievement of long-sought social reforms. Thus trade union

Socialists in increasing numbers deserted their old party for Roosevelt's Democracy or such halfway houses as New York's American Labor party. For Communists, especially after a shift in Comintern policy in 1935, the New Deal emerged as part of a broad anti-Fascist "popular front." Finally, for less ideological trade unionists, Roosevelt symbolized a type of democratic capitalism with the largest possible degree of social justice.

It was natural that in this burst of political activity, the CIO should be far more aggressive than the AFL. The liberal and insurgent spirit which characterized its advocacy of industrial unionism was carried over to the promotion of social reform. While there was not actually any far departure from the old tradition of rewarding labor's friends and punishing its enemies, the CIO was to go much further in trying to make this policy effective. Unlike the AFL, which continued to uphold nonpartisanship in presidential elections, it was prepared to come out in vigorous support of Roosevelt.

There was also greater recognition by the industrial unions of the CIO than on the part of the more strongly established craft unions in the AFL of the extent to which all wage earners had become dependent upon government. The experience of the depression had convinced them of the need for additional controls over the economic life of the nation.

"With the guarantee of the 'right to organize,' such industries may be unionized," Lewis wrote in regard to mass-production enterprises, "but, on the other hand, better living standards, shorter working hours and improved employment conditions for their members cannot be hoped for unless legislative or other provisions be made for economic planning and for price, production and profit controls. Because of these fundamental conditions, it is obvious to industrial workers that the labor movement must organize and exert itself not only in the economic field but also in the political arena."

To carry forward such a program, the CIO leadership was instrumental in establishing Labor's Non-Partisan League in 1936 and also supported the formation of the American Labor party in New York. The primary purpose behind these moves was the reelection of Roosevelt, and every effort was made to win the support of both AFL and CIO unions. The first president of the Non-Partisan League was George L. Berry, of the Printing Pressmen's Union, an AFL affiliate. But while many state labor federations and member unions did cooperate with the league, the AFL itself would not have anything to do with it officially. The executive council was divided on political issues. William Hutcheson headed the Republican Labor Committee and Daniel Tobin the Democratic Labor Committee. While Green personally backed Roosevelt, he condemned the Non-Partisan League as a dual movement in politics, just as the CIO was allegedly a dual labor movement.

There was never any question, however, as to where either the CIO or the new industrial unions stood. They made heavy contributions to the Non-Partisan League's campaign fund (the United Mine Workers alone advanced $500,000), and Lewis called for unequivocal support for the New Deal. "Labor has gained more under President Roosevelt," he declared, "than under any president in memory. Obviously it is the duty of labor to support Roosevelt 100 per cent in the next election."

The Democrats had appealed for labor's backing and had every reason to expect it. The Roosevelt administration had grappled directly with the issues created by the depression and had shown a primary concern with getting people back to work, raising wages, and promoting union organization. "We will continue to protect the worker," the Democratic platform pledged, "and we will guard his rights, both as wage earner and consumer." The Republicans also promised to uphold the right to organize, but neither their previous record nor general attitude was any assurance that labor's broader aims would receive from them the support which had been obtained under the New Deal.

The campaign of 1936 was a bitter one. The divisions of opinion created in American society crossed party lines and aligned class against class, as had not happened since Populism challenged the conservative rule of the dominant business community forty years earlier. While former President Hoover and the Liberty League, an organization of conservative Democrats, charged that the administration sought "to introduce the foreign creeds of Regimentation, Socialism, and Facism," Roosevelt struck back no less vigorously with the countercharge that the "economic royalists" considered government as their own instrument. "Government by organized money," he declared, "is just as dangerous as government by organized mob."

The votes of labor—of AFL as well as CIO union members—played an important part in enabling Roosevelt to sweep the country in 1936. The wage earners had aligned themselves with other liberal elements in the country in a nationwide popular response to a dynamic program of recovery and reform. Labor endorsed agricultural relief and business reform as well as a new order of industrial relations and social security; it endorsed a measure of economic recovery reflected in rising business activity and higher farm income as well as lessening unemployment and increased wages.

The campaign activities of the Non-Partisan League and the vote won for Roosevelt in New York by the American Labor party appeared to demonstrate the effectiveness of direct labor action in politics. The CIO developed a broad and comprehensive legislative program, and, in a new Declaration of Purpose, the Non-Partisan League stated that it would attempt in future elections to insure both the nomination and the election of candidates pledged to support labor and other progressive measures. It was ready to work "with every progressive group whose purpose is to secure the enactment of liberal and humanitarian legislation."

The Non-Partisan League entered into local elections in several states during the next few years, sought to capture control of the Democratic party in Pennsylvania, played an active role in New Jersey politics, and threw its support behind a campaign for a labor administration in Detroit. In New York, the American Labor party drew largely from the socialist-minded members of the needle-trades unions, but it also attracted enough liberal supporters outside the ranks of labor to rally 500,000 votes for the reelection of Mayor Fiorello La Guardia in 1937. On the national stage, there was continued activity in backing up New Deal legislation, supporting Roosevelt's program for the reorganization of the Supreme Court and promoting further reform measures all along the line. The Non-Partisan League entered into the congressional elections of 1938 and energetically tried to defeat all opponents of the New Deal and to elect its adherents regardless of party affiliation.

Sidney Hillman played an important part in this political activity of the late 1930s, although his role was to be even more significant with the formation of the CIO's Political Action Committee in 1944. A strong proponent of "constructive co-operation" between labor and management, he also urged board participation by wage earners in politics to assure the basic conditions which would make such cooperation feasible. Few unions have been more politically conscious than his Amalgamated Clothing Workers. Sometimes characterized as the very embodiment of "social-engineering" union leadership, at once highly practical and idealistic, Hillman was one of the foremost labor strategists of the day with a broad and visionary view of the society which he believed could be created in the United States. "Having realized our dreams of yesterday," Hillman told a union convention in 1938, "let us dedicate ourselves to new dreams of a future where there will be no unemployment; a future where men and women will be economically secure and politically free."

The possibilities of developing an even more active political role for labor than represented by the Non-Partisan League were widely debated at this time. The old issue of the formation of a labor party, which had so often been raised in the past, was once again revived. The League was seen in some quarters as the possible nucleus for a movement in which labor, farmers, and other liberal groups might be brought together in a coalition that would either capture control of the Democratic party or set up an independent third party should it prove desirable.

These ideas did not make any real headway, however. The AFL would have none of them, and the CIO, while repeatedly calling for a constructive program of economic security, did not go so far as to endorse independent political action. Past experience with third-party movements was discouraging for further experiment along these lines, and the friendly attitude toward labor of the New Deal appeared in any event to make it inadvisable. The workers as a whole seemed tightly bound to Roosevelt's Democratic party and unlikely recruits for a new labor or third party. Yet for organized labor the threat of a third party always lurked in the background should the Democrats disappoint the workers.

Third party or no third party, conservative and anti-New Deal forces became increasingly alarmed over the effect of the political pressure which labor was exerting in the late 1930s. To combat such influences, the program of the CIO was singled out as radical and un-American. Charges were made that left-wing elements were wholly in control of the Non-Partisan League and forcing it to follow the Communist party line. The National Association of Manufacturers and other employer groups seized every opportunity to press such attacks. One pamphlet widely circulated by various antiunion groups had the engaging title of "Join the CIO and Help Build a Soviet America." The active leaders of the Non-Partisan League and the American Labor party, particularly Hillman and Lewis, were assailed for their supposed sympathies with Communism and willingness to promote policies dictated from Moscow.

There were some fitfully burning embers where the opponents of the CIO saw such dense clouds of smoke. The radical elements always present in the labor movement, and which in the past had been represented by Chicago anarchists, left-wing Socialists, and the IWW, were now generally enrolled in the Communist camp. Their labor front had originally been the Trade Union Educational League, founded by William Z. Foster after the failure of the steel strike in 1919 and subsequently the Trade Union Unity League set up some ten years later to promote industrial unionism independently of the AFL. The shift in the Moscow party line in the mid-1930s, which swung Communist support to a united democratic front against fascism, then led to the abandonment of dual unionism and a return to the older Socialist techniques of boring from within. The Communists were prepared to do everything that they could to encourage industrial unionism and hoped to win control, or at least to dominate, the CIO and its political affiliates.

Lewis did not hesitate to draw upon their experience and organizing skill in building up the CIO and the Non-Partisan League. He needed help from every quarter. "We have to work," he stated, "with what we have." While he fully recognized that the Communists would seek to use the new unions to strengthen their own position, he nevertheless thought that he could disregard their politics so long as they aided him in promoting industrial unionism. As a result of such hospitality, Communists and other leftists won important positions in some unions and even in the high councils of the CIO itself. Within the UAW, left-wing and anti-Communist factions persistently struggled for power. Communist party members and their allies controlled the United Electrical, Radio, and Machine workers, the Transport Workers, the Maritime Workers, the Fur and Leather Workers, the Mine, Mill and Smelter Workers, and the International Woodworkers. Their zeal and enterprise, particularly in parliamentary strategy and organizational leg-work, as well as the degree to which they served the needs of their members, gave the left-wingers influence over a rank and file generally non- or anti-Communist.

The great bulk of union members, even in Communist-led unions, remained steadfast Democrats. Moreover, the three top CIO leaders—Lewis, Hillman, and Murray—were themselves anti-Communists. In the mid and late 1930s, however, they did not see Communists as a threat to the labor movement. Rather, as long as the Communist Party of America supported the CIO and the New Deal,

Lewis and his associates took full advantage of the dedication and discipline which the young Communists brought to the labor movement.

The political support that the left wing was prepared to give to Roosevelt and the New Deal as part of the program for a united front added further confusion to the labor scene. The anti–New Deal forces made the most of Communist backing for Roosevelt in attacking his administration for what they declared were its Socialistic and radical policies. But while the President could repudiate Communist support as such, he continued to need that of organized labor. It was consequently greatly to his interest to have a united movement strong enough to rally the progressive forces of the nation behind his policies. Since 1937, he had continually urged a reconciliation between the AFL and the CIO with such ideas in view, and in 1939 he again called upon both organizations to make a real effort to settle their differences.

Upon Roosevelt's insistence, peace negotiations were resumed that year, and representatives of the AFL and the CIO tried to get together. The issue of craft unionism versus industrial unionism had long since lost any real validity, as we have seen, but the rival drives for power had been intensified by the conflicts of the past few years. Lewis put forward an ambitious proposal for the merger of the AFL, the CIO, and the railway brotherhoods. It was wholly impractical, for the railway brotherhoods were not even remotely interested in such a project, and Lewis was immediately charged with not acting in good faith.

The AFL counteroffer was for readmission of the CIO unions to the parent organization, but without recognition of their extended jurisdiction. Lewis adjourned the meeting without giving a definite answer to this proposal, but he soon declared that peace was "impossible" because of the obstructive attitude of the AFL leaders who were pursuing a policy of "rule or ruin." The truth of the matter was that neither side was willing to make real concessions. In spite of their professed acceptance of the need for labor unity, both the AFL and the CIO put their own interests first. Green continued to express his "passion for peace," but it was to be upon his own terms. Lewis was perhaps more frank in stating, "we must expand our movement."

The internal difficulties confronting labor were in no way resolved in 1939. In the meantime, however, far more important developments on the world scene were to have their inevitable repercussions on both labor and national politics. Russia and Germany concluded a nonaggression pact in late August 1939, and immediately afterward Europe was plunged into war by Hitler's attack on Poland. The United States found itself menaced by the growing possibility of being drawn into the raging struggle against fascism, and popular attention was increasingly diverted from domestic problems to the larger issues of foreign policy. The country was critically divided into opposing camps on the overshadowing question of whether aid to the Allies could keep war from American shores, or whether the United States should seek to maintain an isolationist position as the only means to safeguard its own peace.

As expressed in resolutions adopted by both the AFL and the CIO, labor was entirely opposed to American entry into war but was prepared to support Roosevelt's policy of extending aid to the Allies and building up American defenses. There were differing viewpoints within union ranks, however, as among other elements in the population, while the Communist party line had abruptly shifted from the united democratic front to virulent isolationism. The Roosevelt administration was attacked as vigorously as it had formerly been defended. With the approach of the election of 1940, the question of how labor would vote consequently became of utmost importance. In these circumstances, the position of Lewis was to attract nationwide attention, and it was a strange, unpredictable role that he chose to play.

In the aftermath of Roosevelt's reelection in 1936, Lewis expected the Democrats to pay their political debts to organized labor. During the summer of 1936, Roosevelt had made numerous promises to the CIO in return for Lewis's endorsement. During the great General Motors sit-down strike, Lewis expressed publicly what he expected the president to do. "For six months the economic royalists represented by General Motors," Lewis told reporters, "contributed their money and used their energy to drive this administration out of power. The administration asked labor for help and labor gave it. The same economic royalists now have their fangs in labor. The workers of this country expect the administration to help the workers in every legal way and to support the workers in General Motors plants."

In this case Roosevelt delivered, although he left to Governor Murphy the actual implementation of a prolabor policy. Less than six months later, however, another strike—the fierce struggle between the SWOC and "Little Steel"—caused a rift between Lewis and Roosevelt. When the CIO leader again turned to the President for help, Roosevelt replied, a "plague o' both your houses." After brooding over this rebuff, Lewis, in a Labor Day 1937 radio speech, in which he enumerated the deaths and injuries suffered by workers in the steel industry, attacked the President: "It ill behooves one who has supped at labor's table and who has been sheltered in labor's house to curse with equal fervor and fine impartiality both labor and its adversaries when they become locked in deadly embrace."

Pundits immediately tried to explain the cause of the rift between Roosevelt and Lewis. All sorts of explanations were offered, but the one which gained the widest credence, perhaps because it seemed most dramatic and made for the best story, concerned Lewis's political ambitions. According to Frances Perkins, the primary source of this tale, Lewis went to Roosevelt in late 1939 or early 1940 with a political proposal.

"Mr. President, I have thought of all that and I have a suggestion to make for you to consider," Mrs. Perkins quotes Roosevelt, who in turn was quoting Lewis. "If the vice-presidential candidate on your ticket should happen to be John L. Lewis, those objections would disappear. A strong labor man would insure the full support, not only of all the labor people, but of all the liberals who worry about such things as third terms."

The suggestion did not appeal to the President, and he ignored it. But there is another account of this incident, probably apocryphal. It has Lewis proposing to Roosevelt that, as the "two most prominent men in the nation" they would make an invincible ticket, and the President blandly asking, "Which place would you take, John?"

Perkins's tale, however, is one of those historical anecdotes which amuses people but misses the truth. Roosevelt and Lewis were indeed coming to a political parting of the ways in late 1939 and early 1940. But it had nothing to do with Lewis's personal political ambitions. In fact, after the Republicans had rejected his desire to serve as Secretary of Labor in the 1920s, Lewis neither sought nor wanted public office. Abundant historical evidence shows that what Lewis wanted from Roosevelt was not a position as his running mate, but rather more governmental assistance for the CIO and organized labor.

Much had changed since Lewis had wholeheartedly supported Roosevelt in 1936. For one thing, the CIO had yet to recover from the recession of 1937–1938. For another, the New Deal had lost momentum as a domestic reform movement. A congressional coalition of northern Republicans and southern Democrats thwarted the CIO's favorite legislation, and the President seemed unable or unwilling to do anything about it. For yet another reason, by 1940 Roosevelt was abandoning domestic reform crusades to concentrate on foreign affairs. And Lewis read the President's diplomacy as an effort to involve the United States in the European war. As the labor movement's most outspoken opponent of American involvement in overseas war, Lewis saw little choice but to break with Roosevelt politically. Thus he now charged the administration with betraying the workers' cause and refusing to give labor representation in either the cabinet or any policy-making government agency. At a United Mine Workers convention in January, he dramatically broke all former ties with the President. "Should the Democratic National Committee," he told his startled audience, "be coerced or dragooned into renominating him, I am convinced. . . his candicacy would result in ignominious defeat."

Lewis's alternative to Roosevelt and the Democrats was less than clear. By 1940 he had developed strange political allies. On the one hand, Communists now applauded Lewis as labor's savior, the one high union leader who resisted the nation's drift into an "imperialist" war. On the other hand, Lewis associated himself with the isolationist America First Committee and some of the most reactionary industrialists in America. To complicate matters further, in the spring and summer of 1940, Lewis delivered a series of speeches to groups of blacks, left-wing youths, and senior-citizens in which he suggested the need for a new third party. What Lewis might do in the autumn of 1940 puzzled everyone who observed the CIO leader's political machinations.

In any event, Lewis openly opposed the President as the 1940 campaign got under way. The New Deal had completely failed to bring about economic recovery, he declared, and it was in fact entirely responsible for the prolongation of the depression. For a time he did not indicate whether opposition to Roosevelt meant support for Wendell Willkie, the Republican nomineee, but he resolved such doubts as to where he stood in a radio speech on October 25th which had been carefully timed for full dramatic effect.

"I think the reelection of President Roosevelt for a third term would be a national evil of the first magnitude," Lewis stated. "He no longer hears the cries of the people. I think that the election of Mr.

Wendell Willkie is imperative in relation to the country's needs. I commend him to the men and women of labor.. . .

"It is obvious that President Roosevelt will not be reelected for a third term unless he has the overwhelming support of the men and women of labor. If he is, therefore, reelected, it will mean that the members of the Congress of Industrial Organizations have rejected my advice and recommendation. I will accept the result as being the equivalent of a vote of no confidence and will retire as president of the Congress of Industrial Organizations in November."

Lewis had miscalculated his influence in the labor movement and over working-class voters. Ignoring the warnings of the CIO president, many of his associates came out openly for Roosevelt, and union after union adopted resolutions favoring a third term. The majority of the AFL leaders and unions also endorsed the President, and there can be no question that the votes of wage earners contributed heavily, as they had in his two earlier elections, to Roosevelt's third triumph. The vote in mining districts, where the leadership of Lewis was generally followed automatically, showed that even members of the United Mine Workers refused to heed his advice in national politics. In contradiction of the Lewis pronouncement, Green declared after the election that working men and working women had voted for Roosevelt because "they believe he is the friend and the champion of social justice and economic freedom."

Lewis had lost his bet. In gambling the presidency of the CIO on the willingness of labor's rank and file to follow him, he had not only taken himself completely out of politics but had also sacrificed control of the organization which he had done so much to build up. For he fulfilled his pledge to retire from the presidency of the CIO at its next convention. He was still able to exert a powerful influence in labor councils, but it was the close of a chapter in his spectacular career. For all the defiant independence and dramatic posturing that were to mark his later activities, he could not recapture the power and prestige of his days as president of the CIO.

Lewis remained, of course, head of the United Mine Workers, and its members continued to follow wherever he led so far as union affairs were concerned. It was a merry chase. Lewis was soon to take them out of the CIO and then in time back into the AFL. The miners could never be sure just where they stood. Lewis made up his own mind and gave short shrift to the ideas of associates or followers. At the end of 1947, the miners were again to find themselves in the labor wilderness when their chieftain walked out of the AFL for the second time with a casual abruptness that was startling even for him. Reporters summoned to the United Mine Workers headquarters were shown a message scrawled in blue crayon on a two-by-four inch slip of paper which read: "Green, AFL. We disaffiliate, Lewis. 12/12/47."

The new CIO president in 1940 was Philip Murray, the leader of the SWOC organizing campaign and for so many years the able and loyal lieutenant of Lewis in the United Mine Workers. His background had a marked similarity to those of Green and Lewis in that his family was of British coal mining stock. Murray, however, was himself born abroad—in Lanarkshire, Scotland, in 1886—and did not come to the United States until he was sixteen. He then followed the family tradition of entering the mines. Two years later he had his first difficulties with management and lost his job as a result of taking part in a strike. "I've never had a doubt since then," he has written, "of what I wanted to do with my life."

In 1916 he was chosen president of District Number 5 of the United Mine Workers and four years later vice-president of the international union. He was known as an extremely able administrator and organizer, but perhaps most of all for his faithful support, in good times and bad, of the policies laid down by his chief. He believed firmly in Catholic social-reform precepts and in the middle ground between socialism and unfettered capitalism expressed in Pope Leo XIII's famous encyclical, *Rerum Novarum*. Labor organization and collective bargaining were essential, in his opinion, to secure social justice for workers.

Long invisible in the shadow cast by Lewis, Murray tried to assert his independence and manhood as the new president of CIO. He urged the CIO to support Roosevelt's foreign policy and program of national defense. "The convictions which I recommend," he was to tell the CIO convention in 1941, "have not come to me as a result of pressure from any group within or without. I am one individual, as you know, who resents the exercise of pressure from individuals or groups. I stand upon my individual integrity as a man."

After the election of 1940, the country in general swung more strongly behind the program of national defense. The successive measures taken by the Roosevelt administration to extend aid to the Allies, particularly the adoption of lend-lease in 1941, became the all-important issues confronting the nation. The division between isolationists and interventionists grew even more embittered, but the urgent necessity to build up national security could hardly be denied by anyone other than outright pacificists. Mounting war orders from abroad began in 1941 to spur the economic recovery that the New Deal had been unable to achieve. The United States felt itself in imminent danger of being drawn into the war, but it was in the meantime beginning to enjoy an improved economy.

Labor felt the impact of these developments in many ways. Increased production not only brought about a rapid decline in unemployment, but also stimulated wage increases. The growing need for skilled workers in the defense industries was a new characteristic of the labor market which sharply contrasted with conditions that had prevailed for over ten years. Between April 1940, and December 1941, total nonagricultural employment rose from thirty-five to over forty-one million, and wage rates generally increased about 20 per cent. In the durable goods industries so basic to the defense program, average earnings spurted from $29.88 to $38.62 a week. War had come to the rescue of American industry and the strength of organized labor, as union members and wage earners shared substantially in the mounting profits of wartime business.

Labor was prepared to cooperate fully to make the United States "the great arsenal of democracy," but, remembering the defeats and setbacks of the 1920s, was also insistent that the benefits attained under the New Deal should not in any way be prejudiced. Further than that, it asserted the right to press forward the campaign to extend union recognition and collective bargaining. And, as the cost of living rapidly rose under wartime conditions, labor demanded further wage increases to maintain its purchasing power. With industry booming and union strength growing, the stage was set for further struggles between management and labor over their respective roles in an expanding economy. The year 1941 was to prove one of the most tumultuous in labor history.

In most instances the new economic circumstances—full production, scarce labor, and rising profits—prompted unions and management to bargain collectively and to reach acceptable agreements on wages, hours, and working conditions. The "Little Steel" companies and the United Steelworkers of America finally came to terms, and Henry Ford completely reversed his antiunion policies to sign a contract unreservedly recognizing the United Automobile Workers and even going so far as to grant it a closed shop. But such progress in allaying the causes of industrial strife was soon overshadowed by the outbreak of fresh disputes. There were still industries and employers which viewed unions as unwarranted intrusions on managerial rights and prerogatives.

Almost hysterical fear of the growing strength of the unions led a few companies not only to refuse new wage demands, but to try in every possible way to clip labor's wings. This group refused further concessions looking toward union recognition, attacked the closed shop as undemocratic and un-American, and circumvented the legal requirements of collective bargaining wherever they could. They covered their antiunion activity in many instances with a mantle of patriotism by insisting that their objectives were merely to maintain uninterrupted industrial production.

The needs of national defense, indeed, tended to make the public impatient of labor's demands, and its cause was in no way helped by wide-spread internal squabbling. The angry recriminations of rival leaders, jurisdictional strikes, and highly publicized exposures of a few instances of union racketeering and graft weakened public confidence in the responsibility of organized workers in the face of the mounting national emergency. And it was true that some of the new, insurgent unions were unable to maintain discipline among their thousands of freshly recruited members. Their belligerent attitude toward employers and their insistence upon wage increases and other concessions were on occasion as destructive of industrial peace as the antiunion policies of reactionary business.

The number of labor disputes in 1941 reached a higher total than in any previous year, with the single exception of 1937. There were strikes in the automobile industry, in the shipyards, in transportation, in the building trades, in textiles, and in steel and coal mining. Hardly an industry escaped work stoppages which for a time seriously interfered with production. In all, there were 4,288 strikes involving over 2,000,000 workers—almost twice the number of disputes and four times the number of workers as in the previous year. Approximately 8.4 per cent of the nation's employed industrial wage earners took part in these outbreaks, and 23,000,000 man-days of work were lost.

The threat to the defense program in these work stoppages led to the creation, in March 1941, of the National Defense Mediation Board. This was a tripartite body, representative of labor, management, and the public, with authority to seek the adjustment of disputes in defense industries through either mediation or voluntary arbitration. Its powers did not include enforcement of its decisions, and, while it was successful in restoring industrial peace in many instances, more drastic action was to prove necessary on several notable occasions.

A strike on the part of aviation workers at Inglewood, California, led to seizure of a North American Aviation plant by the War Department before a negotiated compromise could be effected, and the Navy Department moved in on a strike of shipyards workers at Kearny, New Jersey, after the Federal Shipbuilding and Dry Dock Company rejected a proposed settlement granting the union maintenance of membership.[1] The climax both of labor disputes and of the troubles of the National Defense Mediation Board was to be reached, however, in a coal strike which many persons mistakenly thought seriously interrupted production and imperiled the whole defense program.

The major issue at stake was the establishment of the union shop in the so-called "captive" coal mines operated by the steel industry. The Defense Mediation Board had wavered on the validity of incorporating such a demand in union contracts and, when the mining dispute came before it for action in the fall of 1941, it refused to accept the union shop as a basis for a contract. Lewis consequently ignored the board, and in the face of President Roosevelt's plea that as a loyal citizen he should come to the aid of his country, Lewis called a strike in the captive coal mines on October 27 which threatened to close down the steel industry almost entirely.

Lewis's aims were simple and reasonable, as the President knew. Only the mines operated by the steel companies refused to grant the UMW a union shop contract, although more than 97 per cent of the miners already belonged to the union. In fact the captive-mine owners actually had little interest in defending the minuscule minority among their employees who were nonunion. Rather, their real aim was to preserve the open shop in the steel industry itself. For his part, Lewis wanted to win total union security immediately; he remembered how short-lived had been labor's gains during the First World War. However reasonable Lewis's position and goals may have been, in calling a strike he challenged the President directly. Roosevelt accepted the challenge.

---

[1]See Ch. 18, pp. 323–325.

Roosevelt promptly went on the air after the strike had been called. He declared that the country had to have coal, and that national production could not be hampered "by the selfish obstruction of a small but dangerous minority of labor leaders." There were suggestions that he was finally ready to accept the antistrike legislation which was already being proposed in Congress. But in the meantime, Lewis had been negotiating with Myron C. Taylor, of the United States Steel Corporation, and an agreement was reached whereby the union shop issue was again to be reviewed by the Defense Mediation Board without either party obliged to accept its rulings. Lewis was confident that his demands would now have to be approved because of the country's urgent need for coal, and he called off the strike for a temporary truce period while the board again took the case under consideration.

It gave its decision on November 10—and it was nine to two against the union shop. Only the two CIO members dissented from a report which was upheld not only by the representatives of management and the public, but also by those of the AFL (who acted as much out of their own hostility to Lewis and the CIO as from any commitment to principle or cooperation with the government). Although 97 per cent of the 53,000 workers in the captive coal mines were already members of the United Mine Workers, the position taken was that a union shop was a matter for collective bargaining rather than government order, and that it was unjustifiable for the Defense Mediation Board to force 1,590 men to join a union against their will.

A principle was at stake, and a showdown between Lewis and the President appeared to be unavoidable. Lewis refused to modify orders renewing the strike at the expiration of the truce, and he was backed up by the CIO in spite of the internal feuds within that organization. Its representatives on the Defense Mediation Board promptly resigned, and a resolution of the convention then in session upheld Lewis' stand. For his part, Roosevelt declared that under no circumstances would the government order a union shop, insisted upon further negotiations between the miners and the steel companies, and, at the same time, made preparations for governmental seizure of the mines should an agreement not be reached. Congress was currently debating amendments to the neutrality legislation, and, partly to assure support for his foreign program by congressmen who believed that he was dealing too leniently with labor, the President pledged that, regardless of what Lewis might do, coal would be mined—"the government proposes to see this thing through."

There was a week of feverish negotiations while the country clamored for a settlement, but neither the miners nor the steel companies would give in on the union shop. On November 17 the strike was again on. The workers in the captive mines laid down their tools, and soon sympathetic strikes in other areas swelled the total of idle men in the coal pits to some 250,000. The steel industry was hamstrung in the face of a national emergency. It was reported that Roosevelt was finally ready to act, with 50,000 troops ordered to take over the mines, and the situation grew hourly more tense. Then suddenly and unexpectedly, on November 22, Lewis called off the strike. He had accepted a proposal of the President for binding arbitration of the union shop issue by a three-man tribunal—Lewis himself, Fairless of the United States Steel Corporation, and as the impartial member, John R. Steelman of the United States Conciliation Service.

Had Lewis capitulated? The secret of his abrupt move was the position of the third man on the tribunal. Steelman was a friend of labor, and he was known to be sympathetic toward the union shop. The miners' chieftain felt certain of what his decision would be—and events were to prove him wholly justified. Roosevelt expected the same result. From the start of the controversy, he had urged the captive-mine operators to grant the union shop voluntarily. All he had ever wanted to do was to avoid direct presidential responsibility for ordering nonunion miners to sign up with the UMW. Roosevelt had probably expected the Defense Mediation Board to rule in favor of union security, and was disappointed when it did not. The special arbitrational tribunal thus served Roosevelt's purposes. It had the guise of impartiality, included Lewis as well as an executive of the steel industry, and ruled in favor of the union shop. Lewis was mollified, coal would be mined, and the President could evade direct responsibility for the results.

Lewis's victory benefited his union, but it also intensified a rising antiunion feeling in Congress and within the business community. Newspaper editorials and the statements of national leaders and public opinion polls all showed a pronounced stiffening of attitudes toward labor. In and out of Congress, there was a demand for new legislation to restrict the power of the unions and safeguard the public interest against further interruptions to industrial production. The coal strike, and the spectacle of Lewis arrogantly defying the National Defense Mediation Board and the authority of the President, merely brought matters to a head. Antilabor laws of varying severity had already been passed in twenty-two states, and some thirty bills to curb unions were introduced in Congress.

Against the background of uncertainty over the coal strike and other labor disturbances, including a narrowly averted railroad strike, the House approved one of these antilabor measures on December 3, 1941, by a vote of 252 to 136. It would have banned all strikes in defense industries involving the closed shop or growing out of jurisdictional disputes, and any others unless approved by a majority of workers in government-supervised elections after a thirty-day cooling off period. Green denounced the bill as "an instrument of oppression"; Murray declared that "nothing more subversive to American democracy has ever been prepared." It appeared probable that its terms would be modified by the Senate, and the President was believed to favor a milder measure, but there was little doubt that some law would be speedily enacted to meet what was generally being called "the national menace" of continued strikes paralyzing defense.

As the tide beat against the labor movement, even the friends of labor, fearing that the upsurge against unions might lead to curtailment of basic rights guaranteed by the Wagner Act, called for greater moderation on the part of both AFL and CIO leaders. "The union movement in this country is no longer an infant requiring protection," the *New Republic* editorialized. "It has grown up physically, and if it is to conduct itself like a responsible adult it must be controlled by the same social discipline which governs the rest of the community."

How far the pendulum might have swung against labor can hardly be known. For new events suddenly interposed with dramatic force. On December 7—the same day that the arbitral tribunal announced that Lewis had been granted a union shop in the captive coal mines and while the House antistrike bill was pending in the Senate—Japan struck at Pearl Harbor. The United States was at war.

XVIII

The Second World War

The Second World War proved as fraught with opportunities and perils for workers and organized labor as the First World War had been. Because it lasted more than twice as long, was even more global in scope, and entailed a more total domestic production effort, the Second World War had a more lasting and transforming impact on American workers and their labor movement than did the First World War.

First, the Second World War cured, as none of the New Deal reforms had, the economic miseries of the Great Depression. The Allied military machine needed all that the American economy could produce. Where for a full decade workers had fruitlessly chased jobs, employers now wooed workers. Labor scarcity superceded labor surplus. From 1942 through 1945, the highest level of full employment in American history prevailed. Workers had steady jobs, security of employment, and rising real incomes.

Second, the war drew increasing numbers of men and women from the secondary to the primary labor market. The millions of able-bodied men conscripted into the armed forces had to be replaced in the civilian labor force. Two sources provided the new workers. Women worked for wages as never before. Despite wartime propaganda and the myths associated with gender-typing, which suggested that wartime women workers were former full-time housewives who, for patriotic reasons, volunteered for factory labor only for the duration of the national emergency, the reality was otherwise. Many former "housewives" did go to work in order to help win the war, not simply to increase family earnings. But the great majority of women worked because they had to, and millions of them deserted, not the tidy home, but the low-wage job ghetto heretofore reserved for female workers. Now they took higher-paying jobs in the once all-male preserves of steel mills, auto plants (now tank and airplane factories), shipyards, railroads, and machine shops. By the peak of the war, women formed 36 per cent of the full-time labor force. Blacks provided the other major source of wartime labor, and black women benefited even more dramatically than white women. Blacks left low-wage domestic menial and agricultural jobs for more skilled and better-paying defense work. The "great migration," which had carried about 350,000 southern blacks northward from 1915 to 1918, repeated itself on a far grander scale between 1941 and 1945. This time, three to five million left the South for the promised land to the north and west.

This transformation in the labor force did not occur smoothly and easily. Generally, white women found entry into better jobs easier than black men and women. Yet even in their case, male workers, their unions, and also employers insisted that, at best, women should replace men only for the duration of the war. Blacks met much more resistance. Old-line, all-white AFL craft unions denied membership to blacks and tried to keep them out of skilled work. Even in the more open CIO unions and in nonunion factories, white workers threatened to strike if blacks received more skilled jobs. And many employers retained old prejudices, viewing blacks as fit only for janitorial and other forms of menial labor. It took the threat of a protest march in Washington led by black civil-rights organizations in the midst of war to persuade President Roosevelt to issue an Executive Order (number 8802) which established a Fair Employment Practices Commission. Under federal prodding and in response to the demands of total war, resistance by white workers, unions, and employers abated.

Third, the war rescued the CIO and mass-production unionism from the doldrums. In dire organizational trouble on the eve of war, by the end of 1941 the CIO had finally organized Ford, "Little

Steel," and the major meat-packing firms. It also stablized shaky affiliates, which had previously won recognition and contracts. The CIO's membership gains became even greater as war production intensified. Corporations blessed with cost-plus contracts could simply pass on the expenses of union contracts to purchasers and preferred not to imperil production and profits by antagonizing their workers. Rarely had union organizers operated in such easy circumstances.

Two factors joined to make the wartime changes in the labor force and industrial relations relatively tranquil. Never before had a war found the American people so united behind the government. This time, unlike 1914–1918, few if any workers or union leaders saw the conflict as an imperialist struggle in which capitalists shed workers' blood. The Second World War was a crusade to save democracy from fascism—for workers as well as bosses. And this time, also, unlike the First World War, the federal government was much more prepared to intervene regularly in labor-management relations. To a degree never before equaled, Washington officials and boards managed the national economy, and in no sector more fully and directly than in the setting of labor policy.

Because labor leaders were well aware of what the federal role would be in a wartime economy, they insisted on their right to full representation on the federal agencies created to deal with the crisis. President Roosevelt partly recognized the justice of such demands. In first setting up the Office of Production Management in 1941, he had appointed Sidney Hillman (Hillman's appointment legitimated the CIO in the way in which Gompers's services during the First World War had legitimated the AFL) to serve as its codirector with William S. Knudsen, a General Motors vice-president. Labor representatives were also appointed to the subsequent War Production Board, the Office of Civilian Defense, the Office of Price Administration, the Office of Economic Stabilization, and the War Manpower Commission. Yet something more than this role in helping to order the economy was obviously needed to assure labor's full support for the war effort and to guard against the ever-present danger of strikes which might curtail the production of essential military supplies.

To this end, the President summoned a conference of labor and business leaders just ten days after Pearl Harbor to plan new measures for industrial cooperation. After prolonged discussion, the conferees agreed upon a three-point program: no strikes or lockouts for the duration of hostilities; peaceful settlement of all industrial disputes;

and, more concretely, the creation of a tripartite board, with labor, management, and the public each represented by four members. This agency—the National War Labor Board—would be empowered to handle all labor controversies affecting the war effort which otherwise failed of settlement. In return for assurances that it would have a voice in determining such conditions and terms of employment as might be required by wartime necessity, labor had agreed in the national interest to surrender for the time its right to strike.

A sharp decline in work stoppages throughout the country was the immediate consequence of this agreement. In comparison with the 23,000,000 man-days lost in 1941, the total for 1942 fell to 4,180,000. But as the pressures and tensions of war mounted, this record could not be sustained. Labor's leaders charged that the workers' interests were being ignored in the controls which the government now exercised over wages and prices. William Green declared that it was on the understanding that collective bargaining would be sustained that labor had foregone the right to strike and that the course which Washington was following could not be reconciled with its earlier pledges. John L. Lewis was far more belligerent in his stand and soon showed tht he was ready to defy all governmental authority to protect the interests of the United Mine Workers. In such circumstances, strikes increased notably during 1943, with a total of 13,500,000 man-days lost, and, while they again declined somewhat the next year, rose again as the war drew to an end in 1945.

Nevertheless, labor continued on the whole to support the war effort conscientiously, and a great majority of unions sought in every possible way to restrain strike activity. The man-days lost actually averaged only about one tenth of 1 per cent of the total working time in industry as a whole and were estimated to be the equivalent of no more than one day per worker for the four war years. Many of the strikes were no more than unauthorized walkouts. Their grievances intensified by the strain of long hours and other hardships resulting from wartime conditions, the workers took matters into their own hands. They laid down their tools or quit their jobs in frustrated protest, but once they had let off steam by asserting themselves, they went back to work without serious interruption to production. A few more threatening strikes also occurred, but they were the exception rather than the rule.

As the war finally drew to an end, there was hardly a political or military leader who did not take occasion to pay glowing tribute to the role which labor had played. It was the determination of American workers to preserve their heritage for coming generations, President Roosevelt declared, that had made possible "the greatest production achievement in the world's history."

The key to labor's wartime history was the National War Labor Board, which officially came into being by Executive Order in January 1942. Its primary function was to take over all unsettled industrial disputes certified by the Secretary of Labor as likely to "interrupt work which contributes to the effective prosecution of the war." Its decisions were to be binding in such cases on both management and labor, and, since they were made on a tripartite basis, this in effect gave the public representatives a determining voice on all issues where labor and management could not be brought into accord.

A first and vital problem which the War Labor Board faced was the issue of union security, which had wrecked the old Defense Mediation Board. The National War Labor Board met this problem successfully with adoption of the principle of maintenance of membership. There would be no attempted enforcement of either a closed shop or a union shop in contract negotiations, but union members, or those who subsequently joined the union, would be required to keep up their membership for the contract's life. Should they fail to maintain good union standing, they were subject to dismissal from their employment. The labor members of the Board accepted this solution of the problem without qualification; those representing management acquiesced very reluctantly. Once it had been agreed upon, however, the principle of maintenance of membership was consistently upheld throughout the war. It ultimately applied to some three million workers, or approximately 20 per cent of those covered by collective-bargaining agreements.

The assurances embodied in this program for both union security and individual freedom of action contributed immensely to industrial peace and were greatly responsible for the low level of strikes during 1942. At the end of that year, labor's leaders could boast that the country's workers had maintained "the finest record of continuous, uninterrupted production ever achieved." Addressing the AFL convention, Roosevelt stated that labor's cooperation spoke for itself—"it is splendid."

However, the War Labor Board soon found itself facing an even more troublesome problem than union security. Rising prices, induced by the inevitable inflationary pressures of wartime, led the unions to demand wage increases at least commensurate with the rise in the cost of living, and, when they threatened to strike if necessary to enforce their claims, something had to be done. The board first sought to meet this issue on a union-by-union basis. But when the government, gravely concerned over the effects of a price-wages spiral on the national economy, adopted an overall stabilization program, it was clear that a more consistent and comprehensive policy would have to be worked out. Some sort of formula was needed which would at once hold wages as a whole in line and yet allow such increases as were clearly justified by the rise in the cost of living which had already occurred.

The War Labor Board seized the opportunity to work out and apply such a formula when, in July 1942, the employees of the Little Steel companies demanded a wage increase of $1 a day. After lengthy hearings it was decided that a rise in wages was justified, but that it should be limited to an equivalent of the increase in living costs between January 1941—a time of relative price stability—and May 1942, when the government had instituted its stabilization program. According to the reports of the Bureau of Labor Statistics, the cost-of-living index had risen some 15 points during this period, and consequently any wage increase would have to be held to this same percentage over existing levels. The War Labor Board consequently awarded the workers at Little Steel plants a raise of 44 cents a day rather than the $1 which they originally demanded.

The Little Steel formula now became the basic yardstick for the settlement of all wartime wage disputes. It had been adopted, however, on the assumption that the new stabilization program had brought to an end "the tragic race between wages and prices," and that a 15 per cent wage increase was therefore fair and equitable. This soon proved to be a false assumption. Prices could not be held completely in line. The War Labor Board found itself in the unenviable position of trying to reconcile its formula for wage increases with a further rise in living costs which progressively exceeded the figures on which the formula was based.

Moreover, the board's troubles were compounded when passage of the Economic Stabilization Act in October 1942, which gave congressional sanction to the government's program, expanded its authority beyond the disputed cases which were its original concern. The board was now obliged by government directive to restrict all wage increases, except where flagrantly substandard conditions existed, to the 15 per cent increase in straight-line hourly wages that had been granted in the steel industry. For the remainder of the war, it consequently had two distinct functions: settlement of disputed cases and supervision of voluntary wage agreements. And in both classifications, the Little Steel formula was frozen as the official limitation on all wage adjustments.

Organized labor promptly and vigorously protested against this broadening of the application of the Little Steel formula as an arbitrary and unwarranted interference with the process of collective bargaining which completely undermined the bases of labor's no-strike pledge. As consumer prices continued to rise, reaching an index figure of 124 by the spring of 1943, these protests became more vehement, and a feeling of angry resentment flared up among the rank-and-file of industrial workers. They believed that the government was forcing the wage earners to bear the brunt of an inflationary price rise from which farmers and other producers were actually profiting. Compelled to take some action, the government chose to try to roll back prices rather than permit further wage increases. While a hold-the-line order issued by the President in April was to prove relatively successful in blocking any further increase in living costs, there was no rollback. Labor's grievances still remained as the rise in living costs continued to exceed the allowable increase in wages under the Little Steel formula.

These were the circumstances which encouraged strikes in 1943. For the most part, as has already been noted, they were of brief duration and did not seriously impede the production of essential wartime goods. Moreover, the leaders of both the AFL and the CIO, in spite of continuing criticism of the government's wage policy, did everything they could to keep things under control. But quite a different situation developed in the coal industry. John L. Lewis bluntly stated that the War Labor Board had breached its contract with labor in establishing the Little Steel formula, and that he had no intention whatsoever of submitting to its authority so far as the miners were concerned. Lewis acted as he did because coal miners had suffered much more from the "Little Steel Formula" than other workers and because higher war production levels had increased greatly the number of mine fatalities and injuries. The miners were growing restive and rebellious by 1943. Lewis preferred not to lose control of his followers. Thus, in blunt defiance of the federal government and an apoplectic press, Lewis led a series of strikes which provided the most dramatic chapter in labor's wartime history.

The expiration in April 1943 of the annual contract between the United Mine Workers and the coal operators initiated this drawn-out controversy. Lewis demanded on behalf of the union not only a wage increase of $2 a day but what was termed portal-to-portal pay for the time that the miners spent traveling underground. Lewis was, as usual, prepared to compromise a part of his original demands. However, when the War Labor Board, to which the dispute had been referred, treated the union's case disdainfully, Lewis removed himself from the hearings and contemptuously attacked the Board as "prejudiced" and "malignant." He said that he would not of course call a strike in wartime, but he blandly announced "the miners were unwilling to trespass upon the property of the coal operators in the absence of a contract."

The members of his union needed no further instructions. They began to quit work even before the final expiration of the old contract, and the country found itself faced with an even graver crisis than it had confronted in 1941. Fully aware of the disastrous effects of a stoppage in coal production, President Roosevelt gave immediate orders for the seizure of the coal mines and, on May 2, went on the air to appeal to the strikers to return to work.

Placing full responsibility for the breakdown in contract negotiations on the officials of the United Mine Workers, Roosevelt declared that every man who stopped mining coal was directly obstructing the war effort, gambling with the lives of American soldiers and sailors, and endangering the security of the entire people. He expressed his sympathy for the miners, promising that any new agreement would be made retroactive, but insisted that production must continue pending further negotiations. "Tomorrow the Stars and Stripes will fly over the coal mines," the President concluded. "I hope every miner will be at work under that flag."

The workers returned to the mines. It was, however, on the orders of the president of their union rather than because of the appeal of the President of the United States. Just twenty minutes before Roosevelt had gone on the air, Lewis had announced a fifteen-day truce (later extended to thirty days) to try to work out a new agreement with Secretary of the Interior Harold L. Ickes, under whose direction the mines were to be placed. Lewis made no concessions or promises of what might happen after the expiration of the truce. He stood firmly on his original demands.

The next six months were a hectic period alternatively punctuated by temporary truces and renewed work stoppages. At one point, the government returned the mines to private operation, but when contract negotiations still made no headway and the miners once again laid down their tools, the government moved in for a second time. Roosevelt now ordered Ickes to conclude a special wage agreement, subject to approval by the War Labor Board, which would be limited to the duration of the government's operation of the mines.

Throughout this period, Lewis held the reins in a steady yet forceful fashion. He insisted that a national emergency was no excuse for operators to exploit coal miners callously. He declared that the miners' right to higher wages was a matter of simple justice and plain equity. It was a case in which union president and his rank and file were in total harmony. When Lewis suggested that miners work, they did so. When he suggested that they take off, miners stayed home or went fishing. Knowing full well that they never stayed out of the mines long enough to deplete coal reserves, the miners ignored President Roosevelt's appeals and press criticism of their actions. Battered by inflation, killed and maimed by coal mining, convinced of the justice of their goals, and certain in their patriotism (miners had sent more than their share of sons and brothers to war), the coal miners loyally followed their union president.

Whipping up a mounting tide of national anger, the press criticized Roosevelt for failing somehow to get the coal mines back into steady production, but newspapers leveled their most vehement attacks against John L. Lewis. He was charged with want of patriotism for placing the interests of the miners above those of the country, assailed for his arrogance, and castigated in season and out for endangering national security. Even other labor leaders criticized the miners' embattled chieftain. There was sympathy for the workers, and in some quarters their strike was even welcomed because it dramatized the government's failure to hold down prices. Nonetheless, the CIO executive committee condemned Lewis for his supercilious attitude toward the War Labor Board and for what it described as "his personal and political vendetta against the President of the United States."

The situation could not endure indefinitely. After the second seizure of the coal mines, a compromise was finally hammered out between Ickes and Lewis, but it was one which went very far toward meeting the union leader's original demands. On the basis of some increase in the miners' working hours and the inclusion of portal-to-portal time, this new agreement provided for an increase of $1.50 a day in the prevailing wage rates. By such expedients, it conformed at least nominally to the Little Steel formula, and the War Labor Board, although very reluctantly, approved it. Lewis ordered the miners back to work. He had forced the government's hand. If his victory was not quite as complete as he triumphantly claimed, his stubborn, intractable stand had served the miners well.

The coal strike had greatly aroused corporate and congressional conservatives, and, fearful that other union leaders might be tempted to follow what were felt to be Lewis's outrageous tactics, they began to seek new legislation to curb labor's power. Other work stoppages in the spring of 1943, which antiunion employers seized upon to illustrate labor's irresponsibility, strengthened this demand, but the threatened breakdown in coal production was the single most important factor in creating the popular mood.

A number of restrictive bills were introduced in Congress in response to such gathering pressure, but the one which acquired strongest support was a measure jointly sponsored by Representative Howard Smith of Virginia, and Senator Tom L. Connally, Democrat of Texas. In the first instance, it provided definite statutory authority for the National War Labor Board, but it then went on to incorporate a series of provisions which in tone and content were definitely anti-labor. It empowered the President, whenever governmental mediation in a labor dispute proved unsuccessful, to take control of any plant or industry where a halt in production threatened the war effort and thereupon to enforce criminal penalties against any persons who instigated or promoted a strike. It did not place any ban on strikes where the government had not felt compelled to intervene. In contradiction to what had heretofore been a complete no-strike policy, the Smith-Connally bill in such cases sought merely to restrain possible work stoppages by providing for a thirty-day cooling-off period, during which the National Labor Relations Board was to hold a strike vote among all employees concerned. Finally, among several other minor provisions, union contributions to political campaign funds were expressly forbidden.

In the heat of the excitement occasioned by the coal strikes, Congress passed this measure by decisive majorities in both the Senate and the House. Labor was incensed. Its spokesmen declared that the bill ignored the widespread observance of the no-strike pledge through its criminal provisions and at the same time undermined this voluntary commitment by providing under general circumstances for a strike vote. The AFL executive committee bitterly attacked the bill as "born of hatred and malice on the part of reactionary congressmen"; President Murray told the CIO convention that the country was witnessing "the most vicious and continuous attack on labor's rights in the history of the nation."

Roosevelt vetoed the Smith-Connally bill. Although he recognized the need to control strikes, he agreed with labor that the provision for a cooling-off period with strike votes ran wholly counter to the no-strike program. The proposed law, he stated emphatically, would be conducive to labor unrest rather than industrial peace. In the temper of the times, Congress paid no attention whatsoever to his arguments and, on June 25, 1943, overrode his veto. The *New York Times* described what was officially called the War Labor Disputes Act as "a hasty, ill-considered and confused measure." Nonetheless, it remained on the statute books for the duration of the war.

Whatever the influence of the new legislation, which was hard to assess, strike activity followed an erratic course in succeeding years. As we have noted, it was to decline in 1944 and then, in spite of the new law, to increase in 1945. The most disturbing situation, apart from that in the coal industry, developed in an area which fell outside the jurisdiction of the Smith-Connally Act or other wartime legislation. This was a threatened strike on the part of railway workers, subject to controls provided in the amended Railway Labor Act of 1926, which created a serious crisis in the fall of 1943.

Following a breakdown of contract negotiations between the unions and the railway operators, Roosevelt appointed an Emergency Board under the Railway Act's provisions to settle the dispute. Its award, however, went beyond the limits on wage increases incorporated in the Little Steel formula, and the Office of Economic Stabilization consequently disapproved it. The railway unions thereupon prepared to strike.

Faced with an emergency much more dangerous to the war effort than the strikes in the coal fields, Roosevelt promptly intervened in this confused situation and proposed that he should act as an arbitrator between the opposing positions assumed by the Emergency Board and the Office of Economic Stabilization, with his decision binding on all parties concerned. Although the railroads and most of the railway unions accepted this plan, the Locomotive Firemen, the Railway Conductors, and the Switchmen's unions refused to withdraw their strike orders. The President gave instructions for immediate seizure of the railroads. "The war cannot wait and I cannot wait," he declared. "American lives and victory are at stake."

Before the strike orders actually went into effect or any direct confrontation had developed between the government and the railway workers, announcement was made of the presidential decision in the conflict between the Emergency Board and the Office of Economic Stabilization. It upheld the former. In spite of an apparent violation of the Little Steel formula in the wage award, the President sustained it on the ground that the wage increases for the railway workers were made in lieu of overtime and vacation pay to which they would otherwise have been entitled. In the light of a settlement going so far toward meeting their original demands, the unions, which had refused presidential arbitration, now reversed their position and withdrew their strike orders. There had been no interruption of service. On January 18, 1944, the government thereupon restored the railways to private operation after only a brief period of nominal control, and no further troubles developed on the transportation front during the remainder of the war.

The role of the National War Labor Board had been generally ignored or bypassed in the settlement of the labor disputes in both the coal industry and the railroads. Its authority under these circumstances appeared to have been significantly diminished. Nevertheless, it was still charged with settling other disputes and approving wage agreements reached through collective bargaining. But with every passing month it was more than ever caught in the tightening squeeze between its legal responsibilities under the Little Steel formula and the inequity of limiting wage advances to a percentage which had been far outrun by further increases in the cost of living. Moreover, the approval of wage adjustments for coal miners and railroad workers that actually went beyond the Little Steel formula, however disguised as being made in compensation for travel time or in lieu of vacation pay, made the board's position all the more difficult. It somehow had to devise an escape from an impossible dilemma if it were to exercise any sort of influence in maintaining industrial peace.

The board found the answer by authorizing on a ever-broadening scale new fringe benefits, which substantially supplemented the workers' take-home pay without violating any limitation on increases in straight-time hourly rates. In the collective-bargaining agreements coming under its review, it approved provision for holidays and vacations with pay, allowances for travel time and lunch periods, new adjustments for shift differentials, and the establishment of various systems of incentive and bonus payments. It also in effect encouraged insurance and hospitalization benefits for employees by ruling that the setting up of funds for such purposes through collective bargaining was not subject to its supervision or control. As these fringe benefits became more and more widely granted by employers, wage earners were at least partially compensated for the restrictions on wage increases. Labor unrest was substantially allayed.

Altogether during the war years, the War Labor Board imposed settlements in 17,650 dispute cases which affected over 12,000,000 employees, and in 95 per cent of these cases successfully averted any further threat to production. It also approved 415,000 voluntary wage agreements, which involved about 20,000,000 workers. This was a gigantic and time-consuming task, for which there was no parallel in all the history of labor relations, but on the whole the board operated very efficiently.

Both management and labor repeatedly critized the board's policies. Industry complained that it did not uphold the Little Steel formula as rigidly as it should have, and through approving fringe benefits, had in effect granted wholly unjustified wage increases. From the opposite tack, labor insisted that the cost of living index, on which the Little Steel formula was based, was both inaccurate and unfair, and that the board's interpretation of the formula had become "a thumb-screw with which to torment the working people of America and their families."

Despite such criticism, the great majority of the board's awards were accepted voluntarily. It had the authority, should a decision in a war industry be disputed, to recommend to the President seizure of the affected plants and the consequent application of direct sanctions to compel compliance with its orders. But this proved necessary on only forty occasions. The President took action twenty-six times when unions would not cooperate, twenty-three times when management proved recalcitrant, and once when neither the union nor management would agree to a board decision.

The most dramatic instance of defiance was the refusal of the Montgomery Ward Company to accept the board's jurisdiction on the ground that the mail-order business did not directly affect the war effort. President Roosevelt promptly ordered the seizure of the company's plants. Before the issue was finally settled, the country was treated to the engaging spectacle of Montgomery Ward's violently antilabor president, Sewell Avery, being carried bodily from his office by two stalwart members of the army detachment sent to take over company property.

The full record of the National War Labor Board, for all its difficulties and for all the criticism it aroused, constituted a very real success for this unprecedented experiment in tripartite labor arbitration. The board decisively helped to maintain labor peace and played an important role in sustaining the government's wage and price stabilization program. Through its sponsorship of maintenance of membership agreements to protect union security and its approval of fringe benefits as part of the collective-bargaining process, it also safeguarded labor's basic rights and significantly promoted its long-term interests. "The performance of the War Labor Board," so astute a labor historian as Philip Taft has written, "was one of the more notable accomplishments of a government agency dealing with economic problems during World War II."

As a result, between 1940 and 1945 total union membership rose from just under nine million to almost fifteen million, or from 27 per cent to 36 per cent of nonagricultural employees. Equally important, the CIO doubled its membership during the war years, although it remained only two-thirds as large as the AFL. During the war, then, labor built the mass base that would make it an influential economic, social, and political force in the postwar world.

Organized labor remained active on the political as well as on the economic front during the war years. The expanding role of governmental agencies and the passage of the Smith-Connally Act drove home with compelling force the indubitable fact that union interests were greatly affected by the measure of sympathy and support which labor could command in Washington. As the presidential campaign of 1944 approached, union leaders launched a determined drive to support President Roosevelt and the election of congressional candidates who might be counted upon to defend the labor cause. While the AFL maintained its traditional nonpartisanship and did not officially endorse the Democratic party, most of its member unions worked actively for Roosevelt's reelection. Without any such restraining legacy, the CIO not only endorsed a fourth term for the President by a resolution of its executive committee but also formed a nationwide Political Action Committee with the avowed purpose of getting out the labor vote in his support.

Under the energetic leadership of Sidney Hillman, the PAC laid plans for a national doorbell-ringing campaign to educate the workers in their political responsibilities, publicize the labor records of members of Congress, and encourage a heavy registration. It also sought hearings at both party conventions, as indeed labor groups had done ever since the days of Gompers, and used all its influence in favor of prolabor planks in their platforms. Its influence was greatest with the Democrats, and the PAC was falsely reputed to have played an important role in the selection of Roosevelt's running mate, Harry S Truman of Missouri. While unable to secure the nomination of Henry Wallace, its first choice for the vice-presidential candidacy, it allegedly blocked that of James F. Byrnes of South Carolina and opened the way for Truman. Hillman was the key labor figure in this behind-the-scenes political maneuvering, and his supposed ascendancy was highly dramatized by the published story—denied by all concerned but given nationwide publicity—that, in the vice-presidential struggle, Roosevelt had ordered his aides to "clear everything with Sidney." Actually, Roosevelt and his aides astutely managed the convention and got precisely what they wanted.

During the campaign itself, the PAC not only carried through vigorously its door-to-door canvass to get out the vote but also published and distributed a great mass of prolabor literature—millions of copies of pamphlets, leaflets, and fliers. Declaring that the first task facing the nation was complete victory in the war, these pamphlets further outlined a postwar domestic policy for full employment, fair wages, adequate housing, social security, and further protection of the interests of workers, farmers, and veterans. To attain these objectives, labor's campaign literature constantly reiterated, it was essential to elect a President and a Congress fully committed to progressive ideals. The magazine *Time* wryly commented: "Far and wide the slickest political propaganda produced in the U.S. in a generation."

Such aggressive tactics created great alarm in conservative and anti-labor circles. The PAC was assailed as radical, un-American, and dominated by Communists. The president of the Union Pacific

Railroad solemnly warned that it was "a pernicious innovation that
has literally snaked its way into American politics," and Senator John
W. Bricker, Republican of Ohio, declared that the PAC was seeking
"to dominate our government with radical and communistic
schemes." Sidney Hillman struck back angrily, saying that the smear
campaign was "lies on the top of lies."

In cooperation with other prolabor groups, the PAC undoubtedly
helped to swell the majority whereby Roosevelt was once again swept
into office. Every survey indicated that labor was probably more
united behind a single presidential candidate than ever before. A
questionnaire sent to 140 union newspapers indicated that only one
of them had supported the Republican candidate, Thomas E. Dewey
of New York, while, even more revealing, only eleven upheld the
AFL's official policy of neutrality.

As the war finally drew to an end, the fundamental problem facing
the nation was the readjustment of the economy to the needs of peace
without allowing unemployment to create a depression or permitting
inflation to set off a chain reaction of rising prices and rising wages
which might bring about an equally dangerous cycle of boom and
bust. Organized labor was convinced that a breakdown in the
economy could be avoided only if the government took a strong position in support of full employment and further wage increases in
order to sustain national purchasing power and thereby create an expanding market for industrial goods. It was prepared to fight for such
a program both in the interests of wage earners and in the interests of
the country as a whole. Underlying all such economic considerations,
moreover, was a further issue. After the end of the First World War,
labor had seen the gains made during the period of hostilities gradually whittled away by the aggressive counterattack of industry in
breaking the turbulent strikes of 1919. As the guns fell silent in
Europe and the Pacific a quarter of a century later, labor determined
that there should be no recurrence of this setback to union security.
Labor would militantly defend its rights.

This resolve was strengthened by the immediate consequences of
peace. There were widespread layoffs in the latter half of 1945 as industry closed its factories to retool for normal production, and even
workers holding their jobs found their take-home pay reduced with a
return to the forty-hour week. Moreover, prices once again began to
rise, and the limited wage adjustments allowed by the still functioning

War Labor Board were completely inadequate to meet higher living costs. But in answer to union demands that wages be increased, industry retorted that labor was treating "the economic pool as a grab-bag" and refused any concessions. The lines of battle were being drawn.

President Truman hoped that the issues at stake could be resolved and the reconversion program speeded up by a return to the normal processes of collective bargaining. He was prepared to relax many of the wartime controls over the economy and to transfer the functions of the War Labor Board to a new tripartite National Wage Stabilization Board. Moreover, he stated his conviction that unions were entitled to safeguards which would counteract their feeling of insecurity in the postwar era, and that industry could afford reasonable pay concessions without having to raise prices on manufactured goods. "Wage increases are imperative," he said on October 20, 1945, "to cushion the shock to our workers, to sustain adequate purchasing power and to raise national income. . . . Fortunately there is room in the existing price structure for business as a whole to grant increases in rates."

The country's industrial leaders promptly attacked this statement as an indication that the administration intended to continue the New Deal's favoritism for labor. In the Senate, Robert A. Taft, Republican of Ohio, declared that the President had surrendered to the CIO. Whatever the political implications of Truman's stand, there could in fact be no denying that he had accepted labor's main contentions. His administration appeared ready to act on the premise that the national government had a direct responsibility to try to safeguard the nation's millions of industrial workers from unemployment and otherwise promote their economic well-being. But Truman was also emphasizing the vital importance of maintaining national purchasing power, as Roosevelt had before him, for the benefit of the entire country.

The validity of his thesis that wages could be raised without compensating price increases for industry was lent support by governmental reports which showed that corporation profits during the war period had been two and one-half times the prewar average and were heading toward the highest levels in all history. Business economists, however, flatly denied the accuracy of these governmental surveys. In a quite different analysis of the prevailing situation, they insisted that higher wages would mean added costs which could not possibly be absorbed by industry within the existing price structure.

It soon became apparent in these circumstances that collective bargaining could not be relied upon to settle the mounting number of industrial disputes. Neither management nor labor showed any disposition to work out their problems in a conciliatory spirit. With a basic power struggle underlying the controversy over wages and prices, there was little room for maneuver, and the government saw the whole reconversion program dangerously threatened. As petitions for strike votes submitted to the National Labor Relations Board under the terms of the Smith-Connally Act steadily rose (the pending total was 800 in October 1945), President Truman, as had President Wilson in similar circumstances in 1919, turned to a labor-management conference in the hope of bringing the two sides together.

This conference met in Washington on November 5, 1945, to try to formulate "a broad and permanent foundation for industrial peace and progress." The representatives of labor and management duly met, conferred, and then adjourned—without making any appreciable progress whatsoever. They accepted the validity of collective bargaining, which was more than labor and management had been able to do in 1919, but they could not agree on any procedures which might break the impasse in current negotiations. The failure of the conference gave a new impetus to the rising tide of strikes throughout the country. Even as the labor and management representatives were discouragedly packing their bags to leave Washington, it came into full flood.

Machinists and shipyard workers in San Francisco went on strike; building service operators and longshoremen in New York broke off their contract negotiations; truck drivers in the Midwest quit their jobs; and in other parts of the country oil refinery workers, lumberjacks, and glass workers walked out. Picket lines in city after city and strikers carrying placards demanding union security and take-home pay the equivalent of wartime wages brought home vividly to the public the extent and gravity of industrial unrest. By the end of 1945, the strikes began to assume even greater proportions as the major CIO unions launched an all-out attack against the mass-production industries. Some 200,000 employees of General Motors struck in November; two months later 300,000 meatpackers and 180,000 electrical workers quit their jobs; and then, with even more devastating impact on the economy, 750,000 steel workers walked out. At the beginning of the new year, the staggering total of almost 2,000,000 industrial workers were simultaneously on strike.

There was little violence. What was taking place was a grim endurance contest between the forces of labor and industry rather than a slugging match. But newspaper headlines from coast to coast underscored the mounting gravity of the crisis, and a clamor rose for decisive action to restore industrial peace. Steel held the spotlight. The halt in production of steel was also causing the layoff of additional thousands of workers in other plants as they felt the harsh effects of spreading economic paralysis.

Of all the immediate postwar strikes, the most revealing and significant was the conflict between the UAW and General Motors. In this instance, the strike leader, Walter Reuther, the most daring and ambitious among a new generation of labor leaders, made an innovative and imaginative proposal. He insisted that General Motors could increase wages without raising prices and that corporations should not earn excessive profits at the expense of workers and consumers. Reuther called on General Motors to open its financial records to union economists in order to demonstrate the relationship among wages, prices, and profits. The company's high profits, Reuther asserted, enabled it to increase wages while holding prices stable; in fact, the labor leader suggested that General Motors could probably reduce car prices and still earn substantial profits. The UAW thus identified itself as the advocate of the public's interest in stable prices and mass consumer purchasing power.

In response General Motors maintained that the relationship among wages, prices, and profits fell totally within the prerogatives of management. It refused to open its books to the union and insisted that the rights of property owners to use their assets could not be infringed. To open internal corporate financial records to union or public scrutiny, General Motors executives alleged, would be tantamount to eliminating the basic principles of "free enterprise" capitalism.

There matters stood for more than three months as the union and the company proved unable to reach agreement through voluntary collective bargaining. General Motors, moreover, was adamantly opposed to bringing the dispute before a presidential fact-finding board. But it must be noted that General Motors in 1945–1946, unlike most corportions in 1919–1920, made no effort to operate its struck plants. Nor did it seek to smash the union with which it was locked in combat.

The obduracy of the parties to the General Motors conflict and the rapid spread of strikes to other vital sectors of the economy confronted President Truman with the complete collapse of a postwar labor policy predicated on the resumption of peaceful collective bargaining. While Truman still hoped to keep governmental interference at a minimum, he nonetheless realized that he had to act to restore labor peace and safeguard his economic stabilization program. What he now proposed was a policy providing for a thirty-day cooling-off period before any strike could take place and, in each instance, the submission of the issues in dispute to a presidential fact-finding board. This board would seek to resolve the controversy before it through a formula which would permit wage increases commensurate with the rise in the cost of living and yet hold the line against further inflation.

Neither labor nor management welcomed this plan, but Truman proceeded to set up his fact-finding boards on his own initiative. The board established to investigate the dispute between the United Steel Workers and the steel companies handed down a ruling which became the basis for the settlement of most postwar strikes. Estimating that there had been a 33-per-cent increase in living costs since 1941, it provided a comparable wage increase for steelworkers, with price relief for companies in need of increased earnings. In plain terms, the award meant an 18½-cents rise in basic hourly wage rates, and a $5-a-ton-advance in the price of steel. From steel the terms of the award spread rapidly to the electrical machinery, meatpacking, and oil-refining industries. And, in the end, even the UAW accepted the terms of the postwar strike settlement, finally calling off the General Motors strike after a battle of more than 100 days. By mid-March 1946, the postwar strike wave, the most massive in the history of the United States, had practically ended.

The end had not come yet, however. Even as the major strikes in other sectors of the economy were reaching settlement, a new conflict developed in the coal industry. John L. Lewis could hardly be expected to stand aside as the CIO unions made such substantial gains. He not only demanded further wage increases for the miners but also the establishment of a general welfare fund to which the operators would contribute seven cents a ton for all coal mined. When the operators balked, Lewis promptly broke off further negotiations. "Good day, gentlemen," he was reported as saying. "We trust that time, as it shrinks your purse, may modify your niggardly and antisocial purposes." On April 1, 1946, some 400,000 miners were once again on vacation in the small, drab coal towns of Pennsylvania and West Virginia, Kentucky and Alabama, Illinois and Iowa.

The coal strike continued intermittently for the rest of the year, with Lewis in customary fashion defying the operators, the government, and the public. Once again government took over the mines under the terms of what Lewis called "the infamous Smith-Connally statute," but soon after a highly favorable agreement had been reached with Secretary of the Interior Julius A. Krug, Lewis declared its provisions inadequate. When Krug refused to consider their revision, the strike was resumed.

In these circumstances, the government applied for a federal injunction to restrain all strike activity. Judge T. Alan Goldsborough of the federal district court in Washington, characterizing the strike as "an evil, demoniac, monstrous thing," granted the government's request. Lewis refused to acquiesce in what he called "the ugly recrudescence of government by injunction" and ignored the court's orders. He was thereupon cited for contempt and, after a formal trial, found guilty. The United Mine Workers was fined $3,500,000 and Lewis himself $10,000.

The case was carried to the Supreme Court which, in a five-to-four decision, sustained Judge Goldsborough on the ground that, in spite of the provisions of the Norris–La Guardia Act, the government could indeed obtain an injunction where a strike threatened the national welfare and security. Lewis had for once suffered a sharp reverse. He agreed to call off the strike, the Supreme Court reduced the fine against the United Mine Workers to $700,000, and the miners returned to their jobs. Nevertheless, the union's power had by no means been broken. When the mines were returned to private operation on the expiration of the Smith-Connally Act in June, 1947, Lewis succeeded in winning a new contract which met virtually all his demands both in respect to wages and contributions to the welfare fund.

A further major strike was narrowly averted in May 1946, following a breakdown in wage negotiations between management and workers on the nation's railways. The elaborate machinery of the Railway Labor Act failed to bring about a settlement, and the government once again had recourse to a special emergency board. It finally hammered out a settlement acceptable to the carriers and most of the unions, but the Railroad Trainmen and the Locomotive Engineers—300,000 strong—refused to go along and sent out strike orders.

In this new emergency, President Truman promptly seized the railroads, and, when the trainmen and engineers began to quit work,

Truman went on the air on May 24 to deliver an uncompromising ultimatum. Unless all employees returned to their jobs the next day, the government would operate the railroads and provide the protection of the country's armed forces "to every man who heeds the call of his country in this hour of need." When there was no move to call off the strike on the expiration of this deadline, he went before Congress and, at a tense and expectant session, asked specific authority not only to apply for an injunction, but for further powers to deprive the strikers of their seniority rights and to draft them into the armed forces should they continue on their course.

As the President reached the dramatic climax in this speech, he was suddenly interrupted. A clerk handed him a message, and, in the hushed silence, he quietly announced: "Word has just been received that the rail strike has been settled on the terms proposed by the President." Almost hysterical cheers greeted this announcement, but when they finally died down, Truman deliberately went on with his prepared text. The legislation he sought was still necessary, he stated, in order fully to resolve the crisis.

The House promptly responded to the President's appeal, but, with the strike now over, the Senate let the bill die in committee. The whole atmosphere was one of anticlimax. In both congressional and popular debate, however, Truman found himself strongly attacked for proposing such an unprecedented and forceful measure. He was not only assailed by labor and liberal spokesmen, but, in ironic reversal of their usual positions, conservatives led by Senator Taft attacked the President's plan as unfair to the railway workers and a violation of their civil liberties.

In union circles, opposition could hardly have been more vehement. In spite of everything he had done to uphold labor's cause in the earlier disputes of this tumultuous year, Truman found himself universally condemned for his attitude during the railway crisis. He was accused of having turned completely against the unions and, at the CIO national convention, was scornfully labeled "the Number One strikebreaker of the American bankers and railroads."

The record of the twelve-month period since the end of the war had been a shattering one—4,630 work stoppages and a total of 5,000,000 strikers piling up 120,000,000 days of idleness. Nevertheless, the economy had successfully withstood such heavy battering. Instead of the feared depression and consequent unemployment, the reconversion program was forging ahead, and, at the close of the year, the civilian labor force had risen to an all-time high of 55,000,000 workers.

For workers and the labor movement, the aftermath of the Second World War proved fundamentally different from that of the First World War. Not only did economic expansion, inflation, and relatively full employment distinguish 1945–1946 from the economic contraction, deflation, and unemployment of 1919–1921; the emergence of stable trade unions in the mass-production industries and peaceful collective bargaining had become essential to the smooth functioning of the economy. If organized labor did not fulfill all the promises raised by its wartime aspirations, it did not shrink back to its prewar state.

Indeed, at first, many observers thought that labor had become a new power in the land. The Harvard economist, Sumner Slichter, wrote that "the United States is gradually shifting from a capitalistic community to a laboristic one—that is, to a community in which employees rather than businessmen are the strongest single influence." Corporate executives complained that "efforts are continuing on the part of certain unions to extend the scope of collective bargaining to include matters and functions that are clearly the responsibility of management." And a labor leader asserted that it was the unions' responsibility to regulate the employer "at every point where his action affects the welfare of the men."

In fact, the resolution of the strike wave of 1945–1946 blasted such fears and hopes. All along the line, especially in the General Motors strike, employers held firm on the issue of managerial prerogatives. Having lost much of their shop-floor discipline as a result of wartime labor shortages, corporate managers now sought to reassert their control over labor. The agreements of 1946 set the basic terms of what soon became the governing labor-capital détente. Workers received higher wages and unions institutional security in return for respecting the rights of management. Union leaders, moreover, promised to discipline unruly workers who violated the armistice between labor and capital.

For a quarter of a century, the system of industrial relations initiated during the New Deal, perfected in the Second World War, and legitimated in 1946 worked. The American economy dominated the globe, capital accumulation grew, productivity rose, and profits waxed. Higher productivity and profits, in turn, enabled corporations to negotiate union contracts which guaranteed ever-rising real standards of living. The abolition of poverty in our time, which Herbert Hoover had prematurely promised Americans in 1928, now seemed to have become a reality.

XIX

From Taft-Hartley to
the Merger of the AFL
and the CIO

While organized labor survived the reconversion period with its wartime gains intact and most workers held steady jobs with good wages, their successes cloaked real weaknesses. The postwar strike wave intensified a powerful antiunion drive that had originated in the late 1930s, resulted in the passage of the wartime Smith-Connally Act, and had developed a new vigor in 1946–1947. The corporate community and its conservative congressional allies unleashed a propaganda campaign which portrayed organized labor as a selfish special interest which ill-served the public. Public opinion polls reflected the success of the conservative antiunion campaign. A majority of those polled consistently reported distaste for union militancy and fear of irresponsible labor leaders.

The antiunion drive coalesced in 1946 around the demand for the amendment of the Wagner Act of 1935. It was now said that the basic character of New Deal labor legislation had granted unions too much power, that it even enabled organized labor to dominate the economy. By outlawing unfair management practices only, the union critics contended, the Wagner Act left labor free to engage in all kinds of improper and sometimes coercive behavior. The end result of the mounting agitation to redress the balance of power, which conservatives argued had gone too far to the side of labor, was the enactment in June 1947 of the Taft-Hartley Act.

Before this basic measure became law, Congress had adopted an earlier bill introduced by Representative Francis Case which clearly revealed its temper. This bill had first been passed by the House during the strikes of early 1946. As they were settled under Truman's program, further action lagged. With the subsequent crises in coal and on the railroads, however, the Senate hurriedly fell in line and approved the Case bill. This measure set up a Federal Mediation Board, prescribed a sixty-day cooling-off period before any strike could be called, and decreed loss of all their rights under the Wagner Act for workers who quit their jobs during the cooling-off period. It also banned secondary boycotts and jurisdictional strikes and authorized the use of injunctions to prevent violent or obstructive picketing.

This was a draconian measure which hit hard at labor's historic right to strike. Truman promptly vetoed it. He argued that it dealt with the symptoms rather than the causes of industrial unrest and urged Congress to take a more thorough look at the whole problem. What was really needed, he stated, was a long-range program that would face up to the unresolved issues of labor relations and, at the same time, continue to safeguard the basic principle of union security.

The antilabor forces in Congress could not muster the votes to override this veto, but they had no idea of letting restrictive legislation go by the board. The midterm elections of 1946 strengthened their hand. The Republicans won decisive control of Congress, and their landslide victory was interpreted as a direct popular mandate to take drastic action on the labor issue in spite of President Truman's position. Some thirty states had adopted various forms of restrictive legislation and, in such circumstances, it was hardly surprising that Congress should hasten to fall into line. The leaders of both the AFL and the CIO assailed what they termed a "deliberate and monstrous movement. . . to cripple if not destroy, the labor movement," but they were unable to rally the support, either in Congress or in the country as a whole, to combat the antilabor trend.

The Taft-Hartley Act had a stormy passage through Congress. The more severe provisions first incorporated in the measure by the House were to be somewhat liberalized by the Senate, but in its final form the bill very definitely reflected the conservative reaction. Truman vetoed it as he had the Case bill. He condemned it as primarily designed to weaken the unions, declared that it would in fact encourage rather than discourage strikes, and deplored what he said would be its effect in making government "an unwanted participant at every bargaining table." The bill's provisions, he concluded, were "shocking—bad for labor, bad for management, bad for the country."

This time his opposition was to prove unavailing. Vehemently attacking the President for his prolabor sympathies, the bill's proponents charged that he had completely misrepresented its provisions. They succeeded in winning the necessary support in both the House and the Senate to override his veto, and the Taft-Hartley Act duly became the law of the land.

It was a long and immensely complicated measure whose declared purpose was to restore that equality of bargaining power between employers and employees which it was contended had been sacrificed in the Wagner Act. The rights guaranteed labor in that earlier law were matched by specific safeguards for the rights of management. Employers were guaranteed full freedom of expression in respect to their views on union organization, short of threats of reprisal or promises of benefits, and they were authorized, themselves, to call for elections to determine the appropriate bargaining units in wage negotiations. At the same time, it was declared an unfair labor practice for unions in any way to attempt to coerce employers, engage in either secondary boycotts or jurisdictional strikes, or, in their turn, to refuse to bargain collectively.

The Taft-Hartley Act also incorporated a number of provisions which directly affected union security. It expressly banned the closed shop, required highly complicated voting procedures for the establishment of the union shop, and, perhaps most significantly, left the door open to even more severe antiunion legislation by the states. In Section 14(b), it permitted the states to bypass federal legislation allowing the union shop by themselves banning it. This provision made possible so-called state "right-to-work" laws which were to hamper further union organization more directly than anything in the Taft-Hartley Act itself.

There were further restrictions. Unions were required to give sixty-day notice for the termination or modification of any agreement and were made suable in the federal courts for breach of contract. They were not allowed to make contributions or otherwise expend any of their funds in political campaigns. Their officers were required to file affidavits affirming that they were not members of the Communist party or of any organization supporting it.

In Title II, the Taft-Hartley Act broke entirely new ground with an elaborate formula for dealing with strikes which created a national emergency. It gave the President the authority, after making an investigation through a special board of inquiry, to apply for what in effect constituted an eighty-day injunction against any strike that was found to imperil the national health or safety. Should negotiations during this period still fail to solve the controversy, the President was to submit a report to Congress "with such recommendations as he may see fit for consideration and appropriate action." Finally, Taft-Hartley made a number of significant administrative changes in existing legislation. It provided for the enlargement of the National Labor Relations Board, with the appointment of a new general counsel, and established an independent Federal Mediation and Conciliation Service with authority to step into any labor dispute which threatened a substantial interruption of interstate commerce.

The debate over the bill had been impassioned. The temper of the House was revealed in the report of its Committee on Education and Labor which declared that, as a result of union activity, the individual worker's "mind, his soul, and his very life have been subjected to a tyranny more despotic than anyone could think possible in a free country." The committee would have abolished the National Labor Relations Board, eliminated the requirement of management obligation in collective bargaining, and required a vote of all workers involved before a strike could be called. The position of the Senate Committee on Labor and Public Welfare was more moderate. It recommended that the social gains which employees had received under previous legislation should be maintained and that Congress should seek to remedy existing inequities between employers and employees by precise and carefully drawn legislation. The views of the Senate committee were more nearly to prevail, partly through common sense and partly to assure a majority that could override Truman's expected veto. In the meantime, however, representatives of industry and of labor fought out their own battle in the public forum.

The full strength of employer associations, spearheaded by the National Association of Manufacturers, was thrown behind enactment of a stiff bill. The AFL[1] and the CIO opposed any new legislation whatsoever. Both industry and labor sent their spokesmen to the congressional hearings, inserted full-page advertisements in the country's newspapers presenting their contrasting philosophies, and bought radio time to air their views. While the bills' proponents maintained that the proposed legislation went no further than to equalize bargaining power, its opponents characterized it as a vindictive attack on unionism instigated by those who wished to do away with collective bargaining altogether.

In light of the prevailing political situation, labor's position was very weak. In refusing to compromise in respect to the proposed legislation and seeking to hold reactionary employers wholly responsible for the drive to modify prolabor provisions of the Wagner Act, both the AFL and the CIO misjudged congressional realities. And in refusing to suggest any alternative measure to meet the alleged inadequacies, if not unfairness, of the Wagner Act, they reinforced the widespread view in Congress that organized labor had become increasingly irresponsible in the exercise of monopolistic power.

There was still much latent support for the labor cause. Some three months after final passage of the Taft-Hartley Act, public opinion polls showed that 53 per cent of the persons questioned who knew of its enactment believed that it should be repealed or at least revised. But the campaign to block antilabor legislation had been started too late and had been too uncompromising to overcome the momentum of the conservative reaction which had been building up since 1938. In unjustified self-assurance, union leadership had failed to adjust itself to new times and new circumstances. Labor had suffered a severe setback on the political front.

The passage of the Taft-Hartley Act did not by any means bring to an end the impassioned controversy over its merits. While neither the hopes of its adherents nor the fears of its critics were in practice to be realized, it remained a bone of embittered contention among the prolabor and antilabor forces in the country. Congress faced no more

---

[1]It is worth noting that, between 1938 and 1943, the AFL leaders had themselves helped to draft several of the restrictive clauses incorporated subsequently into the Taft-Hartley Act. See James Gross, *The Reshaping of the National Labor Relations Board* (Ithaca, N.Y., 1981).

sensitive political issue in the whole range of domestic legislation. As the 1948 presidential campaign approached, neither party was able to ignore it. The Republicans cautiously called for continuing study to improve labor-management legislation; the Democrats more forthrightly pledged Taft-Hartley's immediate repeal.

Truman's unexpected and dramatic reelection raised high labor's hopes that repeal would actually be effected. They were disappointed. A conservative coalition of Republicans and southern Democrats remained in control of Congress, and it had little sympathy with organized labor. One amendment to the law was adopted. The required elections for the union shop had in every case shown such overwhelming workers' support (an average 87 per cent among those voting) that it was henceforth provided that such agreements could be concluded without employee polls. Otherwise, every move to revise or repeal the law was beaten back. Taft-Hartley remained on the statute books.

Labor continued to attack it as a "slave-labor" bill. This it certainly was not. There was little question that certain of its provisions, and most notably Section 14(b) with its encouragement of state right-to-work laws, impeded union organization in the South and perhaps some other parts of the country. Nevertheless, there was to be further growth in union membership during the next few years, and the proportion of the nation's workers whose terms of employment were governed by collective bargaining agreements rose steadily.

Where Taft-Hartley proved most disappointing and ineffective was in the application of its provisions for settling strikes that endangered the public welfare. Title II, which labor condemned as reestablishing "the abhorrent principle of government by injunctions," afforded no real solution to the problem which such strikes created. In succeeding years, its provisions were invoked only with great reluctance and often served to confuse rather than to clarify the issues in dispute.

The first major strike that led President Truman to take action under the injunction proceedings occurred in the perennially restless coal fields. In spite of the settlement reached in 1947, intermittent work stoppages continued, and a new controversy developed between the miners and the operators when the ever-aggressive John L. Lewis charged that the latter had "dishonored" their contract in respect to the health and welfare fund. This dispute was finally ironed out, but two years later the miners' chieftain again began to agitate in favor of higher wages. His new technique was to avoid the charge of directly calling a strike but to bring comparable pressure on the operators by periodically ordering out the miners in a series of so-called "memorial" work stoppages protesting against the high rate of deaths and injuries in the coal mines.

As these work stoppages went on, Truman finally felt compelled under public pressure to invoke Title II of Taft-Hartley and, on February 6, 1950, he obtained a temporary injunction against any further strikes. When the union officials sent out instructions ordering the miners back to work, they were largely ignored. The government then instituted contempt proceedings against the United Mine Workers on the ground that the orders calling off the strike had been given only "token compliance." A federal court, however, refused to sustain these proceedings. It asserted that the government had not proved its charge of lack of good faith in the union's issuance of its orders.

In this impasse, Truman turned rather desperately to Congress for authority—as in wartime—to seize the coal mines. While Congress hesitated, a new agreement was finally reached—in March 1950—between the union and the operators, and the work stoppages came to an end without the necessity of further governmental intervention. The experience with Taft-Hartley had proved, to say the least, very inconclusive.

Another strike involving the law's emergency provisions—although they were not actually invoked—took place in the steel industry in 1952. It was to last nearly two months—the longest and costliest work stoppage that the industry had up to that time ever experienced—and taking place as it did against the background of the Korean War, aroused a measure of public concern comparable only to the strike crises during the Second World War. There could be no disputing the fact that the breakdown in steel production created a national emergency.

Wages and hours had at this time once again been brought under governmental control as a result of the Korean hostilities, and, when negotiations for a new contract between the United Steelworkers and the industry broke down at the end of 1951, the dispute was referred to a new Wage Stabilization Board. The union agreed to hold any strike activity in abeyance until the board made its report; when the Board did so some three months later, the union agreed to accept its recommendations. However, the steel industry denounced the report for advocating recognition of the union shop and refused to accept the proposed wage settlement unless it was allowed to make compensatory increases in the price of steel. When the Economic Stabilization Director denied the price increases, the industry rejected the settlement as a whole and the union thereupon made ready to strike.

There was an immediate and widespread demand that Truman should seek an injunction under the Taft-Hartley Act. He bluntly refused to do so. He took the position that the steel workers had already refrained from striking for three months while the Wage Stabilization Board was making its investigations, and to enjoin them further was not warranted. Instead of an injunction, he took the drastic step, on April 8, 1952, of seizing the steel plants on his own authority as the only way to maintain production vital to the war effort. "I feel sure," he stated, "that the Constitution does not require me to endanger our national safety by letting all the steel mills close down at this particular time."

His action created a storm of protest. While the steel workers remained on the job, the industry promptly took the matter to the courts. The legal issue was fought out against a confused background of preliminary injunctions against government operation, temporary stays of the court orders, and a final appeal to the Supreme Court. On June 2, 1952, it ruled that the seizure of the mills was an unconstitutional exercise of executive authority. The President perforce returned them to private operation, whereupon the steel workers— 560,000 strong—resumed their strike and brought production to a complete halt.

As the popular controversy over Truman's refusal to invoke the Taft-Hartley Act and his arbitrary seizure of the steel mills continued to rage throughout the country, the union and the industry renewed their contract negotiations. It was not, however, until July 26 that they came to terms. The settlement which was at last reached generally conformed to that originally proposed by the Wage Stabilization Board, but in the meantime the strike had cost the industry $350,000,000 and the workers $50,000,000 in wages. More important, the strike had not only crippled the steel industry itself but had also caused the shutdown of many steel-using plants and brought automobile assembly lines to a temporary halt. It had seriously endangered the flow of essential military materials to Korea, and only the gradual cessation of hostilities had prevented an even graver crisis.

A third major strike, which in this instance led to action under the Taft-Hartley Act, occurred the next year on the docks and wharves of New York, when the International Longshoremen's Association and the New York Shipping Association found themselves unable to come to terms over wages and hiring practices. This dispute was to become even more complicated than the strike in coal or in steel. With the work stoppage tying up all shipping in New York, the AFL expelled the union on charges of racketeering and chartered a new longshoremen's organization; the state authorities of New York and New Jersey intervened in the interests of law and order; and a Senate investigating committee angrily reported that the waterfront had become "a lawless frontier" plagued by corruption, Communism, and gangsterism. President Dwight D. Eisenhower, who had now succeeded Truman, finally invoked the emergency provisions of the Taft-Hartley Act, but in spite of a federal injunction a series of wildcat strikes continued as a result of the bitter fight between the old and new longshoremen's unions.

Elections under the auspices of the National Labor Relations Board ultimately confirmed the right of the original union, in spite of all the charges that had been brought against it, to represent the longshoremen in bargaining with the shipping industry. Negotiations were then resumed and a settlement reached which barred both strikes and lockouts for a two-year period. Something like peace temporarily descended on the embattled waterfront, but once again governmental intervention under Taft-Hartley had proved to be wholly unsatisfactory.

There were other strikes in the aftermath of the law's passage, and they always made good newspaper copy. Communications workers, textile workers, automobile workers, and construction workers, among others, had relatively brief work stoppages; the railway workers staged a series of "sick" walkouts in 1951 which led to government threats to dismiss all employees who did not stay on the job; and the next year the coal miners had still another strike. What passed largely unnoticed, however, was that, in spite of all the furor over the coal miners, steel workers, longshoremen and other restive unionists, there was actually a sharp decline in work stoppages. The annual total of man-days lost in the years 1947–1951 averaged 40,000,000, in comparison with 116,000,000 in 1946.

The controversy over Taft-Hartley and the headlines concerning a handful of so-called national-emergency strikes cloaked even more significant developments in the arena of labor-capital relations. For one thing, when times were good and the labor market tight, unions continued to grow. They reached their relative membership peak at the end of the Korean War in 1954, when 18,000,000 workers, or 35 per cent of the nonagricultural labor force, belonged to unions. And in the South, where Taft-Hartley probably had a more restrictive impact on labor than elsewhere, union membership grew proportionately more rapidly. Still more important, an entirely new pattern of labor-management collective bargaining agreements had begun to appear, nowhere more significantly than in the automobile industry.

Beginning with the contract between the UAW and General Motors in 1948 and continuing in a series of contracts signed in the 1950s and later, the automobile companies and the union pioneered a new relationship. Interestingly, several of the innovations were a result of company, not union initiatives. The evolving labor-management contract in automobiles encompassed steadily rising real wages and industrial stability. The companies agreed to grant workers annual productivity wage increases and contractual cost-of-living adjustments (COLA) to protect them against price inflation. At the end of the 1950s, the contract came to include Supplementary Unemployment Benefits (SUB)—a form of short-term guaranteed annual wage. The companies also provided their employees with health-care protection, retirement plans to supplement social security, and a combination of paid holidays and annual vacations. In return, the union consented to long-term contracts (two to five years in length), which enabled management to plan for the future more safely, and the UAW policed the agreement by disciplining unruly workers who engaged in unsanctioned wildcat strikes.

In short, in return for promising labor peace to management, unions and their members won a rising real standard of living. As wage increases became the chief goal of the postwar union movement, money took precedence over the older labor demand for industrial democracy. As long as it granted higher real wages, management held a relatively free hand in controlling the labor process. As David Brody has written: "The common tendency everywhere was toward an ever greater extension of the contractual net." At rock bottom, the "companies and unions revealed what was . . . the common intent of their encompassing contractual relationship—the containment of spontaneous and independent shopfloor activity."

Labor's advance on the economic front did not lead it to ignore the less favorable battleground of politics. It had learned a bitter lesson in the passage of the Taft-Hartley Act. The campaign for the repeal of this measure continued unabated and, on a broader front, every effort was made to promote new social legislation. "Labor has long recognized," President Murray of the CIO declared, "that the gains which it wins through economic action can be protected, implemented and extended only if it develops a progressive program of legislation and secures its enactment through effective participation in the political life of the nation."

The Republican victory at the polls in 1952 dashed all hopes for the repeal of Taft-Hartley, but its revision still seemed possible. In a message to Congress on February 2, 1953, President Eisenhower stated that experience had shown the need for corrective measures in existing legislation. Moreover, he appointed Martin P. Durkin, former president of the United Association of Journeymen Plumbers and Steamfitters, as his Secretary of Labor (it was said that the cabinet was made up of nine millionaires and a plumber!), and this appeared to be a further augury for the advancement of labor's interests.

Yet nothing was done. Durkin drew up nineteen proposed amendments to Taft-Hartley and, in the belief that he had the President's approval for them, gave out the draft of a message for their submission to Congress. Eisenhower, however, denied that he had promised his support. Resenting what he interpreted as repudiation of an agreed-upon policy, Durkin thereupon resigned from the cabinet. Although the President tried to justify his policy and reassure labor of his continuing sympathy, union leaders were convinced that the conservative elements surrounding him had forced him to go back on his promises. He was to declare at the AFL convention in September 1953 that he had "a very great comprehension of what organized labor had done for this country," but such vague rhetorical phrases hardly compensated for his failure to back up his own Secretary of Labor in support of remedial legislation.

The leadership of both the AFL and the CIO realized anew in these circumstances that labor would have to build up its political strength if it was not to face the danger of further restrictive legislation. The AFL had already established a League for Political Education paralleling the CIO's Political Action Committee. The two organizations had done yeoman work in the 1952 election, even though not too successful, and they were now prepared to cooperate fully in exerting all possible pressure on Congress in organized labor's interest.

Their lobbying activities helped to bring about a further expansion in the Social Security program. It was extended to cover an increasing number of workers in respect to old-age and survivors' insurance benefits, and the monthly payments on such accounts were substantially increased. In 1955 Congress also raised the minimum wage levels established under the Fair Labor Standards Act from 75 cents to $1 an hour. On another front, although unsuccessful for another decade, union lobbies worked consistently for the old-age health program, which became known as Medicare.

Organized labor's political interests were not limited by social-welfare legislation. It participated actively and sometimes enthusiastically in the politics of the Cold War and the domestic Red Scare. As the global confrontation between the United States and the Soviet Union increasingly became the central issue of postwar American life, the labor movement could not escape its ramifications. In fact, few Americans proved more militantly anti-Communist than labor leaders, especially those within the older AFL unions.

Both the AFL and the CIO fully supported the foreign policies of Presidents Truman and Eisenhower. They endorsed the Truman Doctrine of containing Soviet power by providing military and economic aid to Greece and Turkey; favored the Marshall Plan; approved American participation in NATO; and defended Truman's "police action" in Korea. They also took funds from the CIA and used them to combat left-wing influences in the labor movements of West Germany, France, Italy, Latin America, and elsewhere in the Third World. Labor's leaders stood in the vanguard of those emphasizing the gravity of the Communist threat and repeatedly called for more effective common action in combating it.

Writing in the *American Federationist* in January 1948, George Meany, at that time secretary-treasurer of the AFL, emphasized that, in order to win the peace so essential for American security, the United States should make every effort to keep its sister democracies free. He declared that the Marshall Plan was the best means of halting the surge of totalitarianism in Europe and argued that its annual cost would be no more than the nation spent in a single sixteen-day period during the Second World War. In a later article, he supported the North Atlantic Treaty even more emphatically. "In this grave hour," he stated, "the people of America can be fully assured that in

American labor the cause of democracy at home and abroad has a devoted, determined, and dynamic champion."

Within the ranks of the CIO, both Philip Murray and Walter Reuther were equally forthright in pledging labor's vigorous support for the foreign policies of the Truman administration. An article in the *C.I.O. News* singled out for praise Truman's Point Four program of technical assistance for underdeveloped countries. In providing help for other people, it noted, Point Four would also create additional jobs for American workers. On one occasion, Reuther called for more effective social action "to back the country's defense and foreign aid programs."

In reaffirming support of the Truman policies after the outbreak of the Korean War, both national labor federations adopted new resolutions. In the light of the conflagration in eastern Asia, that of the AFL stated, the paramount task which confronted the free labor movement was to deter and, if need be, decisively defeat Soviet imperialism. The CIO declared that it fully backed the American government and the United Nations in the struggle being waged against Communist aggression.

Within its own house, organized labor broke all ties with Communism and purged its ranks of alleged Communists. It withdrew its representatives from the World Federation of Trade Unions when that organization appeared to be falling under Communist domination and cooperated in the formation of a new International Confederation of Free Trade Unions. On the home front, the CIO disqualified Communists from official positions and expelled unions which it claimed followed the Soviet line.

The CIO, to be sure, had had a mutually beneficial relationship with left-wingers since its founding in 1935. No irremediable problems had arisen between the organization's top leaders and its left-wingers prior to 1947–1948. Communists served loyally and effectively in the CIO national office, and those affiliated unions led by the left bargained with employers and served their members no differently from other unions. What came to separate the left from the remainder of the CIO were nontrade union issues. The labor left, as a rule, opposed the Truman Doctrine and its offshoots, the Marshall Plan and NATO. Had the left limited itself merely to rhetoric and foreign-policy declarations, its behavior might have been tolerated. But in the election of 1948 the CIO left challenged basic policy. Instead of rallying behind Truman and the Democrats, the left enlisted in the campaign of Henry Wallace and his Progressive party. To Philip Murray and other CIO leaders, this action, which imperiled Truman's reelection, betrayed labor's vital interests. Thus at its annual convention in 1949, the CIO revised its constitution to make Communists ineligible for executive office and to provide for expulsion by a two-thirds vote of any affiliate following the "Communist line." Only a year later, the CIO expelled eleven unions which composed almost a fifth of its total membership.

Aside from the United Electrical Workers, most of the expelled unions were small and relatively unimportant. But the CIO chartered new unions to replace those expelled, and in the electrical industry an old-fashioned jurisdictional struggle ensued. The CIO's president, Murray, used the expulsion of the so-called Communist-led unions to slake the ravenous thirst of domestic red-hunters. Characterizing the Communist-dominated unions as "a small but noisy clique" within the ranks of the CIO, he declared that the overwhelming majority of its membership had no sympathy whatsoever with subversive activity.

Throughout these years, which were at once marked by further economic advances and the setback on the political front caused by passage of the Taft-Hartley Act, the forces of American labor remained divided. Of the estimated total of something over 17,000,000 union members in the mid-1950s, the AFL claimed 9,000,000, the CIO some 6,000,000, and approximately 2,500,000 belonged to the United Mine Workers, the Railway Brotherhoods, and other independent unions. There were repeated efforts to establish an organic unity among these divisive elements, and a number of committees were set up to discuss the complicated issues involved. But in spite of general agreement that "the economic, social and industrial interest of labor can best be served through the establishment of a united labor movement," no satisfactory formula for bringing it about could be found.

The original conflict between the AFL and the CIO over industrial unionism had subsided. Both federations had long since recognized that industrial unions had their place alongside, rather than in opposition to, craft unions. There had also been increasing cooperation in many places of labor activity, most notably creation of the United Labor Policy Committee during the Korean War, and the unions generally worked together on such political issues as their continuing battle against Taft-Hartley. It was perhaps the persistence of old rivalries among the leaders of the AFL and the CIO as much as anything else that brought every move toward an effective merger to a dead end.

In 1952, a change in leadership in both federations gave a fresh impetus to the reunification movement. Within the brief span of twelve days in November of that year, William Green, president of the AFL for nearly thirty years, and Philip Murray, president of the CIO since the resignation of John L. Lewis, both died with dramatic unexpectedness. Their sudden passing from the scene was a harsh blow for the American labor movement since it confronted both the AFL and the CIO with the difficult task of choosing new leaders who could face up to the pressing problems of the 1950s. At the same time, handing over responsibility to men who had not played major roles in the original split between the AFL and the CIO provided a unique opportunity for bringing old and outworn rivalries to an end.

After a sharp struggle among contending factions, the CIO elected to its presidency Walter Reuther, the brilliant, hard-hitting, dynamic head of the United Automobile Workers. Having begun as an apprentice die and tool maker, he had played an important part in the organization of his union during the 1930s, at one time being brutally beaten up by the "brass-knuckle-men" of the Ford Company's service department, and had risen to the presidency in 1946. He was a skillful organizer, a persistent, stubborn negotiator in his relations with management, and highly articulate in presenting his views to the public.

In appearance, Reuther looked totally unlike the public image of a hard-fighting labor leader. He dressed conservatively and acted circumspectly. Neither a smoker nor a drinker, he was little given to social diversions. Throughout his whole career, he had worked at the job with a concentrated, single-minded energy that largely accounted for his gradual emergence as one of labor's strongest, as well as most ambitious, leaders.

His ideas of labor's role in society were broad and comprehensive and carried him far beyond the immediate problems of business unionism. Reuther's ideas owed something to socialist theory, but his approach to politics was completely pragmatic. Labor should work within the existing party structure, which in the circumstances of the time meant support for the Democrats, though he occasionally raised the specter of a third party. Although he and a brother had worked in the Soviet Union in the early 1930s and at the time referred favorably to the socialist experiment, Reuther by 1946 was as strongly anti-

Communist as other labor leaders. Indeed, he rose to the presidency of the UAW partly by red-baiting, and he drove Communists out of his union. Yet his imagination led him to envisage social goals for labor which went far beyond its traditional objectives.

"The kind of labor movement we want," he once stated, "is not committed to a nickel-in-the-pay-envelope philosophy. We are building a labor movement, not to patch up the world so men can starve less often and less frequently, but a labor movement that will remake the world so that the working people will get the benefit of their labor." There was never any question of Reuther's complete devotion to labor's cause. At once idealistic and eminently practical, a veteran in union warfare and an experienced leader, he was in every way a logical candidate for the post first held by Lewis.

The AFL chose as its new leader a man of quite a different stripe—George Meany, its secretary-treasurer. Relatively little known outside union ranks, he had had a long career of activity within the organized labor movement ever since his early days as an apprentice plumber. He first became a union business agent and then went on to serve as secretary of the New York Building Trades Council and president of the New York State Federation of Labor before taking over his post in the national organization in 1939. A large, heavily built man, weighing some 228 pounds, he was once described as "a cross between a bulldog and a bull." He looked like the old-fashioned, conventional labor leader of an earlier era and was generally pictured either smoking a big cigar or chewing determinedly on an unlighted one. But he hardly conformed to type in the breadth of his interests. Fond of dancing, a fair pianist, he was also an avid golfer.

In his contacts with other union leaders and the representatives of management, Meany was aggressively outspoken, sometimes truculent. "Blunt as the plumber's wrench," a labor writer characterized his public addresses. He could be as tough as circumstances demanded.

Throughout his career Meany had always been active politically—not always conforming to the more conservative position of the AFL officialdom—and he fought hard for every cause he favored. He was a consistent rhetorical opponent of racial or religious discrimination in union membership, and, again in contrast to many of his colleagues, believed strongly in labor's need to play an active role in politics. Moreover, he believed that unions should enter more actively into community affairs and seek to exercise their influence on the local level as well as on state and national issues.

The new heads of both federations, along with most of their associates, personified the steady professionalization and bureaucratization of the labor movement. In the postwar world, union officials increasingly earned high salaries, received substantial monetary perquisites, and held office for long terms. Labor leadership was now truly a career, not a calling. More often than in the past, labor leaders had post-secondary school educations, and several had earned law degrees. Meeting regularly with corporate executives and high federal officials, top union leaders were far removed from the rank and file. But we must not exaggerate the distance between postwar labor leaders and their predecessors. Recall that Samuel Gompers's alter ego in the AFL, Matthew Woll, was a lawyer, and that, in the 1920s, John L. Lewis on his passport listed his occupation as "labor executive."

Nevertheless, as their backgrounds and temperaments both suggested, Reuther and Meany were determined to do everything that they could to build up the strength of organized labor. They were prepared to institute new organizing campaigns among the unorganized and seek every opportunity to marshal the political support of union members behind further progressive legislation. To this end, they were also committed to the cause of labor unity and ready to break new ground in trying to settle the differences that had divided the AFL and the CIO for nearly two decades. A first step was their conclusion, in June 1953, of a two-year no-raiding agreement among the constitutent unions of the two federations, and the next year both the AFL and the CIO conventions duly ratified it. Union piracy and jurisdictional strikes had long been recognized as a disruptive force within labor ranks and perhaps the greatest continuing obstacle to reunification. But it was Meany and Reuther who had both the vision and the authority to tackle the issue directly and to point the way toward a settlement that held out some promise of an end to this costly and futile interunion warfare. "The signing and ratification of the No-Raiding Agreement between our two organizations," they jointly announced, "is an historic step. We are confident that the No-Raiding Agreement may function in a spirit of understanding and fraternal friendship."

By 1955, eighty affiliated unions of the AFL and thirty-three CIO unions had accepted the agreement's terms. While it was to prove impossible—either then or in later years—to eradicate jurisdictional strikes entirely, their frequency was sharply reduced and a better atmosphere was created among rival unions.

In the meantime, the two federations had also set up a Joint Unity Committee, headed by their new presidents, which undertook to explore possible ways to effect a merger. Its deliberations were kept secret, and outside official labor circles (except insofar as the no-raiding agreement was a straw in the wind), little was known as to what progress the committee might be making. The underlying politics were extremely complicated. The long history of earlier discussions did not inspire any great optimism over the new Joint Unity Committee's ability to surmount the many obstacles in its path.

It was consequently with great dramatic impact that the committee announced, on February 9, 1955. that full agreement had been reached for the merger of the AFL and the CIO into a unified federation. In a joint statement, Meany and Reuther further declared that in the new AFL-CIO the identity of each affiliated national or international union would be preserved, the no-raiding agreement would be continued on a voluntary basis, and special departments within the old AFL would remain, although supplemented by a new Industrial Union Department. In this way, explicit recognition was given to the need for both craft and industrial unions within the ranks of organized labor, and every encouragement was offered to promoting the most effective forms of organization among American workers as a whole.

The program for the new federation, in addition to plans for greater efforts to organize the unorganized, embraced a new approach to the three greatest internal problems plaguing the labor movement—corruption, racial discrimination, and possible Communist infiltration. The AFL negotiators promised to heed the CIO position on labor racketeering and racial discrimination. Indeed, CIO support enabled Meany to promise a sustained campaign against criminal influences in the labor movement and to insist that unions accept members regardless of race. Meantime the CIO deferred to Meany's militant anti-Communism by consenting to a declaration which promised to protect the labor movement from "the undermining efforts of the Communist agencies and all others who are opposed to the basic principles of our democracy and of free and democratic unionism."

As befitted the party to the merger with by far the larger membership and treasury, the AFL obtained both the presidency and the secretary-treasurership. After ratification of the merger agreement at meetings of the two organizations, a first convention of the AFL-CIO held in early December 1955, thereupon elected George Meany president and William Schnitzler secretary-treasurer, with Walter Reuther serving as vice-president in charge of the Industrial Union Department.

In their historic statement announcing the final agreement for the consolidation, Meany and Reuther jointly declared: "We feel confident that the merger of the two union groups which we represent will be a boon to our nation and its people in this tense period. We are happy that, in our way, we have been able to bring about unity of the labor movement at a time when the unity of all American people is most urgently needed in the face of the Communist threat to world peace and civilization."

Shortly after these developments, Meany wrote a significant article in *Fortune* which outlined organized labor's goals and aspirations. It was perhaps most interesting in revealing the continuity in the development of the labor movement and the persistence of the hard-headed pragmatism which Samuel Gompers had brought to it. Meany emphasized the need for further improvement in the status of industrial workers and the consequent importance of further economic and political activity in their behalf. He made no suggestion of a labor party, but he did declare emphatically that, because of an ever-increasing stake in governmental policies, "we shall remain in politics." Summarizing labor's traditional position, he then wrote: "We do not seek to recast American society in any particular doctrinaire or ideological image. We seek an ever rising standard of living. Sam Gompers once put the matter succinctly. When asked what the labor movement wanted, he answered, 'More.' If by a better standard of living we mean not only more money but more leisure and richer cultural life, the answer remains, 'More.'"

In conclusion, Meany reviewed the past with a sense of great achievement. Largely through the efforts of the national and international unions, he declared, American wage earners had since 1900 doubled their standard of living while their working time had been reduced by one third. He looked forward confidently, he told his readers, to further progress within the framework of that system of free enterprise which had made possible labor's favorable status in American society.

In a sense, then, the merger of the AFL and the CIO, instead of symbolizing the great strength of labor united, reflected, in the words of the labor economist, Richard Lester, the triumph of a "sleepy monopoly." Relatively long-term labor-management contracts, union security clauses, and the direct check-off of union dues from the paycheck by employers gave labor leaders a vested interest in developing harmonious relations with capital. Excessive demands might lead to conflict, and strikes threatened equally the survival of union and corporate "executives." Like typical bureaucrats, union officials preferred ease and convenience in administering their institutions rather than innovative breakthroughs. More and more, the primary obligation of labor leaders in a mature movement became to preserve and protect their own particular organizations. Serving larger, more idealistic social purposes became secondary and useful only to the extent that it benefited the primary institutional interests of trade unions.

XX

Disappointed Hopes

The merger of the AFL and the CIO appeared to hold out in 1955 the highest prospects for the still further growth and development of unionism. The leaders of the new federation were confident that the unity finally achieved would enable labor to put its house in order and resolve its nagging internal problems. They hopefully envisioned a doubling of union membership within ten years and a consequent increase in both the economic and political power which might be exerted to strengthen the security of all industrial workers. They also believed that it would at last be possible to bring about either the repeal of the Taft-Hartley Act or substantial modification of its restrictive provisions, encourage recruitment from the ranks of nonunionized workers, and broaden the scope of collective-bargaining agreements.

These bright expectations were not fulfilled. The problems facing organized labor proved to be far more intractable than they appeared to be in 1955, and over the horizon were new developments that served to impede the progress so confidently anticipated. As the national economy continued to grow, subject only to shallow recessions in the mid- and late 1950s, workers, especially those in the unionized sectors, won higher real wages and expanded fringe benefits. The union-management bargain, consummated in the late 1940s, persisted over the next two decades. At the same time, however, workers and their unions were dismayed by the specter of possible unemployment due to technological advance and automation. Moreover, the organized labor movement itself was to experience a decline in membership and potential power which before the end of the 1950s created an atmosphere of deep discouragement in labor circles.

The merger of the AFL and the CIO disappointed the expectations of many of the advocates of labor unity. During its first decade, the merged federation proved largely unsuccessful at organizing the unorganized. The fastest growing sector of the labor force—the white-collar service and professional occupations—remained largely impervious to unionism. Here most workers continued to identify more with employers and managers than with unions. Organized labor proved equally unable to unionize workers in low-wage, labor-intensive, competitive trades. Millions of blacks, other nonwhites, and women toiled on the nation's farms and in its homes, restaurants, laundries, and garment sweatshops without union protection. They earned minimal wages at best (often below federal or state mandated minimums because they were in categories of work legislatively excluded from coverage) under exploitative conditions and without job security.

A dual labor market characterized the American economy by the end of the 1950s. In one part, mostly white male workers earned good wages, held stable jobs, and had the protection of strong unions. In the other, women and nonwhites earned only 50 to 60 per cent as much in wages, lacked job security, and had no unions to defend their interests. In fact, many unions still proved resistant to opening their doors to these groups.

A year after its formation the AFL-CIO was to attain what proved to be its greatest membership—a total of some 15,500,000 in affiliated unions. Succeeding years saw a steady attrition in this figure. While the expulsion of the Teamsters accounted for the greater part of this decline, there had also been substantial losses in the membership of other important industrial unions which continued their affiliation with the parent body. The AFL-CIO had far from attained its optimistic hopes of either representing all labor or experiencing a steady growth in membership.

Even more significant than any such shifts or changes within the national federation, however, was what proved to be the failure of union membership as a whole to continue its record of steady growth. The peak was reached in 1954 with an overall total of almost 18,000,000, or over 35 per cent of the nonagricultural employment. Eight years later, this total had fallen to 16,800,000, or, in percentage terms, only some 30 per cent of the increased labor force and the lowest figure since 1952.

This actual decline and even more drastic drop in percentage terms was to continue in succeeding years. The contrast with the hopes in 1955 that union membership would be doubled in a decade could hardly have been more glaring. In weight of numbers at least, the labor movement appeared to have lost its momentum. In 1960 Walter Reuther bluntly declared: "We are going backward." And he was right. The total size of the work force continued to grow, making the proportion of union members an even smaller part of the whole.

Many factors accounted for what was from labor's point of view such an unhappy situation. The AFL-CIO encountered unexpected obstacles in developing the new organizing campaign in which its leadership had such confidence. In a number of industries, partly due to prosperity and the more generous wage policies followed by employers, there was simply little interest in unionization. Outright opposition remained strong in such geographical areas as the South, and organizers were hampered by state right-to-work laws. In many instances, the labor leaders themselves, both at the top and at local levels, appeared to have lost something of the zeal which had marked their organizing activity in the past. It appeared to be impossible to awaken the enthusiasm or inspire the action that had first given such vitality to the campaign to organize the unorganized.

Over and beyond all such considerations, however, were the changes which had taken place by mid-century in the structure of the civilian labor force. More than anything else, they accounted for the drop in union membership and the seemingly insuperable obstacles which organized labor faced in seeking to combat it. For the number of blue-collar workers, who provided the bulk of union membership, was declining in contrast to a steady rise in the number of nonunionized white-collar workers. In traditional terms, the labor pool from which the unions drew their members was steadily shrinking, and as yet no way had been found to effectively organize the growing number of those workers who had customarily resisted unionism.

More specifically, what had happened since the end of the Second World War was that the proportion of the nation's workers engaged in mining, manufacturing, and transportation had fallen, while that of employees in wholesale and retail trade, the service industries, and government had increased. Technological advance, making possible increased industrial production with fewer workers, accounted for the one phenomenon, and a popular demand for expanded services, both private and public, explained the latter. The effect on the relative proportions of blue-collar and white-collar workers in the total labor force was statistically reflected, between 1947 and 1963, in the former's decline from 40.7 per cent to 36.4 per cent of the total, and in the latter's rise from 45.3 per cent to 57 per cent.

As a consequence, membership in such basic industrial unions as those of the steel workers, automobile workers, and miners was falling, and there were at first no compensating gains in the relatively weak unions which represented retail clerks, department-store and office workers, or government employees. An exception was the vigorous growth of the Teamsters, the country's largest union, but the overall picture was clear. Unless labor could more successfully organize the white-collar workers, the trend toward declining union membership which had begun in 1957 seemed likely to continue.

The disappointments which labor suffered so far as union membership was concerned were paralleled in the field of political action. The AFL-CIO was militantly determined to marshal the full support of labor behind all candidates for public office who showed a sympathy for union aims and aspirations. To this end it established a new Committee on Political Education (COPE). While this committee reaffirmed labor's traditional attitude in stating that it would maintain "a strictly nonpartisan attitude," it was hardly surprising that in practice this meant, as in almost every year since 1936, virtually all-out support for the Democratic ticket in national elections. COPE campaigned vigorously for Adlai E. Stevenson in 1956, and again for John F. Kennedy in 1960. It generally supported Democratic candidates for Congress. In the light of congressional gains by liberals in these years (in spite of the reelection of Eisenhower in 1956), efforts were thereupon renewed through the most intense lobbying activities to get some action on Taft-Hartley's repeal and to promote further legislation favorable to labor and the nation's workers.

Such efforts were unsuccessful, and, before the end of the 1950s, Congress had enacted another piece of labor legislation that the unions attacked as being quite as obstructive to their interests as Taft-Hartley itself. The only political achievement which could be credited to organized labor during this period was that of holding the line against the further proliferation of the state right-to-work laws.

In 1955, seventeen states had such laws which barred not only the closed shop but also the union shop. They were largely in the South or Far West, but conservative business interests mounted an intensive campaign to win over some of the more heavily industrialized states. While labor continued to feel that the only resolution of this issue was repeal of Section 14(b) of the Taft-Hartley Act, it conducted a hard-hitting war against any further state legisation. In only two instances did it fail to defeat proposed new right-to-work laws, and in 1958 it decisively threw back antiunion forces in California, Ohio, Colorado, Idaho, and Washington.

In the meantime, however, labor had suffered that reverse in the field of national legislation which the AFL-CIO roundly denounced as the fruit of an antiunion design "to destroy labor" and "the most severe setback in more than a decade." The background for this new law was the dramatic disclosure of corruption and racketeering in a number of unions and the congressional reaction to labor's apparent inability to clean its own house.

The problem of corruption had a long history which may be traced back at least as far as the disclosures of extortion and other improper activities on the part of local union officials made before the United States Industrial Commission in 1899. Then, as half a century later, the unions most deeply involved were those in the building trades, longshoremen, truck drivers, laundry and dry cleaning employees, and other service workers. The opportunities for racketeering had always been much greater in such unions than in those embracing the workers in productive industry, and corruption could never be totally stamped out.

The AFL had never proved totally successful in cleansing those of its affiliates which were most susceptible to corruption and racketeering. Because of its deeply-held principle of complete union autonomy, the Federation avoided direct intervention in the internal affairs of its affiliates. But as governmental agencies became more concerned with criminal influences in the labor movement, the AFL had no choice but to act more forcefully. Thus in 1953 the Federation expelled the International Longshoremen's Association in response to dramatic revelations of racketeering on the New York–New Jersey waterfront.

The merger of the AFL and the CIO added impetus to labor's anti-corruption crusade. Almost immediately, the AFL-CIO established an Ethical Practices Committee charged with drawing up and seeking to enforce rules of conduct aimed against racketeering and corruption by union officials.

Yet organized labor's own voluntary attempts to root out corruption were insufficient to ward off congressional investigation of union behavior. In 1957 the Senate established a Select Committee on Improper Activities in the Labor or Management Field which was headed by Senator John Mc-Clellan of Arkansas and had as its vigorous chief counsel a youthful Robert F. Kennedy. This committee promptly instituted a series of public hearings, nationally televised, that were to shock and alarm the entire country. The evidence spread upon the public record revealed a larger degree of dictatorial union leadership, which violated every democratic principle, and more corruption, racketeering, and gangsterism on the part of union officials than even labor's severest critics had suspected. Witness after witness testified to rigged elections, the misuse of union funds, embezzlement, and theft. It was true that these disclosures involved only a handful of unions. Nevertheless, they served to cast suspicion on the entire labor movement and placed its leaders very much on the defensive.

One of the chief targets of the congressional investigation was the Teamsters Union. Probing deeply into its internal affairs, the Mc-Clellan committee brought out innumerable cases of political chicanery in the locals, extortion on the part of union officials in their dealings with employers, and close associations (particularly in New York) with known gangsters. Racketeering was rife, with inevitable terrorism and violence. Even more sensationally, the hearings disclosed that corruption extended to the top leadership. The Teamsters' president, David Beck, was running the union very much as he chose and had diverted large union funds to his own private purposes. Self-assured and arrogant, completely disdainful of the Senate committee's powers, Beck repeatedly refused to answer the questions asked him. The evidence brought out against him nevertheless forced him to give up the presidency of his union and led to his indictment—and ultimate conviction—on charges of tax evasion and grand larceny.

Beck's downfall did not, however, lead to any clean-up in the Teamsters' affairs. He was succeeded in office by James R. Hoffa, whose rise in union ranks since his early organization of a warehouseman's union in 1932 had brought him to the Teamsters' vicepresidency. An able, efficient organizer, his career had nonetheless been marked, according to testimony before the McClellan committee, by undercover business relationships with the firms with which his union was negotiating and other private dealings with companies handling its health and welfare funds.

It soon become apparent that the new union president was, if anything, even more determined than Beck had been to defy any interference with how he ran things. After a group of union officials had unsuccessfully contested his election as illegal, the McClellan committee sought to oust him on charges that he was the source of a "cancer" that spread continuing corruption and gangsterism throughout his union. But when his case was taken to the courts and a federal district judge appointed a board of monitors to supervise temporarily the conduct of the Teamsters' affairs, Hoffa fought back with every possible legal device and continued to hold his office.

A bitter feud thereupon developed between the Teamsters' chief and the Department of Justice, which was accentuated when Robert Kennedy became Attorney General in 1961. The former counsel of the McClellan committee continued through repeated prosecutions for malfeasance and corruption to try to break Hoffa's power. The latter nonetheless was reelected to his presidency in 1961 (with a salary of $75,000), successfully combated or appealed every legal move made against him (even when found guilty in 1964 of tampering with a jury), and continued to dominate what Kennedy called his "Hoodlum empire."[1]

The hearings involving the Teamsters were the most sensational of those held by the McClellan committee, but only a little less so were the disclosures of corruption in a number of small unions. The Hotel and Restaurant Employees, the Bakery and Confectionery Workers, the Laundry Workers, the Operating Engineers, the Allied

---

[1]In 1967 Hoffa started to serve a term in federal prison. His handpicked successor, Frank Fitzsimmons, took over the presidency of the Teamsters. Under Fitzsimmons, the union followed the same high-handed and corrupt practices. But the new Teamsters' president proved a loyal Republican and thus was tolerated by the administration of President Richard M. Nixon. In December 1971, Nixon paroled Hoffa from prison on condition that the former union official never again play an active role in the Teamsters. By 1974 rumors arose that Hoffa planned to challenge Fitzsimmons for the union presidency. But in July 1975 Hoffa disappeared without a trace. He has neither been seen nor heard since. Most knowledgeable authorities believe that criminal elements murdered Hoffa. The Teamsters' Union has remained an object of federal investigation and prosecution. In 1982, its new president, Roy Williams, stood trial on charges of having tried to bribe a United States senator from Nevada. A jury found him guilty. Throughout the decade of the 1980s the union found itself beset by charges of corruption, federal investigations, and membership unrest. The Teamsters' sad history culminated in 1989 when it came under a federal judge's trusteeship. See Ch. XXI, pp. 401–402 for some of those developments.

Industrial Workers, and the United Textile Workers all came under attack. Union witnesses again reported cases of the misuse of union funds, of collusion between union officials and employers, and of extortion and violence. Once more there was spread upon the record the picture of a relationship between union officials and underworld elements which made employees and employers alike, as well as the public, victims of a network of festering corruption.

As this evidence came to light, the Ethical Practices Committee of the AFL-CIO was galvanized into new action. It called the unions accused of such improper activities to account and placed them on probation, so far as their membership in the federation was concerned, until they met prescribed terms for internal reform. When the Teamsters Union, the Bakery and Confectionery Workers, and the Laundry Workers signally failed to clean house, the AFL-CIO officially expelled them. It was seeking to do what it could, however limited its powers, to demonstrate that responsible labor leadership deserved public confidence.

In spite of such moves on the part of the AFL-CIO, the first report of the McClellan committee insisted that its fully documented disclosures of union corruption called for governmental action. President Eisenhower agreed. On his urging, Congress began to consider various proposals to stop "corruption, racketeering and abuse of power in labor-management relations." There was widespread support for some measure along these lines, but congressional debate soon opened up the broader question of legislation affecting the unions' legal rights with a demand for tightening the provisions of the Taft-Hartley Act rather than liberalizing them.

The upshot of the struggle in Congress between the friends and foes of organized labor was the passage of the Landrum-Griffin Act, which Eisenhower signed on September 14, 1959. The first sections of this new law dealt with the issue of corruption and incorporated a Bill of Rights for union members. These provisions embodied specific safeguards for democratic procedures in the conduct of union affairs, protected union funds with the imposition of fines and prison sentences for any official guilty of their misuse, made any forceful interference with the rights of union members a federal offense, and prohibited persons convicted of certain crimes, and also members of the Communist party, from serving as union officials for five years after their release from prison or after termination of Communist membership. The Landrum-Griffin Act, however, also went beyond the Taft-Hartley Act by severely tightening a number of its provisions governing union activities.

The existing ban on secondary boycotts was broadened to prevent a union from bringing any pressure to bear on an employer to make him cease doing business with another employer. A new curb was placed on picketing to outlaw any action whereby a union sought to coerce a company where a rival union was lawfully recognized. And, most seriously from the labor point of view, the new legislation stated that in the so-called "no-man's-land"—an area where disputes were judged too unimportant or localized for consideration by the National Labor Relations Board—the states could assume jurisdiction. This latter provision strongly militated against further union organization in the South, where only 2,000,000 out of a possible 12,000,000 workers were organized, because of the wide prevalence in that region of right-to-work laws.

As was the case with Taft-Hartley, the Landrum-Griffin Act satisfied neither the fondest wishes of its advocates nor the worst fears of its critics. Unions did not collapse, nor did the more autocratic ones become perfect democracies. In the mid- and late 1960s, when the economy boomed and the labor market tightened, unions increased their membership substantially, especially in the South. What passage of the act did demonstrate, however, was government's deeper, direct involvement in the field of labor relations. For the first time, federal power claimed a direct responsibility for internal union affairs.

The struggle over union corruption and labor legislation also showed the limits of AFL-CIO political influence. Despite the fact that corruption in the labor movement was limited to only a small number of unions, the AFL-CIO failed to stop federal legislation that affected the internal affairs of every union in the nation. Having discarded all dreams of independent political action by the 1950s, the AFL-CIO now found itself as much a captive as a captain of the Democratic party. Organized labor's almost total integration into the Democratic party structure still left it at the mercy of the southern Democratic-Republican congressional coalition, which ruled Congress on many issues vital to unions during most of the period from 1945 to 1982.

While the political battle over labor waxed and waned, most unions and corporations continued to negotiate mutually acceptable agreements, without strikes or with only brief ritualistic ones. One major exception broke the rule of harmonious labor-management relations—the great steel strike of 1959—and its protracted duration and results disclosed much about the real state of labor relations in modern America.

It was perhaps natural that this contest should take place within the steel industry. The strike recalled those major conflicts of the past—Homestead, the steel strike of 1919, the Little Steel strike of 1937—in which labor had fought so bitterly for its rights against the entrenched power of the country's largest industry. And in 1959, as in these earlier strikes, the forces of all organized labor and those of all industry believed that their interests were deeply involved in the outcome of the struggle—this time a grim endurance contest rather than a flare-up of violence and intimidation.

The real nature of the conflict was not apparent at first. The negotiation of a new contract between the United Steelworkers and the steel industry appeared to be no more than another chapter in the endless bargaining over wages, and it was generally believed that the ultimate outcome would be the sort of compromise settlement which had marked every postwar contract—a further increase in steel wages followed by another mark-up in steel prices.

The industry's position, as developed in the early stages of the negotiations, revealed an apparent determination this time to call a halt to any further increase in wages. Its spokesmen insisted that this was the only way to control inflation. The union, on the other hand, declared that the workers were entitled to higher pay in the light of both increased productivity and higher living expenses and stoutly maintained that the profits of the steel companies made a reasonable wage increase possible without raising steel prices. Agreement on this issue was difficult enough in itself, and it only gradually became apparent that more was at stake. But when industry also demanded modification of the existing work rules, the union stiffened its resistance all along the line. It refused any concessions on what was a more vital issue than wages. The steelworkers sought to retain what control they had over work rules in the face of rapid technological change. The steel companies strove to win a free hand in introducing and controlling new methods of production. Jobs, more than wages and fringes, were at stake in this confrontation between labor and capital.

In these circumstances, the contract negotiations broke off in mid-July, and steel workers throughout the country walked out on strike.

Subsequent attempts to reconcile the divergent positions of labor and industry failed with monotonous regularity; as the strike dragged on for seemingly endless weeks and steel supplies reached near exhaustion, the nation's entire economy began to falter even more dangerously than in 1952. In these circumstances the Eisenhower administration had no choice but to act. On October 9, 1959, Eisenhower invoked the emergency provisions of the Taft-Hartley Act. Declaring that the continuing strike imperiled the national health and safety, he appointed a special board of inquiry, and when it duly reported that it could discover no basis for the strike's settlement, he ordered the Department of Justice to seek an injunction against the union. A federal district court granted the government's plea, and although the union appealed on the ground that the strike had not created a national emergency, the Supreme Court sustained the lower court's decision by an eight-to-one vote on November 7. The strikers thereupon returned to work, but the officers of the United Steelworkers bitterly attacked the administration for strike-breaking and, without conceding a point, appeared to be fully prepared to resume the strike when the injunction had run its course.

The deadlock appeared to be insurmountable. There was much talk of the wage issue, but the real stumbling block, on which neither side was willing to give way at all, remained the dispute over work rules and their possible relationship to automation. As the year drew to an end, the prospect of a renewal of the strike, with even more serious consequences for the economy, became insupportable. Still, the union's lines held firm with the workers' determination to renew the strike strengthened by the industry's obdurate stand on the work rules. For a time the latter's front seemed to waver when the Kaiser Company withdrew from the corporate coalition and reached an independent agreement with the union, but it was soon reestablished. The industry's spokesmen reiterated their insistence upon changes in the work rules as a necessary condition for any contract.

Then on January 5, 1960, came the announcement of a sudden and dramatic breakthrough. In the face of steadily mounting economic and political pressure, and its fear that, if the strike was renewed, government would force an unsatisfactory settlement, the steel industry compromised. It came to terms with the union and signed a new agreement. It provided for increased pension and insurance payments, with a subsequent wage rise, but most importantly it incorporated maintenance of the existing work rules. David McDonald, president of the United Steelworkers, declared that it was the best contract the union had ever concluded.

The victory won by the United Steelworkers in the face of such stubborn opposition on the part of management was far more signifi-cant in its implications for future union controls over work rules than for its wage increases. And it was a victory important for organized labor as a whole since it had been won in the face of the resistance of industry as a whole. Labor had successfully reasserted its compelling economic power to protect the interests of union members. But the struggle between workers' desire to maintain traditional work rules and management's urge to introduce labor-saving technology did not end in 1960. And in the future, labor would lose as often as it won on this front.

Despite the steelworkers' victory, the future seemed fraught with peril for organized labor as the 1950s drew to a close. No wonder that delegates to the AFL-CIO convention of 1959 moved in an at-mosphere thick with gloom. Everywhere the talk was of a conser-vative corporate and congressional campaign to weaken or destroy the entire labor movement. Also looming over the horizon was the deepening problem of how organized labor would combat the threat of technological innovation. Automation made job security a grave issue in a productive economy which still failed to provide work for all.

As the Eisenhower era ended, permanent unemployment seemed to be a fixture of the American economy. At the end of the 1950s, and in 1960–1961, recession caused unemployment to rise as high as 6.8 per cent of the civilian labor force. Even after the fiscal policies of the new Democratic President, John F. Kennedy—which were a com-bination of large corporate and smaller personal income tax cuts—produced an economic boom, unemployment stayed at a historically high level. Thus in December 1964 Lyndon B. Johnson, who had suc-ceeded Kennedy as President after the latter's assassination, declared: "The Number one priority today is more jobs. This is our dominant domestic problem and we have to face it head-on."

What made the job problem even more severe was its direct relation to two of the most significant developments of the 1960s—the widespread introduction of automation into industry and the revolu-tion in race relations. However much experts debated over the long-range impact of automation and whether it increased or decreased total opportunities for employment, it clearly reduced the need for workers in several basic industries and transformed the structure of the labor force. By 1963 the automobile companies produced more automobiles than in 1955 with 17 per cent fewer workers. In the steel industry, half as many workers could meet the production levels of 1946–1947 in the more automated mills. In 1964, President Johnson predicted that, by the end of the 1970s, the United States would be able to match the industrial output of the 1960s with 22,000,000 fewer workers. "The worker's great worry these days," wrote A. H. Raskin, the nation's leading labor journalist, "is that he will be cast onto the slag heap by a robot." A story told about the automobile industry illustrated Raskin's point. Harlow Curtice, president of General Motors, took Walter Reuther for a tour of a new automated automobile plant. Turning to the union leader, Curtice said, "Walter, in the future the UAW will not be able to call the machines out on strike." To which Reuther responded, "Will the machines be able to buy your automobiles?"

Some of the major strikes and labor-management agreements of the 1960s illustrated clearly the impact of technological innovations on workers and unions. Containerization revolutionized the loading and unloading of ships, drastically reducing the need for dockside labor. As a consequence, the International Longshoremen and Warehousemen's Union of the Pacific Coast and the International Longshoremen's Association of the Atlantic and Gulf coasts found themselves locked in conflict with the shipping companies. After a series of strikes and Taft-Hartley injunctions, both unions reached settlements which accepted containerization in return for guarantees of annual earnings, if not jobs, for most current union members. Moreover, as longshoremen retired or died, natural attrition would steadily shrink the ranks of dockers and union members. A similar settlement ended a decades-old dispute on the nation's railroads. Ever since the introduction of diesel engines in the 1920s, firemen occupied a superfluous job. But traditional union contracts and state full-crew laws protected the jobs of firemen and other redundant crewmen. Finally, in the 1960s, after a threatened national strike and the appointment of a presidential fact-finding commission, the dispute was resolved. The presidential commission's recommendations, which were enforced by Lyndon Johnson, did away with firemen on diesel locomotives as well as other unneeded crewmen. Again the unions won job protection for most current members at the expense of allowing attrition to reduce employment on the railroads. Printers in the newspaper business suffered a similar fate. Long among the most traditional, skilled, secure, and status-encrusted workers, printers in the 1960s could not stymie technological innovation. New computers, which transferred reporters' stories and other copy directly from word processors to tape-controlled typesetting electronic systems, eliminated the need for the printer's skills. Some newspapers used the new technology to break the union. Others, like the *New York Times*, after experiencing two long and costly strikes, reached an agreement with the printers' union which effectively made the craft a dying trade. Again, in return for securing the jobs or the income of current regular full-time printers, the union conceded the *Times* and other newspapers the right to introduce the new computer-based technology. Having become superfluous, the remaining printers could sit around the plant cutting out paper dolls, playing cards, or otherwise wasting time until they chose to retire or accept a cash payment for quitting. They also knew that no new printers would replace them in the future.

As longshoremen, firemen, and printers became dying occupations, jobs expanded in other sectors of the economy. But the expansion of white-collar employment did not help the victims of automation. The white-collar service and trades category of employment included an incredibly diverse array of occupations. Unskilled and relatively uneducated men and women could find employment as fast-food restaurant workers, hairdressers, waitresses, sanitation workers, car-washers, and domestics. Those jobs, however, spelled low wages, miserable working conditions, and insecurity of employment. Those private- and public-sector white- collar jobs, which paid best and provided decent conditions and job security were reserved for people with advanced formal education. "Automation has now created an abyss between those with training and education and those without," wrote the Socialist publicist, Michael Harrington. "So a man can be sentenced to life at the bottom of the economy without even becoming a certified, statistical tragedy."

For nonwhites, all those problems were compounded. First, nonwhite workers were heavily concentrated among the ranks of the semi-skilled and unskilled, whose opportunities in the new job universe were most constricted. Second, those nonwhites who had more skilled or secure, hence better-paying, jobs were concentrated in precisely those industries affected by technological innovation. Third, the unemployment rate for nonwhites constantly held at twice the level of that for white workers. "The two-to-one ratio," wrote the sociologist, Daniel Patrick Moynihan, in 1965, "is now frozen into the economy." Commenting on the plight of nonwhite workers, A. Philip Randolph, head of the Brotherhood of Sleeping Car Porters and the nation's most eminent black labor leader, observed, "black workers face a virtually unsolvable problem." Indeed black teenagers endured unemployment rates of 30 to 40 per cent, and this at the moment of the civil-rights revolution and the great transformation in American race relations.

Among the major beneficiaries of the expansion of the labor force were female workers. By 1964, women composed 34 per cent of the labor force as compared to 20 per cent in 1947, and their proportion would rise steadily every year thereafter. Most strikingly, the greatest increase in waged work occurred among older married women, precisely those who in the past had remained at home. But the vast majority of women workers tended to be employed outside the highly unionized, high-wage job world of basic industry. Locked in the female-dominated "pink-collar job ghetto," women workers typically earned only 59 per cent as much as male workers. In fact, the better educated a woman was, the less she earned relative to a similarly educated man. That ratio also seemed to be "frozen into the economy."

In fact, the whole dual labor market appeared impermeable to change. Nonwhites, women, and teenagers all competed for the same unstable, low-wage, nonunion jobs, with women, as a group, making the most "progress." For too long all these low-wage workers toiled away in what Michael Harrington described as "The Other America"—a part of the nation invisible to its more affluent and contented citizens.

Among the so-called affluent and contented were said to be the vast majority of union members in the primary labor market. By the mid-1950s their real wages had advanced 50 per cent over prewar levels, and by the late 1960s had risen almost another 50 per cent. Fringe benefits added to the feeling of security and comfort. More workers than ever before covered by union contracts now received life, sickness, and accident insurance, survivor benefits, improved pensions, and supplementary unemployment benefits. The UAW-General Motors contract of 1964 included benefits for psychiatric treatment, tuition for job-related education, severance pay, and incentives for early retirement. An increasing number of contracts provided for paid holidays (between six and ten in the UAW) and paid vacations, the latter depending on the length of service, but ranging up to four weeks annually. By the mid-1960s, economists estimated that 85 per cent of workers had an average of twenty paid days off a year.

As early as 1959, the Department of Labor had reported that the "wage earner's way of life is well-nigh indistinguishable from that of his salaried co-citizens. Their homes, their cars, their babysitters, the style of clothes their wives and children wear, the food they eat...their days off—all of these are alike and are becoming more nearly identical." Five years later, an article in the *Saturday Review of Literature* echoed the same theme: "The working class as a proportionately large and socially identifiable segment of our society is all but disappearing—the generic middle class now includes skilled and semi-skilled laborers."

A poll conducted by the AFL-CIO in 1968 provided some confirmation for such assertions. The poll reported that 45 per cent of union families earned betwen $7,500 and $15,000 annually, and that another 32 per cent were in the $5,000–7,500 range. Nearly half lived in comfortable suburbs, and most cited taxes and prices—typical middle-class concerns—not jobs and wages, as their primary political worries. George Meany added his own gloss to these findings in a Labor-Day interview with the *New York Times* in 1969. Speaking with pride about the accomplishments of the labor movement, Meany agreed with a reporter that, "Labor, to some extent, has become middle class." "When you become a person who has a home and has property," he added, "to some extent you become conservative. And, I would say to that extent, labor has become conservative. I don't think there is any question of that."

But even before this image of the worker as a satisfied bourgeois citizen indistinguishable from other Americans became commonplace, the novelist and social critic, Harvey Swados, criticized the notion that the worker "is just like the rest of us—fat, satisfied, smug, a little restless but hardly distinguishable from...fellow members of the middle class—whom he earns like, votes like...dreams like." Swados used his own personal experiences as an automobile assembly-line worker during the 1950s to remind people that hand and muscle work remained absolutely subordinate to mind and desk work, that dealing with people conferred much more prestige and satisfaction than manipulating things. He described fellow workers, whose attitudes toward the job were compounded of hatred, shame, and resignation, who knew that they did endless, filthy, and mindless work for less money than so-called professionals. As one worker told him: "I curse the day I ever started, now I'm stuck; any man with brains that stays here ought to have his head examined. This is no place for an intelligent human being."

No wonder so many workers fled as rapidly as they could to their new detached, single-family suburban homes. There they could enjoy such things as basement workshops, or backyard vegetable-flower gardens and the satisfaction of real creation; or a less active form of pleasure in such things as color television and the other appliances available in a mass-consumer society, or power-boating, golfing, or barbecuing during leisure time.

Yet, as sociological study after study showed, working-class suburbs were different from more traditional middle- and upper-class ones. Blue-collar marriages built on more clearly defined male-female sociocultural roles and less on the affective relations so important among middle-class suburban husbands and wives. Workers tended less than middle-class suburbanites to belong to civic clubs. Instead, they preferred more traditional fraternal associations. Workers also preferred to spend most of their leisure time in a family setting and to entertain mostly within the family. Finally, most workers brought union loyalties and Democratic voting preferences with them to the suburbs.

However many American workers in the mid-1960s behaved like middle-class citizens or aspired to such status, millions were trapped in dead-end jobs or mired in real poverty. These were the people Harrington described in *The Other America* (1962); for whom John F. Kennedy provided federal work programs; and for whom Lyndon B. Johnson declared his "war on poverty." Mostly nonwhite, female, or aged, they were outside the direct protection of unions and most in need of governmental assistance. Ironically, it was for precisely this sector of the population, and not for its own institutional needs, that the AFL-CIO accomplished the most politically.

In the congressional struggles over Kennedy's "New Frontier" and Johnson's "Great Society," the AFL-CIO proved the most effective lobbying voice for the "other America." In 1961, Congress broadened the coverage of the Fair Labor Standards Act and raised the minimum wage to $1.25 an hour. This was a triumph for organized labor, although a worker fully employed at the minimum wage would still earn only $2,600 annually, a figure well below the government-defined minimum subsistence level. Consequently, the AFL-CIO continued to put pressure on Congress for expanded social-security coverage, a progressively higher minimum wage, and health-care protection for all Americans. It also sought legislation to ameliorate unemployment through a reduced work week, government-sponsored job-training programs, and countercyclical public works.

Both Presidents Kennedy and Johnson tried to repay politically the trade unionists who had worked so hard for their elections in 1960 and 1964. The Democratic chief executives strongly endorsed extended social security benefits and higher minimum wages. Moreover, in 1962, Congress passed the Manpower Development and Training Act with a three-year appropriation of $35,000,000 to help workers who lost their jobs as a result of automation. Johnson's "war on poverty" met organized labor's aims even more fully.

The concrete results of the Johnson program were new legislation which ranged from aid to education to urban development, from civil rights to Medicare. The Economic Opportunity Act, with appropriations of nearly $1,000,000,000, set up such new projects as a job corps for young people, work-training assistance, and varied urban and rural community action programs. In 1965, Congress made available more money for social welfare in general than ever before in all its history. All this was greatly in the interests of union members. Their own high wages and improved status in society would assuredly go by the board if unemployment and poverty were allowed to undermine the basic economic structure of the country.

As one observer wrote, labor is "the largest single organized force in this country pushing for progressive social legislation." On few issues was this truer and more paradoxical than in the battle over civil-rights legislation. Itself a laggard internally and institutionally on the "race" question—it had refused to participate in Martin Luther King, Jr.'s march on Washington in 1963, had a long history of tolerating racially discriminatory practices by its affiliates, and was to have persistent problems with its black members—the AFL-CIO nonetheless proved itself unstinting in lobbying for the passage of civil-rights laws in 1964 and 1965.

On another issue tangential to its institutional needs, the AFL-CIO also made sacrifices. Faced with the choice of obtaining the elimination of Section 14(b) of the Taft-Hartley Act ("the right-to-work" clause) or allowing legislation which guaranteed equal voting rights (one person, one vote) to pass Congress, the labor federation chose the latter. In this case, the principle of democracy triumphed at the expense of trade unionism.

Internally, however, the race issue divided the AFL-CIO. As early as 1955 it had established a civil-rights committee to eliminate racial discrimination among its affiliates. But its control over international unions and their locals was limited, and Meany was also personally loath to act on such matters. Thus the building and some of the other skilled trades excluded blacks from membership, and in the South a dual system of seniority often governed promotion and wages. The failure of the AFL-CIO to act more decisively prompted A. Philip Randolph in 1960 to form the Negro American Labor Council in order to keep "the conscience of the AFL-CIO disturbed."

The rise of black consciousness and militancy in the 1960s further roiled the labor movement. Herbert Hill, the NAACP's labor adviser, clashed with Meany at the convention of 1962 over the Federation's racial practices. Randolph, too, often found himself at odds with Meany. The building trades unions were constantly embroiled in street protests with black militants and under governmental orders to recruit more minority members. In 1968, the New York City teachers' union led a strike which put it in conflict with a part of the city's black community. And in Detroit, where black workers formed a large and vital sector in the automobile industry, militants among them created so-called revolutionary factions within the UAW—DRUM (Dodge Revolutionary Union Movement) and FRUM (Ford Revolutionary Union Movement). These black militants seemed at times to devote more effort to fighting UAW leaders than to taking on General Motors, Chrysler, or Ford.

Other nonracial problems bedeviled organized labor in the 1960s. The most severe was its continued inability to organize workers as rapidly as the labor force grew, or to penetrate substantially the dynamically growing sales, service, and public-employment sectors. Between 1960 and 1965, total union membership remained relatively stable but continued its decline as a proportion of the civilian labor force, dropping to 25 per cent, the lowest level since 1950. Only about 10 per cent of the workers who fell into the white-collar category (2,300,000 out of about 22,000,000) belonged to unions.

For a time—from 1965 to 1970—organized labor reversed somewhat the pattern of its relative decline in membership. What happened in those years was quite simple. As a consequence of the

Vietnam War and the Johnson administration's loose fiscal and monetary policies, the domestic economy boomed. Unemployment declined, the demand for skilled labor exceeded the supply, and trade unions operated in the most favorable situation since the end of the Korean War. Also, many political jurisdictions, especially the federal government, instituted new employee relations codes which granted public servants the right to join unions and bargain collectively, though almost never the right to strike. Unions consequently added more than two million members to their ranks. Significantly, however, the rise in membership only kept pace with the increase in the size of the labor force. As the 1960s ended, organized labor's relative size and strength remained where it had been at the start of the decade, and the future did not look bright.

The war in Vietnam brought setbacks as well as successes to the labor movement. The AFL-CIO (and Meany in particular) remained the nation's most steadfast anti-Communist institution in the 1960s. The Federation's leaders outdid Kennedy and Johnson in their attacks on Soviet Russia and Communism and in their willingness to restrict trade with Communist nations. In October 1965, the executive council reaffirmed its total support for Johnson's policies in Vietnam.

As the struggle in Southeast Asia became the single most contentious issue in American domestic affairs, the AFL-CIO remained committed to the war effort. No matter how many Democrats, Republicans, current and former American diplomats, and business people decried United States policy in Southeast Asia, George Meany held firm to the containment of Communism and Lyndon B. Johnson's foreign policy. No matter how unpopular the war became at home and how much it sowed the seeds of domestic violence, the AFL-CIO chief refused to change his mind about Vietnam. The gap between old-guard labor's view of world affairs and that of other Americans was revealed graphically by events on Wall Street in the spring of 1970. There unionized building trades workers, wearing hard hats and carrying American flags, shouted patriotic slogans and clubbed and beat antiwar demonstrators.

The refusal of the AFL-CIO to modify its strident anti-Communism and its inability to organize the most rapidly growing sector of the labor force led Walter Reuther to take the UAW out of the Federation. In a letter released in February 1967, Reuther charged: "The AFL-CIO, in policy and program, too often continues to live with the past. It advances few new ideas and lacks the necessary vitality, vision, and imagination and social invention to make it equal to the challenging problems of a changing world. It is sad but nevertheless true that the AFL-CIO is becoming increasingly the comfortable, complacent custodian of the status quo." The UAW leader promised that his union would fight for more democracy in the labor movement, finance and support a more aggressive organizing campaign, lobby for an expanded welfare state, and "resist communism and all forms of totalitarianism that would enslave the human spirit."

To accomplish his stated goals, Reuther invited the Teamsters to join with the automobile workers in an Alliance for Labor Action (ALA), which would ally the nation's two largest unions. If ever an unholy labor alliance existed, it was the one between the Teamsters and the auto workers. It brought together one of the most democratic unions and one of the most autocratic unions, a practitioner of reform unionism with an exponent of business unionism, the most Democratic of labor organizations with one of the most Republican, one of the cleanest unions and one with a long history of racketeering and corruption. This is perhaps why, in practice, the ALA did not amount to much and had no impact on the future of the labor movement.

In fact, one of the most important breakthroughs in unionism came on a totally unexpected front. The Mexican-American, or Chicano workers who toiled in California's "factories in the fields" for the first time in their lives built a successful union. Finding a leader in Cesar Chavez, himself a Mexican American of farm-worker origins, the migrant farm workers of California formed the United Farm Workers' Organizing Committee (later the United Farm Workers of America) to carry on their struggle with the state's grape growers. With funds from the AFL-CIO, organizational assistance provided by the UAW, moral support from such politicans as Robert F. Kennedy and many Catholic prelates and priests, the farm workers pursued *La Causa* (the cause) and *La Huelga* (the strike). Because conventional strikes and picketing tactics were of little use in the countryside, Chavez's union perfected a consumer boycott of California grapes. So successful was the boycott strategy that in 1967 California grape growers began to sign contracts with the farm workers—a triumph won by no previous organization of such workers. Buoyed by his union's success in the vineyards, Chavez in 1969 and 1970 pushed ahead to demand contracts from other California commercial farmers, especially lettuce growers who were also subjected to a consumer boycott. But by then the farm workers' organizing campaign had been slowed partly as a result of jurisdictional conflict with the Teamsters and partly as a consequence of internal organizational disarray. For Chicano workers, too, the 1970s posed perils.

Yet, all in all, by the end of the 1960s American workers and their unions seemed firmly integrated into a corporate welfare state. A variety of federal programs set minimum wages, stabilized incomes, provided job security, offered social security to the aged, infirm, and dependent, and redistributed a small share of the national income to the truly needy. The major unions, meantime, negotiated long-term contracts with binding no-strike clauses that provided stability for large enterprises and income gains for workers. As the Harvard economist, John Kenneth Galbraith noted, workers and their unions had become cooperative members of *The New Industrial State* (1967)—a junior but vital part of his ruling "technostructure."

Little, then, could American workers and their labor leaders imagine the blows which they and their organizations would suffer in the vastly different circumstances of the 1970s and 1980s.

XXI

An Uncertain Future:
Labor Since the 1970s

For twenty-five years after the Second World War, the western nations and Japan enjoyed a wave of economic expansion and prosperity unparalleled in the history of modern capitalism. It was this boom which enabled the United States to create an affluent society and which also enabled trade unions in the basic industries to provide their members with steadily rising real wages, expanding fringe benefits, and job security. Economic growth, moreover, created the resources with which postwar federal administrations from Eisenhower through Nixon expanded welfare benefits and transferred some of the surplus accumulated by the successful to the poor and unfortunate. By the end of the 1960s, the combination of economic prosperity and federal transfer payments had pulled millions of Americans above the poverty line.

The surge of economic expansion and prosperity ended, however, in the 1970s. Throughout the advanced industrial world, the United States included, supply outpaced demand, inflation replaced price stability, and mass unemployment again became a reality. Throughout the 1980s, only Japan among the leading industrial nations, and Austria and Sweden among smaller ones, seemed able to maintain high productivity and relatively full employment. The United States, for example, entered the decade of the 1980s plagued by a conjunction of double-digit inflation, declining industrial productivity, and the highest level of unemployment since the Great Depression of the 1930s.

Between 1973 and 1991 sweeping changes in the nation's social, economic, and political landscapes threatened American workers and their labor movement with a crisis of unprecedented proportions. Unions ended the 1970s with more members than ever before in their history and with the Democratic party, the labor movement's preferred political partner, in control of the White House and both houses of Congress. As the 1990s began, unions had fewer members than at any time since the end of the Korean War in 1953, Republicans were in firm control of the presidency, and the labor movement's alliance with the Democratic party was a frail political reed. What had happened over the course of two decades to sap the strength of trade unionism and render the future of the labor movement uncertain?

No simple summary of facts can explain the history of American workers and their unions between 1970 and 1990. A few features, however, stand out. After nearly a quarter of a century of steady economic expansion, rising real incomes, and stable prices, Americans experienced during the 1970s a more erratic pattern of economic change. The decade opened with a burst of inflation, which President Richard M. Nixon tried to combat through mandated price and wage controls in the summer of 1971. For a time, such federal policies restrained inflation, but a year later Nixon lifted the controls and prices soared once again. This new round of inflation was aggravated by the first energy crisis, which followed hard on the heels of the 1973 war in the Middle East between Israel and the Arab nations. Using American support for alleged Israeli aggression against the Arab states as a pretext, the oil-producing and exporting states (predominantly Persian Gulf Arab nations) used their cartel (OPEC) to embargo oil shipments to the United States. OPEC simultaneously introduced steep price rises for crude oil, which steadily increased, ultimately to over 1000 per cent, thereby also increasing the price of everything dependent on the use of petroleum—from public and private transportation to home heating, lighting, and food. Then Gerald Ford replaced Nixon as president in 1974 when the latter was compelled to resign from office as a result of the Watergate scandal. Ford made the fight against inflation his first priority. He did so by dampening economic growth, thus inducing a recession and compelling unemployed workers to enlist in a war against inflation. In 1975, the unemployment level exceeded 8 per cent of the labor force, and for the first time since the mid-1960s, the number of families which the Bureau of the Census classified as living in poverty actually increased. In fact, beginning with the first round of inflation in 1972 and 1973, even fully employed workers had begun to experience declines in real take-home pay as prices soared and social-security payroll taxes climbed.

The years that followed only worsened the economic situation for many working families. By the end of the 1970s, the real purchasing power of family income had declined, and the Joint Economic Committee of Congress warned in 1979 that Americans were likely to see their standard of living drastically reduced during the 1980s if current economic trends persisted. The Joint Committee's prediction was right on the mark. When a Republican president, Ronald Reagan, came to power in January 1981, he, like Paul Volcker, Carter's chair of the Federal Reserve Board, chose to combat the double-digit inflation and interest rates of the late 1970s through monetary and fiscal policies guaranteed to produce deep recession. The Reagan administration cooled inflation, but once again only at the expense of millions of workers who suffered the heaviest unemployment since the Great Depression. By December 1981, unemployment reached 10.8 per cent nationally and levels far in excess of that in such states as Michigan, Ohio, Pennsylvania, and Alabama which were heavily dependent on the deeply troubled automobile, steel, and mining industries (the figure for African Americans soared to over 18 per cent and for black teenagers it approached 50 per cent).

Having tempered inflation, the Reagan administration implemented a policy of deficit spending contrary to the stated supply side economic ideology of the Reagan revolution. Instead, Reaganomics became in practice old-fashioned Keynesian economics, in which deficit spending and the remilitarization of the economy fueled economic recovery. Between 1983 and 1988, as unemployment fell and the number of Americans employed rose, wages and incomes failed to rise sufficiently for most workers to improve their real standards of living. "Young, male, blue-collar workers . . . suffered devastating financial setbacks during the 1980s," wrote an economics columnist for the *New York Times*. Over that time, the earnings of high school dropouts fell 15 per cent, and even graduates of secondary schools experienced a loss of 9 per cent in earnings. Indeed, according to a report prepared by the Bureau of Labor Statistics, among ten industrial or recently industrializing nations between the years 1985 and 1988, only in the United States did workers experience a loss in their rate of compensation. While such increases varied from a low of 22 per cent in Korea to a high of 78 per cent in Germany, American real wage rates actually fell marginally. Many American families could only tread water economically or enjoy minimal improvements in living standards by having multiple wage earners in the same household. As the living wage* became an historical relic, the two wage-earner household increasingly became the norm. As a consequence, husbands worked more than one job, wives increasingly worked for wages outside the household, and for some, family life disintegrated. Child poverty soared (some reports suggested that a quarter of all American children lived at or below the poverty level), especially among households without male heads and without multiple wage earners.

Perhaps a good share of the stagnation in wage rates and family income growth resulted from measurable changes in the character and composition of the American labor force. Between the 1940s and 1970s, the workers who had experienced the greatest rise in real standards of living had been concentrated in the unionized mass-production industries or the skilled trades whose members had exceptional bargaining power in the labor market. Even nonunion employers who competed for the same sources of labor had to meet union standards or deal with the loss of their best employees and a discontented work force. During the 1970s and 1980s, however, precisely those sectors of the economy (mass-production and skilled trades) and their unions suffered the heaviest job and membership losses respectively.

A combination of domestic economic stagnation and global competition for markets at home and abroad accelerated the factors restructuring the American labor force. Such industries as automobile, steel, rubber, and textile, to name only a few, faced global overcapacity. Higher quality, lower-priced products from East Asian competitors, especially Japan, and European industrial nations captured markets from American mass-production enterprises. In order to survive in the competitive world marketplace, American enterprises had to introduce technological innovations which substituted capital (automated machinery and computerized robots) for human labor. Hence employment opportunities in the basic mass-production industries decreased steadily.

Only in the clerical, retail, and service sectors, which were not subject to comparable global competition, did employment expand. Not surprisingly, in July 1982 for the first time in U.S. history, total employment in

---

*The living wage traditionally referred to the concept that a single wage earner, normally a male head-of-household, earned enough income to support a spouse and children in reasonable security and comfort, that is, to enjoy an equally traditional "American standard of living."

the consumer, financial, and service sectors surpassed the job total in primary production—manufacturing, mining, and construction. In the three-plus decades after World War II, employment in the white-collar sector tripled to account for more than 27 per cent of nonfarm payroll jobs, while primary sector blue-collar employment fell from 41 per cent to under 27 per cent. By 1981 such fast-food enterprises as McDonald's and Burger King employed more workers than either the automobile or steel industries. The forces of global economic competition continued to shrink the active labor force in basic industry throughout the decade of the 1980s as the number of employees in the clerical and service trades rose.

The restructuring of the American economy did not eliminate labor force segmentation or its basis in racial and gender differences. White males still dominated the shrinking sector of high-wage, union-protected jobs. As the labor market remained slack throughout the 1980s, African American and Hispanic American males saw their earnings fall to 73 per cent and 71 per cent respectively of white male's average earnings. Women, by contrast, experienced a relative rise in comparative earning power. White women saw their wages rise to 67 per cent of men's earnings; African American women to 83 per cent; and Hispanic American women to 78 per cent. Women benefited from the concentration of their employment in the only expanding sectors of the economy (clerical, retail, service) and from the decline in the earnings of male workers. Still, women, whatever their race, remained concentrated in the lowest paying, least unionized sectors of the economy, while nonwhite males could no longer rely on employment opportunities in the high-wage, unionized mass-production sector.

A new wave of immigration stimulated by changes in the laws restricting it also played a part in transforming the labor force. Until 1960, the vast majority of newcomers to the United States had originated in Europe. Between 1961 and 1971, owing to the elimination of nationality quotas, half of all new immigrants came from Latin America and East and South Asia. Over the next two decades, 80 per cent of all immigrants left Latin America and Asia. By 1986, 17 per cent of the total population and an even higher proportion of the labor force was nonwhite. Added to the legal immigrants from nations to the south and from Asia were millions of illegal newcomers predominantly from Mexico, El Salvador, and Haiti. These illegal immigrants filled the needs of employers for cheap field and domestic labor in the Southwest and along the East Coast. Both the legal and the illegal new immigrants engendered resentment among large numbers of white and African American workers who blamed the newcomers for falling wages and unemployment. Partly to deal with such resentment and also to regulate the flow of illegals across the border with Mexico, Congress in 1986 passed legislation which regularized the status of such immigrants by offering them amnesty from deportation and the chance to qualify for citizenship.

The security and rewards of American workers were also increasingly affected by foreign workers who remained in their homelands. For most of the modern industrial era, certainly from the late eighteenth century through the 1960s, cheap labor had moved around the globe to satisfy the appetite of capital for workers. Since the 1970s, however, American business has moved production abroad to find cheaper labor, and has exported jobs to the *maquiladoras* on the Mexican border and to East Asian assembly lines.

The political universe also shifted to the disadvantage of the labor movement. Ever since its founding in 1955, the AFL-CIO had worked with and through the Democratic party to advance welfare legislation and to protect labor's interests. After 1968, that political alliance grew increasingly frayed at the edges. Nixon and the Republican party merged the themes of race, crime, and welfare dependency to woo white workers who identified themselves more as consumers than as producers, more as taxpayers than as welfare recipients. Even when Democrats returned to power with the election of Jimmy Carter as president in 1976, organized labor's gains were few and far between. Democrats in Congress increasingly represented constituents who disliked taxes, detested welfare expenditures for those whom they identified as parasites, and frowned on legislative favors for such special interests as minorities and organized labor. All this led the *AFL-CIO News* to describe the results of the first congress in ten years under a Democratic administration as "not a monument to forward-looking legislation but a tombstone."

Labor's unhappiness resulted largely from its inability to achieve congressional passage of reforms in national labor law. All the AFL-CIO had sought were reforms in the administration of the National Labor Relations Act, which would have stiffened the penalties for employer unfair labor practices and made representation election procedures speedier and more equitable for workers and unions. Truly, as union leaders asserted, "Labor law reform would not have organized a single worker or put unions at any new kind of advantage," yet employers fought with unprecedented solidarity to defeat the reforms. What George Meany characterized as "a heavily-financed, well orchestrated coalition between big business and right-wing extremists" produced a victory for employers.

In the aftermath of the defeat of labor law reform in Congress, on July 19, 1978, Douglas Fraser, president of the United Automobile Workers, resigned from the prestigious Labor-Management Group. In a widely publicized open letter, Fraser accused business leaders of breaking the fragile, unwritten compact which had bound labor and management together since the end of World War II and which the Labor-Management Group exemplified. "I believe," Fraser wrote, "that leaders of the business community...have chosen to wage a one-sided class war today in this country." He had no choice but to divorce himself from industrial leaders while they tried to destroy unions and ruin the lives of working people. Fraser proved equally denunciatory of Democrats who practiced a kind of politics without clear-cut ideological differences with Republicans "because of business domination."

Yet, in the election of 1980, organized labor allied with the Democratic party and its candidate Jimmy Carter. Ronald Reagan and the Republicans swept into office, however, with the victor carrying the votes of more than half of all white union members and their families. Reagan Republicans appealed with consummate skill to the resentments of northern white ethnic workers and poor white Southerners. Like Nixon before him, Reagan claimed to represent the "forgotten" Americans who worked hard, paid their taxes, and obeyed the law. In practice, far more than Nixon ever had, Reagan assaulted organized labor, which he identified as the "special interest" whose selfish wage demands were most responsible for inflation. Lane Kirkland, the new president of AFL-CIO, charged that the Republican party's economic program "fails every test of justice and equity."

Over the next eight years, Reagan and his Republican allies validated Kirkland's condemnation. One of the new president's first decisive actions in labor affairs in the summer of 1981 exposed Reagan's antiunion animus. The first chief executive to have himself been a former union member and officer (president of the Screen Actors Guild), Reagan used his vast presidential powers to break a strike by the Professional Air Traffic Controllers' Organization (PATCO). The President and members of his administration declared the strike illegal, defined the men and women on strike as outlaws, sought legal injunctions against the strikers, and had a number of PATCO leaders arrested, chained, and imprisoned. Having broken the strike, Reagan announced that strikers would never be rehired for their former positions or pardoned for their behavior and that PATCO would be decertified as a legitimate bargaining agent.

More disquieting for organized labor than PATCO's defeat was the reality that Americans overwhelmingly endorsed their president's policies and also that private sector union members turned their backs on public employees, whose salaries were paid through taxes. In 1981, solidarity remained a chimera for American workers.

Such unpleasant realities caused the AFL-CIO to take an unprecedented step for the modern labor movement. It called for a mass demonstration by trade unions and their allies in Washington on September 19, 1981. What soon came to be called Solidarity Day drew between 350,000 and 500,000 people to the nation's capital to protest the Reagan administration's domestic policies. The demonstration united young and old, white and nonwhite, male and female. Even the conservative and cautious building trades unions joined the protest.

As the Reagan administration's economic policies induced recession and deepened unemployment, labor's protests and political responses grew. The AFL-CIO and its affiliates concentrated on defeating Republican candidates in the election of 1982. The Democrats gained twenty-six seats in the newly elected House, mostly among liberals sympathetic to labor. Democrats did even better in gubernatorial elections, sweeping into power in many of the most populous industrial states. Labor looked forward to playing a decisive part in the selection of the Democratic candidate for president in 1984.

The AFL-CIO's joy over its political success in 1982 proved short-lived. Together with its friends and allies, the labor federation did play a decisive role in winning the 1984 Democratic presidential nomination for Walter Mondale. Mondale, however, proved a weak opponent for Reagan, who won a remarkable landslide victory at the polls. Once again, Reagan appealed with consummate skill to white workers' jealousy of the gains won by minorities, to the resentment of hard-working blue-collar laborers who felt that their precious tax-dollars had been squandered on "welfare parasites," and to powerful strains of nationalism and patriotism latent within the white working class. And, once again, a majority of white union members and their families delivered their votes to the Republican candidate for president. Equally important, during the campaign of 1984, as never before, the Republicans succeeded in identifying organized labor as a selfish special interest whose programs came at the expense of the majority of citizens.

Returned to office in 1984 with a clear mandate, Reagan continued the economic policies that took from the poor and gave to the rich. By the end of his second term, the distribution of income and wealth in the United States had grown more unequal than it had been for more than sixty years.

What had been happening and what was made even more obvious by the election of the Republican George Bush in 1988 was that as the Democratic and Republican parties had increasingly become two wings of a single political organization—or, as the financier Felix Rohaytan put it, a one-party condominium system in which Republicans govern from the White House and Democrats from Congress. Political participation fell most sharply among lower-income voters. The political scientist Walter Dean Burnham has traced the depoliticization of the American masses from the immediate post–World War II elections to the Republican presidential triumph in 1988. Among those workers who continued to vote, issues that might be characterized as consumer-taxpayer cum racial grew more salient than class-producer issues. The politics of low taxes, price stability, and race operated against the interests of organized labor and to the advantage of more conservative influences in both political parties.

A similar longterm shift in judicial interpretations of labor law and in appointments to the federal judiciary also spelled trouble for labor. Ever since the 1940s, the federal judiciary had been reinterpreting New Deal labor law in a manner which curtailed the rights of workers as individuals and unions as institutions. A series of Supreme Court decisions from the late 1960s through the 1970s practically outlawed strikes where union contracts and/ or arbitration machinery existed. These decisions breathed new life into the labor injunction, which the Norris-LaGuardia Act of 1932 had banned. Other decisions brought union practices once more under antitrust legislation or common-law restraint-of-trade violations. On occasion, workers and unions won favorable decisions, such as when the Supreme Court found the J. P. Stevens textile company guilty of violating federal labor law. Overall, however, especially as such Republican presidents as Nixon, Reagan, and Bush reshaped the composition of the federal judiciary through the power of appointment, legal doctrine steadily diminished the rights of organized labor.

The conjuncture of recurrent economic crises, the restructuring of the labor force, and an altered legal-political universe implied disaster for the American labor movement. For a time between 1968 and 1978, the unionization of public employees disguised the relative decline of trade unionism. White-collar workers, especially the public employees among them, became the most rapidly expanding sector of the labor movement.

Teachers, nurses, and social service professionals began to act like traditional trade unionists and often transformed their hitherto ineffective professional associations into potent labor unions. Altogether, public worker unions and employee associations increased their membership by over two million, and by 1978, represented 36 per cent of all state and local public employees. Among the eight unions with the largest gains in membership between 1968 and 1978, the most successful were the American Federation of State, County, and Municipal Employees (AFSCME), with 650,000 new members, a growth of 180 per cent, and the American Federation of Teachers (AFT) whose membership tripled from 165,000 to 500,000. By 1980, the two largest unions in the AFL-CIO, one of which was AFSCME, represented white-collar workers in public and private employment. Moreover, in that same year, the National Education Association, which represents teachers and bargains like a trade union, claimed 1,800,000 members, making it larger than any union in the AFL-CIO.

The progress made in union growth by public employees was not matched by workers in the private sector. Consequently, organized labor's share of the work force continued to decline. By 1978, only 26.6 per cent of nonagricultural workers belonged to trade unions, as compared to 34.7 per cent in 1954 and 35.5 per cent, the peak during World War II. It was in manufacturing, the traditional stronghold of the labor movement since the 1930s, that unions suffered worst during the 1970s. Between 1974 and 1978 alone, unions in manufacturing lost more than one million members (from 9,144,000 to 8,119,000), a loss of over 11 per cent. In the twenty-four years since the end of the Korean War, the trade unions' share of the total labor force had fallen almost 25 per cent.

Equally threatening to the future of the labor movement was the inability of unionism to keep pace with the growth of the labor force in the nonmanufacturing sector, where the bulk of job growth occurred. While employment in that sector rose 37 per cent in the decade 1968–1978, union membership increased only 13 per cent, resulting in a decline in organized labor's share of that market from 24.6 to 20.3 per cent. Many of the workers in that sector, typically teenagers earning minimum wages, tended to enter and leave the job market rapidly and were scattered in so many small isolated locations that the cost of organizing them appeared to exceed the potential benefits. Others were women, who often found their concerns neglected by a male-dominated union movement, and still others were people who through family origins, culture, and education identified more with management than labor.

An equally ominous sign for organized labor was its inability to recruit among workers in the healthiest sector of manufacturing—the so-called high-technology firms. These enterprises had long practiced what came to be called during the 1980s alternative industrial relations systems. Indeed, as the research of Sanford Jacoby has demonstrated, even during the turbulent years of the New Deal and World War II, many American industrial enterprises successfully practiced a form of labor relations which kept them union-free. These companies sought to guarantee their employees job security through noncontractual forms of seniority and internal job ladders. Typically, they paid their workers wages comparable to union levels. They also provided a wide array of fringe benefits, everything from health-care insurance and attractive retirement benefits to country clubs and company-financed higher education. Such enterprises, particularly in the high-technology sector, practiced a corporate culture which extolled teamwork, cooperation between workers and managers, and identification of all employees as members of a common professional or managerial family.

Beginning slowly in the mid-1970s and accelerating rapidly at the end of the decade, the decline of trade unionism proceeded apace. The public fiscal crisis of the years 1975–1977 fueled resentment against high taxes and highly paid unionized public employees, a combination linked in the public mind. New York City's near bankruptcy in 1976–1977 and popular rebellions against taxes in California (1978) and Massachusetts (1980), which limited the state's power to tax, started a trend toward retrenchment in public employment and resistance to pay increases for such employees. Unionism's once untapped frontier in public employment was now shrinking. At the same time, the stagflation (inflation unaccompanied by economic growth) of the late 1970s in a universe of intensifying global economic competition ended unionism's absolute increase in membership. After 1978, membership began to fall absolutely as well as relatively. Between 1980 and 1982 alone, total union membership fell by almost three million (22,366,000 to 19,763,000) and to only 17.7 per cent of the total labor force (22.1 per cent of the nonagricultural labor force). The economic recovery of 1984–1986 failed to add members to union ranks as ordinarily happened in times of business expansion. Instead union ranks dwindled as the 1980s passed into the 1990s and every major sector of the economy experienced such losses in union membership. Job losses were especially severe in the trade unions' former strongholds, namely the automobile, steel, electrical goods, and clothing industries.

Other indicators revealed the severe plight of trade unionism in the

United States as the decade of the 1990s opened. The number of strikes, especially those involving large numbers of workers, declined precipitately. Much of that reflected worker and union awareness of management's willingness to hire permanent replacement workers when employees walked out, a policy that grew increasingly effective in a loose labor market and a political milieu in which politicians and jurists lauded the power of free choice in a free society. Unions now also found themselves far less successful in winning NLRB representation elections and instead more often found their bargaining units decertified by employer-initiated elections. From the NLRB's founding in 1935 until the passage of the Taft-Hartley Act in 1947, unions won 75 per cent of all NLRB elections. Until 1975 they continued to win half. Since then, however, unions have never won as many as 50 per cent of such elections, and the trend line has moved inexorably downward.

Such trends have clearly damaged the ability of unions to bargain collectively. The recession of 1981–1982 resulted in union contracts which actually reduced real wages on the order of 7 to 8.5 per cent. In addition, many union contracts negotiated between 1982 and 1985 implemented two-tiered wage agreements which paid new hires lower wages, conceded employers greater power over work rules and job assignments, relinquished a number of paid holidays and personal days, and tolerated reductions in medical and retirement benefits. In 1984 and 1985, for the first time in decades, the rate of wage increases granted nonunion employees exceeded those negotiated by unions. Increasingly, moreover, unions since 1985 have surrendered cost-of-living (COLA) wage rises, accepted annual bonuses in lieu of increases in the base wage or salary, and negotiated contracts in which wage increases have lagged behind the inflation rate.

Such indicators had struck some of the more astute observers of the labor movement even before business and the Republicans began to assault trade unions in the 1980s. As early as 1978, a journalist writing in *Harper's Magazine* titled his article, "The Last Days of the American Labor Movement." The president of AFSCME, Jerry Wurf, lamented that "the American labor movement is having less and less impact on society." And, as the decade of the 1970s ended, the dean of American labor reporters, A. H. Raskin, noted that "far from serving as the cutting edge of social change . . . trade unionism appears today to be a largely spent force in the national life."

Several bright spots, however, illuminated the otherwise bleak prospects of organized labor as it entered the decade of the 1980s. One positive sign was the installment of the new president of the AFL-CIO, Lane Kirkland, who replaced George Meany upon the latter's retirement in 1979. Although Meany handpicked his successor, Kirkland was a different sort of person. Indeed, he appeared more the contemporary professional executive than the old-fashioned, hard-bitten labor boss. Whereas Meany reeked of cigars, brusque words, and stale ideas, Kirkland exuded polish, spoke smoothly, and enjoyed the play of ideas. While Meany had been the child of poor, big-city, working-class parents, Kirkland came from a comfortable South Carolina family and had graduated from the United States Merchant Marine Academy as well as having earned a master's degree from Georgetown University's School of Foreign Affairs. These differences in social background, education, and temperament made Kirkland more open to new forces and tendencies in American society. He realized that the labor movement had to appeal more strongly to white-collar professional employees, that it had to find more room in the leadership for nonwhites, and that it had to work harder to attract the fastest growing sector of the labor force—women. Kirkland also understood that labor unity was more essential than ever before, and he immediately invited both the UAW and the Teamsters to reaffiliate with the AFL-CIO. In the case of the UAW, Kirkland's plea fell on sympathetic ears. At the AFL-CIO convention of 1981, the automobile workers resumed full and active membership. Before the decade ended, moreover, both the Teamsters (in 1988) and the United Mine Workers (a year later) reaffiliated with the AFL-CIO.

Kirkland's stewardship offered two other areas of promise for the future. Labor in America had advanced in the past by regularly incorporating new, underrepresented groups into the movement. For the 1980s and the foreseeable future, white-collar people, nonwhites, Hispanics (including the large number of illegal immigrants), and women especially, appear as unionism's most attractive frontier. Kirkland's receptivity to the organization of these groups augured well. As women came to compose 40 per cent of the total labor force and more than 50 per cent of all women sought full-time waged work, their importance to the labor movement grew ever more decisive. In the decades between 1958 and 1978, for example, the number of women in unions doubled, from 3,300,000 to 6,600,000, and the proportion of women in the labor movement rose from 18 to 27 per cent overall. Among women workers more than men, union membership bore some relationship to the expansion in the size of the labor force. And, for the first time in the history of the AFL-CIO, a woman, Joyce Miller, of the ACTWU and the Coalition of Labor Union Women, sat on its executive council.

Kirkland has also opened the AFL-CIO to the influence of academics, historians, and sociologists, as well as to economists and industrial relations experts. Members of the executive council have met privately and informally with such intellectuals to pick their minds about how to improve labor's image and how to organize nonunion workers. More formally, in 1983, the AFL-CIO appointed a Committee on the Evolution of Work, composed of union officials and academics. This new committee focussed on the factors which had created the contemporary labor force and how trade unions could best attract nontraditional workers. In 1985, it published a report, *The Changing Situation of Workers and their Unions*, which called on the affiliates of the AFL-CIO to devise different tactics and strategies for a labor force which had grown more educated and also more diverse in race and gender. It called on unions to acknowledge that more educated workers sought self-respect and fulfillment at work, that they expected jobs to be meaningful and to offer opportunities for challenge and growth. The report reminded labor leaders that not all workers were alike and that traditional adversarial collective bargaining arrangements were not always in order. Unions had to remember that many workers, especially white-collar, professional and technical employees, wanted to be involved with management in planning the labor process and the flow of work, and that the customary union-management contract, which bound both sides tightly in a web of rules, had to give way to more flexible and elastic arrangements of power sharing. And, finally, the report called on the AFL-CIO and its affiliates to create new forms of associate membership for workers, who sympathized with the spirit and goals of unionism, but who worked either in blatantly nonunion enterprises or in firms which offered their employees a considerable measure of involvement in matters which would ordinarily be the province of collective bargaining.

However well-intentioned the principles and goals enunciated by the Evolution of Work Committee, its recommendations had little immediate impact on the short-run fate of trade unionism. In the years which immediately followed the 1985 report, unions continued to lose members and to represent a smaller proportion of the total labor force. Simply put, most U.S. unions found it exceedingly difficult to adapt to the tactics of antiunion managements. Corporations and their managers proved much more successful than labor leaders in adapting their values and strategies to an external environment of global economic competition.

Labor leaders seemed frozen into the large, impersonal union bureaucracies which they had created to win concessions from the equally gargantuan corporate enterprises with which they were compelled to bargain. A style of unionism which had worked in the heyday of American mass-production industry and global economic dominance seemed anachronistic in the emerging era of specialized batch-production industry and worldwide competition for markets. Just as union leaders found it increasingly difficult to recruit new members from enterprises which practiced sophisticated human resources management techniques and sought the cooperation of their employees in planning work, they also discovered widespread alienation among their existing memberships. Rank-and-file union members often saw their union leaders as more distant and more autocratic than their bosses at work. In many cases, workers needed protection as much against union bosses as corporate bosses, a reality well evidenced in the history and practices of the Teamsters' union. Just as the AFL style of business unionism suited the needs of skilled workers in the late nineteenth and early twentieth centuries, and the CIO style of industrial unionism fit the mass-production workers of the mid-twentieth century, only a new form of unionism can address the concerns of the more highly educated, professionalized, and individualized labor force of the late twentieth century.

Throughout the 1980s and into the 1990s unions have been stymied in their efforts to adapt to an economic environment characterized by intense competition globally and deregulation domestically. In such industries as automobiles and steel, unions have survived, but only at great cost. In 1978, *Forbes* magazine had observed that "organized labor is so . . . interwoven into the fabric of the U.S. economy, especially in basic industries, that any sudden and serious loss of its authority would probably distress management more than please it. . . . A high GM executive once remarked, if the UAW did not 'police' the contract. . . GM plants would be chaotic." That reality remained true throughout the decade of the 1980s, as the big three domestic automobile manufacturers, GM, Ford, and Chrysler, continued to bargain collectively with the UAW. Such bargaining, however, now had to respond directly to the rising threat of Japanese competition. Japanese automobile firms, led by their own big three —Toyota, Nissan, and Honda—had captured nearly one-third of the domestic American market by 1991. To meet Japanese competition, U.S. firms had to eliminate excess capacity and lower their costs of production. That meant inducing the UAW to accept contracts that introduced Japanese methods of production into American automobile plants. The contracts negotiated between the automobile companies and the UAW in the 1980s replaced regular increases in the base wage with annual bonuses related to gross profits, eliminated or modified cost-of-living increases,

reduced paid personal leave days and annual paid holidays, redefined heretofore tightly circumscribed job categories to make work assignments and
responsibilities more flexible, and introduced so-called quality circles and
other forms of employee group participation in the production process in
order to bridge the chasm between management and labor.

These contractual innovations or concessions on the part of labor may
have saved the union's place in the automobile industry, but they failed to
save jobs for workers or the union from losing members. The industry's
capacity to produce cars continued to exceed its ability to sell them, and,
as a consequence, the Big Three closed its more antiquated assembly
plants and downsized its labor force. Ford, GM, and Chrysler also shifted
away from manufacturing parts and accessories in their own unionized fa-
cilities to subcontracting their manufacture to smaller, lower-cost nonunion enterprises. Because the new style of collective bargaining and labor
relations in the automobile industry purchased union security at the price
of jobs and benefits for workers, some insurgents in the UAW at the end
of the 1980s formed a New Directions movement, which demanded
greater militancy by the union and a more antagonistic approach by labor
to management instead of a cooperative one.

How a more militant, antagonistic brand of unionism as promoted by
New Directions might save the UAW, American jobs, and American
standards from the Japanese threat remains uncertain. By 1990, Japanese
competition in the automobile industry meant not cars imported into the
U.S. but manufactured here with the labor of American workers. All the
major Japanese companies and some of the lesser ones had established assembly plants in the U.S. by 1990, and the largest among them operated
on a nonunion basis. Only in those cases in which Japanese firms formed
a direct partnership with one of the Big Three—as for Mitsubishi with
Chrysler and Mazda with Ford, and on a larger scale, Toyota with General Motors (who formed the New United Motor Manufacturing, Inc. in
Fremont, California)—was the UAW tolerated. And in the case of
NUMMI, which Toyota used to determine whether American labor
could be as productive as Japanese labor, the UAW had to agree to accept
Japanese methods of production. Overall, however, the Japanese Big
Three chose to operate their American plants on a nonunion basis.
Honda, the first company to open an assembly plant in the United States
early in the 1980s, kept the union out of its Ohio facility. Having worked
hard to influence Honda's indigenous American labor force, the UAW in
1985 refused to risk an NLRB representation election. The union tried
harder to organize workers at Nissan's new plant in Smyrna, Tennessee,

where in 1989 the NLRB conducted a representation election. The UAW lost the election by a margin of better than two to one.

The ability of the Japanese transplants to operate nonunion shops threatens the UAW's future in the American automobile industry. The Japanese firms operating in America have a younger, better-educated, and more carefully screened labor force than do their Big Three competitors. This means higher per capita productivity and lower costs for health and retirement benefits. Because the Japanese plants have less excess capacity than their American competitors, they guarantee employees job security in return for management's ability to use labor more flexibly. Finally, the fact that Japanese firms produce cars on a nonunion basis renders it more difficult for the UAW to use the strike threat when negotiating with American companies. If the militants in the New Directions faction were to shut down plants through aggressive strikes, how would they preserve what remains of Ford's, GM's, and Chrysler's share of the American market from further Japanese penetration?

Deregulation of the domestic transportation industry in the United States produced a comparable trauma for unions in that sector. Throughout the 1950s and 1960s, the Teamsters had been the most successful union at organizing new members. Despite the union's expulsion from the AFL-CIO, its links to crime and criminal syndicates, and its sordid leaders, the Teamsters became the largest union in the country. At the end of the 1970s, however, the Interstate Commerce Commission began to deregulate trucking from federal control and open it to new forms of competition. Nonunion operations grew at the expense of their unionized competitors. Small, independent trucking firms and individual drivers acting as subcontractors took business away from higher-cost, national union firms. Soon, the Teamsters, like many other unions, began to experience a decline in membership, and in 1982 and 1985 faced the reality of negotiating contracts that reduced wages for new hires by 30 per cent, eliminated the annual COLA, and reduced other fringe benefits drivers had long taken for granted. In the case of the Teamsters, as had also been true for the UAW, concessionary bargaining failed to save union jobs.

The Teamsters also experienced a membership rebellion. Fueled initially by the corrupt practices of the union leadership and the Teamsters' autocratic governance, the insurgency led by younger, more educated members coalesced into a movement called Teamsters for a Democratic Union (TDU). TDU gained added momentum and a larger following when the Teamsters' officials during the 1980s negotiated concessionary contracts. Beset by deregulation on one front and insurgency on another, the union's leaders again found themselves the targets of a federal campaign against union corruption. In 1988, the Department of Justice began proceedings to place the Teamsters under a federal court trusteeship, which was one of the reasons the Teamsters finally decided to accept Lane Kirkland's invitation to reaffiliate with the AFL-CIO. Reaffiliation, however, did not protect the Teamsters from the Justice Department. In 1989, a federal judge placed the union under his direct jurisdiction, required the union to implement more open and democratic governance procedures, and mandated the first direct membership election for international office. By 1991, TDU committed itself to back a reform candidate for president of the Teamsters. Yet, even after that candidate, Ron Carey, and his slate won election by a large plurality, it remains unclear how a new, more democratic administration will respond to the problems of deregulation and increased competition in the trucking industry.

A similar pattern appeared in the airline industry. There, too, federal deregulation of a formerly controlled economic sector opened the path for competition from new nonunion enterprises. Here the catalyst was one Frank Lorenzo, who from his base of operations in lower-cost, nonunion Texas Air challenged his larger unionized competitors for a market share. Lorenzo also acquired two larger unionized enterprises, Continental and Eastern Airlines, which he determined to make nonunion. At Continental, his stewardship precipitated a strike which plunged the airline into bankruptcy, an opportunity which Lorenzo then used to break all union contracts. Lorenzo's control of Eastern Airlines produced a similar result, in this case driving the company into bankruptcy, federal receivership, and by 1991 total dissolution. The inroads of nonunion competition compelled unions at such traditional old-line carriers as TWA, Pan American, and United to negotiate concessionary contracts under which new hires received lower salaries and veteran employees surrendered a part of their fringe benefits. Concessions by their unions, however, could not save TWA and Pan American from economic decline and failure. In 1991, Pan American had to sell the bulk of its overseas and domestic routes to Delta. And TWA itself survived precariously. The future of U.S. air travel seemed likely to be dominated by three giant enterprises, American, United, and Delta, the latter of which had always operated nonunion and the former two in which unions had lost a part of their influence.

As the year 1991 passed the future prospects of organized labor remained dim. In some cases, old-fashioned militant and adversarial tactics still benefited unions. In 1988 and 1989, the UMW successfully fought the attempt by Pittston Coal to run its operations nonunion in western Virginia and to withdraw from its obligations to the union health fund. When Pittston attempted to operate with permanent replacement workers, the UMW threw up mass picket lines, challenged legal injunctions and state troopers, in one instance seized company property, built a firm base of local community support, and elicited sympathy and solidarity from elsewhere in the labor movement. Under the leadership of its new, educated young president, Rich Trumka, the miners' union adapted the tactics of civil disobedience used in the civil rights and peace movements to labor conflict with great effect. In the end, Pittston conceded to the union.

The New York *Daily News* also lost its battle with the unions in 1990 after a protracted lockout strike. Having first instigated a strike by its press operators, the newspaper then locked out its loyal union employees and replaced them with new hires or renegade union members. In response, the unions called for a community boycott both of advertising in the newspaper and purchase of the *News*; they used moral suasion and, on occasion, physical force to halt circulation and sales of the paper, and they rallied support from the citywide labor movement. In the end, the owners of the newspaper sold their enterprise to the English publisher Robert Maxwell who proceeded to negotiate successfully with the unions. But with Maxwell's death and bankruptcy in late 1991, the fate of the *Daily News* is once again in doubt.

For every union success story, however, there has been an equal failure. If the Pittston and *Daily News* strikes proved how militancy and community campaigns might produce worker victory, the strike in Austin, Minnesota, between packinghouse workers organized in Local P-9 of the Food and Commercial Workers' Union and the Hormel Company established the limits of militancy and community-based struggles. After a struggle which lasted nearly two years (1985–1986) in which they evinced indomitable resolve, the Hormel workers found themselves defeated decisively by a recalcitrant employer supported by the leaders of the strikers' own international union. Several years later, in 1990, the Greyhound Bus Company precipitated a strike by its employees and then immediately hired replacement workers. As the year 1991 drew to its close, the strikers remained out of jobs, Greyhound busses continued to roll, and the union had little prospect of sitting at the bargaining table. Pilots, cabin attendants, and machinists at Continental and Eastern Airlines, as we have already seen, suffered a similar fate. As a union consultant remarked in 1985, "Management is feeling very feisty and confident these days about their ability to exert their muscle and break a union, with no fear of the consequences." And one wonders why not, when they have the ability and the will to hire permanent replacement workers during strikes, to threaten to close factories or to move production to nonunion sites at home or overseas, and to raise the specter of foreign competition for American jobs.

The potential of creating an impasse explains why, according to three of the nation's leading experts on industrial relations, Thomas Kochan, Robert McKersie, and Harry Katz, the more innovative unions and union-free large enterprises now have similar agendas. As another well-known labor economist, James L. Medoff, observed in 1985, owing to the twin competitive threats of foreign competition and successful nonunion domestic enterprises, "unions and managements are working better together to preserve jobs, to save companies and keep plants from closing, and that's what is really reducing the number of strikes."

Barely hanging on in the realms in which they have long had influence, the unions appear impotent to penetrate many giant enterprises whose employees are content or to recruit members in small firms who, according to survey data, are more favorably disposed to unions. The larger enterprises pay a price to keep unions out by offering job security, company-mandated welfare benefits, profit sharing, and a corporate culture in which all participants are made to feel part of a common family engaged in a cooperative endeavor. The small, less welfare-oriented, less innovative firms in the service and retail sectors keep unions out with less effort or planning. Widely scattered, employing few workers at any one location, and relying on the labor of new immigrants, women, and teenagers, mostly part-timers who turn over at geometric rates, such enterprises rarely attract the interest of union organizers. The costs of seeking to unionize such small units appear to exceed the potential benefits for the unions with jurisdiction.

The prospects for the American labor movement at the start of the 1990s remind one of those in the 1920s. Unions again seem on the defensive, both unable to attract members in the growth industries, where employers successfully practice human resources management and alternative industrial relations, and threatened by job losses in the declining mass-production industries. Once again the nation's political and business leaders look at unions with jaundiced eyes and believe that the conditions and fate of workers should be left to the marketplace and not to the mercies of government regulators or union officials. And, in the 1980s and

1990s, as in 1928 and 1929, astute critics assail unionism as "a largely spent force," one "having less and less impact on society."

Will the labor movement's contemporary critics prove more prescient than were their predecessors? If the past has shaped the present and acts as guide to the future, the history of contemporary American workers remains to be made and written. Only the subjects of that future history, male and female, white and nonwhite, young and old, union and nonunion, can determine how it will in fact be made. Of one thing, however, we can be sure: organized labor will make history in the future only to the extent that it becomes an ally of the new social movements among women, nonwhites, and environmentalists, and only to the extent that it proves to the American people that trade unionism serves the entire community and not its own narrow interests.

Further Reading

General

The best bibliographical guide to American labor history is now Maurice Neufeld, Daniel J. Leab, and Dorothy Swanson, *American Working Class History: A Representative Bibliography* (New York, 1983), which includes novels and plays as well as more conventional scholarly works. Other general bibliographies include: Gene S. Stroud and Gilbert E. Donahue, *Labor History in the United States: A General Bibliography* (Urbana, Ill., 1961); Fred D. Rose, *American Labor in Journals of History: A Bibliography* (Urbana, Ill., 1962); and Andor and Judith W. Skotnes, *American Working-Class History in Historical Journals, 1961–1972: A Bibliography* (New Brunswick, N.J., 1974).

The classic sources for general labor history remain John R. Commons and Associates, *History of Labor in the United States*, 4 vols. (New York, 1918–1935), and *A Documentary History of American Industrial Society*, 10 vols. (New York, 1958). Philip Taft has written several books that provide the most recent version of Commons's approach to American labor history: *The A. F. of L. in the Time of Gompers* (New York, 1957), *The A. F. of L. from the Death of Gompers to the Merger* (New York, 1959), and a full and comprehensive one-volume textbook on the labor movement as a whole, *Organized Labor in American History* (New York, 1964).

For a multivolume history whose structure and subject matter are comparable to those of Commons and Taft, but one that offers an orthodox Marxist version of American labor history through the World War I years, see Philip S. Foner, *History of the Labor Movement in the United States*, 8 vols. (New York, 1947–1988).

Other briefer general histories include Henry Pelling, *American Labor* (Chicago, 1960); Joseph Rayback, *A History of American Labor* (New York, 1959); Thomas R. Brooks, *Toil and Trouble: A History of American Labor* (New York, 1964); and a Marxist synthesis, Herbert Morais and Richard O. Boyer, *Labor's Untold Story* (New York, 1971). For more recent general histories that incorporate the insights of the "new" labor history, see Bruce Laurie, *Artisans into Laborers: Labor in Nineteenth-Century America* (New York, 1989); James R. Green, *The World of the Worker: Labor in Twentieth-Century America* (New York, 1980); and Robert Zieger, *American Workers; American Unions, 1920–1985* (Baltimore, 1986).

Three somewhat dated books still offer the best introduction to theoretical and ideological issues in the history of the American labor movement: Selig Perlman, *A Theory of the Labor Movement* (New York, 1928); Frank Tannenbaum, *A Philosophy of Labor* (Cambridge, Mass., 1955); and Mark Perlman, *Labor Union Theories in America: Background and Development* (Evanston, Ill., 1958).

The best introduction to the innovative and stimulating work done during the last two decades in labor history can be found in the following collections of essays: Herbert G. Gutman, *Work, Culture, and Society in Industrializing America* (New York, 1975), and *Power and Culture: Essays on the American Working Class*, ed. Ira Berlin (New York, 1987); David Montgomery, *Workers' Control in America* (New York, 1979); David Brody, *Workers in Industrial America* (New York, 1980); Michael Frisch and Daniel Walkowitz, eds., *Working-Class America* (Urbana, Ill., 1983); Daniel J. Leab, ed., *The Labor History Reader*, (Urbana, Ill., 1985); and J. Carroll Moody and Alice Kessler-Harris, eds., *Perspectives on American History: The Problems of Synthesis* (DeKalb, Ill., 1989).

Women

The history of women, work, and unions has generated an unusual amount of excellent literature recently. The best of the more general histories and essay collections on the subject include: Alice Kessler-Harris, *Out to Work: A History of Wage-Earning Women in the United States* (New York, 1982); Barbara Wertheimer, *We Were There: The Story of Working Women in America* (New York, 1977); Rosalyn Baxandall, Linda Gordon, and Susan Reverby, eds., *America's Working Women: A Documentary History* (New York, 1976); Meredith Tax, *The Rising of the Women* (New York, 1980); Philip S. Foner, *Women and the American Labor Movement*, 2 vols. (New York, 1979–1980); Lynn Y. Weiner, *From Working Girl to Working Mother: The Female Labor Force in the United States, 1820–1980* (Chapel Hill, N.C., 1984); Ruth Milkman, ed., *Women, Work, and Protest: A Century of Women's Labor History* (Boston, 1985); Milton Cantor and Bruce Laurie, eds., *Class, Sex, and the Woman Worker* (Westport, Conn., 1977); Joan Jensen and Sue Davidson, eds., *A Needle, a Bobbin, a Strike: Women Needleworkers in America* (Philadelphia, 1984). And for a truly stunning book that integrates women's and African American labor history, Jacqueline Jones, *Labor of Love, Labor of Sorrow: Black Women, Work, and the Family from Slavery to the Present* (New York, 1985).

More specialized studies examine a wide variety of aspects of women's relationship to labor history, including among other subjects: the role of women in different eras of history; their history in various trades and unions; and their activities in different communities. The following are among the best of such histories: Christine Stansell, *City of Women: Sex and Class in New York, 1789–1960* (New York, 1960); Thomas Dublin, *Women at Work: The Transformation of Work and Community in Lowell, Massachusetts, 1826–1860* (New York, 1979); Mary H. Blewett, *Men, Women, and Work: Class, Gender, and Protest in the New England Shoe Industry, 1780–1910* (Urbana, Ill., 1988); Susan Levine, *Labor's True Woman: Carpet Weavers, Industrialization, and Labor Reform in the Gilded Age* (Philadelphia, 1984); Cindy S. Aron, *Ladies and Gentlemen of the Civil Service: Middle-Class Workers in Victorian America* (New York, 1987); Stephen H. Norwood, *Labor's Flaming Youth: Telephone Operators and Worker Militancy, 1878–1923* (Urbana, Ill., 1990); Dolores E. Janiewski, *Sisterhood Denied: Race, Gender, and Class in a New South Community* (Philadelphia, 1985); Susan A. Glenn, *Daughters of the Shtetl: Life and Labor in the Immigrant Generation* (Ithaca, N.Y., 1990); Susan P. Benson, *Counter Cultures: Saleswomen, Managers, and Customers in American Department Stores, 1890–1940* (Urbana, Ill., 1986); Kathy Piess, *Cheap Amusements: Working Women and Leisure in Turn-of-the-Century New York* (Philadelphia, 1986); Patricia A. Cooper, *Once a Cigar Maker: Men, Women, and Work Culture in American Cigar Factories, 1900–1919* (Urbana, Ill., 1987); Nancy S. Dye, *As Equals and as Sisters: Femi-*

nism, Unionism, and the Women's Trade Union League of New York (Columbia, Mo., 1980); Marjory W. Davies, *Woman's Place is at the Typewriter: Office Work and Office Workers, 1870–1930* (Philadelphia, 1982); Ileen DeVault, *Sons and Daughters of Labor: Class and Clerical Work in Turn-of-the-Century Pittsburgh* (Ithaca, N.Y., 1990); Barbara Melosh, *"The Physician's Hand": Work Culture and Conflict in American Nursing* (Philadelphia, 1982); Judith Sealander, *As Minority Becomes Majority: Federal Reaction to the Phenomenon of Women in the Work Force, 1920–1963* (Westport, Conn., 1983); Vicki L. Ruiz, *Cannery Women, Cannery Lives: Mexican Women, Unionization, and the California Food Processing Industry, 1930–1950* (Albuquerque, 1987); Ruth Milkman, *Gender at Work: The Dynamics of Job Segregation by Sex during World War II* (Urbana, Ill., 1987); and Nancy Gabin, *Feminism in the Labor Movement: Women and the United Workers, 1935–1975* (Ithaca, N.Y., 1990).

African Americans

A variety of books, some new, some old, cover the history of African American workers from different perspectives. The best of the older studies is Sterling D. Spero and Abram L. Harris, *The Black Worker* (New York, 1931). Among the better of the new books are the following: William H. Harris, *The Harder We Run: Black Workers since the Civil War* (New York, 1982); Julius Jacobson, ed., *The Negro and the American Labor Movement* (New York, 1965); and Philip S. Foner, *Organized Labor and the Black Worker, 1619–1973* (New York, 1974). One should also note here again, J. Jones, *Labor of Love, Labor of Sorrow.*

Among the finer more specialized studies, one might consult the following: Joe William Trotter, Jr., *Black Milwaukee: The Making of an Industrial Proletariat, 1915–1945* (Urbana, Ill., 1985) and *Coal, Class, and Color: Blacks in Southern West Virginia, 1915–1932* (Urbana, Ill., 1990); Peter J. Rachleff, *Black Labor in the New South: Richmond, Virginia, 1865–1890* (Philadelphia, 1984); Peter Gottlieb, *Making Their Own Way: Southern Blacks' Migration to Pittsburgh* (Urbana, Ill., 1987); and James R. Grossman, *Land of Hope: Chicago, Black Southerners, and the Great Migration* (Chicago, 1989).

The Premodern Era: To the 1870s

For the colonial and revolutionary eras one should consult Marcus W. Jernegan, *Laboring and Dependent Classes in Colonial America, 1707–1783*

(New York, 1960); David Galenson, *White Servitude in Colonial America: An Economic Analysis* (New York, 1981); Richard B. Morris, *Government and Labor in Early America*, (New York, 1946); Gary B. Nash, *The Urban Crucible: Social Change, Political Consciousness, and the Coming of the American Revolution* (Cambridge, Mass., 1979); Eric Foner, *Tom Paine and Revolutionary America* (New York, 1976); Charles G. Steffen, *The Mechanics of Baltimore: Workers and Politics in the Age of Revolution, 1763-1812*; Graham Hodges, *New York City Cartmen, 1667-1850* (New York, 1986); Marcus Rediker, *Between the Devil and the Deep Blue Sea: Merchant Seamen, Pirates, and the Anglo-American Maritime World, 1700-1750* (New York, 1987); and Billy G. Smith, *The "Lower Sort": Philadelphia's Laboring People* (Ithaca, N.Y., 1990).

For workers in the new nation and the era of early industrialization, the following books provide the best introduction: Howard Rock, *Artisans of the New Republic: The Tradesmen of New York City in the Age of Jefferson* (New York, 1979); Edward Pessen, *Most Uncommon Jacksonians: The Radical Leaders of the Early Labor Movement* (Albany, N.Y., 1967); Bruce Laurie, *Working People of Philadelphia, 1800-1850* (Philadelphia, 1980); Allan Dawley, *Class and Community: The Industrial Revolution in Lynn* (Cambridge, Mass., 1976); Paul G. Faler, *Mechanics and Manufacturers in the Early Industrial Revolution: Lynn, Massachusetts, 1780-1860* (Albany, N.Y., 1981); Susan Hirsch, *Roots of the American Working Class: The Industrialization of Crafts in Newark, 1800-1860* (Philadelphia, 1978); Sean Wilentz, *Chants Democratic: New York City and the Rise of the American Working Class, 1788-1850* (New York, 1984); Richard B. Stott, *Workers in the Metropolis, Class, Ethnicity, and Youth in Antebellum New York City* (Ithaca, N.Y., 1990); Steven J. Ross, *Workers on the Edge: Work, Leisure, and Politics in Industrializing Cincinnati, 1788-1890* (New York, 1985); Jonathan Prude, *The Coming of the Industrial Order: Town and Factory Life in Rural Massachusetts, 1810-1860* (New York, 1983). For an older, dated but still useful synthesis consult Norman Ware, *The Industrial Worker, 1840-1860* (Boston, 1924).

On the era of the Civil War and Reconstruction the following books should be used: David Montgomery, *Beyond Equality: Labor and the Radical Republicans, 1862-1872* (Urbana, Ill., 1981); Jonathan Grossman, *William Sylvis: Pioneer of American Labor* (New York, 1945); Daniel Walkowitz, *Worker City, Company Town: Iron and Cotton Worker Protest in Troy and Cohoes, New York, 1855-1884* (Urbana, Ill., 1978); Iver Bernstein, *The New York City Draft Riots* (New York, 1990); and Grace Palladino, *Another Civil War: Labor, Capital, and the State in the Anthracite Regions of Pennsylvania, 1840-1868* (Urbana, Ill., 1990).

The Era of the Knights of Labor and the American Federation of Labor, from the 1870s to 1919

The best introduction to the period is now David Montgomery, *The Fall of the House of Labor: The Workplace, the State, and American Labor Activism, 1865-1925* (New York, 1987). Norman Ware's old history of the struggle between the Knights of Labor and the AFL, *The Labor Movement in the United States, 1860-1895* (New York, 1929), remains a useful account of the first half of the period. A far briefer, more modern synthesis can be found in Melvyn Dubofsky, *Industrialism and the American Worker, 1865-1920* (Arlington Heights, Ill., 1985). The best history of the emergence of stable craft unions remains Lloyd Ulman, *The Rise of the National Trade Union* (Cambridge, Mass., 1955). Other rewarding volumes include Gerald Grob, *Workers and Utopia: A Study of the Ideological Conflict in the American Labor Movement, 1865-1900* (Evanston, Ill., 1961); Irwin Yellowitz, *Industrialization and the American Labor Movement, 1850-1900* (Port Washington, N.Y., 1977); Melton A. McLaurin, *The Knights of Labor in the South*, (Westport, Conn., 1978); Leon Fink, *Workingmen's Democracy: The Knights of Labor and American Politics* (Urbana, Ill., 1983); Richard Oestreicher, *Solidarity and Fragmentation: Working People and Class Consciousness in Detroit, 1875-1900* (Urbana, Ill., 1986); and Roy Rosenzweig, *Eight Hours for What We Will: Workers and Leisure in an Industrial City, 1870-1920* (New York, 1983). Two books by Daniel Nelson analyze management strategies in this period, *Managers and Workers: The Origins of the New Factory System in the United States, 1880-1920* (Madison, Wis., 1975) and *Frederick W. Taylor and Scientific Management* (Madison, Wis., 1980). For perhaps the best single book on the labor policies of employers one should read Sanford Jacoby, *Employing Bureaucracy: Managers, Unions, and the Transformation of Work in American Industry, 1900-1945* (New York, 1985). Two books that treat the efforts of public officials and corporate leaders to implement welfare reform for workers are James Weinstein, *The Corporate Ideal in the Liberal State* (Boston, 1968) and Stuart Brandes, *American Welfare Capitalism, 1880-1940* (Chicago, 1976). For the upheaval of 1919 consult David Brody, *Labor in Crisis: The Steel Strike of 1919* (Urbana, Ill., 1987); Francis Russell, *A City in Terror: 1919, The Boston Police Strike* (New York, 1975); and David Goldberg, *A Tale of Three Cities: Labor Organization in Paterson, Passaic, and Lawrence, 1916-1921* (New Brunswick, N.J., 1989).

The Interwar Years: 1919–1939

Irving Bernstein's two volumes offer the most complete treatment of the entire era: *The Lean Years: A History of the American Worker, 1920–1933* (Boston, 1960) and *Turbulent Years: A History of the American Worker, 1933– 1941* (Boston, 1969). General trends in the labor movement can be followed in Melvyn Dubofsky and Warren Van Tine, *John L. Lewis: A Biography* (New York, 1977; abridged paperback edition, Urbana, Ill., 1986). Among the best sources for the social history of workers during the 1920s and 1930s are still Robert and Helen Lynd, *Middletown* (New York, 1929) and *Middletown in Transition* (New York, 1937). For the 1930s see also E. W. Bakke, *Citizens without Work* (New Haven, Conn., 1940) and *The Unemployed Worker* (New Haven, Conn., 1940). Two excellent new books integrate the social, political, and institutional history of workers: Gary Gerstle, *Working-Class Americanism: The Politics of Labor in a Textile City, 1914–1960* (New York, 1989), and Lizabeth Cohen, *Making a New Deal, Industrial Workers in Chicago, 1919– 1939* (New York, 1990). James N. Gregory, *American Exodus: The Dust Bowl Migration and Okie Culture in California* (New York, 1989), treats an important social phenomenon of the 1930s.

An excellent contemporary collection of essays on labor in the 1920s is J.B.S. Hardman, ed., *American Labor Dynamics* (New York, 1928). The larger national political arena is treated in Robert Zieger, *Republicans and Labor, 1919–1929* (Lexington, Ky., 1969).

The great upheaval of the 1930s has been described and analyzed in many books. James O. Morris, *Conflict within the AFL: A Study of Craft versus Industrial Unionism, 1901–1938* (Ithaca, N.Y., 1958) and Walter Galenson, *The CIO Challenge to the AFL: A History of the American Labor Movement, 1935–1941* (Cambridge, Mass., 1960) respectively, and in the latter case encyclopedically, portray the origins and results of the split in the AFL and the ensuing civil war in the labor movement. Key developments in the automobile industry are brilliantly handled in two books by Sidney Fine: *The Automobile Under the Blue Eagle* (Ann Arbor, Mich., 1963) and *Sit-Down: The General Motors Strike of 1936–1937* (Ann Arbor, Mich., 1969). An equally good book treats the maritime industry: Bruce Nelson, *Workers on the Waterfront: Seamen, Longshoremen, and Unionism in the 1930s,* (Urbana, Ill., 1988). Two books by James A. Gross cover in detail aspects of the New Deal revolution in labor law: *The Making of the National Labor Relations Board* (Albany, N.Y., 1974) and *The Reshaping of the National Labor Relations Board*

(Albany, N.Y., 1981). For other aspects of New Deal labor policy see Jerold S. Auerbach, *Labor and Liberty: The LaFollette Committee and the New Deal* (Indianapolis, 1966); James A. Hodges, *New Deal Labor Policy and the Southern Cotton Textile Industry, 1933–1941* (Knoxville, Tenn., 1986); Stanley Vittoz, *New Deal Labor Policy and the American Industrial Economy* (Chapel Hill, N.C., 1987). Three books capture some of the contemporary flavor of the labor upheaval: Edward Levinson, *Labor on the March* (New York, 1937); Mary Heaton Vorse, *Labor's New Millions* (New York, 1938), and Benjamin Stolberg, *The Story of the C.I.O* (New York, 1938).

The Maturation of the American Labor Movement

The best synthesis for the period still remains Chapters 5 and 6 in David Brody, *Workers in Industrial America* (New York, 1980). They may be supplemented by Joel Seidman, *American Labor from Defense to Reconversion* (Chicago, 1953) and Colston Warne, ed., *Labor in Postwar America* (Boston, 1949). A more recent book by Nelson Lichtenstein offers an astute scholarly history of the impact of federal wartime labor policies on mass-production unionism: *Labor's War at Home: The CIO under the No-Strike Pledge* (New York, 1982).

Labor and the Cold War has been the subject of several studies of varying quality. Two early and conventional anticommunist accounts of the Cold War in the labor movement are David J. Saposs, *Communism in American Unions* (New York, 1959) and Max M. Kampelman, *The Communist Party vs. the C.I.O* (New York, 1957). More dispassionate and perhaps more judicious later versions of the struggle can be found in Bert Cochran, *Labor and Communism: The Conflict that Shaped American Unions* (Princeton, N.J., 1977); Harvey Levenstein, *Communism, Anticommunism, and the CIO* (Westport, Conn., 1981); and Roger Keeran, *The Communist Party and the Auto Workers Unions* (Bloomington, Ind., 1980). Two books present sharply conflicting portraits of American labor's role in the Cold War overseas. Ronald Radosh, *American Labor and United States Foreign Policy* (New York, 1969) blisters labor's foreign policy. Roy Godson, *American Labor and European Politics: The AFL as a Transnational Force* (New York, 1976) defends the AFL-CIO. For a more recent and highly critical scholarly study of the subject see Ronald Filipelli, *American Labor and Postwar Italy, 1943–1953: A Study of Cold War Politics* (Stanford, Calif., 1989).

A group of books written in the 1950s and early 1960s takes a jaundiced view of labor's successes in the postwar period. Among the best in this genre are Bert Cochran, ed., *American Labor in Midpassage* (New York, 1959); Paul Jacobs, *The State of the Unions* (New York, 1963); Paul E. Sultan, *The Disenchanted Unionist* (New York, 1964); Sidney Lens, *The Crisis of American Labor* (New York, 1959); B. J. Widick, *Labor Today: The Triumphs and Failures of Unionism in the United States* (New York, 1964); Richard A. Lester, *As Unions Mature* (New York, 1958); and William Serrin, *The Company and the Union: The "Civilized" Relations of the General Motors Corporation and the United Automobile Workers* (New York, 1970).

For a closer look at postwar workers, rather than the institutions of labor, one might turn to Richard Sennett and Jonathan Cobb, *The Hidden Injuries of Class* (New York, 1972); Robert Blauner, *Alienation and Freedom* (Chicago, 1964); William Kornblum, *Blue-Collar Community* (Chicago, 1974); Bennett Berger, *Working-Class Suburb: A Study of Auto Workers in Suburbia* (Berkeley, Calif., 1960); Stanley Aronowitz, *False Promises: The Making of American Working-Class Consciousness* (New York, 1973); Irving Howe, ed., *The World of the Blue-Collar Worker* (New York, 1972); Lillian B. Rubin, *Worlds of Pain: Life in the Working-Class Family* (New York, 1976); and the insightful interviews gathered by Studs Terkel in *Working* (New York, 1972). See also Andrew Levinson, *The Working-Class Majority* (New York, 1974).

Many excellent books describe, analyze, and interpret the transformation of the labor force since the 1970s, the increasing globalization of economic competition, and the contemporary crisis of American workers and their labor movement. The following are the best of such studies: Kim Moody, *An Injury to All: The Decline of American Unionism* (New York, 1988), which also suggests policies to combat decline; Michael Goldfield, *The Decline of Organized Labor in the United States* (Chicago, 1987); Richard B. Freeman and James L. Medoff, *What Do Unions Do?* (New York, 1984), which defends the contributions of unions to the economy; Michael J. Piore and Charles Sabel, *The Second Industrial Divide: Possibilities for Prosperity* (New York, 1984), which examines the shift from mass-production to specialized batch-production and its impact on workers; Thomas A. Kochan, et al., *The Transformation of American Industrial Relations* (New York, 1986) which together with Charles C. Hecksher, *The New Unionism: Employee Involvement in the Changing Corporation* (New York, 1988) calls for new forms and styles of collective bargaining and industrial relations; and Paul C. Weiler, *Governing the Workplace: The Future of Labor and Employment Law* (Cambridge, Mass., 1990) which suggests how changes in labor law can protect workers and benefit unions. A somewhat different angle on contemporary workers and their unions can be explored in Leon Fink's and Brian Greenberg's book on hospital workers and their struggle to build a union, *Upheaval in the Quiet Zone: A History of the Hospital Workers' Union, Local 1199* (Urbana, Ill., 1989).

Special Studies

There are many special studies dealing with various aspects of the history of workers and the labor movement. The following represents a highly selective sampling. For older treatments of employer antiunion tactics see Robert W. Dunn, *Company Unions* (New York, 1927) and Leo Huberman, *The Labor Spy Racket* (New York, 1937). For a more recent scholarly and sophisticated approach to corporate labor policies consult Howell John Harris, *The Right to Manage: Industrial Relations Policies of American Business in the 1940s* (Madison, Wis., 1982). Charles O. Gregory, *Labor and the Law* (New York, 1946) remains the most accessible general history of the subject, but three newer books offer more interesting insights into the relationship between the law and labor history: James B. Atleson, *Values and Assumptions in American Labor Law* (Amherst, Mass., 1983); William E. Forbath, *Law and the Shaping of the American Labor Movement* (Cambridge, Mass., 1991); and Christopher L. Tomlins, *The State and the Unions: Labor Relations, Law, and the Organized Labor Movement in America, 1880–1960* (New York, 1985). Two books investigate the impact of unemployment and living standards on American workers: Alex Keyssar, *Out of Work: The First Century of Unemployment in Massachusetts* (New York, 1986) and Peter R. Shergold, *Working-Class Life: The "American Standard of Living" in Comparative Perspective, 1899–1913* (Pittsburgh, 1982). On labor and politics see J. David Greenstone, *Labor in American Politics* (New York, 1969), James C. Foster, *The Union Politic: The CIO Political Action Committee* (Columbia, Mo., 1975), and Gary M. Fink, *Labor's Search for Political Order: The Political Behavior of the Missouri Labor Movement, 1890–1940* (Columbia, Mo., 1973). On ideological conflicts see Milton Derber, *The American Idea of Industrial Democracy, 1865–1965* (Urbana, Ill., 1970). And for the story of corruption in the labor movement consult Robert F. Kennedy, *The Enemy Within* (New York, 1960) and John Hutchinson, *The Imperfect Union: A History of Corruption in American Trade Unions* (New York, 1970).

On ethnicity and labor see Victor Greene, *The Slavic Community on Strike: Immigrant Labor in Pennsylvania Anthracite* (South Bend, Ind.,

1968); John Bodnar, *Immigration and Industrialization: Ethnicity in an American Milltown* (Westport, Conn., 1977); Gerd Korman, *Industrialization, Immigrants, and Americanizers: The View from Milwaukee* (Madison, Wis., 1967); Tamara Hareven, *Family Time and Industrial Time: The Relationship between Family and Work in a New England Industrial Community* (New York, 1982); and Ewa Morawska, *For Bread with Butter: The Life-Worlds of East Central Europeans in Johnstown, Pennsylvania, 1890–1940* (New York, 1985).

On African American workers and civil rights consult Herbert Hill, *Black Labor and the American Legal System* (Washington, 1977) and August Meier and Elliot Rudwick, *Black Detroit and the Rise of the UAW* (New York, 1979).

A truly interesting study of occupational health and safety and labor's response to industrial injuries and illness is Alan Derickson, *Workers' Health, Workers' Democracy: The Western Miners' Struggle, 1891–1925* (Ithaca, N.Y., 1988).

A series of books probes occupational, social, and geographical mobility among American workers. The best of them include Stephan Thernstrom, *Poverty and Progress: Social Mobility in a Nineteenth-Century City,* (Cambridge, Mass., 1964) and *The Other Bostonians: Poverty and Progress in an American Metropolis* (Cambridge, Mass., 1973); Clyde and Sally Griffen, *Natives and Newcomers: The Ordering of Opportunity in Mid-Nineteenth Century Poughkeepsie* (Cambridge, Mass., 1978); Thomas Kessner, *The Golden Door: Italian and Jewish Immigrant Mobility in New York City, 1880–1915* (New York, 1977); and John Bodnar, et al., *Lives of their Own: Blacks, Italians, and Poles in Pittsburgh, 1900–1960* (Urbana, Ill., 1982).

Biography and Autobiography

A highly interesting approach to labor history is through biography and autobiography. Brief sketches of hundreds of labor leaders can be found in Gary M. Fink, ed., *Biographical Dictionary of American Labor Leaders* (Westport, Conn., 1984). Melvyn Dubofsky and Warren Van Tine have edited a collection of essays which examine a diverse group of labor leaders: *Labor Leaders in America* (Urbana, Ill., 1987). Material on William H. Sylvis is available in James C. Sylvis, *The Life, Speeches, Labor, and Essays of William H. Sylvis* (Philadelphia, 1872) and in the biography by Jonathan Grossman, *William Sylvis: Pioneer of American Labor* (New York, 1945). Terence V. Powderly wrote two autobiographical books: *Thirty Years of Labor* (Columbus, Ohio, 1889) and *The Path I Trod* (New York, 1940). Stuart B. Kaufman, has been editing *The Samuel Gompers Papers*, 3 vols. (Urbana, Ill., 1986–) with seven more volumes to follow. Samuel Gompers wrote a two-volume autobiography titled *Seventy Years of Life and Labor* (New York, 1925); a one-volume edition was published in 1986, edited by Nick Salvatore (Ithaca, N.Y.). The most complete biography of Gompers is Bernard Mandel, *Samuel Gompers* (Yellow Springs, Ohio, 1963). A spritely, briefer treatment is Harold Livesay, *Samuel Gompers and Organized Labor in America* (Boston, 1978). Elsie Gluck wrote the only biography of the early United Mine Workers president, *John Mitchell, Miner* (New York, 1929). A readable, dramatic account of Eugene V. Debs can be found in Ray Ginger, *The Bending Cross: A Biography of Eugene Victor Debs* (New Brunswick, N.J., 1949). A more recent, scholarly, and accurate life is Nick Salvatore, *Eugene V. Debs: Citizen and Socialist* (Urbana, Ill., 1982). Two autobiographies by radical labor leaders are William D. Haywood, *Bill Haywood's Book* (New York, 1929) and Ralph Chaplin, *Wobbly: The Rough and Tumble Story of an American Radical* (Chicago, 1948). Peter Carlson has written a lively journalistic version of Haywood's life: *Roughneck: The Life and Times of Big Bill Haywood* (New York, 1983). Melvyn Dubofsky has written a briefer version of the same life story: *"Big Bill" Haywood* (Manchester, England, 1987).

Among the better biographies of more recent labor leaders are Saul Alinsky, *John L. Lewis: An Unauthorized Biography* (New York, 1949); Melvyn Dubofsky and Warren Van Tine, *John L. Lewis: A Biography* (New York, 1977; abridged paperback edition, Urbana, Ill., 1986) which is more thorough, accurate, and documented; Robert H. Zieger, *John L. Lewis: Labor Leader* (Boston, 1988); Steven Fraser, *Labor Will Rule: Sidney Hillman and the Rise of American Labor* (New York, 1991) has now surpassed Matthew Josephson, *Sidney Hillman: Statesman of American Labor* (Garden City, N.Y., 1952); John Barnard's *Walter Reuther and the Rise of the United Auto Workers* (Boston, 1983) has replaced Irving Howe and B. J. Widick, *The UAW and Walter Reuther* (New York, 1949) and Victor Reuther, *The Brothers Reuther and the Story of the UAW* (New York, 1976); Ralph and Estelle James, *Hoffa and the Teamsters* (Princeton, N.J., 1965); Jervis Anderson, *A. Philip Randolph: A Biographical Portrait* (New York, 1972) and Paula F. Pfeffer, *A. Philip Randolph, Pioneer of the Civil Rights Movement* (Baton Rouge, 1990); Charles Larrowe, *Harry Bridges: The Rise and Fall of Radical Labor in the United States* (New York, 1972); and Joseph Goulden, *Meany* (New York, 1972).

Three excellent autobiographies by radical labor leaders are Len DeCaux,

Labor Radical (Boston, 1970); Wyndham Mortimer, *Organize!* (Boston, 1971); and Nell Irvin Painter, *Hosea Hudson: His Life as a Negro Communist in the South* (Cambridge, Mass., 1979).

Radicalism and Strikes

The story of radicalism and strikes within the labor movement is told in such general studies as Louis Adamic, *Dynamite* (New York, 1931); Samuel Yellen, *American Labor Struggles* (New York, 1936); and David J. Saposs, *Left-Wing Unionism* (New York, 1926). Recent books have become more scholarly and nuanced. For a collection of essays covering almost all aspects of the relationship between the left and labor see Seymour Martin Lipset and John H. M. Laslett, eds., *Failure of a Dream: Essays in the History of American Socialism* (Berkeley, Calif., 1984). An excellent study focused on the relationship between the Socialist Party of America and the trade unions is John H. M. Laslett, *Labor and the Left* (New York, 1970). More general studies that touch on labor and the left include Daniel Bell, *Marxian Socialism in the United States* (Princeton, N.J., 1967); James R. Green, *Grass-Roots Socialism: Radical Movements in the Southwest, 1895–1943* (Baton Rouge, La., 1978); Carlos A. Schwantes, *Radical Heritage: Labor, Socialism and Reform in Washington State and British Columbia, 1885–1917* (Seattle, 1979); and for a scathing critique of the old American left, see Aileen Kraditor, *The Radical Persuasion* (Baton Rouge, La., 1981).

The story of the most romantic of all American radical labor organizations, the IWW, is covered in the following: Melvyn Dubofsky, *We Shall Be All: A History of the IWW* (Chicago, 1969); Joseph R. Conlin, *Bread and Roses Too: Studies of the Wobblies* (Westport, Conn., 1969) and ed., *At the Point of Production: The Local History of the I.W.W.* (Westport, Conn., 1981); and Patrick Renshaw, *The Wobblies* (Garden City, N.Y., 1967). For a perceptive study of one of the IWW's most famous struggles see Steve Golin, *The Fragile Bridge: Paterson Silk Strike, 1913* (Philadelphia, 1988), and for a fascinating collection of IWW documents, Joyce Kornbluh, *Rebel Voice: An IWW Anthology* (Ann Arbor, Mich., 1964).

For the tale of strikes and violence see Jeremy Brecher, *Strike!* (San Francisco, 1972); Rhodri Jeffreys-Jones, *Violence and Reform in American History* (New York, 1978); Wayne G. Broehl, Jr., *The Molly Maguires* (Cambridge, Mass., 1964); Robert V. Bruce, *1877: Year of Violence* (Indianapolis, 1959); Donald L. McMurray, *The Great Burlington Strike of 1888* (Cambridge, Mass., 1956); Henry David, *History of the Haymarket Affair* (New York,

1936), now surpassed by Paul Avrich, *The Haymarket Tragedy* (Princeton, N.J., 1984); Almont Lindsay, *The Pullman Strike* (Chicago, 1942); Leon Wolff, *Lockout: The Story of the Homestead Strike of 1892* (New York, 1965); Graham Adams, Jr., *Age of Industrial Violence, 1910–1915* (New York, 1966); John Hevener, *Which Side Are You On? The Harlan County Coal Miners, 1931–1939* (Urbana, Ill., 1978); and David A. Corbin, *Life, Work, and Rebellion in the Coal Fields: The Southern West Virginia Coal Miners, 1880–1922* (Urbana, Ill., 1981).

Individual Unions and Industries

The histories of individual unions and industries provide a special and often rewarding approach to any study of the labor movement as a whole. Among the best published during the past three decades are David Brody, *Steelworkers in America: The Nonunion Era* (Cambridge, Mass., 1960) and *The Butcher Workmen: A Study of Unionization* (Cambridge, Mass., 1964); Robert Christie, *Empire in Wood: A History of the Carpenters' Union* (Ithaca, N.Y., 1956); Daniel J. Leab, *A Union of Individuals: The Formation of the American Newspaper Guild, 1933–1936* (New York, 1970); Martin Segal, *The Rise of the United Association: National Unionism in the Pipe Trades* (Cambridge, Mass., 1970); Thomas R. Brooks, *Communications Workers of America: The Story of a Union* (New York, 1977); Richard Lingenfelter, *The Hardrock Miners: A History of the Mining Labor Movement in the American West, 1863–1893* (Berkeley, Calif., 1974); Mark Wyman, *Hard Rock Epic: Western Miners and the Industrial Revolution, 1860–1910* (Berkeley, Calif., 1979); Steven Brill, *The Teamsters* (New York, 1978); Robert Ozanne, *A Century of Labor-Management Relations at McCormick and International Harvester* (Madison, Wis., 1967); Mark Perlman, *The Machinists: A New Study in American Trade Unionism* (Cambridge, Mass., 1967); David Bensman, *The Practice of Solidarity: American Hat Finishers in the Nineteenth Century* (Urbana, Ill., 1985); Daniel Nelson, *American Rubber Workers and Organized Labor, 1900–1941* (Princeton, N.J., 1988); Gerald Zahavi, *Workers, Managers and Welfare Capitalism: The Shoeworkers and Tanners of Endicott-Johnson, 1890–1950* (Urbana, Ill., 1988); Jacquelyn D. Hall, et al., *Like a Family: The Making of a Southern Cotton Mill World* (Chapel Hill, N.C., 1987); James R. Barrett, *Work and Community in the Jungle: Chicago's Packinghouse Workers, 1894–1922* (Urbana, Ill., 1987); Robert H. Zieger, *Rebuilding the Pulp and Paper Workers' Unions, 1933–1941* (Knoxville, Tenn., 1984); Stephen Meyer, III, *The Five-Dollar Day: Labor Management and*

Social Control in the Ford Motor Company, 1908–1921 (Albany, N.Y., 1981); Ronald W. Schatz, *The Electrical Workers: A History of Labor at General Electric and Westinghouse, 1923–1960* (Urbana, Ill., 1983); Michael Kazin, *Barons of Labor: The San Francisco Building Trades and Union Power in the Progressive Era* (Urbana, Ill., 1987); Walter Licht, *Working for the Railroad: The Organization of Work in the Nineteenth Century* (Princeton, N.J., 1983); Shelton Stromquist, *A Generation of Boomers: The Pattern of Railroad Labor Conflict in Nineteenth-Century America* (Urbana, Ill., 1987); William Harris, *Keeping the Faith: A. Philip Randolph, Milton Webster, and the Brotherhood of Sleeping Car Porters* (Urbana, Ill., 1977); Dick Meister and Anne Loftis, *A Long Time Coming: The Struggle to Unionize America's Farm Workers* (New York, 1977); Cletus Daniel, *Bitter Harvest: A History of California Farm Workers, 1870–1941* (Ithaca, N.Y., 1981); David Katzman, *Seven Days a Week: Women and Domestic Service in Industrializing America* (New York, 1978); Daniel Sutherland, *Americans and their Servants: Domestic Service in the United States from 1800 to 1920* (Baton Rouge, La., 1981); Ray Marshall, *Labor in the South* (Cambridge, Mass., 1967); and Philip Taft, *Organizing Dixie: Alabama Workers in the Industrial Era* (Westport, Conn., 1981).

Labor in Fiction

Although workers have never been a featured subject in American fiction, a few novels do provide especially illuminating insights into the human dimensions of labor history. Among the best of the early novels are Upton Sinclair, *The Jungle* (New York, 1906), reprinted by the University of Illinois Press in 1989 and edited by the historian James Barrett; and Ernest Poole, *The Harbor* (New York, 1915). Two novels especially informative about the experiences of immigrant workers are Thomas Bell, *Out of this Furnace* (Pittsburgh, 1976), a story that covers three generations of Slovak-American steelworkers; and Anzia Yezierska, *Bread Givers* (New York, 1975), about Jewish immigrant workers and their families. A more recent novel also treats the world of Jewish immigrant garment workers in New York: Meredith Tax, *Rivington Street* (New York, 1982). Enlightening fictional treatments of the 1920s and 1930s are Jack Conroy, *The Disinherited* (New York, 1963); Albert Halper, *The Foundry* (New York, 1934); Ruth McKenney, *Industrial Valley* (New York, 1939); and John Steinbeck, *In Dubious Battle* (New York, 1936). For the Second World War and after, the following might be read: Harriette Arnow, *The Dollmaker* (New York, 1972), a story of Appalachian migrants in wartime Detroit told from a woman's perspective; K. B. Gilden, *Between the Hills and the Sea* (Ithaca,

N.Y., 1990), a tale of the Cold War in the Connecticut labor movement; and Harvey Swados, *On the Line* (Urbana, Ill., 1990), fictional sketches of automobile assembly-line workers. A little-known novel explores one of the most violent and dramatic episodes in American labor history, Robert Houston, *Bisbee '17* (New York, 1979).

INDEX

Adair v. *United States*, 187
Adams, Charles Francis, 178*n*
Adams, Samuel, 16
Adamson Act, 195–196, 216
Adkins v. *Children's Hospital*, 193, 241
Agrarianism, 79–80
Agrarian Workingmen's Party, 43
agricultural workers, 383–384
aircraft workers' strike, 315
airline industry, 402, 403–404
Alarm, The, 117
Alien Contract Labor Law, 173
Alliance for Labor Action, 383
Allied Industrial Workers, 369–370
Alsop, George, 8–9
Altgeld, John Peter, 118, 167, 172
Amalgamated Association of Iron, Steel and Tin
 Workers, 150, 158, 160–161, 178, 225, 264,
 289
Amalgamated Clothing Workers, 198, 214, 259,
 285, 304
American Alliance for Labor and Democracy, 219
American Anti-Boycott Association, 188
American Emigrant Company, 92
American Federationist, 189, 191, 192, 354
American Federation of Labor, 109, 120, 122,
 139; organization of, 149–155; early political activity of, 171–172; leadership of, 153–154,
 248–250, 358; and Pullman strike, 168; membership of, 174, 196, 259, 298, 356; during progressive period, 177, 190–199; attitude toward
 industrial unionism, 249, 259–260, 278–279,
 283–286, 297–298; attitude toward IWW, 211;
 and welfare capitalism, 250; and unemployment
 insurance, 251–252, 254; rivalry with CIO,
 278–288, 297–298, 300; peace negotiations

with CIO, 287–288, 307; in Second World
 War, 332–333; and Taft-Hartley Act, 345–349;
 corruption condemned by, 360; postwar policies
 of, 353–355; fight against communism,
 354–356; merger with CIO, 356–361
American Federation of Labor-Congress of Industrial Organizations (AFL-CIO): establishment of,
 360–361; problems of, 363–367, 396–398;
 membership of, 364–365, 381–382; political ac-
 tivity of, 366, 379–380, 390–393, 400; corrup-
 tion fought by, 367–371; and Landrum-Griffin
 Act, 371; on racial discrimination, 381; foreign
 policy support by, 382
American Federation of State, County, and Munic-
 ipal Employees, 394, 396
American Federation of Teachers, 394
American Labor Party, 301, 302, 304
American Labor Union, 202
American Miners' Association, 88
"American Plan," 238
American Railway Union, 156, 164, 165–170
American Revolution, 16–17
American Woolen Company, 207, 208, 210
anarchism, 109, 116, 117, 118
Ancient Order of Hibernians (Molly Maguires),
 111
Anderson, Albert B., 228
Anthony, Susan B., 99
Anti-Trades Union Association, 61
anti-unionism: of court decisions, 62–64, 169,
 187–190, 240–241, 393; from strikes, 137,
 222–223, 317–318; 343; of employer cam-
 paigns, 185–187, 237, 314, 391, 395–396, 399,
 404; steel industry campaign, 225–227; after
 Wagner Act, 268; postwar, 343–344
apprenticeship system, 14, 26

arbitration: in 1902 coal strike, 183–184; in Second World War, 329–330; in railroad strike threat (1946), 339
Associationists, 77–78
automation: unemployment from, 235–236; and collective bargaining negotiations, 374–377; as strike issue, 374–375; and work rules, 373; and government action, 374–375
automobile industry: union organization in, 264, 290, 398; strikes in, 290–294, 337–338; fringe benefits in, 377–378, 399–401; work-rule agreements in, 399–401
Avery, Sewell, 332

Baer, George F., 182–183, 184
Bakery and Confectionary Workers Union, 369–370
Baltimore and Ohio Railroad strike, 113
Beck, David, 368, 369
Beecher, Henry Ward, 92, 115–116
Bellamy, Edward, 91
Berkman, Alexander, 159
Berry, George L., 247, 302
"bespoke work," 14, 21, 25
Bethlehem Steel Corporation, 299
"Bill of Grievances" (1906), 190, 194
Black, Hugo, 256
Black-Connery bill, 256–257
"Black International," 117
Bolshevism, see communism
bookbinders, 64
Bootmakers, Journeyman Society of, (Boston), 63
Boston, Mass.: slums in, 75–76; policy strike in, 223–224
Boston Courier, 59
Boston Massacre, 16–17
Boston Prison Discipline Society, 48
Boston Transcript, 58, 231, 252
bound labor, see indentured servants
boycotts, 29, 89, 188–189
Brandeis, Louis D., 197
Bricker, John W., 334
Bridges, Harry, 263
Brisbane, Albert, 77–78
Brody, David, 245, 352
Broehl, Wayne G., Jr., 112n
Browder, Earl, 280
Brown, Thomas H., 286
Brownson, Orestes, 72
Bryan, William Jennings, 172, 191
Bryant, William Cullen, 62, 67
Buchanan, Joseph R., 132
Buck's Stove and Range Company, 189
building trades, 23, 27, 60
Burnham, Walter Dean, 393

Bush, George, 393
Byrd, William, 8
Byrnes, James F., 333

cabinetmakers, 24, 27, 54
California, and anti-unionism, 367
Carey, Ron, 402
Carnegie, Andrew, 91, 160
Carnegie Steel Company, 158–160
carpenters, 23, 26, 27, 59, 61
Carpenters and Joiners, United Brotherhood of, 144
Carter, Jimmy 390, 391
Carter, Robert, 14
Carwardine, W. H., 163
Case bill, 344
Catholic Church, and Knights of Labor, 127, 129
central trades council, 56
Chambersburg Public-Opinion, 229
Chavez, Cesar, 383–384
Chevalier, Michael, 71
Chicago Daily News, 229, 231
Chicago Herald, 164, 168
Chicago Tribune, 159–160, 212
child labor, 4, 192, 260
Chinese Exclusion Acts, 173
Chinese workers, 92–93
Chrysler Corporation, 295, 400, 401
cigar makers' unions, 106, 142
CIO, see Committee for Industrial Organization; Congress of Industrial Organizations
C.I.O. News, 355
Citizen's Industrial Association, 185–186
Civilian Conservation Corps, 272
civil rights committee (AFL-CIO), 381
Civil War, 87–89
Clayton Act, 194–195, 216
Cleveland, Grover, 166–167, 170, 178, 179
Cleveland Leader, 162
Cleveland News, 212
Cleveland Plain Dealer, 253
closed shop, 28, 61, 84, 98, 106, 313, 314, 318, 323, 345, 366
coal industry; strikes in, 111–112, 179–184, 186–187, 227–229, 315–317, 338–339, 348–349, 402–403; union organization in, 111, 179–184, 239–240, 259; anti-union campaigns in, 239–240
Coalition of Labor Union Women, 397
collective bargaining, 28; and NRA, 266ff; and Wagner Act, 265–268; in Second World War, 325–328; and Taft-Hartley Act, 349; work rule issue in, 373–374, 396; for job security, 374–377, 399–401; fringe benefits in, 399–401
colonial labor, 1–20

Colorado, and anti-unionism, 367
Colorado Fuel and Iron Company, 186–187, 242
Commercial and Financial Chronicle, 261
Commerford, John, 80
Committee for Industrial Organization (1935–1938) 260, 278–300; *see also* Congress of Industrial Organizations
Committee on Political Education (AFL-CIO), 366
Committee on the Evolution of Work, 398
Commonwealth v. *Hunt*, 63
communism; in 19th century, 115, 119; in 1919, 221–222, 228–229; in 1920s, 252; and the CIO, 289, 301, 305–307, 355–356; and Taft-Hartley affidavit, 346; union battle against 354–356, 360, 382; and Landrum-Griffin Act, 370
company towns, 162–163
company unions, 181, 242–243, 261
Conference for Progressive Political Action, 246, 247
Congress, U.S.: investigating committees of, 142, 187, 268–269, 368–370; attitude toward unions in, 343–348; *see also* labor legislation; social legislation
Congress of Industrial Organizations, 288–300; leadership of, 286–289; membership of, 286–289, 297; establishment of, 288; and strikes of 1937, 291–296, 299; political activity of, 300–311; and communism, 289, 301, 305–307, 355–356, peace negotiations with AFL, 287–288, 307; in Second World War, 321–336, passim; postwar strikes by, 338–341; and merger with AFL, 356–361
conspiracy laws, 62–65, 116, 173, 189
Constitution, U.S. adoption of, 17–18
contract labor, 92
contracts: special, and ten-hour laws, 82–83
Coolidge, Calvin, 224, 233, 246, 390
cooling-off periods, 318, 328–329, 338, 344
cooperatives, 78, 103–104; and Knights of Labor, 130–131
Coppage v. *Kansas*, 187
cordwainers, *see* shoemakers
corporation, rise of the, 91
corruption, union, 238, 314, 360, 367–371
cost of living, 22, 26–27, 52, 87–88, 220, 352; and Second World War, 324–325, 331; in postwar reconversion, 341; and steel negotiations (1960), 373; under wages (1960s), 377–378; in 1970s–1980s, 386–387
court decisions: anti-labor policies in, 30–31, 62–63; 187–189; on legality of unions, 62–63; for labor interests, 270, 275–276, 393; *see also* Supreme Court
Coxey's Army, 170

craftsmen, colonial, 1–3, 13–14, 16–17
craft unionism, 127, 249, 278–279, 283–286, 298
Croly, Herbert, 179
Cuomo, Mario, 400
currency reform, 104–105
Curtice, Harlow, 375
Curtis, George Ticknor, 162

Danbury Hatters' case, 188–189
Darrow, Clarence, 166
Daugherty, Harry M., 231
Davis, David, 100
Debs, Eugene V., 156, 164–166, 167, 168–169, 170, 172, 202
debt, imprisonment for, 48–49
Declaration of Independence, 19, 47
defense production, 313–315
De Leon, Daniel, 202, 204
Democratic Party: labor support of 314ff, 380, 390–393, 400; and John L. Lewis, 308–311
depressions: (1819), 31–32; (1837), 68–69; (1870s), 105–107; (1880s), 132; (1890s), 155–156; (1921), 230; (1930s), 237, 250–254; (1980s), 387–388
Dewey, Thomas E., 334
Dickens, Charles, 70–71, 72
discrimination, 360, 380–381
dockyard workers, *see* longshoremen
Donovan, Raymond, 395
Douglas, Charles, 65
Dual labor market, 364, 377, 399–400
Dubinsky, David, 285, 286, 289
Duncan, James, 178
Duncan, James A., 283
Duplex Printing Press v. *Deering*, 240
Durkin, Martin P., 353

Economic Opportunity Act, 380
Economic Stabilization, Office of, 324, 329–330
Economic Stabilization Act, 324
Edgerton, John E., 238
education: public, 46–48, 59; retraining programs, 380
eight-hour day, 101–103, 125, 245
Eisenhower, Dwight D., 351, 353, 354, 366, 370, 373, 385
Eliot, Charles W., 178
employer associations, 185–187, 237–238, 346–347, 393–394
energy crisis, 386
English, William, 65
Erdman Act, 187
Ethical Practices Committee (AFL-CIO), 367, 370
ethnic factors, 76, 84, 181, 211, 224, 234

Ettor, Joseph J., 207, 208, 210, 211
Evans, George Henry, 40, 43, 79–80, 83

fact-finding boards, 338
Factory Girls' Association, 54
factory system, *see* industrial revolution
Fair Labor Standards Act, 274, 354, 379–380
Fairless, Benjamin, 294
Federal Emergency Relief Administration, 272
Federal Mediation Board, 344
Federal Mediation and Conciliation Service, 346
federal unions, 259–260
Federation of Organized Trades and Labor Unions, 149–151, 152
Ferral, John, 60, 65, 80
Fincher, Jonathan, 89
Fincher's Trade Review, 89
firemen, railroad, 156, 374–375
Fitzsimmons, Frank, 369*n*
Flint Alliance, 292–293
Foner, Eric, 87
Forbes, 399
Ford, Gerald, 386
Ford, Henry, 313
Ford Motor Company, 320
foreign policy: and Second World War, 310–318; labor's support of, 354–355, 382
Fortune, 280, 361
forty-hour week, 260, 274, 275
Foster, William Z., 225, 307
Fourier, Charles, 77–78
Franklin, Benjamin, 6
Fraser, Douglas, 391
"freedom's dues," 10–11
Free Enquirer, 40, 42
"free speech fights," 206–207, 212
Fremming, Harvey C., 286
French Revolution (1830), 54–56
Frey, John P., 285
Frick, Henry Clay, 158, 159, 160
Friendly Society of Tradesmen House Carpenters, 24
fringe benefits, 331, 332, 363, 377–378, 396, 400, 401, 402

Galbraith, John Kenneth, 384
garment worker's unions, 197–198
Gary, Elbert H., 221, 225, 227
General Managers' Association, 164, 166
General Motors Corporation, 291–294, 336, 337–338, 352, 375, 389, 399–401
general strike (Seattle), 222–223
general trades' unions, 56, 65
George, Henry, 93
Gibbons, James, Cardinal, 127, 129

Giovannitti, Arturo, 207, 208, 210
Girder, Tom M., 299
Goldman, Emma, 159
Goldsborough, T. Alan, 339
Gompers, Samuel: and labor radicalism, 110–111, 190, 204, 222; role in formation of AFL, 150–155; character and career, 120, 143–149, 171–172; on Homestead and Pullman strikes, 161, 168; policies during progressive period, 178, 179, 185, 189–192; on Clayton Act, 195; and First World War, 215–219; death of, 248; and labor philosophy, 190–192, 247, 282
Gould, Jay, 90, 133, 134, 136, 137, 138
government: labor attitude toward (1830s), 36–37; work day on public projects 61; investigating committees, 142, 187, 268–269, 368–370; labor representation in, 216–219, 321–322; and war-time controls, 216–219, 323ff, 334–40, 349–350; and social welfare, 255–257, 272, 275, 380; *see also* labor legislation; social legislation
government intervention: Lincoln on, 88; troops used in, 88, 112–115, 166–167, 226, right of, 170; coal strike arbitration (1902), 183–184; in First World War, 217–218; in Second World War, 323ff; in steel disputes (1950s), 349–350, 372–374; in railroad automation dispute, 374–375; *see also* injunctions
Greeley, Horace, 75, 77–78, 82
Green, William: becomes president of AFL, 248–250; and depression, 252; on security, 273; and CIO, 279–289; on Roosevelt, 311; on anti-labor bills, 318; and Second World War strikes, 322; death of, 357
Greenbackism, 104–105
Greenback-Labor parties, 105
Greyhound Bus Company, 403
Grosscup, Peter J., 168, 169

Hagerty, T. J., Father, 203
Hamilton, Alexander, 18, 26
Hanna, Mark, 163, 164, 172, 178, 180
Hanson, Ole, 223
Harding, Warren G., 231, 233
Harper's, 87, 252, 396
Harriman, E. H., 91
Harrington, Michael, 376, 377, 379
Harrison, William Henry, 38
Hasenclever, Peter, 15
hatters, boycott by, 188–189
Hay, John, 177
Hayes, Rutherford B., 115
Haymarket Square riot, 116–119, 120, 139
Haywood, William D., 203–206, 208, 210, 211, 213

Hill, Herbert, 381
Hill, James J., 91
Hillman, Sidney, 285, 286, 289, 297, 304–305, 306, 321, 333, 334
Hoffa, James R., 368–369
Holmes, Oliver Wendell, 188, 241
Homestead Act, 80
Homestead strike, 157, 158–162
Hone, Philip, 58
Hoover, Herbert, 233, 254, 303, 342
Hormel Company, 403
Hotel and Restaurant Employees Union, 369
Howard, Charles P., 285
Hughes, Charles Evans, 270
Hutcheson, William L., 247, 285, 286, 303

Ickes, Harold I., 326, 327, 328
Idaho, and anti-unionism, 367
Immigration: during colonial period, 2–8; effect on textile industry, 73; during 1850s, 74–76; influence in late 19th century, 93; during progressive period, 177; restriction of, 196, 234; 1970s–1980s, 389–390
indentured servants, 3–11
Industrial Alliances, 185
Industrial Brotherhood, 105, 125
Industrial Commission, 173
industrial congresses, 83, 105
"industrial democracy," 242, 282
Industrial Relations Commission (1912–1915), 194, 215–216
industrial revolution, 73ff; and industrial expansion, 90–91
Industrial Union Department (AFL-CIO), 360
industrial unionism, 121–122, 198, 200, 214, 249, 278–279, 283, 297–298
Industrial Workers of the World, 201–214
inflation: of 1830s, 52; post-Second World War, 341; 1970s, 386–387
injunctions: during Pullman strike, 168–170; labor attacks on, 170, 189–190, 228; and Clayton Act, 240; in post-First World War strikes, 228–229, 231; and Norris-La Guardia Act, 253; and coal strike (1946), 339; and Taft-Hartley Act, 346, 348–350; and steel strike (1959), 373; 1980s, 393
Inland Steel Company, 299
Interchurch World Movement, Commission of Inquiry of, 226–227
International Confederation of Free Trade Unions, 355
International Ladies' Garment Workers' Union, 197, 214, 259, 285
International Longshoreman's Association, 263, 351, 367, 375

International Typographical Union, 178
International Union of Cigar Makers, 142, 143–145, 147
International Workingman's Association, 100, 109, 110, 146
International Working People's Association, 117
Ireland, John, Archbishop, 178, 182
Iron Age, The, 208, 261
Iron and Steel Institute, 290
"iron-clad oaths," 116
Iron Molders Union, 88, 98–99, 103, 143, 152
Irons, Martin, 136

Jackson, Andrew, 38, 45, 49
Jacksonian democracy, 36–38, 45
Jacoby, Sanford, 395
Japanese automobile companies, 400–401
Jay, John, 19
Jefferson, Thomas, 18, 76
Job security, and automation, 374–376
Johnson, Hugh, 258
Johnson, Lyndon B., 374, 375, 379, 380, 382
Johnson, Samuel, 6
Johnston, William H., 246
Jones, Hugh, 11
Jones, Mother, 203
Journal of Commerce, 183
Journal of United Labor, 123, 129
Journeymen Bootmakers' Society of Boston, 63
Journeymen Cordwainers, Society of, 23, 29
jurisdictional disputes, 155, 345, 360

Kaiser Company, 373
Katz, Harry, 404
Kellogg, Edward, 104
Kennedy, John F., 366, 374, 379, 380
Kennedy, Robert, 368, 369, 383
Keynesian economics, 387
King, Martin Luther, Jr., 380
Kirkland, Lane, 391, 396–398
Knights of Labor, 109, 119, 120–141, 143; and strikes, 126, 131–134; decline of, 135–140; rivalry with national unions, 148–152, 154; failure of, 140–141
Knights of St. Crispin, 106
Knudsen, William, S., 291, 293, 321
Kochan, Thomas, 404
Korean War, 349–351
Krug, Julius, 339

labor: political vs. economic activity for, 49–50; organization terminology in, 56; philosophy and goals for, 68, 106–107, 142–143, 214, 357–358, 361–362; future of, 397–405
Labor, Department of, 194, 353, 395

labor force: colonial sources of, 1–11; under industrial expansion, 91–94; unorganized, 174, 198–199, 364-367, 391, 397; shift in status of, 364–367, 374–379, 388–389

labor legislation: colonial, 12–14; ten-hour laws, 82–83; contract labor law, 92, 173; eight-hour laws, 102; in 1890s, 173; Erdman Act, 187; in progressive period, 176–177, 192–193; Norris-La Guardia Act, 253; under New Deal, 256–258, 265–267; on defensive industry strikes, 317–318; restrictive trend, 317–318, 390; in Second World War, 328–329; Taft-Hartley Act, 344–348; and union corruption, 367–371; Landrum-Griffin Act, 370–371; and labor law reform, 390–391

Labor-Management Group, 391

labor-management relations: movement for bargaining in, 177–179; in First World War, 216–219; under welfare capitalism, 242–245; in Second World War, 322–324; in postwar reconversion, 340–342; in 1980s, 399–404; *see also* collective bargaining

labor parties: workingmen's parties, 37–50, 51, 57, 79; and National Labor Union, 95–96, 99–100, 105; National Labor Reform Party, 100; and Populism, 170–173; and La Follette candidacy, 246–248; third party, and John L. Lewis, 308–310; American Labor Party, 301, 302, 304

labor press, *see* newspapers

Labor Reform Association, 101

"Labor's Bill of Rights," 230

Labor Statistics, Bureau of, 173

labor unions, *see* unions

La Follette, Robert M., 246, 247

La Follette, Robert M., Jr., 268–269

La Follette Civil Liberties Committee, 268–269

La Follette Seamen's Act, 195

La Guardia, Fiorello H., 304

laissez faire, 91–92

land reform, *see* agrarianism

Landrum-Griffin Act, 370–371

Lassallean socialism, 117, 145

Laurrell, Ferdinand, 143, 146

Lawrence, Abbott, 72

Lawrence, Mass., textile strike, 207–211

League for Political Education (AFL), 353

legislation, *see* labor legislation; social legislation

leisure time, 59, 379

Lend-Lease, 312

Lester, Richard, 361–362

Lewis, John L., 280–283; coal strike (1919), 228–229; in 1920s, 239–240, 247; and CIO, 279–299; steel strike (1937), 309; and Roosevelt, 283, 303, 308–311; and communists, 306–307; and AFL conflict, 307; resignation

from CIO, 311; coal strike (1941), 315–317; and Second World War strikes, 322, 325–328; coal strikes (1946–1950), 338–339, 348

Liberty League, 303

Lincoln, Abraham, 86–88

Little Steel formula, 324–325

Lloyd, Henry Demarest, 169

lobbying, *see* political action

Lochner v. New York, 193

lockouts, 98, 158–159

Locomotive Engineers, Brotherhood of, 88, 155, 339

Locomotive Fireman and Enginemen, Brotherhood of, 165, 330, 374–375

Loewe and Company, 188

Long, Huey, 280

longshoremen, 351, 367, 375

Looking Backward (Bellamy), 91

Lorenzo, Frank, 402

Lowell, Mass., textile mills, 70–73

Luther, Seth, 65–66

Lynn Record, 72

maquiladoras, 390

Maxwell, Robert, 403

McBride, John, 172

McClellan Committee, 368–370

McCormick Harvester plant, 117

McDonald, David, 373–374

McGuire, Peter J., 144, 145, 149

McKersie, Robert, 404

Machinists' and Blacksmiths' National Union, 85, 88, 106

McKinley, William, 172, 173

McMahon, Thomas F., 286

McParlan, James, 112

maintenance of membership principle, 315, 323, 332

Maintenance of Way Employees, 230

management: rights of, in Taft-Hartley Act, 349–351; and Landrum-Griffin Act, 370–371; and technological advance, 374, 377, 388; *see also* employer associations, labor-management relations

Manpower Development and Training Act, 380

Manufacturers' Record, 231, 258

Marble, Slate and Stone Polishers, Rubbers and Sawyers, Tile and Marble Setters Helpers and Terrazo Helpers, International Association of, 155

Marshall Plan, 354

Martin, Homer S., 291

Marx, Karl, 78, 100, 109, 146

Maryland, colonial labor in, 5, 15

Maryland Gazette, 10

Massachusetts, workingmen's parties in, 45

Massachusetts Supreme Court, 63–64
Mather, Cotton, 3
Maximum-hour laws, *see* work hours
Meany, George, 354–355, 358, 359, 360–361, 378, 381, 382, 391
mechanics' lien laws, 49
Mechanics' Union of Trade Associations, 33–34, 56, 58
Medicare, 354
Medoff, James L., 404
Middletown (Lynd and Lynd), 235
migrant workers, 201, 204–206, 213–214
militia system, 49
Miller, Joyce, 397
Miners' and Mine Laborer's Benevolent Association, 111, 112, 152
Miners' Association, 88
Miners' National Association, 111
Mine Workers, *see* United Mine Workers
minimum wages, *see* wages
mining industry: strike suppression in, 186–187; western strikes, 201–202; and IWW, 212–213; *see also* coal industry
Mitchell, John, 178, 181–182
Mohawk Valley formula, 269
Molders' International Union, 88, 98–99, 103, 143, 152
Moley, Raymond, 265
Molly Maguires, 111–112, 127
Molly Maguires, The (Broehl), 112n
Mondale, Walter, 392
monopoly, industrial, 91
Monroe, James, 55
Montgomery Ward Company, 332
Moore, Ely, 66–67
Morgan, J.P., 184, 227
Morris, Gouverneur, 17
Most, Johann, 117
Moynihan, Daniel Patrick, 377
muckrakers, 179
Murphy, Frank, 293
Murray, Phillip, 280, 288, 289, 306; becomes head of CIO, 312; and anti-labor bills, 318, 329, 353; on foreign policy, 312, 355; on communist-controlled unions, 357; death of, 357
Muste, A. J., 262

Nation, The, 113, 137
National Association of Manufacturers, 186, 237, 243, 244, 269, 305, 346
National Civic Federation, 177–178, 182, 185
National Defense Mediation Board, 314–315, 316–317
National Education Association, 394

National Industrial Conference, 221
National Industrial Recovery Act, 256–258, 265
National Labor Board, 261
National Labor Reform Party, 100
National Labor Relations Act, *see* Wagner Act
National Labor Relations Board: (1934), 261–263; (1935), 266–267; 270–271, 298, 336, 346, 351, 371, 396
N.L.R.B. v. Jones and Laughlin Steel Company, 270
National Labor Union, 95–100, 105, 121, 125
National Maritime Union, 306
National Molders' Union, 85
National Recovery Administration, 257, 258, 261–262, 264
National Reform Association, 79–80, 83
national security, and strikes, 349, 352
National Stove Manufacturers' and Iron Founders' Association, 98
National Trades Union, 56, 64–67
National Typographical Union, 85, 106
national unions: early organization of, 57, 85, 88, 94–107; revival in 1880s, 120, 143, 149–153, 155–156
National Wage Stabilization Board, *see* Wage Stabilization boards
National War Labor board: (1918), 218, 220; (1942), 322, 323–332, 335
National Workingmen's Convention, 86
Negro American Labor Council, 381
Newark News, 231
New Deal, 255–277
"New Directions," 400, 401
New England: colonial labor in, 3, 14–15; industrial revolution in, 70–73
New England Artisan, 65
New England Association of Farmers, Mechanics, and Other Workingmen, 45, 65
New England Courant, 22
New England Workingmen's Association, 77, 83
New Republic, 318
New United Motor Manufacturing (NUMMI), 400
Newspaper Publishers' Association, 178
newspapers: public opinion, role of, 29; labor, 35, 40, 79, 89; and strikes, comment on, 113, 115, 161–162, 168, 229, 231; on labor attitude (1932), 252–253; on injunction, 231–232; strikes by, 377, 403
New York, N.Y.: Workingmen's Party in, 38–44, 46, 58; French Revolution demonstration in, 54–56; slums of, 75–76, dock strike in, 351; printers' strike in, 376
New York *Daily News* strike, 403
New York Evening Post, 62, 67, 183, 208, 231
New York Gazette, 14

New York General Trades' Union, 56, 61, 64–65, 66
New York Herald, 83, 86, 99, 115, 168, 183
New York Herald Tribune, 247, 252
New York Industrial Congress, 83–84
New York Review, 391
New York Shipping Association, 351
New York Sun, 97, 134–135
New York Times, 52, 75, 110, 115, 168, 182, 208, 214, 329, 376
New York Tribune, 75, 77–78, 113, 115, 167, 229, 231
New York Typographical Society, 28
New York World, 162, 214
Nixon, Richard M., 369*n*, 386, 390
Non-Partisan League, 302–303, 304–305
no-raiding agreement, 359, 360
Norris-La Guardia Act, 188, 253, 256, 339, 393
North American Party, 43
North American Review, 162
North Atlantic Treaty Organization, 354, 355

O'Connell, James, 178
Office of Civilian Defense, 321
Office of Economic Stabilization, 321, 329, 330
Office of Price Administration, 321
Office of Production Management, 321
Ohio, and anti-unionism, 367
Ohio People's Press, 38
old-age programs, 272–273, 354
Olney, Richard, 166, 168, 170
open shop, 186, 237–238, 294, 398
open-shop association, 185–186, 237–238
Operating Engineers Union, 369
Owen, Robert Dale, 40–41, 43

Paine, Thomas, 19
Palmer, John McAuley, 161
Parry, David M., 186
Parsons, Albert, 117
Paterson, N.J., silk strike, 211–212
Pearl Harbor, 318
Peck, S.B., 243
Pennsylvania Gazette, 6
People's Party, 171–172
People v. Fisher, 62
Perkins, Frances, 249, 256, 274, 309
Philadelphia, Penn.: union associations in, 33–34, strikes in (1830s), 60–61
Philadelphia Aurora, 31
Philadelphia Bulletin, 247
Philadelphia General Trades' Union, 65
Philadelphia Inquirer, 231

Philadelphia and Reading Railroad, 112
Philadelphia Public Ledger, 229
picketing, 271, 276, 371, 403
Pinkerton detectives, 112, 136, 138, 158–159, 161
Pittsburgh, Penn., strike violence in, 114–115
Pittsburgh Leader, 161
Poindexter, Miles, 229
Point Four Program, 355
police strike, Boston, 223–224
political action, labor: colonial, 16–18; vs. economic, 95; by industrial congresses, 83; of National Labor Union, 96, 99–100, 105; by Knights of Labor, 126, 139–140, 171; by AFL, 230, 246–248, 254; and New Deal, 300–311; by CIO, 300–311; and campaign contributions, 303; in 1944 campaign, 332–334; in 1950s, 353–354; Meany's belief in, 358, 361; and technological unemployment, 380; in 1980s, 390–393; *see also* labor parties
Political Action Committee (CIO), 304, 333–334, 353
Political Education, Committee on (AFL-CIO), 366
Populist Party, 171
portal-to-portal pay, 326
Post, C. W., 186
poverty, war on, 380
Powderly, Terence V., 127–132, 133, 134, 135, 136–137, 138, 139, 140, 141, 143, 149, 154
Presidential Railroad Commission, 375
prices, *see* wage-price policy
Printing Pressmen's Union, 247, 302
printing trades, 22, 24, 28, 57, 74, 106, 375–376
prison: labor contract system, 26, 53, 96, 126; for debt, 48–49
Professional Air Traffic Controllers' Association, 391–392
profit-sharing plans, 243–244, 251
Progressive Cigar Makers' Union, 151–152
Progressive Political Action, Conference for, 246–247
prosperity, and labor organizations, 52, 84, 313, 341–342, 377–379, 385
public interest, strikes against, 346, 349–350, 373–374
public opinion: acceptance of force of, 29; for labor, 67, 179; anti-labor, 183, 229, 231–232, 395–396; against sit-down strikes, 296; against defense strikes, 318; and Taft-Hartley Act, 347
Public School Society, 46
Pullman, George M., 162ff
Pullman strike, 157, 162–170
purchasing power: high wages for, 274–275; maintenance of, 313, 334; loss of, 387–388

racial discrimination, 360, 377, 380–381
racketeering, *see* corruption
railroads: strikes, 109, 112–116, 132–137, 162–170, 230–232; union organization in, 155–156, 165, 174, 356, 375; legislation for workers on, 195–196, 241–242, 265; strike threats, 329–330, 339; "sick" walkouts on, 351: automation disputes in, 375
Railroad Trainmen, Brotherhood of, 155–156, 339
railway brotherhoods, 155–156, 174; membership of, 155–156, 179, 356, 375
Railway Conductors, Order of, 155, 330
Railway Labor Act, 241–242, 265, 329, 339
Railway Labor Board, 230, 231
Randolph, A. Philip, 377, 381
Raskin, A. H., 375, 396
Reagan, Ronald W., 387, 391–393
redemptioners, 4, 7–8; *see also* indentured servants
Reed, John, 211
reform movements, 36–38, 40–44, 45–49, 76–84, 99, 145, 175–177; and Knights of Labor, 121, 126–127; and New Deal, 255–256
Remington Rand Company, 269
Republican Party, 172–173, 344, 348, 353, 371, 391–393
Republic Steel Corporation, 299
retirement incentives, 376
retraining programs, 380
Reuther, Walter, 337, 357–358, 359, 360–361, 365, 375, 382–383
Rhodes, James Ford, 170
Richmond Times Dispatch, 248
Rights of Men to Property, The (Skidmore), 39, 79
right-to-work laws, 345, 348, 365, 366–367, 380
Rivington, James, 23
Rockefeller, John D., 91
Rockefeller, John D., Jr., 178, 187, 221
Roosevelt, Franklin D.: and New Deal labor policies, 256–258, 265; on Fair Labor Standards Act, 274–275; on labor unions, 276–277; and General Motors Strike, 293; labor's political support for, 303–304, 311; relations with Lewis, 282, 308–311; and coal strike (1941), 315–317; and wartime labor relations, 321–322, 326–369; fourth-term election of, 333–334
Roosevelt, Theodore, 175, 179, 183–184, 200
Root, Elihu, 184
Rohaytan, Felix, 393

sailors: strikes by, 29; legislation for, 195
St. Louis Republican, 113
San Diego Tribune, 206
"scabs," 29, 98

Schnitzler, William, 361
Seattle, Wash., general strike, 222–223
Seattle Times, 247
Sedition and Espionage Acts, 212–213
seniority rights, 374–375
service industries, 236, 366, 376–377
Shaw, Lemuel, 63
Sherman, Charles O., 203
Sherman Anti-Trust Act, 169, 173, 189
Ship Carpenters and Caulkers, International Union of, 100
shipping industry, *see* longshoremen
shoemakers, 24, 73–74, 85–86, 106
Siegfried, Andre, 234
Simons, A. M., 203
Sinclair, Upton, 296
sit-down strikes, 291–294, 295–296
Skidmore, Thomas, 39–40, 43, 79
slavery, 1, 3, 41–42, 86
Sleeping Car Porters, Brotherhood of, 377
Slichter, Sumner, 341
Smith, John, Captain, 3
Smith-Connally Act, 328–329, 336, 339, 343
Social Destiny of Man, The, 77
socialism, 77, 119, 145, 200
Socialist Labor Party, 146
Socialist Party of America, 202, 204
social legislation: for social reform, 175–176, 191–195; the social security program, 272–273, 354, 380; labor's support of, 354, 380–381
Social Security Act, 272–273, 354, 380
"Solidarity Day," 392
Sons of Liberty, 16–17
Sons of Vulcan, 88
Soule, George, 252
South, the unions in, 352, 365, 371
Sovereign, James R., 140
Sovereigns of Industry, 105
speed-up, 73, 245
Springfield Republican, 179
stabilization program, 335–340
"stagflation," 395
standard of living in 19th century, 26–27, 75–76, 93–94; in 1960s, 377–379; in 1970s, 1980s, 386–390
Stanton, Elizabeth Cady, 99
states: price-wage compacts between, 15–16; labor legislation by, 253, 390; right-to-work laws in 345, 348, 366–367, 380; "no-man's land" jurisdiction for, 371
Steel, 261
steel industry: organization in, 178, 225, 246, 289–290, 294–295; strikes in, 158–162, 224–227, 269, 299, 336–337, 349–350; Little

Steel Formula in, 324–325; price increases in, 338, 372; automation in, 375
Steelman, John R., 317
Steel Workers' Organizing Committee, 289, 294–295, 299
Steigel, Henry, 15
Stephens, Uriah, S., 122–123, 127, 140
Stevens, J. P., 393
Stevenson, Adlai, 366
Steward, Ira, 101–102
Strasser, Adolph, 142, 143, 144, 146, 151
strikes: 18th to 19th century, 22–23, 32–33; as criminal conspiracy (1806), 30–31; in 1830s, 57–61; of shoemakers (1860), 85–86; during Civil War, 88; of molders, 98; mining, 111–112, 179–184, 186–187, 227–229, 315–317, 338–339, 348–349; railroad, 109, 112–116, 132–137, 162–170, 230–232; and Knights of Labor, 132–134, 136–138; anti-union feeling from, 162, 222, 231–232, 317–318, 343, 347; steel, 158–162, 224–227, 269, 299, 336–337, 349–350, 372–374; and the IWW, 206, 212; of Lawrence textile workers, 207–210, 211; of Paterson silk workers, 211–212; during First World War, 212, 217–218; in 1919, 220–229; in 1920s, 244, 251; during depression, 251–252; under NRA, 262–264; of Little Steel workers, 269, 299; after Wagner Act, 270; in automobile industry, 291–294, 337–338, 389; in 1941, 313–321; in Second World War, 322, 325–328; man-days lost in, 322, 340, 351; and postwar reconversion, 336–340; and Taft-Hartley Act, 349–351; jurisdictional, 155, 345, 360; declines in, 351, 396; and automation, 375–376; 1980s, 403–404
Supreme Court cases: on union membership, 188–189; on union boycotts, 188–190, 240; on wage and hour laws, 193, 240–241; on injunctions, 169, 187–188, 240; NRA decision, 270; decisions for labor in, 275–276; and steel strikes (1950s), 350, 373; in 1970s, 393
sweatshops, 26, 144
Swinton, John, 128, 138
Switchmen's Union, 330
Sylvis, William H., 97–100, 103, 104, 140, 143

Taft, Philip, 332
Taft, Robert A., 335, 340
Taft, William Howard, 191, 218, 241
Taft-Hartley Act, 344–348, 349–351, 352, 353, 356, 366, 370–371, 373, 380
Tammany Hall, 44, 49, 54, 66, 83
Taylor, Frederick W., 242
Taylor, Myron C., 294, 316

"Taylorism," 242
Teamsters, International Brotherhood of, 285, 366, 368–369, 383, 401–402
Teamsters for a Democratic Union (TDU), 401–402
technological change, *see* automation
teenagers, unemployment among, 377
ten-hour day, 58–61, 80–83
textile industry, 70–73
Textile Labor Relations Board, 264
Textile Workers' Organizing Committee, 297
third party, *see* labor parties
thirty-hour week, 256–257
Thornhill v. Alabama, 276
Time, 333
Tobin, Daniel J., 285, 303
Tompkins Square riot, 110–111
Trades' Advocate, 89
trades' assemblies, 89
trade societies, 23–29, 56–57
Trade Union Educational League, 306
Trade Union Unity League, 306
Trautmann, William E., 203, 204
Trenton Daily State Gazette, 85
Trevellick, Richard F., 100
Truax v. Corrigan, 240
Truman, Harry S: as vice-presidential candidate, 333; labor policy of, 335–336, 338, 339–340; and labor legislation, 344–348; and strikes (1950s), 348–350; foreign policy of, 354–355
Trumka, Rich, 403
typographical unions, 85, 106, 178

unemployment: in 19th century, 110, 162, 173; in 1920s, 235–236; New Deal measures for, 272–274; from automation, 374–375; for unskilled and blacks, 374–375; and legislation, 379–380; in 1980s, 387–389
unemployment insurance, 253, 254
Union Pacific strike, 132
Union Pacific Employees' Protective Association, 132
unions: early patterns of, 24–25, 27–29; growth of (1830s), 51–57; court decisions on, 63–64, 188–190, 270, 275–276; Civil War revival of, 88–89; membership figures, 88, 106, 154, 173–174, 184–185, 196, 219, 232, 236, 251, 259, 333, 352, 364–365, 381–382, 393–396, 400; and new unionism, 122, 143–145, 150, 198, 214; reasons for membership in, 196; industrial vs. craft, 121–122, 249, 278–279, 283, 297–298; company, 189, 242–243, 261; New Deal gains for, 259–264; right to organize legalized, 265–266; and unskilled workers, 259;

post-Second World War hostility toward, 343–347; communists purged from, 355–356; acceptance of, 341–342; white-collar resistance to, 364, 382; investigation of, 368–370; status of (1960s), 381–384, (1980s), 393ff

union security, 323–325, 333–335, 341–342, 362, 384

union shop, 315, 316–317, 323, 345, 348, 349, 366

United Association of Journeymen Plumbers and Steamfitters, 353

United Automobile Workers, 290–294, 337–338, 352, 382–383, 391, 397, 399–401

United Brewery Workers, 203

United Brotherhood of Carpenters and Joiners, 144–149

United Brotherhood of Railway Employees, 202

United Farm Workers of America, 383–384

United Garment Workers, 197

United Hatters, 188, 286

United Labor Policy Committee, 356

United Metal Workers, 202

United Mine Workers: and early coal strikes, 177–184; in progressive period, 179–184, 186–187, 196; and 1919 strike, 227–229; in 1920s, 239–240; under New Deal, 259; strikes (1941–1950), 315–317, 325–328, 338–339, 348–349; membership of, 356; outside AFL-CIO, 312; 1980s, 397, 402–403

United Nations, 355

United States Bank, 45, 52

United States Chamber of Commerce, 256, 393

United States Steel Corporation, 160, 178, 185, 225, 227, 294–295, 316, 317

United Steelworkers of America, 313, 338, 372–374

United Textile Workers, 207, 208, 264, 286, 370

vacations, 331, 378

Van Buren, Martin, 61

Van Cleave, J. W., 189

Vietnam War, 380, 385

violence: of 1870s, 108–119; of 1880s, 136–137; Homestead strike, 158–159; Pullman strike, 166–167; Colorado mining strikes, 187, 202; and the IWW, 206–208; strikes (1937), 299

Virginia Company, 3–5

Virginia Gazette, 8

Voice of Industry, 72, 76

Volcker, Paul, 387

"voluntarism," 191–192, 250

Wabash Railroad strike, 133–134

wage-price policy: colonial, 12–13; and national market, 94; Little Steel formula, 324–325; and steel strike (1952), 350; in 1970s, 386–387

wages: colonial, 12–13; Revolutionary period, 15–16; early 19th century, 26–27, 52–53; and industrialism, 74–75; immigration effect on, 76, 92–93; strikes for increases in (1850–1860s), 88; late 19th century, 173; minimum legislation on, 274–275, 354, 379–380; rise in (1920s), 244; Second World War increases, 313, 324; fringe benefits as, 377–378; postwar increases, 335, 341–342; Korean War control of, 349–350; in mid-1950s, 352; in 1960s, 377–378; in 1970s–1980s, 386–390

Wage Stabilization boards, 335, 349, 350

Wagner, Robert F., 265

Wagner Act, 265–266, 267, 268, 343–344, 347, 390

Wallace, Henry A., 333, 356

Wall Street Journal, 195

Walsh, Frank P., 218, 225

Walsh-Healey Public Contracts Act, 274

Ware, Norman J., 141

War Labor Board, *see* National War Labor Board

War Labor Conference Board, 217–218

War Labor Disputes Act, *see* Smith-Connally Act

War Manpower Commission, 321

War Production Board, 321

Washington, D.C., marches on, 170, 380, 392

Washington Post, 168, 252

Washington Star, 247

Webster, Daniel, 47–48

Weekly Miner, 89

welfare, *see* fringe benefits; social legislation

welfare capitalism, 175, 242–244, 245, 251, 391, 395, 404

welfare funds: early mutual aid societies, 23–24; union, 144

Western Federation of Miners, 201–202, 203, 204

Wheeler, Burton K., 246

white-collar workers, 364–365, 376–377, 388–389; and unions, 393–394, and strikes, 390

Whitman, Walt, 41

wildcat strikes, 351

Wilkerson, James H., 231

Willard, Daniel, 232

Williams, Roy, 369n

Wilkie, Wendell, 282, 310–311

Wilson, Woodrow, 191, 194, 216, 217, 222, 229

Winthrop, John, 3

"Wobblies," *see* Industrial Workers of the World

Woll, Matthew, 285, 359

women: first strike of, 32–33; during 1830s, 53–54, 58; in Lowell cotton mills, 70–73; in Na-

tional Labor Union, 95–96; suffrage for, 99; and Knights of Labor, 134; and World War I, 220; and 1920s, 234–235; and CIO, 297; in World War II, 319–320; in labor force of 1960s, 377; in labor force of 1970s–1980s, 389, 394, 397
Women's Trade Union League, 246
Wood, Leonard, 226
work hours: colonial, 12–13; the ten-hour day, 38, 58–61, 80–83; and industrial revolution, 72, 81; the eight-hour day, 101–103, 125, 138–139; late 19th century, 156, 173; maximum, state laws on, 192–193; in 1920s, 245; the thirty-hour week, 256; and NRA, 257–258; and Fair Labor Standards Act, 274, 354, 379–380; the forty-hour week, 260, 274; and New Deal, 274
Workingmen's Advocate (Chicago), 89
Working Man's Advocate (New York), 40, 43–44, 54, 56, 79, 100
Working Men's Association, New England, 77, 81, 83

workingmen's parties (1830), 35–50
Working Men's Party (1876), 116
Workingmen's Party of New York, 38–44
workmen's compensation laws, 192, 253
work rules: as strike issue, 372–374; automobile industry, 398–400; negotiations over, 374–375, 398–400; in railroad disputes, 375
Works Progress Administration, 272
World Federation of Trade Unions, 355
World War, First, 212–213, 215–220
World War, Second, 319–334
Wright, Frances, 40–42
Wurf, Jerry, 396

"yellow-dog" contracts, 185, 188, 238, 242, 271
Youngstown Sheet and Tube Company, 269, 299

Zaritsky, Max, 286